DATE DUE

AUG 0 5 2009

FREEDOM OF THE PRESS 2008

FREEDOM OF THE PRESS 2008

A Global Survey of Media Independence

EDITED BY

KARIN DEUTSCH KARLEKAR AND SARAH G. COOK

FREEDOM HOUSE
NEW YORK ■ WASHINGTON, D.C.

ROWMAN & LITTLEFIELD PUBLISHERS, INC.
LANHAM ■ BOULDER ■ NEW YORK ■ TORONTO ■ PLYMOUTH, UK

ROWMAN & LITTLEFIELD PUBLISHERS, INC.

Published in the United States of America
by Rowman & Littlefield Publishers, Inc.
A wholly owned subsidiary of The Rowman & Littlefield Publishing Group, Inc.
4501 Forbes Boulevard, Suite 200, Lanham, Maryland 20706
www.rowmanlittlefield.com

Estover Road, Plymouth PL6 7PY, United Kingdom

Copyright © 2009 by Freedom House, Inc.

British Library Cataloguing in Publication Information Available
Library of Congress Cataloging-in-Publication Data Available

ISBN-13: 978-0-7425-6308-7 (cloth : alk. paper)
ISBN-10: 0-7425-6308-1 (cloth : alk. paper)
ISBN-13: 978-0-7425-6309-4 (pbk. : alk. paper)
ISBN-10: 0-7425-6309-X (pbk. : alk. paper)
ISBN-13: 978-0-7425-6629-3 (electronic)
ISBN-10: 0-7425-6629-3 (electronic)
Printed in the United States of America

$\ominus$™ The paper used in this publication meets the minimum requirements of
American National Standard for Information Sciences—Permanence of Paper for
Printed Library Materials, ANSI/NISO Z39.48-1992.

Table of Contents

We would also like to acknowledge comments and input on various reports from the following members of the International Freedom of Expression Exchange (IFEX) network: Owais Aslam Ali of the Pakistan Press Foundation, Carlos Cortes Castillo of the Fundacion para la Libertad de Prensa (Colombia), Corina Cepoi of the Independent Journalism Center (Moldova), Ronald Koven of the World Press Freedom Committee, Edetaen Ojo of Media Rights Agenda (Nigeria), Julie Payne of Canadian Journalists for Free Expression, Mak Yin Ting of the Hong Kong Journalists' Association, Jose Roberto de Toledo of the Brazilian Association of Investigative Journalism (Abraji), Nabil Rajab of the Bahrain Center for Human Rights, Moataz El Fegiery of the Cairo Institute for Human Rights Studies (Egypt), Khadga Sen Oli of the Center for Human Rights and Democratic Studies (Nepal), Oleg Panfilov of the Center for Journalism in Extreme Situations (Russia), Melinda de Jesus of the Center for Media and Responsibility (Philippines), Malcolm Joseph of the Center for Media Studies and Peace Building (Liberia), Item Eko Maryadi of the Alliance of Independent Journalists (Indonesia), Andres A. Solis of the Centre for Journalism and Public Ethics (Mexico), Kifle Mulat of the Ethiopian Free Press Journalists' Association, Uvindu Kurukulasuriya of Free Media Movement (Sri Lanka), Boris Timoshenko of the Glasnost Defense Foundation (Russia), Emin Huseynov and Sarah Paulsworth of the Institute for Reporter Freedom and Safety (Azerbaijan), Erol Onderoglu of the IPS Communication Foundation (Turkey), Roula Mikhael of the Maharat Foundation (Lebanon), Kaitira E. Kandjii of the Media Institute of Southern Africa (Namibia), Omar Faruk Osman of the National Union of Somali Journalists, and Sihem Bensedrine of L'Observatoire pour la liberte de press, d'edition, et de creation (OLPEC–Tunisia).

Freedom House would like to thank the Annenberg Foundation for its generous grants in support of our freedom of expression work. Additional support for this year's survey was provided by the Lynde and Harry Bradley Foundation, the F. M. Kirby Foundation, the Lilly Endowment, Free Voice, the Freedom Forum, and Bette Bao Lord.

The Survey Team

Contributing Authors

Fadeel Al-Ameen is a journalist and author who writes extensively about the status of the contemporary Arab media and has conducted several media-training workshops and seminars for Arab journalists. He worked as editor in chief of *Hi* magazine for three years and is currently a consultant for several media organizations in the D.C. area and the Middle East. He holds an MA in journalism and mass communication from the University of Northern Colorado and completed his graduate degree in international media from Indiana University at Bloomington. He served as a Middle East analyst for *Freedom of the Press*.

Alexis Arieff received her MA in international relations from Yale University and is a former senior research associate for the Africa program at the Committee to Protect Journalists. She served as an Africa analyst for *Freedom of the Press*.

Charles Arthur is an analyst and journalist specializing in Caribbean politics and economics. He holds an MA in Latin American government and politics from the University of Essex, United Kingdom. He is a contributing writer for the Economist Intelligence Unit, *Latinamerica Press*, and the International Press Institute's *World Press Freedom Review* and is the author of two books about Haiti. He served as the Caribbean analyst for *Freedom of the Press*.

Luis Botello is the director of Latin American programs at the International Center for Journalists. A native Panamanian, he has worked throughout the Americas, conducting training programs and conferences on freedom of expression and of the press as well as journalism ethics. He previously served as morning newscast producer, host, and television reporter for Televisora Nacional in Panama, where he covered assignments in Colombia, the United States, and Europe. He received a BA in journalism and an MA in mass communications from Louisiana State University and has also held several teaching positions. He served as the Central America analyst for *Freedom of the Press.*

Sarah Cook is a research assistant at Freedom House. Her research focuses on Asia and the Middle East. Prior to joining Freedom House, she coedited the English version of Chinese attorney Gao Zhisheng's memoir *A China More Just.* She holds an MSc in Middle East politics and an LLM in public international law from the School of Oriental and African Studies in London, where she was a Marshall Scholar. She served as an East Asia and Middle East analyst for *Freedom of the Press.*

Jake Dizard is a research analyst at Freedom House and assistant editor of the annual Freedom House publication *Countries at the Crossroads.* His area of focus is Latin America, with a specific emphasis on the Andean region. He is a 2005 graduate of the Johns Hopkins School of Advanced International Studies. He served as an Americas analyst for *Freedom of the Press.*

Camille Eiss is a former research analyst at Freedom House and assistant editor of *Freedom in the World,* with a focus on political and human rights developments in Southeast Asia. She previously worked as associate managing editor of the *Washington Quarterly* at the Center for Strategic and International Studies. She holds an MSc in the history of international relations from the London School of Economics, with a focus on political Islam. She served as a Southeast Asia analyst for *Freedom of the Press.*

Ashley Esarey received his PhD in political science from Columbia University and is An Wang Postdoctoral Fellow at Harvard University's Fairbank Center for Chinese Studies, where his research concerns mass media, the internet, and blogging in China and their effect on political discourse and democratization more generally. He served as East Asia analyst for *Freedom of the Press.*

Elizabeth Floyd is editor of special reports at Freedom House. Her areas of interest include Europe, education, and cultural history. She has an MA in modern European history from Hunter College, CUNY, with a focus on German history; her BA is in history from California State University at Sacramento. She served as a Western Europe analyst for *Freedom of the Press.*

Thomas Gold is a former assistant professor of comparative politics at Sacred Heart University and author of *The Lega Nord and Contemporary Politics in Italy.* He earned his PhD from the New School for Social Research and received a Fulbright Fellowship to conduct research in Italy. He served as a Southern Europe analyst for *Freedom of the Press.*

Sallie Hughes is an associate professor in the Journalism Program and Spanish-Language Journalism Master's Program at the School of Communication, University of Miami. Her PhD from Tulane University is in Latin American studies, with an emphasis on the media and politics of the region. Her book on the transformation of journalism in Mexico, *Newsrooms in Conflict: Journalism and the Democratization of Mexico,* was published in 2006 by the University of Pittsburgh Press. She served as an Americas analyst for *Freedom of the Press.*

Ana Jelenkovic is an associate at Eurasia Group, focusing on the Caucasus, Southeast Europe, and the broader Black Sea region. She holds an MA in international relations from Columbia University. She has worked on Balkan human rights and media issues at the Committee to Protect Journalists, the Harriman Institute, the Open Society Institute, and Freedom House's New York and Belgrade offices. She served as a Balkans and Caucasus analyst for *Freedom of the Press.*

Karin Deutsch Karlekar is a senior researcher at Freedom House and managing editor of the *Freedom of the Press* survey. She has conducted fact-finding missions on press freedom, human rights, and governance issues to a number of countries in Africa and South Asia and has written reports for several Freedom House publications. Currently, she also serves as chair of the governing council of the International Freedom of Expression Exchange network. She holds a PhD in Indian history from Cambridge University and previously worked as a consultant for Human Rights Watch. She served as a South Asia and Africa analyst for *Freedom of the Press.*

Daniel Kimmage is currently a senior analyst at Radio Free Europe/Radio Liberty, where he previously specialized in covering Central Asian affairs. He received his BA from Binghamton University and his MA from Cornell University. He served as the Central Asia analyst for *Freedom of the Press*.

John Kubiniec is a partner in Klos Training, a company specializing in building communication skills. He was formerly Freedom House's regional director for Central and Eastern Europe and the former Soviet Union and currently serves as a board member of Freedom House Europe. He has lived in several countries in Central and Eastern Europe, where he has worked for human rights and advocacy organizations supporting democratic development and civil society in the Balkans and the former Soviet Union. He studied economics and Slavic languages and literature and speaks Russian and Polish. He served as an Eastern Europe analyst for *Freedom of the Press*.

Astrid Larson is pursuing her master's in international affairs from the New School University. She holds a BA from Smith College and studied international communication at American University. She served as a Western Europe and South Pacific analyst for *Freedom of the Press*.

Alexander Lupis is a journalist and human rights researcher who is fluent in Russian and Serbo-Croatian. During the 1990s, he worked for the International Organization for Migration, Open Society Institute, Human Rights Watch, and Organization for Security and Cooperation in Europe, focusing on human rights issues in the former Yugoslavia. More recently, he worked as the Europe and Central Asia program coordinator at the Committee to Protect Journalists, followed by a one-year fellowship in Moscow at the Russian Union of Journalists. He served as a former Soviet republics analyst for *Freedom of the Press*.

Ekaterina Lysova is a human rights lawyer from the Russian Far East who holds a PhD in law from Far Eastern State University. She spent five years working as a media lawyer for the Press Development Institute and for the IREX Media Program in Vladivostok and Moscow. After serving as a full-time researcher at the University of Cologne's Institute for East European Law, she now works as a researcher for the Moscow Media Policy & Law Institute. She served as a former Soviet republics analyst for *Freedom of the Press*.

Eleanor Marchant is a specialist in African media issues. Most recently, she served as a fellow with the East African press freedom organization the Media Institute, based in Nairobi, where she wrote regularly about regional media issues and helped to advocate for media freedom. Prior to that, she served as a research analyst at Freedom House and assistant editor of the *Freedom of the Press* survey. She holds an MA in international relations from New York University and a BSc in economics and politics from the University of Bristol, United Kingdom. She served as an Africa analyst for *Freedom of the Press*.

Caroline Nellemann is an international consultant specializing in digital media and democratization. Previously, she has worked for the Berkman Center for Internet & Society at Harvard University, the Danish Aid Agency, and International Media Support. Currently, she is working as head of section at the IT-Strategic Division at the Danish Ministry of Science, Technology, and Innovation. She holds an MA in international development and cultural studies from Roskilde University, Denmark. She served as a Middle East analyst for *Freedom of the Press*.

Katrina Neubauer is a research analyst at Freedom House and assistant editor of *Freedom in the World*. Her area of focus is sub-Saharan Africa, with a particular emphasis on the Sahelian region. She holds an MA in international relations from George Washington University. She served as an Africa and South Asia analyst for *Freedom of the Press*.

Chris W. Ogbondah is a professor of journalism and coordinator of the Mass Communication Program in the Department of Communication Studies at the University of Northern Iowa. He holds a PhD in journalism from Southern Illinois University at Carbondale and is author of *The Press in Nigeria: An Annotated Bibliography; Military Regimes and the Press in Nigeria, 1966 to 1993: Human Rights and National Development;* and *State-Press Relations in Nigeria, 1993–1998: Human Rights and Democratic Development*. He has published articles on press freedom in scholarly journals. He served as a West Africa analyst for *Freedom of the Press*.

Folu Ogundimu is a professor of journalism and former senior research associate for Afrobarometer at Michigan State University(MSU). He holds a PhD in mass communication from Indiana University at Bloomington and is coeditor of *Media and Democracy in Africa*. He was founding director of the Ghana Multidisciplinary Studies Program at MSU. He served as a West Africa analyst for *Freedom of the Press*.

Ory Okolloh is a Kenyan lawyer and blogger. She is a graduate of Harvard Law School and blogs atKenyan Pundit. She is the co-founder of Kenya's Parliament watch website Mzalendo.com and the website Ushahidi.com, which allowed people to report atrocities committed in Kenya after the recent elections. She was a contributor to the book *Worldchanging: A User's Guide for the 21st Century* and is a frequent speaker at conferences, including Ted Global Africa and Poptech. When she is not working on her projects, she consults on digital access and citizen journalism issues. She served as an East Africa analyst for *Freedom of the Press*.

Aili Piano is a senior researcher at Freedom House and managing editor of *Freedom in the World*. She was a country report author for several editions of *Nations in Transit*, a Freedom House survey of democratization in Central and Eastern Europe and Eurasia, and for Freedom House's *Countries at the Crossroads 2004* survey of democratic governance. Before joining Freedom House, she worked as a diplomatic attaché at the Estonian Mission to the United Nations. She holds an MA from Columbia University's School of International and Public Affairs. She served as the Baltic states analyst for *Freedom of the Press*.

Arch Puddington is director of research at Freedom House and coeditor of *Freedom in the World*. He has written widely on American foreign policy, race relations, organized labor, and the history of the cold war. He is the author of *Broadcasting Freedom: The Cold War Triumph of Radio Free Europe and Radio Liberty* and *Lane Kirkland: Champion of American Labor*. He served as the United States analyst for *Freedom of the Press*.

David Robie is associate professor of journalism in the School of Communication Studies at New Zealand's Auckland University of Technology and director of the Pacific Media Centre. He holds a master's in journalism from the University of Technology, Sydney, and a PhD in history/politics from the University of the South Pacific, Fiji, where he was former coordinator of the Pacific Region Journalism Program. Dr. Robie was awarded the Pacific Islands Media Association Pacific Media Freedom Award in 2005. He is founding editor of *Pacific Journalism Review* and has written several books on Pacific media, including *Mekim Nius: South Pacific Media, Politics, and Education*. He served as an Asia-Pacific analyst for *Freedom of the Press*.

Mark Y. Rosenberg is a doctoral student of political science at the University of California at Berkeley. He is a former researcher at Freedom House and assistant editor of *Freedom in the World*. He served as a Southern Africa analyst for *Freedom of the Press*.

Tyler Roylance is a research and editorial assistant at Freedom House. He holds an MA in history from New York University. He served as a Central and Eastern Europe analyst for *Freedom of the Press*.

Hani Sabra is a former Middle East and North Africa researcher at the Committee to Protect Journalists, where he worked from 2001 to 2005. He served as the North Africa analyst for *Freedom of the Press*.

Janet Steele is an associate professor of journalism in the School of Media and Public Affairs at George Washington University. She received her PhD in history from Johns Hopkins University and has taught courses on the theory and practice of journalism in Southeast and South Asia as a Fulbright senior scholar and lecturer. Her book *Wars Within: The Story of Tempo, an Independent Magazine in Soeharto's Indonesia* focuses on *Tempo* magazine and its relationship to the politics and culture of new-order Indonesia. She served as a Southeast Asia analyst for *Freedom of the Press*.

Nicole Stremlau is director of the Africa media programme at the Stanhope Centre for Communications Policy Research. She holds a PhD from the London School of Economics in Development Studies. Her research focuses on media during and in the aftermath of guerrilla struggles in the Horn of Africa. She served as an East Africa analyst for *Freedom of the Press*.

Leigh Tomppert is a reporting assistant with the United Nations International Research and Training Institute for the Advancement of Women. She holds an MA in the social sciences from the University of Chicago. She previously worked as a researcher at Freedom House and assistant editor of Freedom House's *Women's Rights in the Middle East and North Africa* survey. She served as a Middle East analyst and an editor for *Freedom of the Press*.

Silvio Waisbord is assistant professor in the School of Media and Public Affairs at George Washington University. He is editor of the *International*

Journal of Press/Politics. Previously, he was associate professor at Rutgers University and director of the Journalism Resources Institute. Among other publications, he is the author of *Watchdog Journalism in South America,* published by Columbia University Press. His current research focuses on civic media advocacy, democracy, and the press in Latin America. He served as a South America analyst for *Freedom of the Press.*

Thomas Webb is a law student at Fordham Law School. He is a former research assistant at Freedom House and a graduate of Vassar College. He served as a Western Europe analyst for *Freedom of the Press.*

Elijah Zarwan is a Cairo-based consultant to Human Rights Watch and Amnesty International. He previously worked as a researcher for the Arabic Network for Human Rights Information, Harvard University, as managing editor of *Cairo* magazine, as an editor at *World Press Review,* and as a freelance journalist in the Middle East. He served as a Middle East analyst for *Freedom of the Press.*

Ratings Review Advisers

Jon B. Alterman is director of the Middle East Program at the Center for Strategic and International Studies in Washington, D.C. He received his PhD in history from Harvard University, and he has worked on the personal staff of Senator Daniel Patrick Moynihan and on the policy-planning staff at the U.S. Department of State. He is the author of *New Media, New Politics?: From Satellite Television to the Internet in the Arab World.* He served as Middle East and North Africa adviser for *Freedom of the Press.*

Rosental Alves is a professor of journalism at the University of Texas at Austin, where he created the first course in online journalism. For over a decade, he was a foreign correspondent based in Spain, Argentina, Mexico, and the United States, working for *Jornal do Brasil,* one of the most important Brazilian newspapers in Rio de Janeiro. In 1994, he managed the creation of the *Jornal do Brasil* online edition, making it the first Brazilian newspaper available on the internet. A working journalist since he was 16, he received a BA in journalism from Rio de Janeiro Federal University. He was the first Brazilian awarded a Nieman Fellowship to spend an academic year (1987–88) at Harvard University. He served as an Americas adviser for *Freedom of the Press.*

Festus Eribo is professor of international communication and head of African studies at East Carolina University, Greenville, North Carolina. He received his PhD from the University of Wisconsin at Madison and his MA from St. Petersburg State University and has worked as a journalist in Africa and Russia. He has authored and coauthored five books, including *Press Freedom and Communication in Africa* and *Window on Africa: Democratization and Media Exposure.* He served as an Africa adviser for *Freedom of the Press.*

Marilyn Greene is an independent media consultant based in Washington, D.C. She is an adviser to the World Press Freedom Committee and served for seven years as its executive director. As a 2005 Knight International Press Fellow in Cameroon, she worked with Francophone and Anglophone journalists to enhance journalistic professionalism in that country. She is also a former international affairs reporter for *USA Today,* covering conflicts in Somalia, Kuwait, and Haiti as well as situations throughout Europe, Asia, and the Middle East. She is a graduate of the Medill School of Journalism at Northwestern University and a former fellow in Asian studies at the University of Hawaii and the East-West Center in Honolulu. She served as a global adviser for *Freedom of the Press.*

Daniel C. Hallin is professor and chair of the Department of Communication at the University of California at San Diego. His research focuses on media and politics and comparative analysis of media systems, particularly in Europe and Latin America. He is the author, with Paolo Mancini, of *Comparing Media Systems: Three Models of Media and Politics.* He holds a PhD in political science from the University of California at Berkeley. He served as an Americas adviser for *Freedom of the Press.*

Marwan M. Kraidy is an expert on Arab media and a scholar of global communication. He is associate professor of communication at the Annenberg School for Communication at the University of Pennsylvania. Previously a fellow at the Woodrow Wilson International Center for Scholars and director of the Arab Media and Public Life project, both in Washington, D.C., Kraidy has published two books, *Global Media Studies: Ethnographic Perspectives* (2003) and *Hybridity, or, The Cultural Logic of Globalization* (2005), and more than 40 articles and essays. He has two forthcoming books on Arab media and politics. He served as a Middle East and North Africa adviser for *Freedom of the Press.*

Josh Kurlantzick is a visiting scholar in the Carnegie Endowment's China Program and also serves as a special correspondent for the *New Republic,* a columnist for *Time*, and a senior correspondent for the *American Prospect.* His recent research focuses on China's relationship with the developing world—including Southeast Asia, Africa, and Latin America—and is summarized in a new book, *Charm Offensive: How China's Soft Power Is Transforming the World.* Kurlantzick was previously foreign editor at the *New Republic* and also reported on Southeast Asia for the *Economist* as a correspondent based in Bangkok, Thailand. He served as an Asia adviser for *Freedom of the Press.*

Tendayi Kumbula is an assistant professor of journalism at Ball State University, Muncie, Indiana. He received his PhD from the University of Southern California and two MA degrees from the University of California at Los Angeles. He has authored or coauthored four books. He has been a reporter and editor in Los Angeles and Indiana and was an editor for four years in Zimbabwe. In 1991 and 2003, he participated in the American Society of Newspaper Editors' Institute of Journalism Excellence, which sends selected journalism educators to spend six summer weeks working in a newsroom. He served as an Africa adviser for *Freedom of the Press.*

Kavita Menon is a senior program officer at the Committee to Protect Journalists (CPJ), an international press freedom organization. She previously headed CPJ's Asia program and later worked as a campaigner and researcher on South Asia at Amnesty International. She holds an MS in journalism from Columbia University and received a Pew Fellowship in International Journalism in 2003. She served as the South Asia adviser for *Freedom of the Press.*

Bettina Peters is director of the Global Forum for Media Development, a network of organizations involved in media assistance programs around the world. Until 2007, she worked as director of programs at the European Journalism Center (EJC), in charge of its international journalism training program. Before joining the EJC, she worked for 10 years at the International Federation of Journalists headquarters in Brussels. She holds degrees in political science and journalism from the University of Hamburg and has edited several publications on journalism, such as the EJC's handbook on civic journalism. In 2007, she wrote the conclusion to a book on media policy in Europe titled *European Media Policy: The Brussels Dimension*. She served as Western Europe adviser for *Freedom of the Press*.

Byron T. Scott is professor emeritus of journalism and director emeritus of the European Union Center at the University of Missouri at Columbia and is a former newspaper and magazine journalist. His special area of interest is the media in transitional nations of the former Soviet bloc. He has worked as a journalist and teacher of journalism throughout the former Soviet bloc, including stints at the American University in Bulgaria, the University of Tirana, Tbilisi State University, and Moscow State University. He served as Central and Eastern Europe/former Soviet Union adviser for *Freedom of the Press*.

Survey Methodology

The 2008 survey, which provides analytical reports and numerical ratings for 195 countries and territories, expands a process conducted since 1980 by Freedom House. The findings are widely used by governments, international organizations, academics, and the news media in many countries. Countries are given a total score from 0 (best) to 100 (worst) on the basis of a set of 23 methodology questions divided into three subcategories. Assigning numerical points allows for comparative analysis among the countries surveyed and facilitates an examination of trends over time. The degree to which each country permits the free flow of news and information determines the classification of its media as "Free," "Partly Free," or "Not Free." Countries scoring 0 to 30 are regarded as having "Free" media; 31 to 60, "Partly Free" media; and 61 to 100, "Not Free" media. The criteria for such judgments and the arithmetic scheme for displaying the judgments are described in the following section. The ratings and reports included in *Freedom of the Press 2008* cover events that took place between January 1, 2007, and December 31, 2007.

Criteria
This study is based on universal criteria. The starting point is the smallest, most universal unit of concern: the individual. We recognize cultural differences, diverse national interests, and varying levels of economic development. Yet Article 19 of the Universal Declaration of Human Rights states:

> Everyone has the right to freedom of opinion and expression; this right includes freedom to hold opinions without interference

and to seek, receive, and impart information and ideas through any media regardless of frontiers.

The operative word for this survey is "everyone." All states, from the most democratic to the most authoritarian, are committed to this doctrine through the UN system. To deny that doctrine is to deny the universality of information freedom—a basic human right. We recognize that cultural distinctions or economic underdevelopment may limit the volume of news flows within a country, but these and other arguments are not acceptable explanations for outright centralized control of the content of news and information. Some poor countries allow for the exchange of diverse views, while some economically developed countries restrict content diversity. We seek to recognize press freedom wherever it exists, in poor and rich countries as well as in countries of various ethnic, religious, and cultural backgrounds.

Research and Ratings Review Process

The findings are reached after a multilayered process of analysis and evaluation by a team of regional experts and scholars. Although there is an element of subjectivity inherent in the survey findings, the ratings process emphasizes intellectual rigor and balanced and unbiased judgments.

The research and ratings process involved 33 analysts and 10 senior-level ratings advisers—the largest number to date. The 10 members of the core research team headquartered in New York, along with 23 outside consultant analysts, prepare the draft ratings and country reports. Their conclusions are reached after gathering information from professional contacts in a variety of countries, staff and consultant travel, international visitors, the findings of human rights and press freedom organizations, specialists in geographic and geopolitical areas, the reports of governments and multilateral bodies, and a variety of domestic and international news media. We would particularly like to thank the other members of the International Freedom of Expression Exchange (IFEX) network for providing detailed and timely analyses of press freedom violations in a variety of countries worldwide on which we rely to make our judgments.

The ratings are reviewed individually and on a comparative basis in a series of six regional meetings—Asia-Pacific, Central and Eastern Europe and the Former Soviet Union, Latin America and the Caribbean, Middle East and North Africa, Sub-Saharan Africa, and Western Europe—involving the analysts, ratings advisers with expertise in each region, other invited participants, and Freedom House staff. The ratings are compared with the previous year's findings, and any major proposed numerical shifts or category changes are subjected to more intensive scrutiny. These reviews are followed by cross-regional assessments in which efforts are made to ensure comparability and consistency in the findings. Many of the key country reports are also reviewed by the academic advisers and by other IFEX members.

Methodology

Through the years, we have refined and expanded our methodology. Recent changes are intended to simplify the presentation of information without altering the comparability of data for a given country over the 28-year span or the comparative ratings of all countries over that period.

Our examination of the level of press freedom in each country currently comprises 23 methodology questions divided into three broad categories: the legal environment, the political environment, and the economic environment. For each methodology question, a lower number of points is allotted for a more free situation, while a higher number of points is allotted for a less free environment. Each country is rated in these three categories, with the higher numbers indicating less freedom. A country's final score is based on the total of the three categories: A score of 0 to 30 places the country in the Free press group; 31 to 60 in the Partly Free press group; and 61 to 100 in the Not Free press group.

The diverse nature of the methodology questions seeks to encompass the varied ways in which pressure can be placed upon the flow of information and the ability of print, broadcast, and internet-based media to operate freely and without fear of repercussions: In short, we seek to provide a picture of the entire "enabling environment" in which the media in each country operate. We also seek to assess the degree of news and information diversity available to the public in any given country, from either local or transnational sources.

The **legal environment** category encompasses an examination of both the laws and regulations that could influence media content and the government's inclination to use these laws and legal institutions to restrict the media's ability to operate. We assess the positive impact of legal and constitutional guarantees for freedom of expression; the potentially negative aspects of security legislation, the penal code, and other criminal statutes; penalties for libel and defamation; the existence of and ability to use freedom of information legislation; the independence of the judiciary and of official media regulatory bodies; registration requirements for both media outlets and journalists; and the ability of journalists' groups to operate freely.

Under the **political environment** category, we evaluate the degree of political control over the content of news media. Issues examined include the editorial independence of both state-owned and privately owned media; access to information and sources; official censorship and self-censorship; the vibrancy of the media and the diversity of news available within each country; the ability of both foreign and local reporters to cover the news freely and without harassment; and the intimidation of journalists by the state or other actors, including arbitrary detention and imprisonment, violent assaults, and other threats.

Our third category examines the **economic environment** for the media. This includes the structure of media ownership; transparency and concentration of ownership; the costs of establishing media as well as of production and distribution; the selective withholding of advertising or subsidies by the state or other actors; the impact of corruption and bribery on content; and the extent to which the economic situation in a country impacts the development and sustainability of the media.

For a complete list of the criteria used to score each of the methodology questions listed below, please see our website at www.freedomhouse.org.

Checklist of Methodology Questions for 2008

A. LEGAL ENVIRONMENT (0–30 POINTS)

1. Do the constitution or other basic laws contain provisions designed to protect freedom of the press and of expression, and are they enforced? (0–6 points)
2. Do the penal code, security laws, or any other laws restrict reporting, and are journalists punished under these laws? (0–6 points)
3. Are there penalties for libeling officials or the state, and are they enforced? (0–3 points)
4. Is the judiciary independent, and do courts judge cases concerning the media impartially? (0–3 points)
5. Is freedom of information legislation in place, and are journalists able to make use of it? (0–2 points)
6. Can individuals or business entities legally establish and operate private media outlets without undue interference? (0–4 points)
7. Are media regulatory bodies, such as a broadcasting authority or national press or communications council, able to operate freely and independently? (0–2 points)
8. Is there freedom to become a journalist and to practice journalism, and can professional groups freely support journalists' rights and interests? (0–4 points)

B. POLITICAL ENVIRONMENT (0–40 POINTS)

1. To what extent are media outlets' news and information content determined by the government or a particular partisan interest? (0–10 points)

2. Is access to official or unofficial sources generally controlled? (0–2 points)
3. Is there official censorship? (0–4 points)
4. Do journalists practice self-censorship? (0–4 points)
5. Is media coverage robust, and does it reflect a diversity of viewpoints? (0–4 points)
6. Are both local and foreign journalists able to cover the news freely? (0–6 points)
7. Are journalists or media outlets subject to extralegal intimidation or physical violence by state authorities or any other actor? (0–10 points)

C. Economic Environment (0–30 Points)
1. To what extent are media owned or controlled by the government, and does this influence their diversity of views? (0–6 points)
2. Is private media ownership transparent, thus allowing consumers to judge the impartiality of the news? (0–3 points)
3. Is private media ownership highly concentrated, and does it influence diversity of content? (0–3 points)
4. Are there restrictions on the means of journalistic production and distribution? (0–4 points)
5. Does the state place prohibitively high costs on the establishment and operation of media outlets? (0–4 points)
6. Do the state or other actors try to control the media through allocation of advertising or subsidies? (0–3 points)
7. Do journalists receive payment from private or public sources whose design is to influence their journalistic content? (0–3 points)
8. Does the economic situation in a country accentuate media dependency on the state, political parties, big business, or other influential political actors for funding? (0–4 points)

Legend

Country

Status: Free (0–30)
     Partly Free (31–60)
     Not Free (61–100)

Legal Environment: 0–30 points
Political Environment: 0–40 points
Economic Environment: 0–30 points

Total Score: 0–100 points

Press Freedom in 2007:
A Year of Global Decline

Karin Deutsch Karlekar

Press freedom declined on a global scale in 2007, with particularly worrisome trends evident in the former Soviet Union, Asia, and sub-Saharan Africa. This marked the sixth straight year of overall deterioration. Improvements in a small number of countries were overshadowed by a continued, relentless assault on independent news media by a wide range of actors, in both authoritarian states and countries with relatively open media environments. Unsurprisingly, many declines—such as those in Pakistan, Bangladesh, and Georgia—took place in the context of broader political crises that led to crackdowns on the media. A number of these crackdowns appeared to focus on newer forms of media, such as satellite television and internet-based news outlets, which are helping to provide more diverse and independent sources of information in otherwise restrictive media environments.

These disturbing developments constitute the principal findings of *Freedom of the Press 2008: A Global Survey of Media Independence*, an annual index published by Freedom House since 1980.

The *Freedom of the Press* index assesses the degree of print, broadcast, and internet freedom in every country in the world, analyzing the events and developments of each calendar year. Ratings are determined through

---

Karin Deutsch Karlekar, a senior researcher at Freedom House, served as managing editor of Freedom of the Press 2008. *She holds a PhD from Cambridge University.*

an examination of three broad categories: the legal environment in which media operate; political influences on reporting and access to information; and economic pressures on content and the dissemination of news. Under the legal category, we assess the laws and regulations that could influence media content as well as the extent to which the government uses these tools to restrict the media's ability to function. The political category encompasses a variety of issues, including editorial pressure by the government or other actors; censorship and self-censorship; the ability of reporters to cover the news; and the extralegal intimidation of and violence against journalists. Finally, under the economic category we examine issues such as the structure, transparency, and concentration of media ownership; costs of production and distribution; and the impact of advertising, subsidies, and bribery on content. Ratings reflect not just government actions and policies, but the behavior of the press itself in testing boundaries, even in more restrictive environments. Each country receives a numerical rating from 0 (the most free) to 100 (the least free), which serves as the basis for a press freedom status designation of "Free," "Partly Free," or "Not Free."

The Global Picture

Of the 195 countries and territories assessed in the latest survey, 72 (37 percent) were rated Free, 59 (30 percent) were rated Partly Free, and 64 (33 percent) were rated Not Free. This represented a modest decline from the 2007 survey, covering the year 2006: 74 Free, 58 Partly Free, and 63 Not Free countries and territories. The findings for the year 2007 also represent a negative shift from the survey results of six years ago, which was the last recent high point of press freedom.

In terms of population, the survey found that only 18 percent of the world's inhabitants live in countries that enjoy a Free press, while 40 percent have a Partly Free press and 42 percent have a Not Free press. These figures are notably affected by two countries—China, with a Not Free status, and India, with a Partly Free status—which together account for more than two billion of the world's six billion people. The percentage of those enjoying Free media in 2007 remained steady, while the percentage of people who live in countries with a Partly Free media environment improved slightly from 39 percent in 2006.

The overall level of press freedom worldwide, as measured by the global average score, worsened slightly in 2007, continuing a six-year downward trend. The averages for the legal, political, and economic categories all worsened as well, with the political category showing a particularly sharp decline.

As demonstrated by the score movements, there were few dramatic openings or closures in the world's media environments—changes that are typically seen in cases of coups, new governments, or serious political conflicts. However, there were significant movements, in some cases a continuation of past trends, in a large number of countries. In terms of countries whose score shifted by three or more points in 2007, declines outnumbered gains by a two-to-one margin.

Key Trends in 2007

Although decline is the overarching theme of this year's index, it is not a simple story of government-led crackdowns that manage to permanently restrict media freedom. The declines are driven by a complex set of factors, including broader authoritarian crackdowns on civil society, political upheaval, violence targeting the media by both state and nonstate actors, the imaginative use of legal mechanisms against journalists, and subtle economic pressures. In many cases, an overall decline in numerical score encompasses both positive and negative factors, including sustained efforts by journalists themselves to push back against a panoply of restrictions.

We have identified several trends that underpin the numerical movements in the latest index:

> **Media have played a key role in countries racked by political unrest and upheaval.** Coups, states of emergency, and electoral disputes have taken place in a growing number of settings. In many cases, the media have played a central role in covering political conflict and are a prime target when a crackdown sets in. Overt restrictions have included shutdowns of leading or pro-opposition news outlets and other forms of direct censorship. In the past year, this was a major factor in the Caucasus, Central and South Asia, and sub-Saharan Africa. Meanwhile, somewhat less egregious instances of pressure and editorial interference occurred in a number of highly ranked countries in Central Europe and the Caribbean.

> **Violence against journalists and impunity regarding past cases of abuse are important factors in a country's level of press freedom.** The level of violence and physical harassment directed at the press continues to rise in many countries, contributing to a number of score declines. In conflict zones such as Iraq and Somalia, the press

is in constant danger. Other regions of concern are Latin America (especially Mexico), the former Soviet Union (most notably Russia), and South and Southeast Asia (particularly the Philippines, Sri Lanka, and Pakistan). Apart from the direct impact on individual journalists, these attacks have a chilling effect, adding to larger problems of self-censorship. Conversely, declines in violence and/or impunity, as occurred in Haiti in 2007, can lead to a wide-ranging numerical improvement.

➤ **Media freedom remains seriously constrained by a panoply of laws used to punish critical journalists and outlets.** Both governments and private individuals continue to restrict media freedom through the use of laws that forbid "inciting hatred," commenting on sensitive topics such as religion or ethnicity, or "endangering national security." The abuse of libel laws has also increased in a number of countries, most notably in Africa.

➤ **Newer media forms—such as satellite television and internet-based newspapers, blogs, and social-networking sites—have emerged as an important force for openness in restricted media environments as well as a key area of contestation.** In the battle between government control and media freedom, relatively unrestricted access to these sources has broadened the diversity of available news and opinion. It was a driving force behind numerical improvements in the Middle East and North Africa region in 2007, and it contributed to Egypt's upgrade to Partly Free status. At the same time, an increasing number of governments—particularly in the former Soviet Union, the Middle East, Asia, and Africa—are employing or expanding methods of control over these potentially disruptive media. While crude blocking or filtering of particular websites remains common, some authoritarian states have also produced or financed progovernment propaganda designed specifically for these new formats.

Regional and Country Declines

The year featured few positive regional trends, with declines predominating in almost every part of the world. The largest regionwide decline was seen in the former Soviet Union, while smaller negative trends were apparent in the Americas, Asia, and sub-Saharan Africa.

There were setbacks in a number of influential countries, many of which had already been on downward trajectories in recent years. A number of declines occurred in South Asia, with restrictions on media coverage imposed in Pakistan, Bangladesh, and Sri Lanka, and Vietnam's government cracked down on dissident writers. Backsliding in the former Soviet Union continued, with Russia, Georgia, and Kyrgyzstan showing declines.

The Americas and sub-Saharan Africa registered both negative status changes for particular countries and broader numerical slippage. In the Americas, Guyana's status shifted from Free to Partly Free, while the score for Mexico deteriorated by a further three points. Sub-Saharan Africa accounted for three of the year's five status changes: Benin declined from Free to Partly Free, and both the Central African Republic and Niger moved into the Not Free column owing to authorities' attempts to limit news coverage, particularly in conflict areas.

Regional and Country Gains

The Middle East and North Africa region stood out by showing both overall improvement and significant gains in a specific country. The average regional score reflected the fact that in a number of countries, the media environment has benefited from greater access to satellite television service and the internet, including new formats such as blogs and social-networking websites. In addition, in the only positive status change of the year, Egypt was upgraded from Not Free to Partly Free as local journalists proved willing to cross the "red lines" that had previously restricted their work, and a greater range of viewpoints emerged not only in the traditional Egyptian media, but also in the pan-Arab press, informal media, and blogosphere. This upgrade occurred despite a continuation of, and in some cases an increase in, government harassment, repression, and imprisonment of journalists.

Numerical improvements also occurred in several fragile states where the government has relatively tenuous control, such as Haiti, East Timor, and Lebanon; one country emerging from a coup, Thailand; and another Asian country, Malaysia, where journalists, particularly those in the new media, have recently shown greater aggressiveness in covering politically sensitive stories despite authorities' attempts to restrict such expression.

Worst of the Worst

The world's worst-rated countries continue to include Burma, Cuba, Libya, North Korea, and Turkmenistan. In 2007, Eritrea joined the ranks of these exceedingly bad performers, while a crackdown in Burma worsened that country's already repressive media environment, leaving its score second only to that of North Korea. In these states, which are scattered across the globe, independent media are either nonexistent or barely able to operate, the press acts as a mouthpiece for the ruling regime, and citizens' access to unbiased information is severely limited. Nevertheless, the numerical scores for Cuba and Libya did improve slightly in 2007 to reflect the marginal openings provided by new and transnational media forms such as the internet and satellite television. Rounding out the 10 most repressive media environments are two countries in the former Soviet Union—Belarus and Uzbekistan—and two other countries in Africa—Equatorial Guinea and Zimbabwe—where media remain heavily restricted.

Regional Trends

Americas: In the Americas, 16 countries (46 percent) were rated Free, 17 (48 percent) were rated Partly Free, and 2 (6 percent) were rated Not Free in 2007. These figures are significantly influenced by the open media environments of the Caribbean, which tend to offset the less rosy picture in Central and South America. There was one negative status change during the year, and numerical declines outweighed gains. The average regional score worsened modestly compared with 2006, as marginal improvements in both the legal and economic categories were overshadowed by a decline in the political category.

The only two countries in the region rated Not Free are **Cuba**, which has one of the most repressive media environments worldwide, and **Venezuela**, where the government of President Hugo Chavez continued its efforts to control the press. Despite significant government restrictions in both countries, the growing number of blogs in Cuba provide some space for free expression, while the vigor of opposition-aligned print media in Venezuela has endured despite the forced closure of key private television outlet RCTV.

Several important countries in the region repeated declines seen in the previous year, often for the same reasons. **Mexico**'s score dropped a further three points, to 51, to reflect the extremely high level of drug-related violence against journalists as well as the continued atmosphere of impunity surrounding attacks on the media. Intimidation and physical attacks were also a major concern in **Bolivia**, whose score worsened a further two points, to 39, owing to increased polarization among media outlets and a rise in attacks against journalists by both government and opposition supporters. In neighboring **Peru**, an increase in threats and physical attacks against media workers, an atmosphere of impunity, and the government's closure of several local radio and television stations—reportedly in retaliation for critical coverage—led to a further slippage, from 42 to 44 points.

Meanwhile, **Colombia**, which had been upgraded to Partly Free in 2006, experienced some backsliding and a numerical deterioration from 57 to 59 points owing to a rise in attacks against journalists by both state and nonstate actors as well as mounting economic uncertainty for media outlets amid the ongoing civil war.

Declines occurred not only in the Americas' midrange performers, but also in several relatively free media environments in the Caribbean. In the region's only status change, **Guyana**'s score worsened from 29 to 31 and its status declined from Free to Partly Free owing to a government decision to withdraw advertisements from the influential newspaper *Stabroek News*, apparently in response to critical reporting, as well as an armed attack against another leading paper. Preelection political tension, which included heightened pressure on and intimidation of the press, was primarily responsible for declines in both the **Bahamas**, whose score moved from 17 to 20, and **Barbados**, whose score worsened from 17 to 19. Meanwhile, **Dominica**'s score fell from 20 to 22 owing to a libel suit filed by the prime minister against a weekly newspaper for articles alleging corruption. The suit had a chilling effect on investigative journalism in the country.

Although the **United States** continues to be one of the better performers in the survey, there were continuing problems in the legal sphere, particularly concerning cases in which the authorities tried to compel journalists to reveal confidential sources or provide access to research material in the course of criminal investigations. In 2007, the numerical score for the United States worsened by one point, to 17, to reflect a slight increase in physical attacks on the press, including one murder and several cases of intimidation.

In a departure from the regional downward trend, **Haiti** showed continued improvement following substantial positive movement and a status upgrade during the previous year. In 2007, its score improved from 59 to 56 owing to a more secure political atmosphere and the launch of the Independent Commission to Support the Investigation of Assassinations of Journalists, which yielded prison sentences for several individuals found guilty of past murders. **Argentina**, after several years of decline spurred by persistent government manipulation of advertising to influence media content, showed a positive score improvement in 2007, from 49 to 47, to reflect a Supreme Court decision favoring nondiscrimination in the allocation of state advertising as well as the granting of the first five broadcasting licenses to noncommercial radio stations.

Asia-Pacific: The Asia-Pacific region as a whole exhibited a relatively high level of press freedom, with 16 countries (40 percent) rated Free, 10 (25 percent) rated Partly Free, and 14 (35 percent) rated Not Free. Yet the regionwide figures are deceptive, as they disguise considerable subregional diversity. For example, the Pacific islands, Australasia, and parts of East Asia have some of the best-ranked media environments worldwide, while conditions in South Asia, Southeast Asia, and other parts of East Asia are significantly poorer. The balanced country breakdown also obscures the fact that only 7 percent of the region's population have access to Free media, while 42 percent live in Partly Free media environments and the majority, 51 percent, live in Not Free media environments. The overall level of press freedom in Asia, in terms of the average regional score, declined marginally from the previous year, with small drops seen in both the legal and political categories.

Asia is home to the two worst-rated countries in the world, Burma and North Korea, as well as other poor performers like China, Laos, and Vietnam, all of which use state or party control of the press as the primary means of restricting media freedom. **Burma**'s score deteriorated in 2007 from 96 to 97 (leaving it in second to last place worldwide) owing to increased state violence against journalists and additional restrictions imposed on internet access during and after prodemocracy demonstrations in August and September. **Vietnam** witnessed a larger numerical decline, from 77 to 82, as the government cracked down on peaceful dissent with a severity not seen in several years. Over a dozen individuals who had pushed for a more open media environment or posted prodemocracy writings online were sentenced to long prison terms. Ironically, the move came shortly after Vietnam gained membership in the World Trade Organization. Conditions in the world's largest poor performer, **China**, did not lead to a numerical change; increased media commercialization balanced tighter official control over content and a general crackdown on dissent, especially online, in the run-up to the 17th Party Congress.

Asia saw many negative developments in 2007, continuing the downward regional trajectory noted in the previous year's survey. Conditions in South Asia were particularly worrisome, with four countries registering significant declines. In Bangladesh and Pakistan, political crises accompanied by the imposition of emergency decrees negatively affected media freedom, while both Sri Lanka and Afghanistan were troubled by ongoing civil conflicts. **Pakistan**'s score worsened from 63 to 66 to reflect increased attacks on journalists who attempted to cover the growing political and constitutional crisis, in addition to overt censorship and other restrictions, particularly on the broadcast media, associated with the imposition of martial law in November. In **Bangladesh**, heightened media restrictions following the January 2007 emergency declaration, including censorship and controls on permissible content, were reflected in a numerical slippage from 66 to 68 points. After a status downgrade in 2006, **Sri Lanka**'s numerical score declined by a further four points, to 67, to reflect a worsening media environment throughout the country, including enhanced legal restrictions, verbal and physical harassment by authorities, and an increase in attacks on and murders of journalists—particularly ethnic Tamil reporters in the north and east, where the government and the Tamil Tiger rebels are fighting an escalating civil war. **Afghanistan**'s score fell from 69 to 71 as a result of journalists' increased difficulties in covering the news, particularly in lawless or rebellious areas of the country, as well as a rise in attacks on reporters and media outlets.

Declines were also apparent elsewhere in Asia. After a status upgrade in 2006, **Cambodia**'s numerical score slipped from 58 to 60 to reflect increased censorship and attacks on journalists, especially in the wake of the publication of a report on illegal logging by the London-based nongovernmental organization Global Witness. In **Mongolia**, ongoing legal harassment of journalists and the judiciary's inability or unwillingness to prevent it led to a numerical slippage from 36 to 38 points.

While the majority of score changes in 2007 were negative, several bright spots are worth noting. A number of these gains came in countries whose scores in 2006 had been negatively affected by coups or other political conflicts. Despite intimidation of journalists by the military in the early months of the year following a December 2006 coup, **Fiji**'s score improved from 39 to 37 points owing to reduced government pressure on the media over the course of 2007 and an improved legal environment as the new regime asserted that the constitution had not been suspended. In **East Timor**, the transition to a new coalition government headed by former president Xanana Gusmao led to an improved political atmosphere and initiatives that enhanced access to information for those outside the capital, boosting the country's score from 42 to 38. **Thailand**, which also experienced a coup in 2006, reversed course slightly with the passage of a new constitution in October that included protections for freedom of expression, leading to an improvement in the legal environment and a score adjustment from 59 to 56 points.

In two other Asian countries, numerical improvements stemmed from the tenacity of journalists, particularly from online and new private media outlets, in reporting on sensitive topics despite the authorities' attempts to restrict such expression. **Malaysia's** score moved from 68 to 65 owing to more aggressive coverage of official corruption and antigovernment protests by online media, even in the face of continuing restrictions on content. In the **Maldives**, a modest opening in the media environment included the launch of new private radio stations and continuing efforts by pro-opposition outlets to present coverage that was critical of the government, leading to more diversity and debate in a changing political arena.

Central and Eastern Europe/Former Soviet Union: For the combined CEE/FSU region, 8 countries (28 percent) remain classified as Free, 10 (36 percent) were Partly Free, and 10 (36 percent) were Not Free. However, a majority of the people in this region (56 percent) live in Not Free media environments, while only 18 percent have access to Free media. In 2007, the regionwide average score showed the biggest drop of any region. Declines were particularly noticeable in the legal and political categories.

While the region shares a common history of communist oppression, the trajectory of countries in the former Soviet Union has diverged significantly from that of Central and Eastern Europe in terms of respect for fundamental political rights and civil liberties. The press freedom ratings for these subregions reflect a similar divergence. All of the countries of Central Europe and the three Baltic states, which have managed to overcome a decades-long legacy of Soviet media culture and control, are assessed as Free. In contrast, 10 of the 12 non-Baltic post-Soviet states are ranked as Not Free. Of the 195 countries and territories examined in the survey, 3 of the 10 worst press freedom abusers—Belarus, Uzbekistan, and Turkmenistan—are found in the former Soviet Union.

In 2007, the region featured no status shifts in either direction, and all of the significant numerical changes were negative. This trend was apparent in the best-performing countries, including several in Central and Eastern Europe and the Baltic states; countries that had recently showed positive improvement, such as Kyrgyzstan and Georgia; and some of the region's worst performers, including Russia, Azerbaijan, and Belarus.

Slippage was apparent in a number of countries with Free media environments, and in most cases it reflected increasing government influence over content at public media outlets. **Latvia**'s score moved from 19 to 22 owing to apparent government intervention in the editorial decisions of public broadcasters, particularly regarding coverage of Russia, and a lack of transparency on private media ownership. Similar concerns over government influence at public broadcasters were an issue in **Slovakia, Slovenia**, and **Poland**, whose scores all dropped two points to 22, 23, and 24, respectively. Meanwhile, **Romania**'s score fell from 42 to 44 to reflect a Constitutional Court decision that reinstated criminal defamation.

Political strife and polarization negatively affected media freedom in several midrange performers. After a promising opening in its media environment two years ago, **Kyrgyzstan** saw continued backsliding in 2007 amid an increase in attacks on journalists and the confiscation of the print runs of several newspapers; the country's score dropped another three points, to 70. In the Caucasus, **Georgia**'s score moved from 57 to 60 to reflect increased polarization of the media environment, the forced closure of the pro-opposition Imedi television station, and the suspension of all broadcast media during a temporary state of emergency. In neighboring **Armenia**, increased government pressure on the media ahead of parliamentary and presidential elections—including legal harassment of journalists and severe financial pressures on the independent Gala TV station—led to a slippage from 64 to 66 points.

Press freedom also suffered in a number of countries with already restrictive media environments. **Azerbaijan**'s score worsened from 75 to 77 owing to the forced closure of two Russian-language newspapers and the sentencing of at least eight journalists to prison during the year. In **Kazakhstan**, the forcible closure of two media outlets after they defended their owner (a member of the presidential family who had fallen from grace), a rise in progovernment media coverage prior to parliamentary elections, and increasing harassment of journalists all pulled the country's score down to 78. **Belarus**'s score worsened from 89 to 91 to reflect an increase in legal harassment and intimidation of independent media outlets as well as the strengthening of restrictions on the internet.

Most important, **Russia**, which serves as a model and sponsor for a number of neighboring countries, saw continued and substantial declines in 2007. Its score worsened from 75 to 78 to reflect a significant deterioration in the legal and political environment for the media, with hundreds of journalists facing criminal or civil cases and at least two taken into temporary psychiatric detention after criticizing local authorities. Reporters continue to suffer from a high level of personal insecurity, and impunity for past murders or physical attacks against journalists is the norm. State control or influence over almost all media outlets remains a serious concern, particularly as it affects the political landscape and Russians' ability to make informed electoral choices.

Middle East and North Africa: The Middle East and North Africa continued to show the lowest regional ratings, with just 1 country (5 percent) rated Free, 3 (16 percent) rated Partly Free, and 15 (79 percent) rated Not Free in 2007. The average regionwide score improved slightly and was the only one to do so in a year marked by global and regional declines. The gains fall within a pattern of longer-term positive movement in the region, owing to the continued spread and influence of pan-Arab satellite television networks and internet-based media such as blogs and social-networking sites, which serve as alternative sources of news and information. In some countries, print media have also become more critical as journalists push the boundaries of acceptable coverage, even when faced with varied forms of harassment or reprisals by autocratic governments.

However, media in the region generally remain constrained by extremely restrictive legal environments in which laws concerning libel and defamation, the insult of monarchs and public figures, and emergency rule hamper the ability of journalists to report freely. Of particular and long-standing concern are Libya, Iran, Syria, Tunisia, Saudi Arabia, and the Israeli-Occupied Territories/Palestinian Authority. Although **Iraq** remained by far the most dangerous country in the world for media workers, a reduction in the number of arrests and detentions of journalists by Iraqi and U.S. security forces contributed to a marginal improvement in Iraq's score for 2007.

In addition to the overall regional improvement, the Middle East saw positive change in a number of key countries, including both relatively good and weak performers. In the only positive status upgrade of the year, **Egypt**'s score improved from 62 to 59 points, lifting it from Not Free to Partly Free. The upgrade reflected Egyptian journalists' increased willingness to cross the "red lines" that previously restricted their work. It was also linked to the greater range of viewpoints represented not only in the traditional Egyptian media, but also in the pan-Arab press, informal media, and blogosphere. It is important to note that the change occurred despite a continuation of, and in some cases an increase in, government harassment, repression, and imprisonment of journalists during 2007.

Other country improvements during the year included a four-point gain to 55 for **Lebanon** owing to a substantial decrease in violence against journalists and a drop in government censorship of the media, and a two-point increase to 54 for **Kuwait** as a result of the licensing of six new Arabic-language dailies—the first licensing of any new paper in 30 years—a positive step that increased media diversity. Scores also improved marginally in two of the region's most restricted media environments, largely to reflect citizens' access to new and freer media forms. **Tunisia**'s score improved from 83 to 81 owing to the launch of an independent journalists' union and the increased availability of satellite television, despite authorities' continued prosecution of critical reporters. The score for the region's worst-rated country, **Libya**, improved from 96 to 94 owing to a lack of government blocking of websites and increased availability of satellite television.

While transnational factors have led to improvements in many countries, the level of press freedom in much of the region continues to be seriously constrained by a restrictive legal framework and by authorities' consistent efforts to limit critical reporting through either legal or physical harassment of journalists. **Morocco** saw further declines in 2007, from 62 to 64 points, as legal harassment led to the forced closure of two prominent publications—*Le Journal Hebdomadaire* and *TelQuel*—following coverage that was critical of the government. In **Jordan**, whose score worsened from 61 to 63, security agencies were primarily responsible for harassing journalists, while the government interfered to prevent the launching of ATV, the country's first private television station.

Sub-Saharan Africa: Overall, 7 countries (15 percent) were rated Free, 18 (37 percent) were rated Partly Free, and 23 (48 percent) remained Not Free in sub-Saharan Africa. The average regionwide level of press freedom declined during the year, as did the average score in the legal and political categories. Trends in individual countries presented a mixed picture, with some improvements but a greater number of declines, including three negative status changes. Press freedom conditions continue to be dire in Equatorial Guinea, Eritrea, and Zimbabwe, where authoritarian governments use legal pressure, imprisonment, and other forms of harassment to sharply curtail the ability of independent media outlets to report freely. All 3 countries continue to rank among the bottom 10 performers worldwide.

Reasons for the negative movement during 2007 varied from country to country, but it appeared to be driven by either legal or political factors and in many cases a combination of the two. **Benin**'s score worsened from

30 to 31, which tipped it over the cusp from Free to Partly Free status, owing to the continuation of criminal libel cases and polarization in a growing number of politically funded media outlets. An increase in legal harassment, particularly through libel cases, was also an issue in **Mali**, whose score worsened from 24 to 27; **Burkina Faso**, whose score decline from 39 to 41 was aggravated by several cases of physical harassment; **Senegal**, whose score moved from 46 to 49 amid biased judgments by the regulatory commission and attacks on the press; and **Djibouti**, whose score fell from 69 to 72, in part because of the shutdown of the country's only private newspaper.

In a number of other countries, political polarization and conflict, sometimes centered on elections, and the authorities' resulting desire to limit press coverage of certain issues had a negative effect on media outlets' ability to cover key news stories and on the diversity of information available to the public. Following a promising upgrade in 2006 owing to legal improvements, the **Central African Republic** slipped back into Not Free status as the authorities attempted to limit coverage of the continuing armed conflict in the north of the country. Meanwhile, **Niger**, which has for some time been rated in the Partly Free category, witnessed a score decline from 58 to 63 points and a downgrade to Not Free status owing to the government's attempts to control information on the civil conflict in the north, including suspending the operation of critical media outlets, prosecuting journalists for libel, and harassing those who produced controversial reports.

Political conflict was a primary factor in the **Comoros'** score decline from 48 to 54 points, the survey's largest drop. The country has seen increased polarization and a parallel increase in censorship and harassment of media by the security forces. Election-related polarization also occurred in **Sierra Leone**, whose score dropped from 56 to 59 to reflect a tense preelection political atmosphere that negatively affected media freedom, including biased reporting, threats, and physical violence, as well as directives from the media commission regarding news coverage. In **Lesotho**, an election-related crackdown that included the shutdown of a radio station and the deportation of one of its journalists led to a numerical slippage from 42 to 46. Threats and attacks from nonstate actors, particularly regarding journalists' efforts to cover the growing problem of drug trafficking, were a key factor in **Guinea-Bissau**, whose score moved from 48 to 53. Finally, conditions in one of Africa's worst performers, **The Gambia**, worsened further during 2007, leading to a drop in score from 77 to 79, owing to a combination of legal and extralegal intimidation of journalists and media outlets that included court cases, arbitrary arrests and imprisonment, and complete impunity in past cases of press freedom abuse. At year's end, media freedom was under threat in **Kenya** in the wake of a disputed election and widespread violence that led to the shutdown of media outlets.

Although they were far outweighed by declines, Africa did see a number of improvements during 2007. In many cases, these positive movements reflected a decline in the physical harassment of journalists or the increased ability of reporters to cover sensitive political stories. Attacks on the press declined in **Tanzania**, whose score improved from 51 to 48; **Nigeria**, whose score improved from 55 to 53; and **Cameroon**, whose score improved from 67 to 65. Cameroon also benefited from the licensing of four new private broadcast outlets. Meanwhile, **Sudan** saw continued numerical improvement owing to further growth in media diversity in the south of the country. Finally, two countries that had seen declines in 2006 reversed course in 2007. A crackdown on the press was eased in **Burundi**, with fewer cases of physical harassment or jailing of journalists, leading to a positive numerical shift from 77 to 74 points. An improved political situation in **Cote d'Ivoire**, in which journalists were less prone to attack and better able to cover news events throughout the country, resulted in a positive score change from 68 to 66.

Western Europe: Western Europe continued to boast the highest level of press freedom worldwide; in 2007, 24 countries (96 percent) were rated Free and 1 (4 percent) was rated Partly Free. Although the level of press freedom remained largely steady, the average regional score did decline slightly from that of 2006. Countries registering declines included **Portugal**, whose score worsened owing to a new law that could strip journalists of their right to protect confidential sources and gives employers the right to reuse journalists' work in any way for 30 days following its initial publication; and **Malta**, whose score deteriorated by several points owing to a series of threats and attacks against journalists covering public demonstrations and debates.

In **Turkey**, the only country ranked as Partly Free in the region, the continued prosecution of large numbers of journalists and the high-profile January 2007 assassination of Armenian editor Hrant Dink, apparently with some involvement by state actors, were the primary factors behind a two-point score decline from 49 to 51.

GLOBAL AND REGIONAL TABLES

Rank	Country	Rating	Status
1	Finland	9	F
	Iceland	9	F
3	Denmark	10	F
	Norway	10	F
5	Belgium	11	F
	Sweden	11	F
7	Luxembourg	12	F
8	Andorra	13	F
	Netherlands	13	F
	New Zealand	13	F
	Switzerland	13	F
12	Liechtenstein	14	F
	Palau	14	F
14	Ireland	15	F
	Jamaica	15	F
16	Estonia	16	F
	Germany	16	F
	Monaco	16	F
	Portugal	16	F
	St. Lucia	16	F
21	Marshall Islands	17	F
	San Marino	17	F
	St. Vincent & Grenadines	17	F
	United States	17	F
25	Canada	18	F
	Czech Republic	18	F
	Lithuania	18	F
	United Kingdom	18	F
29	Barbados	19	F
	Costa Rica	19	F
	St. Kitts & Nevis	19	F
32	Bahamas	20	F
	Malta	20	F
	Taiwan	20	F
35	Australia	21	F
	Austria	21	F
	Hungary	21	F
	Japan	21	F
	Micronesia	21	F
40	Belize	22	F
	Cyprus	22	F
	Dominica	22	F
	France	22	F
	Latvia	22	F
	Slovakia	22	F
46	Slovenia	23	F
	Spain	23	F
	Suriname	23	F
	Trinidad & Tobago	23	F
	Vanuatu	23	F
51	Grenada	24	F
	Poland	24	F
53	Kiribati	26	F

Rank	Country	Rating	Status
	Mauritius	26	F
	Tuvalu	26	F
56	Ghana	27	F
	Greece	27	F
	Mali	27	F
59	Cape Verde	28	F
	Israel	28	F
	Nauru	28	F
	Papua New Guinea	28	F
	Sao Tome & Principe	28	F
	South Africa	28	F
65	Italy	29	F
	Samoa	29	F
67	Chile	30	F
	Hong Kong	30	F
	Namibia	30	F
	Solomon Islands	30	F
	South Korea	30	F
	Uruguay	30	F
73	Benin	31	P F
	Guyana	31	P F
	Tonga	31	P F
76	Bulgaria	33	P F
77	India	35	P F
78	Botswana	36	P F
	Croatia	36	P F
80	Fiji	37	P F
81	East Timor	38	P F
	Mongolia	38	P F
	Montenegro	38	P F
84	Antigua & Barbuda	39	P F
	Bolivia	39	P F
	Dominican Republic	39	P F
	Serbia	39	P F
88	Mozambique	40	P F
89	Burkina Faso	41	P F
	Ecuador	41	P F
91	Brazil	42	P F
	El Salvador	42	P F
93	Nicaragua	43	P F
94	Panama	44	P F
	Peru	44	P F
	Romania	44	P F
97	Bosnia	45	P F
	Philippines	45	P F
99	Lesotho	46	P F
100	Argentina	47	P F
	Macedonia	47	P F
102	Madagascar	48	P F
	Tanzania	48	P F
104	Senegal	49	P F
105	Albania	50	P F
106	Congo-Brazzaville	51	P F

18

Table of Global Press Freedom Rankings

Rank	Country	Rating	Status	Rank	Country	Rating	Status
	Honduras	51	P F		United Arab Emirates	68	N F
	Mexico	51	P F	153	Gabon	69	N F
	Turkey	51	P F		Iraq	69	N F
110	Guinea-Bissau	53	P F		Singapore	69	N F
	Nigeria	53	P F	156	Kyrgyzstan	70	N F
	Uganda	53	P F	157	Afghanistan	71	N F
	Ukraine	53	P F		Bahrain	71	N F
114	Comoros	54	P F		Oman	71	N F
	Indonesia	54	P F	160	Djibouti	72	N F
	Kuwait	54	P F	161	Burundi	74	N F
117	Lebanon	55	P F		Chad	74	N F
	Malawi	55	P F		Togo	74	N F
119	Haiti	56	P F		Venezuela	74	N F
	Mauritania	56	P F	165	Brunei	75	N F
	Thailand	56	P F	166	Ethiopia	76	N F
122	Nepal	57	P F		Swaziland	76	N F
123	Guatemala	58	P F	168	Azerbaijan	77	N F
124	Colombia	59	P F		Tajikistan	77	N F
	Egypt	59	P F	170	Kazakhstan	78	N F
	Seychelles	59	P F		Russia	78	N F
	Sierra Leone	59	P F		Sudan	78	N F
128	Cambodia	60	P F		Yemen	78	N F
	Georgia	60	P F	174	The Gambia	79	N F
	Kenya	60	P F	175	Congo-Kinshasa	81	N F
	Paraguay	60	P F		Saudi Arabia	81	N F
132	Bhutan	61	N F		Tunisia	81	N F
	Central African Republic	61	N F	178	Vietnam	82	N F
134	Algeria	62	N F	179	Laos	83	N F
135	Angola	63	N F		Syria	83	N F
	Jordan	63	N F	181	China	84	N F
	Niger	63	N F		IOT/PA*	84	N F
138	Morocco	64	N F		Rwanda	84	N F
	Qatar	64	N F		Somalia	84	N F
	Zambia	64	N F	185	Iran	85	N F
141	Cameroon	65	N F	186	Equatorial Guinea	89	N F
	Liberia	65	N F		Zimbabwe	89	N F
	Malaysia	65	N F	188	Belarus	91	N F
144	Armenia	66	N F	189	Uzbekistan	92	N F
	Cote d'Ivoire	66	N F	190	Cuba	94	N F
	Guinea	66	N F		Eritrea	94	N F
	Maldives	66	N F		Libya	94	N F
	Moldova	66	N F	193	Turkmenistan	96	N F
	Pakistan	66	N F	194	Burma	97	N F
150	Sri Lanka	67	N F	195	North Korea	98	N F
151	Bangladesh	68	N F	*Israeli-Occupied Territories/Palestinian Authority			

Status	Number of Countries	Percent of Total
Free	72	37%
Partly Free	59	30%
Not Free	64	33%
TOTAL	195	100%

Press Freedom Rankings by Region

Sub-Saharan Africa

Rank	Country	Rating	Status	Rank	Country	Rating	Status
1	Mauritius	26	F	25	Kenya	60	P F
2	Ghana	27	F	26	Central African Republic	61	N F
	Mali	27	F	27	Angola	63	N F
4	Cape Verde	28	F		Niger	63	N F
	Sao Tome & Principe	28	F	29	Zambia	64	N F
	South Africa	28	F	30	Cameroon	65	N F
7	Namibia	30	F		Liberia	65	N F
8	Benin	31	P F	32	Cote d'Ivoire	66	N F
9	Botswana	36	P F		Guinea	66	N F
10	Mozambique	40	P F	34	Gabon	69	N F
11	Burkina Faso	41	P F	35	Djibouti	72	N F
12	Lesotho	46	P F	36	Burundi	74	N F
13	Madagascar	48	P F		Chad	74	N F
	Tanzania	48	P F		Togo	74	N F
15	Senegal	49	P F	39	Ethiopia	76	N F
16	Congo-Brazzaville	51	P F		Swaziland	76	N F
17	Guinea-Bissau	53	P F	41	Sudan	78	N F
	Nigeria	53	P F	42	The Gambia	79	N F
	Uganda	53	P F	43	Congo-Kinshasa	81	N F
20	Comoros	54	P F	44	Rwanda	84	N F
21	Malawi	55	P F		Somalia	84	N F
22	Mauritania	56	P F	46	Equatorial Guinea	89	N F
23	Seychelles	59	P F		Zimbabwe	89	N F
	Sierra Leone	59	P F	48	Eritrea	94	N F

Status	Number of Countries	Percent of Total
Free	7	15%
Partly Free	18	37%
Not Free	23	48%
TOTAL	48	100%

The Americas

Rank	Country	Rating	Status	Rank	Country	Rating	Status
1	Jamaica	15	F		Bolivia	39	P F
2	St. Lucia	16	F		Dominican Republic	39	P F
3	St. Vincent & Grenadines	17	F	21	Ecuador	41	P F
	United States	17	F	22	Brazil	42	P F
5	Canada	18	F		El Salvador	42	P F
6	Barbados	19	F	24	Nicaragua	43	P F
	Costa Rica	19	F	25	Panama	44	P F
	St. Kitts & Nevis	19	F		Peru	44	P F
9	Bahamas	20	F	27	Argentina	47	P F
10	Belize	22	F	28	Honduras	51	P F
	Dominica	22	F		Mexico	51	P F
12	Suriname	23	F	30	Haiti	56	P F
	Trinidad & Tobago	23	F	31	Guatemala	58	P F
14	Grenada	24	F	32	Colombia	59	P F
15	Chile	30	F	33	Paraguay	60	P F
	Uruguay	30	F	34	Venezuela	74	N F
17	Guyana	31	P F	35	Cuba	94	N F
18	Antigua & Barbuda	39	P F				

Status	Number of Countries	Percent of Total
Free	16	46%
Partly Free	17	48%
Not Free	2	6%
TOTAL	35	100%

Middle East & North Africa

Rank	Country	Rating	Status	Rank	Country	Rating	Status
1	Israel	28	F	11	Bahrain	71	N F
2	Kuwait	54	P F		Oman	71	N F
3	Lebanon	55	P F	13	Yemen	78	N F
4	Egypt	59	P F	14	Saudi Arabia	81	N F
5	Algeria	62	N F		Tunisia	81	N F
6	Jordan	63	N F	16	Syria	83	N F
7	Morocco	64	N F	17	IOT/PA*	84	N F
	Qatar	64	N F	18	Iran	85	N F
9	United Arab Emirates	68	N F	19	Libya	94	N F
10	Iraq	69	N F				

*Israeli-Occupied Territories/Palestinian Authority

Status	Number of Countries	Percent of Total
Free	1	5%
Partly Free	3	16%
Not Free	15	79%
TOTAL	19	100%

Asia-Pacific

Rank	Country	Rating	Status	Rank	Country	Rating	Status
1	New Zealand	13	F		Mongolia	38	P F
2	Palau	14	F	22	Philippines	45	P F
3	Marshall Islands	17	F	23	Indonesia	54	P F
4	Taiwan	20	F	24	Thailand	56	P F
5	Australia	21	F	25	Nepal	57	P F
	Japan	21	F	26	Cambodia	60	P F
	Micronesia	21	F	27	Bhutan	61	N F
8	Vanuatu	23	F	28	Malaysia	65	N F
9	Kiribati	26	F	29	Maldives	66	N F
	Tuvalu	26	F		Pakistan	66	N F
11	Nauru	28	F	31	Sri Lanka	67	N F
	Papua New Guinea	28	F	32	Bangladesh	68	N F
13	Samoa	29	F	33	Singapore	69	N F
14	Hong Kong	30	F	34	Afghanistan	71	N F
	Solomon Islands	30	F	35	Brunei	75	N F
	South Korea	30	F	36	Vietnam	82	N F
17	Tonga	31	P F	37	Laos	83	N F
18	India	35	P F	38	China	84	N F
19	Fiji	37	P F	39	Burma	97	N F
20	East Timor	38	P F	40	North Korea	98	N F

Status	Number of Countries	Percent of Total
Free	16	40%
Partly Free	10	25%
Not Free	14	35%
TOTAL	40	100%

22

Western Europe

Rank	Country	Rating	Status	Rank	Country	Rating	Status
1	Finland	9	F		Monaco	16	F
	Iceland	9	F		Portugal	16	F
3	Denmark	10	F	16	San Marino	17	F
	Norway	10	F	17	United Kingdom	18	F
5	Belgium	11	F	18	Malta	20	F
	Sweden	11	F	19	Austria	21	F
7	Luxembourg	12	F	20	Cyprus	22	F
8	Andorra	13	F		France	22	F
	Netherlands	13	F	22	Spain	23	F
	Switzerland	13	F	23	Greece	27	F
11	Liechtenstein	14	F	24	Italy	29	F
12	Ireland	15	F	25	Turkey	51	P F
13	Germany	16	F				

Status	Number of Countries	Percent of Total
Free	24	96%
Partly Free	1	4%
Not Free	0	0%
TOTAL	25	100%

Central and Eastern Europe / Former Soviet Union

Rank	Country	Rating	Status	Rank	Country	Rating	Status
1	Estonia	16	F	15	Macedonia	47	P F
2	Czech Rep.	18	F	16	Albania	50	P F
	Lithuania	18	F	17	Ukraine	53	P F
4	Hungary	21	F	18	Georgia	60	P F
5	Latvia	22	F	19	Armenia	66	N F
	Slovakia	22	F		Moldova	66	N F
7	Slovenia	23	F	21	Kyrgyzstan	70	N F
8	Poland	24	F	22	Azerbaijan	77	N F
9	Bulgaria	33	P F		Tajikistan	77	N F
10	Croatia	36	P F	24	Kazakhstan	78	N F
11	Montenegro	38	P F		Russia	78	N F
12	Serbia	39	P F	26	Belarus	91	N F
13	Romania	44	P F	27	Uzbekistan	92	N F
14	Bosnia	45	P F	28	Turkmenistan	96	N F

Status	Number of Countries	Percent of Total
Free	8	28%
Partly Free	10	36%
Not Free	10	36%
TOTAL	28	100%

Summary of Results

Regional Press Freedom Breakdown

Region	Free	Partly Free	Not Free	Number of Countries
Americas	16 (46%)	17 (48%)	2 (6%)	35
Asia-Pacific	16 (40%)	10 (25%)	14 (35%)	40
CEE/FSU	8 (28%)	10 (36%)	10 (36%)	28
Middle East & North Africa	1 (5%)	3 (16%)	15 (79%)	19
Sub-Saharan Africa	7 (15%)	18 (37%)	23 (48%)	48
Western Europe	24 (96%)	1 (4%)	0 (0%)	25
TOTAL	72 (37%)	59 (30%)	64 (33%)	195

Press Freedom by Population

Status	By Country	By Population (billions)
Free	72 (37%)	1.18 (18%)
Partly Free	59 (30%)	2.67 (40%)
Not Free	64 (33%)	2.77 (42%)
TOTAL	195 (100%)	6.62 (100%)

COUNTRY
REPORTS AND
RATINGS

Afghanistan

LEGAL ENVIRONMENT: 21
POLITICAL ENVIRONMENT: 30
ECONOMIC ENVIRONMENT: 20

Status: Partly Free

TOTAL SCORE: 71

Survey Edition	2003	2004	2005	2006	2007
Total Score, Status	74,NF	72,NF	68,NF	69,NF	69,NF

As the media environment has continued to grow and diversify, journalists faced rising threats in 2007, mostly in the form of physical attacks and intimidation. Article 34 of the new constitution, passed in January 2004, provides for freedom of the press and of expression. A revised 2005 Press Law guarantees the right of citizens to obtain information and prohibits censorship. However, it retains broad restrictions on content that is "contrary to the principles of Islam or offensive to other religions and sects" and "matters leading to dishonoring and defaming individuals." It also establishes five commissions intended to regulate media agencies and investigate complaints of misconduct; one of the commissions has the power to decide if journalists who contravene the law should face court prosecution or a fine. Critics of the law have alleged that its prohibition of "anti-Islamic" writings is overly vague and has led to considerable confusion within the journalistic community on what constitutes permissible content. Amendments to the Media Law proposed in May 2007 could give authorities greater control over content and include vague prohibitions on defamation; these were opposed by local journalists, and the government had withdrawn the proposal by year's end.

Media outlets are occasionally fined or given warnings for broadcasting "un-Islamic" material or offending local culture. Cases of journalists and others being arrested on blasphemy charges have had a chilling effect on press freedom, with an accompanying rise in self-censorship. Many avoid writing about sensitive issues such as Islam, national unity, or crimes committed by specific warlords. In 2006, intelligence officials at the National Security Directorate issued "guidelines" to a number of news media outlets to restrict their coverage of security issues, terrorist incidents or groups, the conduct of foreign troops, or other subjects perceived to harm the national interest or erode the people's morale. The concept received support from other government officials, providing an indication to some observers that an atmosphere of official support for press freedom has diminished in the years following Taliban rule.

A growing number of journalists were threatened or harassed by government ministers, politicians, police and security services, U.S. forces, and others in positions of power as a result of their reporting, while others have been arrested and detained. Kamran Mir Hazar, editor of a popular online news website, was detained several times during the year by national security forces following several critical stories. Staff of the outspoken Tolo network have been particularly targeted. In an April 2007 incident, Tolo's main offices were raided by dozens of police officers, who detained seven staff and took them to be questioned by the attorney general regarding a news report that he had complained about; a similar case occurred in August, leading some commentators to point to a trend of growing official intolerance for critical news reports and abuse of government power to suppress the media. Reporters have also faced difficulties in covering proceedings at the newly established parliament, with several being assaulted and many more denied access on various occasions. In general, according to the Committee to Protect Journalists, official information is not readily available to members of the press. Media diversity and freedom are markedly higher in the capital, Kabul, and some warlords and provincial governors exercise authority over media in the areas under their control.

Journalists were also increasingly targeted by insurgents in 2007. In a horrific case, the Taliban kidnapped Italian journalist Daniele Mastrogiacomo, along with his Afghan driver and his fixer and interpreter, Ajmal Naqshbandi, on March 6. The driver was immediately beheaded, while Mastrogiacomo was released two weeks later after a deal was struck involving the release of five Taliban fighters. However, when authorities refused to accede to further Taliban demands, Naqshbandi was also killed. A prominent female radio journalist, Zakia Zaki, was murdered by unknown gunmen in June, while a female TV presenter was killed in the same week. Others went into hiding as a result of threats from extremists or narco-traffickers. In addition, radio stations faced attacks from insurgents intent on destroying their equipment and limiting their ability to broadcast. However, Reza Khan, sentenced to death for the murder of four journalists in 2001, was executed in October.

Although registration requirements remain in place, authorities have granted more than 400 publication licenses, and over 60 radio channels and 8 television stations are now broadcasting, providing an expanding diversity of views. National and local governments own or control several dozen newspapers and many electronic media outlets, including Radio Television Afghanistan. In the country's underdeveloped economic environment, the majority of media outlets remain dependent on the state, political parties, or international donors for financial support. One prominent exception is the popular and progressive Tolo network of television and radio stations, which provides dynamic coverage and scrutiny of current events and politics in a format that has proved to be financially viable. International radio broadcasts in Dari or Pashto, such as those from the BBC, Voice of America, Radio Liberty, and Radio Free Afghanistan, remain a key source of information for many Afghans. Access to the internet and to satellite TV dishes remains largely unrestricted, although their use is confined predominantly to Kabul and other major cities (only 1 percent of the total population was able to access the internet in 2007). Use of the internet and mobile phones continues to grow rapidly and has broadened the flow of news and other information, particularly for urban Afghans. In October, journalism student Sayed Perwiz Kambaksh was arrested for distributing information he downloaded from the internet regarding the role of women in Islamic societies; the case was ongoing at year's end.

Albania

Status: Partly Free

LEGAL ENVIRONMENT: 16
POLITICAL ENVIRONMENT: 16
ECONOMIC ENVIRONMENT: 18
TOTAL SCORE: 50

Survey Edition	2003	2004	2005	2006	2007
Total Score, Status	50,PF	49,PF	51,PF	50,PF	50,PF

The media environment in Albania remained stable during 2007, though political polarization and economic pressure on private outlets continued to limit media independence. The constitution guarantees freedom of the press, and the government generally respects it in practice. Despite pressure by press freedom groups for parliament to approve draft legislation that would decriminalize defamation, at year's end, it remained a criminal offense with a maximum sentence of two years. Nevertheless, no such cases were reported in 2007 and Prime Minister Sali Berisha's government appeared to adhere to a 2005 commitment to use the right of reply rather than defamation suits to address perceived bias or inaccuracy in the media. Freedom of information is guaranteed in the constitution, but officials often resist media requests and journalists complain of limited access to government ministries. The country's parliament-appointed broadcast regulator, the National Council for Radio and Television, continued to face accusations of political bias in favor of the government, and its staff levels and funding remained inadequate. However, appointees nominated by the parliamentary opposition were added to the council as provided for in a 2006 agreement. In May 2007, the parliament passed a Digital Broadcasting Law to regulate terrestrial and satellite broadcasts. The law was widely seen as damaging the interests of Top Media, a company whose popular stations were consistently critical of Berisha, and whose number would be significantly reduced under the new legislation.

The media continued to reflect a diversity of viewpoints in 2007, but key outlets tended to support one political faction or another. Journalists practiced self-censorship to support the political or economic interests of their employers. The Organization for Security and Cooperation in Europe reported that broadcast media curbed their usual bias to provide balanced coverage ahead of local elections in February, although smaller parties did not receive their fair share of airtime and reporting focused on personalities rather than on policy issues. In addition, rules on allocation of advertisement sales and media silence immediately before voting were not respected. The Berisha government put selective pressure on opposition-oriented media throughout the year, accusing unidentified outlets of receiving funding from organized crime groups. In July 2007, authorities sought to impose a 12 million euro ($16.6 million) fine on Top Media for unpaid taxes, prompting objections and demonstrations by civil rights and press freedom groups. While violence against journalists has reduced in recent years, in April 2007, an explosion damaged the car of Erion Brace, a parliament member and editor of the opposition newspaper *Zeri i Popullit*.

Albania has a diverse, although politically polarized, media landscape. In addition to public television and radio broadcasters, there are dozens of private television stations, radio stations, and print publications, including at least 30 daily newspapers. A lack of transparency of ownership and funding leaves the media open to unsubstantiated accusations of criminal influence or ulterior motives. Public broadcasters are typically biased in favor of the authorities and suffer personnel changes under each new government. Print outlets often have explicit ties to political parties or other interest groups, and virtually none are able to survive on advertising and subscription revenue alone. Larger private television stations are more profitable, but they are subject to pressure from major advertisers. The radio market is dominated by music and entertainment, with only 4 of about 40 stations producing original news content. Most journalists in Albania work without contracts, adding to job insecurity and encouraging self-censorship. All media have difficulty reaching rural areas owing to poor infrastructure and economic considerations. This particularly affects the internet, which is accessed by roughly 13 percent of the population and is without restrictions.

		Legal Environment: 22
		Political Environment: 23
Algeria		Economic Environment: 17
Status: Not Free		Total Score: 62

Survey Edition	2003	2004	2005	2006	2007
Total Score, Status	62,NF	63,NF	64,NF	61,NF	62,NF

While the constitution guarantees freedom of expression, the government has often used legal and extralegal means to harass and restrict the media. A state of emergency decreed in 1992 remained in effect in 2007, authorizing the government to legally penalize any speech deemed threatening to the state or public order. In addition, a separate February 2006 presidential decree authorized the imprisonment for up to five years of journalists who criticized the conduct of the security forces during the country's civil conflict of the 1990s. Similarly, articles from the 1990 Communication Law were amended in 2001 to criminalize defamation of the president, parliament, the judiciary, or the military, and the penal code imposes penalties ranging from fines to prison terms of up to two years for defamation of high-ranking government officials. In May 2006, President Abdelaziz Bouteflika pardoned journalists sentenced to prison terms; however, no efforts have been made to decriminalize press offenses in the first place.

While the number of defamation and legal charges brought against journalists declined in 2007 from previous years, the quantity is still high as the government continues to actively use these laws to threaten and arrest journalists. For example, since 2002 Yasser Abdelhai of the daily *Echourok el-Youmi* has faced 26 defamation cases for his critical reporting. Most recently, in 2007 he was ordered to pay 4 million dinars (US$56,000) by March 15 for damages relating to four separate cases. *Echourok el-Youmi* was further targeted when its managing editor, Ali Fodil, and a journalist, Naila Berrahal, lost their appeal on April 4; each received a suspended sentence of six months' imprisonment and fines of 500,000 dinars (US$7,400) for 2006 convictions of defaming Libyan leader Muammar al-Qadhafi and endangering the security of the Algerian and Libyan states. Separately, on

May 27 Omar Belhouchet, editor of the daily *El Watan*, and columnist Chawki Amari were sentenced for libel to two months in jail and fined 1 million dinars (US$14,000) each for comments published in *El Watan* in June 2006. Noureddine Boukraa of the daily *Ennahar* was similarly arrested on November 14 after publishing an article alleging corruption within the local security services of Annaba, and less than a week later, Ouahid Oussama, correspondent for the daily *Al Bilad*, faced defamation charges brought by the Department of Education of Djelfa for an article criticizing the education system. Despite such persistent government harassment and the resultant self-censorship that often follows, many Algerian journalists aggressively cover government and international affairs and offer diverse opinions and political commentary. Some topics, however, are more sensitive and are subject to censorship, legal repercussions, or harassment. Coverage of issues relating to national security and terrorism is still highly restricted and a dangerous undertaking for any journalist. For example, Anis Rahmani, editor of *Echourok el-Youmi*, and Naila Berrahal, a journalist with the paper, were the targets of death threats in June from individuals claiming to be affiliated with al-Qaeda for their reporting criticizing the organization and Islam. In August, Rahmani was informed by state security services that a "terrorist" in custody confirmed that the editor was indeed a target. Journalists also received pressure from the government not to report on the 2007 bomb attacks in the country, and *El Watan* correspondent Jamal Belkadi was charged with "crossing a security barrier" in May for taking photographs of the site of the attacks in Constantine.

Algeria began allowing for the licensing of private newspapers in 1990, and there are currently more than 100 private daily and weekly newspapers presenting a variety of political perspectives. The government uses its control over the country's printing presses and a state advertising agency to influence the independent print media. On several occasions, authorities have punished critical newspapers by suddenly demanding payment for debts owed to the state printer. While radio and television are completely government owned, political parties and candidates reportedly received equal access to these outlets in the campaign periods leading up to both the May 17 multiparty parliamentary elections and the November 29 multiparty local elections. However, outside of election periods, opposition parties are rarely permitted access to radio or television. Nonetheless, widespread satellite dishes provide alternate sources of information, such as popular Pan-Arab stations like Al-Jazeera and European-based channels. Non-Berber-language channels have increasingly introduced programming in Tamazight (the Amazigh or Berber language), including television and radio advertisements.

The government exercises little control over the internet, but online news is not a major source of information for most Algerians. In 2007, 10.4 percent of Algeria's population accessed the internet, which reflected a 7,000 percent increase since 2000. However, the government does monitor e-mail and internet chat rooms. Internet service providers are legally liable for the content on their websites, and bloggers are not immune to defamation charges. On June 11, blog administrator Abdulsalam Baroudi was fined 10,000 dinars (US$148) on charges brought by the director of religious affairs for having posted defamatory material on his blog in February.

Andorra

LEGAL ENVIRONMENT: 1
POLITICAL ENVIRONMENT: 4
ECONOMIC ENVIRONMENT: 8

Status: Free

TOTAL SCORE: 13

Survey Edition	2003	2004	2005	2006	2007
Total Score, Status	8,F	13,F	14,F	14,F	13,F

Freedom of expression is protected under Article 12 of the Andorran constitution, which also allows for laws that regulate the right of reply, correction, and professional confidentiality. The Universal Declaration of Human Rights is binding in Andorra and also ensures media freedom. No major incidents relating to press freedom were reported in 2007. Owing to Andorra's size, neighboring France and Spain heavily influence the media landscape. The majority of television transmissions are provided through technical accords with the Spanish and French government networks. Domestically, there are two daily papers, *Diari d'Andorra* and *El Periodic*, as well as two major weekly newspapers, *Informacions* and *7 Dies*. The public service broadcaster, Radio i Televisio d'Andorra, operates one radio station and one television station, both of which broadcast in Catalan. The government also releases a daily news bulletin. Internet access is open and unrestricted, and 32 percent of the population had access in 2007.

LEGAL ENVIRONMENT: 19
POLITICAL ENVIRONMENT: 23

Angola

ECONOMIC ENVIRONMENT: 21

Status: Not Free

TOTAL SCORE: 63

Survey Edition	2003	2004	2005	2006	2007
Total Score, Status	72,NF	66,NF	66,NF	65,NF	62,NF

Despite constitutional guarantees, freedom of the press is restricted in Angola. A 2006 Press Law ended the state monopoly on television broadcasting; partially opened the FM bandwidth to independent broadcasters; called for the creation of an independent public broadcaster; rescinded travel restrictions on journalists; and allowed journalists to use the truth defense in libel and defamation trials. However, the law also includes several restrictive provisions concerning journalists' access to information, the right to practice journalism and to establish new media outlets, and the registration of both journalists and media outlets with the government. Moreover, the government has yet to implement legislation required for the execution of the more positive reforms (including application for independent television and radio licenses). Libel of the president or his representatives remains a criminal offense, punishable by high fines and imprisonment. In September, Graca Campos—director of the private weekly *Semanario Angolense*—was found guilty of criminally defaming a former minister of justice, Paulo Chipilica. Campos was sentenced to an eight-month jail term and fined 18.7 million kwanza (US$250,000); he was released in November pending an appeal.

Authorities can suspend a publication for up to a year if it has published three articles that lead to defamation convictions within a three-year period. Particularly in the interior of the country, the judicial system has little independence to enforce legislation guaranteeing press freedom. The Law on State Secrecy permits the government to classify information, at times unnecessarily, and prosecute those who publish classified information. Private media are often denied access to official information or events.

Although generally tolerant of criticism from private media, officials often pressure independent media to cover the government in a more favorable light. While less common than in previous years, arbitrary detention, harassment, and attacks on journalists continue to take place. For fear of reprisals, many journalists practice self-censorship, particularly outside of Luanda, the capital. In late December, a reporter for Radio

Ecclesia—an outspoken Roman Catholic radio station—was sentenced to 30 days in prison for "inciting violence and disobedience" while covering a street vendor protest in Namibe. Foreign media are able to operate with fewer government restrictions than their local counterparts. However, journalists must first secure work visas to enter the country and then must receive authorization from the Ministry of the Interior to meet government officials or travel within Angola.

The government continues to dominate both print and broadcast media. While a few of the six privately owned weekly newspapers do routinely criticize the government, the largest media sources are the state-run outlets that allow very little criticism of government officials. The official Radio Nacional de Angola is the only radio station with national coverage; other radio stations, including the four based in Luanda, may broadcast only in their home province. The state also controls the only nonsatellite television station. While the new Press Law opens television broadcasting to the private sector, the effective promulgation and implementation of the law is another matter. Four private radio stations operate under government license from Luanda. The country's seven private weeklies have low circulation and face financial constraints as well as high costs of production and distribution. Few outside the capital can afford private newspapers. Internet access is generally unrestricted and is available in several provincial capitals, though less than 1 percent of the population was able to make use of this medium owing to cost constraints.

Antigua & Barbuda

LEGAL ENVIRONMENT: 10
POLITICAL ENVIRONMENT: 16
ECONOMIC ENVIRONMENT: 13

Status: Partly Free

TOTAL SCORE: 39

Survey Edition	2003	2004	2005	2006	2007
Total Score, Status	45,PF	43,PF	40,PF	38,PF	38,PF

Although the constitution provides for freedom of speech and of the press, and the government generally respects these rights, the islands drew international attention and criticism after the expulsion of two Caribbean journalists from Antigua in June. Relations between the United Progressive Party (UPP) government and the privately owned media also remained strained throughout the year. In November, the government announced forthcoming legislation to remedy what it labelled "irresponsible media" and proposed a Broadcasting Law to establish standards of conduct to govern both print and electronic media. The Antigua and Barbuda Media Congress (ABMC) expressed its concerns that the planned legislation would result in media censorship. The case against ZDK Radio announcer James "Tanny" Rose finally came before the courts in June and was promptly dismissed. Rose had been arrested in 2005 for "misbehavior in public office" and faced criminal charges in 2006 in relation to his job as chief information officer of the state-owned radio and television authority under the previous government in 1994.

While private print media offer a diversity of opinion, government officials occasionally harass local and foreign journalists who openly criticize the government. In June, the detention and expulsion of two prominent Caribbean journalists brought a storm of protest at home and across the region. Prime Minister Baldwin Spencer claimed that Vernon Khelawan, a Trinidadian, and Lennox Linton, a Dominican, had failed to comply with immigration laws and lacked necessary work permits. Protests centered on the government's direct violation of the Caribbean Community and Common Market, a regional agreement that guarantees media workers free movement within the region. Both the ABMC and the Association of Caribbean Media Workers expressed grave concerns over this attack on press freedom.

The islands have 2 daily newspapers, 1 biweekly paper, and more than 10 radio stations, including the state-owned Antigua and Barbuda Network (ABN), the UPP's Crusader Radio, the opposition Antigua Labour Party (ALP)'s ZDK Liberty Radio International, and the independent Observer Radio. ABN runs the islands' only freely available television service, and there is one cable television company. Most private media outlets are owned by firms affiliated with either the current government or its predecessor. The family of Lester Bird, the former prime minister and leader of the opposition ALP, maintains a high concentration of ownership in both radio and cable television. There are no government restrictions on the internet, which was accessed by over 44 percent of the population in 2007.

Argentina

Status: Partly Free

LEGAL ENVIRONMENT: 11
POLITICAL ENVIRONMENT: 21
ECONOMIC ENVIRONMENT: 15
TOTAL SCORE: 47

Survey Edition	2003	2004	2005	2006	2007
Total Score, Status	39,PF	35,PF	41,PF	45,PF	49,PF

President Nestor Kirchner's four-year term ended in December 2007 with the inauguration of his wife, former senator Cristina Fernandez, but the media environment for much of the year was affected by his particular news management style. Known as the *"estilo K,"* Kirchner's media strategies included the use of government advertising money, reduced media access to the president, and intimidating calls to critical news directors. Although President Fernandez is a beneficiary of this strategy, there was hope (but little immediate evidence) that she would improve press relations. Overall, the year witnessed both positive and negative developments, with the courts interceding against discriminatory advertising practices, while legal and extralegal harassment of journalists continued.

Freedom of speech and of the media are guaranteed under the constitution; however, press freedom is occasionally restricted in practice. While federal insult laws that criminalize defamation of a public official no longer exist in Argentina, government officials have been known to use other federal "crimes against honor" laws that more generally prohibit accusing someone of committing a crime or impugning a person's honor. Such civil laws call for the accuser to pay fines for any material or "moral" damages caused, while criminal laws carry jail time of up to three years. The use of criminal legal action against the press is more prevalent at the state level than at the federal level. Among the many legal cases brought against journalists throughout the year, a judge in the northwestern Salta province convicted radio journalist Sergio Poma of criminal slander in September and gave him a one-year suspended prison sentence and a one-year working ban for calling Governor Juan Carlos Romero "a crook of the worst kind." Poma was also facing three separate criminal slander cases at the end of the year. The Inter American Press Association called on Argentina to use civil penalties to settle such disputes. Charges of inciting violence and arson brought against radio journalists Nestor Pasquini and Hugo Francischelli following a 2006 demonstration were dismissed owing to lack of evidence; the two were released in March after spending more than three months in jail. In July, state authorities in Santa Fe province ordered the closure without notification of printing facilities at the city's only newspaper, *El Observador*, after a permit dispute. The Argentine Journalists Forum (FOPEA) accused authorities of ignoring a provincial constitutional ban against shuttering presses, and owner Andres Sharretta obtained an injunction from a local appeals court.

Media groups arguing that state advertising allocation practices were overly influenced by partisan political incentives sued on constitutional grounds. In an important decision in September, the Argentine Supreme Court ruled that while the media have no right to a specified amount of state advertising, "the government may not manipulate advertising by giving it to or taking it away from media outlets on the basis of discriminatory criteria." The ruling, in a case filed by media group Editorial Rio Negro, ordered provincial Neuquen authorities to rewrite its regulations, which could set a precedent for a similar pending federal case filed by media company Grupo Editorial Perfil.

Some instances of physical harassment of journalists continue to take place. Media watchdog group Reporters Sans Frontieres cited 20 cases of attacks on reporters in 2007, down from 34 in 2006. Among them, police shot Santa Cruz radio reporter Adela Gomez in the foot with rubber bullets on September 13 after she identified herself as a journalist. Gomez was covering a protest of union workers who happened to be blocking the route of Kirchner supporters heading to a presidential rally. A commander reported that the operation's leader and the border guard who shot the journalist were fired. Dario Illanes of the Salta province daily *El Tribuno* was arrested and beaten on August 1 after trying to report from a juvenile detention center. Charges were later dropped, and three police officers were suspended. Police in Entre Rios province physically assaulted and later released radio reporter Carlos Furman in September after he accused them of downplaying the desecration of a cemetery.

There are more than 150 daily newspapers, hundreds of radio stations, and dozens of television channels in Argentina. The country's print media are all privately owned, while the numerous privately owned radio and television stations are able to broadcast without restrictions. While national publications have been hampered by discretionary use of state ad budgets, provincial publications have been even more vulnerable owing to weak local private sectors and politically cautious owners. In Kirchner and Fernandez's hometown of Santa Cruz, for example, investigative journalist Maria O'Donnell reported that media owner and former Kirchner chauffeur Rudy Ullos Igor received almost US$1 million in state advertising in 2006 alone. His media group consistently featured Kirchner, and later Fernandez, prominently and favorably. The political use of state advertising seemed only to increase as the October presidential elections neared. According to a study by the Argentine nonprofit Association for Civil Rights, outgoing president Kirchner's administration increased advertising spending 63 percent in the first half of 2007, as compared with the figure for 2006, in the run-up to the election of Kirchner's wife, former senator Cristina Fernandez. The Argentine Community Radio Forum celebrated the first five broadcasting licenses to be granted to noncommercial radio since the Broadcasting Law was enacted 25 years ago under the Videla dictatorship, but it vowed to continue to pressure Congress to rewrite the law altogether. The licenses included an AM station for the famous Mothers of the Plaza de Mayo. The great majority of radio stations continue to operate in legal limbo two years after the law's provision prohibiting noncommercial radio was declared unconstitutional. In addition to the foreign news broadcasts that are widely available in Argentina, the internet served as an unrestricted source of information and was accessed by nearly 40 percent of the population.

Armenia

LEGAL ENVIRONMENT: 21
POLITICAL ENVIRONMENT: 25
ECONOMIC ENVIRONMENT: 20

Status: Not Free

TOTAL SCORE: 66

Survey Edition	2003	2004	2005	2006	2007
Total Score, Status	65,NF	64,NF	64,NF	64,NF	64,NF

The media environment deteriorated slightly in 2007 as incidents of violence, legal intimidation, and financial pressure continued to restrict the free flow of information, particularly among broadcast media, the primary source of news for most Armenians. The constitution and other statutes protect freedom of the press, but in practice these rights are often threatened. Libel remains a criminal offense and despite legislation that provides access to public information, such access is frequently denied to journalists. In February, the government adopted amendments to the Law on Rules of Procedure of the National Commission on Television and Radio, which defined the commission as an independent body. However, with half its members appointed by the president and the other half by the government-controlled parliament, the body's actual degree of independence from political influence and its level of input from the public remain limited. Two other government-sponsored draft laws proposed during the year threatened to effectively ban foreign broadcasts on Armenian public television and radio by imposing heavy taxes on private companies that aired such broadcasts. After strong international opposition, the amendments were not adopted. However, in July, Radio Free Europe/ Radio Liberty was informed it would no longer be broadcast on Armenian public radio, its avenue for reaching the majority of its audience in the country. The independent news agency A1+, which has engaged in a legal battle with the government since its television station was shut down in 2002, remained without a license during 2007.

While a wide variety of views are expressed in broadcast and print media, the media environment remained highly politicized throughout the year, particularly as government pressure rose ahead of the May parliamentary elections and again at the end of the year just prior to the February 2008 presidential election. During the campaign period, media watchdog groups reported that broadcast media outlets were generally progovernment in their coverage, although more coverage was allocated to opposition politicians and the full spectrum of political parties prior to the parliamentary elections than during previous cycles. Reports monitoring broadcast media indicate that there was a strong bias in coverage in favor of the government-backed presidential candidate, incumbent Prime Minister Serzh Sarkisian, who received mostly positive coverage, as compared to opposition candidate and former president Lev Ter-Petrossian, about whom coverage was highly critical. In addition, media were under pressure not to broadcast comments by opposition candidates after the independent Gala TV was harassed after it aired a speech by Ter-Petrossian. In what appeared to be a government-backed effort to shut down the station, tax authorities launched an audit investigation into the company; eventually, charges were filed against the station's parent company and its assets were frozen. As a result of its troubles, Gala lost a significant amount of its advertising revenues.

Several journalists were imprisoned or facing charges at year's end. In October 2007, police filed criminal charges against two opposition editors, Nikol Pashinyan of *Hayakakan Zhamanak* and Shogher Matevosyan of *Chorrord Ishkhanutyun*, after they had participated in an opposition march that was broken up by riot police. In June, opposition journalist Gagik Shamshian, victim of a 2006 assault by relatives of a local official, was given a suspended sentence of two and a half years for fraud in a case many observers believe was politically motivated. Journalist Arman Babajanian, convicted in 2006 of document forgery and evasion of military service with a particularly harsh sentence, remained in jail at year's end. Violence against the media also continued to be a concern, with several physical attacks on journalists and their offices occurring during the year. In September 2007, the editor in chief of the opposition *Iskakan Iravuk* was badly beaten by unidentified assailants outside the paper's offices and hospitalized as a result. In December, the office of the opposition newspaper *Chorrord Ishkanutyun* was damaged following an explosion that observers linked to the paper's critical coverage of the government. No perpetrators were identified or arrested. Several other physical attacks, particularly against photojournalists, took place at election-related rallies or during government functions that media outlets attempted to cover. Because of such violence, as well as media owners' close government connections, many journalists practice self-censorship.

With television as the country's dominant medium, there are dozens of stations, including several with national coverage. The majority of broadcast media and newspapers are privately owned, but mostly by politicians or businessmen with close government ties. Some public media receive funding from the state budget and state-owned newspapers include the government-sponsored *Hayastani Hanrepatutyun* and the Russian-language version, *Respublika Armenia*. Few private newspapers are financially self-sustainable and able to effectively distribute their editions outside major cities. Ahead of the elections, opposition newspapers were frequently confiscated. There are no formal restrictions for internet access, though regular usage is limited to an estimated 6 percent of the population.

Australia

Status: Free

LEGAL ENVIRONMENT: 6
POLITICAL ENVIRONMENT: 8
ECONOMIC ENVIRONMENT: 7
TOTAL SCORE: 21

Survey Edition	2003	2004	2005	2006	2007
Total Score, Status	14,F	14,F	18,F	19,F	21,F

Press freedom in Australia operates by convention rather than by constitutional guarantees, except in the state of Victoria, where it is protected under the Charter of Human Rights and Responsibilities. The right to information is protected, though lengthy delays and high costs impede access. Several documents were denied to journalists in 2007 because disclosure was deemed "contrary to the public interest." The

Australian Press Council and the Media, Entertainment, and Arts Alliance (MEAA) monitor journalistic freedom and access to information. In 2007, several top media companies and press freedom groups allied to form the Australia's Right to Know coalition. The group published a comprehensive report on the state of free speech in Australia in response to concerns over declining press freedom.

Restrictive legislation has been enacted over the past several years, including the Antiterrorism Act of 2005 and the Telecommunications (Interception) Amendment Act of 2006. In 2007, the government introduced a bill, known as the Communications Legislation Amendment (Crime or Terrorism Related Internet Content), that would give federal police discretionary authority to censor websites considered to contain material that "encourages, incites or induces" offenses against the commonwealth. In May, the Evidence Amendment (Journalists' Privilege) Bill 2007 was proposed. That measure would allow judges to excuse journalists from revealing confidential sources, but press freedom groups advocated greater legislative protection for journalists and whistleblowers. In June, two journalists from the *Herald Sun* were convicted of contempt for refusing to reveal a source before a judge in 2005 and were fined US$6,300 each. Separately, according to a May statement by Australia's Right to Know, a newsroom in Sydney had been raided twice in the past year as federal agents tried to identify the source of an official leak. In June, former customs official Allan Kessing received a suspended sentence of nine months in prison for leaking information to *The Australian* concerning lax airport security, although the leak ultimately led to major security upgrades. Authorities backed down under public pressure from pursuing *The Australian* reporters who published the story.

Private media ownership is concentrated, with the print media dominated by the Fairfax Group and Rupert Murdoch's News Ltd. In 2007, the Australian Competition and Consumer Commission allowed a merger between Fairfax Group and Rural Press. Australia has a strong tradition of public broadcasting, though the Australian Broadcasting Corporation has faced dramatic funding cuts. In May, international press freedom watchdog Reporters Sans Frontieres expressed concern over authorities' threats to withdraw state funding from the newspaper *The West Australian* if it did not fire editor Paul Armstrong. The internet is a vibrant medium in Australia, accessed by 75 percent of the population.

Austria

Status: Free

LEGAL ENVIRONMENT: 8
POLITICAL ENVIRONMENT: 8
ECONOMIC ENVIRONMENT: 5

TOTAL SCORE: 21

Survey Edition	2003	2004	2005	2006	2007
Total Score, Status	23,F	23,F	21,F	21,F	21,F

The federal constitution and the Media Law of 1981 provide the basis for free media in Austria. Freedom of information legislation is in place, and the government generally respects these provisions in practice. Libel and slander laws protect politicians and other government officials and in some cases lead to self-censorship. In the last eight years, the European Court of Human Rights (ECHR) has overturned the guilty verdicts in 15 Austrian defamation cases. According to a new 2007 report released by Article 19, "a large number of [these] defamation cases in Austria are brought by public officials and even judges themselves." In fact, in November 2006 the ECHR overturned the decisions in three cases brought to trial by public figures on defamation charges related to articles published in a single newspaper, *Der Standard*. These most recent ECHR verdicts, coupled with the fact that six new Austrian defamation cases were brought before the ECHR this year, have led many press freedom advocates to push the Austrian government to revise its stringent libel laws. Any form of pro-Nazism or anti-Semitism is prohibited by law, as is Holocaust denial. After two high-profile cases in 2006, including the sentencing of British author David Irving to three years in prison, there was only one Holocaust denial conviction in 2007. Gerd Honsik, who published books in the late 1980s questioning the facts of the Holocaust, was sentenced in December 2007 to 18 months in jail. Separately, a Danish cartoonist, Jan Egesborg, was arrested in a Vienna subway station while putting up posters depicting Russian president Vladimir Putin at the center of a target prior to Putin's visit. The posters were intended to question Putin's involvement in the shooting of journalists. Egesborg was charged with possible incitement allegedly because the use of the target might encourage others to commit a crime, but the charges were later dropped.

Since 2004's Broadcasting Law amendments, Austria's public broadcaster, which operates two television stations and four radio channels, faces growing competition for audiences from private broadcasters. Cable and satellite are widely available and are often used to watch German stations, some of which tailor programming for the Austrian audience. Daily newspapers, both national and regional, are very popular and contest fiercely for readers. Foreign investors have a solid presence in the predominantly privately owned print market, and ownership concentration is high. Many radio stations have ties to print outlets, and additionally there is cross-ownership of daily and weekly newspapers. Press subsidies help newspapers survive and are designed to encourage pluralism. Internet access is unrestricted and was made use of by more than 56 percent of the population in 2007.

Azerbaijan

LEGAL ENVIRONMENT: 25
POLITICAL ENVIRONMENT: 30
ECONOMIC ENVIRONMENT: 22

Status: Not Free   TOTAL SCORE: 77

Survey Edition	2003	2004	2005	2006	2007
Total Score, Status	73,NF	71,NF	72,NF	73,NF	75,NF

Despite constitutional and legal protection for freedom of speech and of the press, media freedom in Azerbaijan continued to decline in 2007. The government has no tolerance for criticism and uses libel suits, unfair trials, physical attacks, and financial pressure to clamp down on opposition media. A draft law on defamation has yet to be adopted. As a result, libel remains a criminal offense, punishable with high fines and up to three years' imprisonment. Nine journalists were in prison during 2007, including one who had been behind bars since 2006, making Azerbaijan the world's fifth-ranked jailer of journalists, according to the Committee to Protect Journalists. Three remained in jail at year's end. The government wields significant control over the National Television and Radio Council (NTRC), the broadcast watchdog and licenser. The Frequency Commission provides the NTRC with a list of available frequencies to assign, but only two licenses were granted in 2007. ANS TV received a six-year broadcast license in April after being shut down for several months in 2006 by the NTRC.

In the year's first prosecution of a reporter, *Nota Bene* journalist Faramaz Allahverdiyev was convicted of libeling the minister of internal affairs and sentenced to two years in prison in January. In May, *Sanat* journalist Rafig Taghi and editor in chief Samir Sadagatoglu were convicted of inciting religious hatred and sentenced to three and four years in prison, respectively. Also that month, *Mukhalifet* journalist Yashar Aghazade and editor in chief Rovshan Kabirli were convicted of libel and sentenced to 30 months' imprisonment as a result of a lawsuit filed by a member of parliament. These five journalists were released by a December presidential pardon. *Bizim Yol* journalist Mushvig Huseynov was arrested in July on bribery charges that he claimed were part of a frame-up, and he remained in pretrial detention for the rest of the year. Eynulla Fatullayev, editor of the Russian-language weekly *Realny Azerbaijan* and the Azerbaijani daily *Gundelik Azerbaijan*, was sentenced in October to eight and a half years in prison on charges of threatening terrorism, inciting ethnic hatred, and tax evasion. The charges stemmed from an article criticizing Azerbaijan's relations with Iran. Fatullayev had received a death threat in March, and he was sentenced to 30 months in prison in April for defamation in an internet post he denied writing. His two newspapers were evicted from their offices and closed in May over alleged fire-safety violations, prompting more than two dozen of the papers' journalists to apply for political asylum abroad. In November, a Baku court sentenced *Ideal* editor in chief Nazim Guliyev to 30 months in prison for libel, but he was released in December after an appeals court overturned the initial ruling. Also in November, police arrested *Azadliq* editor in chief Ganimat Zahidov on what he claimed were fabricated charges of hooliganism and inflicting minor bodily harm; he remained in pretrial detention at year's end. Radio Free Europe/ Radio Liberty (RFE/RL) correspondent Ilgar Nasibov was convicted of libel in December. Although the ruling was overturned just days later, he was immediately sentenced to a year of probation for a separate libel case involving a 2006 *Azadliq* article he said he did not write.

While journalists in Azerbaijan frequently face prison time, those who carry out physical attacks on them enjoy almost total impunity. There were several reports of violence against journalists in 2007, most of them involving beatings by policemen. Meanwhile, there was no progress in solving crimes committed against journalists in previous years, including the March 2006 kidnapping of *Azadliq* journalist Fikret Huseynli, a gruesome May 2006 attack on *Bizim Yol* editor Bahaddin Haziyev, and the 2005 murder of *Monitor* editor Elmar Huseynov.

Despite the intimidation they face, a relatively large number of opposition and independent media outlets continue to function. However, with distribution channels run by progovernment companies and most newspapers having to use government-owned printing presses, opposition print media are not readily available across the country. The government continues to pressure independent vendors who distribute opposition newspapers. There were a total of 21 television stations and 10 radio stations in 2007. State channels compete with private stations, but those featuring opposition views are not available nationwide. The government has used libel laws to punish critical writing online, and in January 2007 it reportedly blocked access to a website featuring criticism of state economic policy. The site's creator was sentenced to 12 days in jail for resisting arrest, though he was quickly released on appeal. A satirical site was also blocked that month, and after a brief reappearance it remained blocked at year's end. Internet usage remains low, with an estimated 13 percent of the population accessing the medium on a regular basis.

Bahamas

Status: Free

LEGAL ENVIRONMENT: 3
POLITICAL ENVIRONMENT: 10
ECONOMIC ENVIRONMENT: 7
TOTAL SCORE: 20

Survey Edition	2003	2004	2005	2006	2007
Total Score, Status	11,F	14,F	14,F	16,F	17,F

The environment for press freedom deteriorated slightly owing to heightened government pressure on the press in the run-up to the country's general elections and steps taken toward a monopolization of the island's print media. The constitution provides for freedom of speech and of the press, and the government mostly respects these rights in practice. Nevertheless, while the media are free to criticize the government and its policies, the incumbent Progressive Liberal Party (PLP) exerted undue pressure on the media in the run-up to May's general election, as it has in the past, by characterizing newspaper coverage critical of the government as failing to be objective or lacking balance and fairness. Meanwhile, partisanship increased throughout the media as the election approached, and the state-owned media were accused of unbalanced favorable coverage of the PLP. A particular source of tension between the state and the press was the *Tribune* newspaper's February publication of photographs showing the minister of immigration, Shane Gibson, and former model Anna Nicole Smith embracing on a bed. Gibson eventually resigned from his position as minister. Prime Minister Perry Christie denounced the *Tribune*, accusing it of serving the interests of the opposition party, the Free National Movement (FNM). After winning back the government in the May elections, the FNM promised to regularly report to the public on the state of the country and to uphold a code of ethics for ministers and members of parliament. The attorney general also announced that she expected a draft of a freedom of information bill to be presented to the House of Assembly before the end of the year, although this did not happen. After taking office, the new prime minister, Hubert Ingraham, suspended two journalists from the Broadcasting Corporation of the Bahamas, alleging their involvement with the PLP.

In July, the announcement that three of the country's four daily newspapers—the *Tribune*, the *Nassau Guardian*, and the *Freeport News*—had agreed to a partnership for sales, purchases, and printing production raised concerns about a looming media monopoly. Although the partners of the merger assured the public that the editorial departments will function independently, critics claimed that the move could only be to the detriment of media independence and diversity in the Bahamas. The state-owned Broadcasting Corporation of the Bahamas operates a television station and the ZNS Radio Bahamas network. There are also numerous privately owned radio stations. The internet was unrestricted and was accessed by close to 31 percent of the population.

		LEGAL ENVIRONMENT: 24
Bahrain		POLITICAL ENVIRONMENT: 27
		ECONOMIC ENVIRONMENT: 20
Status: Not Free		TOTAL SCORE: 71

Survey Edition	2003	2004	2005	2006	2007
Total Score, Status	68,NF	70,NF	71,NF	72,NF	71,NF

Despite constitutional protections guaranteeing freedom of expression and of the press, the government continued to enforce the 2002 Press Law to restrict the rights of the media. Bahrain's Press Law contains 17 categories of offenses and allows for up to five years' imprisonment for publishing material criticizing Islam or the king, inciting actions that undermine state security, or advocating for change in the government. Journalists may be fined up to 2,000 dinars (US$5,300) for an additional 14 offenses. The press can also be prosecuted under the penal code. On May 28, the upper house of parliament passed a revised Press Law that would decriminalize press offenses, protect the confidentiality of sources, ensure access to official information, and end criminal responsibility for publishers. Nevertheless, the draft law still needs to be passed by the lower house, an elected body heavily influenced by conservative religious perspectives, which rejected a similar bill three years prior.

In February, the editor in chief of both *Akhbar Al-Khaleej* and the *Gulf Daily News* wrote an editorial accusing 'Abd al-Hadi Khawaja, president of the Bahrain Center for Human Rights, of conspiracy and treason based on his participation in a seminar sponsored by the American Enterprise Institute. While Bahrain's prime minister commended this particular criticism, journalists who criticize government officials more often receive libel convictions or censorship instead of such praise. A total of 47 complaints were filed against journalists and publishing houses in the courts in 2007, many filed by private individuals. In one case, Dr. Mohammed Saeed Al-Sahlawi and Hussain Abdul Aziz Al Hebshi, who were arrested in November 2006 for possessing 1,500 leaflets of literature deemed to be "subversive," were sentenced at the end of January to one year and six months in prison, respectively. However, they were pardoned by the king in February. Separately, a media 'blackout' was issued against longtime women's rights activist Ghada Jamsheer, who in April sent a letter to the king criticizing the effectiveness of the Supreme Council for Women chaired by the king's wife. According to Article 19, Jamsheer was not published or referenced in any print or broadcast media after April, a move that was in violation of Bahrain's international legal obligations.

Journalists who covered contentious topics like protests were occasionally subject to assault as well as libel allegations. Three journalists from the newspapers *Al-Ayam, Al Waqt,* and *Al Wasat* were physically assaulted and had their mobile phones confiscated by members of the Bahraini security forces on December 25 while trying to cover a peaceful protest outside the Office of the Public Prosecutor. The protest was being held by family members of those who had been arrested for participating in demonstrations over the unnecessarily violent dispersal of a December 17 protest. Similarly, two journalists with Al Alam television were arrested by police, interrogated, and had their equipment stolen as they planned to cover a protest outside a United Nations building.

The Ministry of Information may censor and prevent the distribution of local and foreign publications, close newspapers through court proceedings, ban books and films, block websites, and prosecute individuals. Bahrain's conservative populations also act as independent censors, reporting to the authorities material considered to be indecent or against religious principles. A continued ban on any media discussion of the 2006 "Bandargate" scandal was reaffirmed by the High Criminal Court in November. The "Al Bandar report," written by Sudanese-born British citizen Salah Al Bandar, used leaked government documents to allege election fraud and the involvement of members of the royal family and high-level politicians in fomenting anti-Shia sectarian strife. On April 19, Al Bandar, who was deported in 2006, was convicted in absentia and sentenced to four years in prison and a 100-dinar fine. Numerous websites that had been shut down in 2006 for mentioning the report remained blocked and a number of journalists and human rights activists have been detained and interrogated in 2007 for writing about the scandal.

Despite all of these threats and restrictions, the Bahraini press still offers a more diverse and critical perspective of news and politics than most other Gulf countries. Nonetheless, newspapers tend to avoid reporting on "sensitive" issues such as sectarian tensions, foreign relations with surrounding Gulf countries, governmental corruption, demonstrations, and human rights violations. There is also a dearth of critical coverage of local issues such as land and demographic distribution as well as problems confronting the large immigrant worker population. The lack of any private news agency serves to exacerbate this situation.

There are six privately owned daily newspapers, four in Arabic and two in English, several of which are critical of the government. While there are no state-owned papers, the government has a monopoly on all broadcast media. The country's first private radio station, Sawt al-Ghad, launched in 2005, but the authorities shut it down in 2006 alleging irregularities. A few international radio stations are allowed to broadcast, and foreign satellite television provides the public with their main source of news.

Bahrain was the highest-ranked Arab country on the International Telecommunication Union's Digital Opportunity Index, which measures progress in relation to infrastructure, opportunity, and use of digital media. Of Bahrain's population, 22.2 percent currently use the internet, reflecting an almost 300 percent growth rate since 2000. In addition to the 2002 Telecommunications Law, which imposes civil and criminal penalties for violations, the term *electronic media* was inserted into the 2002 Press Law, allowing the government to regulate this sector under vague legislation. Website administrators may be prosecuted under the same libel laws as journalists and are responsible for all content posted on their sites. On October 21, three journalists were convicted and fined for defaming the director of an elder-care center in an article published in the online newspaper *Al-Saheefa*, one of Bahrain's numerous banned websites. In February, the municipalities and agricultural affairs minister filed a similar criminal libel complaint against blogger Mahmood al-Yousif, who had criticized the minister's praise of the government's handling of earlier flooding; following a campaign by local press freedom groups, the minister dropped the case in May 2007. The government is a major shareholder in Batelco, the country's principal telecommunications company. Batelco monitors e-mail and filters internet content by routing internet activity through proxy/cache servers. All websites are required to register with the Information Ministry. Bahrain has a very active online community with about 200 blogs; however, religious and political content is heavily censored. At least 22 local and international websites were blocked during the year, including the website of the Arabic Network for Human Rights Information, the Bahrain Center for Human Rights, and the International Freedom of Expression Exchange.

Bangladesh

LEGAL ENVIRONMENT: 22
POLITICAL ENVIRONMENT: 30
ECONOMIC ENVIRONMENT: 16

Status: Not Free

TOTAL SCORE: 68

Survey Edition	2003	2004	2005	2006	2007
Total Score, Status	65,NF	68,NF	68,NF	68,NF	66,NF

Following worsening political violence and instability in late 2006, which culminated in the postponement of planned elections, the imposition of a state of emergency, and the installation of a new military-backed interim government on January 11, 2007, the environment for media freedom changed considerably, with additional legal restrictions balanced by a decline in murders and violence against members of the press. Although the constitution provides for freedom of expression subject to "reasonable restrictions," the press is constrained by national security legislation as well as sedition and criminal libel laws. Journalists can be slapped with contempt of court and defamation charges or arrested under the 1974 Special Powers Act (which allows detentions of up to 90 days without trial) in reprisal for filing stories critical of government officials or policies. In February and March, a number of journalists were detained or charged with defamation. Sedition charges were dropped against seven journalists in May, but Salah Uddin Shoaib Choudhury, who was first arrested in 2003, still faces sedition, treason, and blasphemy charges. In September, cartoonist Arifur Rahman was jailed, ostensibly for 30 days, for allegedly insulting Islam through a cartoon depicting a cat named Mohammad. The newspaper that published the cartoon faced protests and temporary suspension, its editors were forced to issue an apology, and Rahman remained in prison at year's end.

Overt censorship and other instances of heightened restriction on the media were imposed in the context of the political turmoil early in the year. Immediately following the emergency declaration, television channels were asked to broadcast news produced by the state-run BTV, and all media were requested to refrain from any criticism of the authorities. The Emergency Powers Rules, announced in late January, restricted coverage of sensitive topics, allowed censorship of print and broadcast outlets, criminalized "provocative" criticism of the government, and imposed penalties, including up to five years in prison and hefty fines, for violations. The government was sensitive to international scrutiny; according to the U.S. State Department, on several occasions during the year authorities banned or delayed distribution of foreign magazines such as the *Economist*, *Time*, and the regional journal *Himal Southasian* or removed pages containing articles about Bangladesh before releasing them. Local media content was also monitored, and in general the print media were allowed more leeway than broadcasters and new media, particularly private television channels that provide 24-hour news coverage. During and following the student-led protests in August, authorities asked television channels not to broadcast images of the riots or air live talk shows and assaulted and detained dozens of journalists. In September, the new 24-hour news channel, CSB, owned by a former lawmaker and businessman who was detained as part of the government's anticorruption crackdown, was shut down altogether on a technicality after airing coverage of the August unrest. Other stations were allowed to resume airing talk shows only after repeated appeals by senior journalists and after agreeing to abide by informal guidelines circulated by the information minister that included bans on live, unedited shows, phone-in and interactive segments, and any statements that could create resentment of the government.

Numerous journalists reported an increase in threatening phone calls from intelligence agencies seeking to prevent critical coverage of the new government or military or encouraging editors to file positive stories on certain topics. Some who refused to comply were targeted with reprisal; in March, Atiqullah Khan Masud, editor and publisher of the popular *Janakantha* daily, was arrested during a high-profile raid on his office and was subsequently accused of corruption, criminal activities, and "tarnishing the country's image abroad." The fear of negative repercussions caused many journalists to practice increasing self-censorship when covering sensitive topics.

Journalists continue to be harassed and attacked by a range of actors, including organized crime groups, political parties and their supporters, and leftist and Islamist militant groups, although no journalists were killed in 2007 and the overall level of violence declined. Most commonly, they are subjected to such attacks as a result of their coverage of corruption, criminal activity, Islamic fundamentalism, or human rights abuses. Police brutality toward photographers attempting to document protests or other political events also remained a concern. In August, security forces assaulted and injured several journalists who were covering protests at Dhaka University, temporarily taking several dozen into custody. On a number of other occasions, journalists were threatened or detained by authorities or the security forces. Cases include that of *Daily Star* reporter E. A. M. Asaduzzaman Tipu, arrested in Nilphamari in March, and Jahangir Alam Akash, a CSB reporter in the northwestern city of Rajshahi, who was arrested and beaten while in custody in October. In a high-profile case that was documented extensively by Human Rights Watch (HRW), Tasneem Khalil, who worked as a journalist for the *Daily Star* and U.S.-based CNN as well as a researcher for HRW, was detained, tortured, and threatened by the Directorate General of Forces Intelligence in May 2007, primarily regarding his news reporting as well as an HRW report he contributed to that focused on extrajudicial killings by the security forces. After international pressure helped secure his release, Khalil sought asylum in Sweden. Impunity for those who perpetrate crimes against journalists is the norm, and investigations into the cases of reporters killed in previous years generally proceeded slowly, if at all.

With hundreds of daily and weekly publications, the privately owned print media continue to present an array of views, although political coverage at a number of newspapers is highly partisan and those outlets that presented views critical of the new government faced sustained pressure. Private broadcasting has expanded in recent years, with eight satellite television stations and three radio stations now broadcasting. The state owns or influences several broadcast media outlets, and private outlets are required to air selected government-produced news segments as a condition of their operation. Political considerations influence the distribution of government advertising revenue and subsidized newsprint, upon which many publications depend. According to the Committee to Protect Journalists, the arrest of several media owners and executives as part of an overarching anticorruption drive served to weaken several outlets financially, as it deprived them of their major backers.

Access to the internet, although generally unrestricted, is limited to less than 1 percent of the population, and some journalists' e-mail is reportedly monitored by police. During and following the August protests, authorities switched off mobile phone networks and routed all internet traffic through the state telecommunications company (leading to a temporary slowdown or shutdown of the internet).

Barbados

LEGAL ENVIRONMENT: 3
POLITICAL ENVIRONMENT: 10
ECONOMIC ENVIRONMENT: 6

Status: Free

TOTAL SCORE: 19

Survey Edition	2003	2004	2005	2006	2007
Total Score, Status	14,F	17,F	17,F	17,F	17,F

Preelection political tension, which included heightened pressure on and intimidation of the media, was primarily responsible for declines in press freedom in 2007. Freedom of the press is constitutionally guaranteed, and while there is no freedom of information legislation, the media generally operate without restriction. However, one case of physical and legal harassment of journalists occurred during the year. On May 25, police manhandled three journalists trying to cover the arrival of traffic accident victims at the Queen Elizabeth Hospital. Jimmy Gittens, CBC correspondent, was arrested and charged with trespassing and later released on bail. Gittens's lawyer reported that a civil suit would be filed against the police. In the run-up to the January 2008 general elections, the media environment became increasingly polarized. Both the ruling Barbados Labour Party (BLP) and the main opposition party, the Democratic Labour Party, made increasing use of the internet in their campaigns. Political blogs also grew in popularity, with two sites in particular, Barbados Free Press and Barbados Underground, drawing large numbers of visitors for their exposés of government misdemeanors and hypocrisy. In late December, one contributor to these two blogs, hotelier Adrian Loveridge, informed the police that he and his wife had been subjected to repeated death threats, including promises to burn down their hotel. The threats appeared to be politically motivated on behalf of the ruling BLP. There are two daily newspapers and two weeklies, all privately owned. A new weekly was launched in January but soon folded. Foreign publications deemed pornographic are restricted by the government. Of the 11 radio frequencies, 3 are run by the state-owned Caribbean Broadcasting Corporation, which also operates the sole television station. In 2006, the Barbados-based Caribbean Media Corporation launched CaribVision, a new 24-hour Caribbean television channel, which is available in over 10 Caribbean countries and in North America. There are no government restrictions on the internet, which was accessed by nearly 60 percent of the population in 2007.

Belarus

Status: Not Free

LEGAL ENVIRONMENT: 28
POLITICAL ENVIRONMENT: 35
ECONOMIC ENVIRONMENT: 28
TOTAL SCORE: 91

Survey Edition	2003	2004	2005	2006	2007
Total Score, Status	82,NF	84,NF	86,NF	88,NF	89,NF

Belarus's limited level of press freedom deteriorated further in 2007 as President Alyaksandr Lukashenka's government suppressed the few remaining independent media outlets and strengthened restrictions on the internet. Despite constitutional provisions for freedom of the press, criticism of the president and his government is considered a criminal offense, and libel convictions can result in prison sentences or high fines. Judges and police officers regularly used politicized court rulings and obscure regulations to harass independent newspapers during the year. In August, court officials in Minsk cited an allegedly unpaid fine from 2006 as a pretext to raid the offices of opposition newspaper *Narodnaya Volya* and confiscate computers and publishing equipment. Minsk police raided the editorial office of the Communist Party's newspaper, *Tovarishch*, in September, confiscating 10,000 copies of the latest edition on the grounds that it failed to properly identify the printing house on the front page. In October, *Narodnaya Volya* was fined 25 million rubles ($11,650) for allegedly defaming the head of Lukashenka's Main Ideological Office.

The government subjected the independent media to systematic political intimidation, while the state media consistently glorified Lukashenka and vilified the political opposition. Local reporters working for foreign media with programming aimed at Belarus—like Radio Free Europe/Radio Liberty, Deutsche Welle, and the Warsaw-based Radio Polonia—and those working for local Polish-language publications faced arbitrary arrests and aggressive harassment from the security services. A number of reporters were detained to prevent them from covering opposition protests. For example, in March 2007 police in Minsk arrested Valery Shchukin to prevent him from covering an unsanctioned rally, marking the country's 1918 independence day, for *Narodnaya Volya*. There was no progress during the year on solving the cases of two journalists who had reported extensively on government corruption and human rights abuses: Veronika Cherkasova, a journalist with the Minsk-based opposition weekly *Solidarnost* who was murdered in 2004, and Dmitry Zavadsky, a cameraman for Russia's ORT television station who disappeared in 2000 and is presumed dead.

The state maintains a virtual monopoly on domestic broadcast media; only state outlets broadcast nationwide, and the content of smaller stations is tightly restricted. In an April 2007 news conference, Lukashenka restated his government's goal of maintaining control over the broadcast media. Several radio news programs broadcast from neighboring countries remained available, while television broadcasts from Euronews and Russian channels were sometimes blocked. The government did not issue any permits for new independent or opposition newspapers in 2007, and it used a range of economic pressures to weaken the country's surviving independent media. Most independent outlets have been banned from the state-dominated printing and distribution system and denied access to government advertising and subsidies. For years, opposition newspapers relied on printing houses in neighboring Russia, but the contracts were terminated in 2006. Independent papers responded by selling directly from the newsroom and using volunteers to deliver copies, but regional authorities have harassed and arrested some of the private distributors.

Because the internet is used by some 56 percent of the population and Belarusian websites are not yet obliged to register with the authorities, many print publications have moved online. However, the state-owned telecommunications company Beltelekom controls all internet access and blocks some critical websites, while the security services reportedly monitor internet communications. In February 2007, the government approved new regulations requiring internet café owners to keep records of their customers' identities and the websites they visited for inspection by the security services. In March, Beltelekom blocked access to several independent websites, including the newspapers *Solidarnost* and *Nasha Niva* and the human rights group Charter 97, prior to the opposition's annual Freedom Day rally. Writer and political activist Andrei Klimau was arrested in April and charged with inciting the regime's overthrow in an article posted on the internet, marking the country's first arrest for comments published online. He was sentenced to two years in prison after a closed trial in August. As a result of these abuses, some media websites have moved to domains in neighboring countries.

Belgium

Status: Free

LEGAL ENVIRONMENT: 2
POLITICAL ENVIRONMENT: 4
ECONOMIC ENVIRONMENT: 5
TOTAL SCORE: 11

Survey Edition	2003	2004	2005	2006	2007
Total Score, Status	9,F	9,F	11,F	11,F	11,F

The constitution guarantees freedom of speech and of the press, and these rights are generally respected by the government. The law prohibits hate speech, including Holocaust denial, which holds a maximum sentence of one year's imprisonment. The Belgian Chamber of Deputies voted unanimously in March 2005 to approve a law that protects journalists' sources. The new law protects reporters from home searches and seizures and gives them the right to silence if called as a witness. The vote came after police raids in 2004 on the home and office of a Brussels-based German reporter, Hans Martin Tillack, which shocked the community of international journalists. In October 2006, Tillack brought his case before the European Union's Court of First Instance, where he argued that the action against him by Belgian police violated his rights. Although the court recognized that his complaints of mistreatment were legitimate, in the end it ruled that the case was outside its jurisdiction. In November 2007, however, the European Court of Human Rights ordered Belgium to pay Tillack 40,000 Euros (US$62,903) in damages.

Newspaper ownership concentration has increased since the 1960s as corporations have steadily been buying up papers. As a result, today a handful of corporations run most of the country's newspapers. In the broadcasting sector, unlike most other European nations, Belgium has two separate public broadcasting organizations (one operating in French and the other in Flemish), each with its own domestic and international broadcasting network.

The government does not limit access to the internet, which was used by close to 53 percent of the population in 2007. However, after being physically attacked, threatened, and having his family threatened, journalist Mehmet Koksal was forced to shut down his blog in October 2007. The blog had reported on events in the Turkish community in Belgium, and Koksal's opinions had angered local politicians as well as the extremist Turkish group Grey Wolves, who attacked Koksal in front of the police, who did little to protect him. Koksal had been filming a riot instigated by the Grey Wolves. No further action was reported.

Belize

LEGAL ENVIRONMENT: 8
POLITICAL ENVIRONMENT: 9
ECONOMIC ENVIRONMENT: 5

Status: Free

TOTAL SCORE: 22

Survey Edition	2003	2004	2005	2006	2007
Total Score, Status	23,F	22,F	20,F	21,F	21,F

The constitution of Belize protects the right to freedom of expression, although there are several legal limitations to that right. The government may fine up to US$2,500 and imprison for up to three years anyone who questions the financial disclosures of public officials. Newspapers are subject to libel laws, and the Belize Broadcasting Authority holds the right to preview broadcasts with political content and remove material it deems libelous. Some isolated attacks against journalists were reported during the year. Local paper *Amandala* reported that in September, two homemade bombs were found in the car of Evan "Mose" Hyde, host of the popular Krem Radio program *Wake Up, Belize*. Upon investigation, authorities indicated that an attempt was made to ignite one of the explosive devices. In October, local Krem TV and Radio co-host Rufus X, of the politically charged *Kremandala Show*, was attacked by an unknown assailant with a metal rod, breaking his arm in two places. The journalist claimed the attack was in response to his expression of political views on the airwaves.

While there are no daily newspapers in Belize, there is a vibrant market for weeklies. Papers are privately owned, with two weeklies directly affiliated with political parties. In general, reporting covers a wide range of opinions. Government-operated radio was privatized in 1998, and today there are 8 television stations and 33 licensed radio stations. The People's United Party and the United Democratic Party both have radio stations with which they are affiliated. While the government does not restrict internet access or use, lack of infrastructure and high costs limited usage to just over 12 percent of the population in 2007.

Benin

Status: Partly Free

LEGAL ENVIRONMENT: 11
POLITICAL ENVIRONMENT: 10
ECONOMIC ENVIRONMENT: 10

TOTAL SCORE: 31

Survey Edition	2003	2004	2005	2006	2007
Total Score, Status	28,F	30,F	30,F	30,F	30,F

Status change explanation: Benin's status declined from Free to Partly Free owing to the continuation of criminal libel cases and increased polarization due to the growing number of politically funded media outlets.

Benin has traditionally ranked among the best-performing African countries for press freedom, with freedom of speech protected by the constitution and normally respected by the government. However, a number of worrying trends that began in the 2006 election year continued to plague the press in 2007. Although the country's 1997 Press Law criminalizing libel has generally been used more as a warning than as actual punishment, it was implemented in December 2006 against the editor and a journalist of the private *L'Informateur* newspaper for refusing to retract a story accusing a court bailiff of rape; both served two months in prison out of a six-month sentence. In February 2007, the trend continued when a court sentenced four top officers of the prominent Golfe Media Group to six months in prison and an exorbitant US$10,000 fine each on charges of criminal defamation. Golfe Media appealed, but the case had not been heard in court by year's end.

Unlike during 2006, when Mathieu Kerekou's regime made several direct attempts to limit critical media content ahead of the presidential election held that year, there were fewer instances of overt harassment by authorities in 2007. However, in December, police arrested and assaulted a cameraman with Golfe Media while confiscating his camera.

Benin's numerous established media outlets have a history of providing aggressive reporting and robust scrutiny of both government and opposition leaders. However, the media market has recently become saturated by a large number of publications that emerged in the month preceding the 2006 election, a majority of which received direct political funding and had an overtly partisan slant. Many of these news outlets were still operating in 2007, leading to the polarization of media content and, to a certain extent, the corrosion of impartial reporting. Although the proliferation of news outlets has contributed to a greater diversity of content, the inability of most of Benin's media operators to garner a consistent profit also limits accuracy and fairness in reporting by making poorly paid reporters susceptible to bribery. The High Authority for Audio-Visual Media and Communications requires media outlets to provide a list of planned programs and publications, claiming that the material is used primarily for administrative purposes. Nonetheless, most media practitioners consider this to be an attempt at censorship and refuse to comply, generally without penalty. While internet access is still available primarily through slow dial-up internet cafés, it remains unhindered by government censorship. At 700,000 users, or nearly 9 percent of the population (almost double that of the previous year), Benin had one of West Africa's highest rates of internet penetration in 2007.

Bhutan

LEGAL ENVIRONMENT: 19
POLITICAL ENVIRONMENT: 23
ECONOMIC ENVIRONMENT: 19

Status: Not Free

TOTAL SCORE: 61

Survey Edition	2003	2004	2005	2006	2007
Total Score, Status	70,NF	68,NF	66,NF	65,NF	62,NF

Freedom of expression and of the press, as well as media diversity, continued to be limited in Bhutan in 2007, despite some improvements during the previous year. The Bhutan Information, Communications, and Media Act, passed in July 2006, was designed to regulate these industries and contains general provisions for freedom of expression and of the press. However, many observers have expressed concerns that it does not provide adequate protection for journalists or guarantee freedom of information. The 1992 National Security Act prohibits criticism of the king and the political system.

Physical attacks on the press in Bhutan are rare, and there were no reported cases of attacks occurring in 2007. Bhutan's main print publication, the state-owned biweekly *Kuensel*—now funded entirely by advertising and subscription revenues—generally reports news that puts the kingdom in a favorable light but has increasingly been highlighting societal problems and carrying stories critical of the government. According to the U.S. State Department, following a number of editorials critical of a proposal to impose restrictions on advertising, the government abandoned the plan in May 2007. In 2006, two private newspapers began operating, *Bhutan Times* and *Bhutan Observer*, which occasionally publish articles critical of the government in spite of their general progovernment content. In November 2006, *Bhutan Now*, a monthly periodical, was launched. State-owned broadcast media, which consist of a radio and a television station operated by the Bhutan Broadcasting Service, carry broadly progovernment programming and do not air opposition positions and statements. The July 2006 Media Act led to the establishment of two independent radio stations, and in April 2007, another private radio station, Radio Valley FM, began broadcasting. There are no private television broadcasters, but cable television services carry uncensored foreign programming, albeit with bans on channels that provide "controversial content" as well as high sales taxes and regulatory obstacles that render costs prohibitive for many citizens.

The internet is gaining use in Bhutan but was accessed by less than 4 percent of the population in 2007. The government occasionally restricts certain websites considered to be offensive to the government or pornographic. In June 2007, authorities blocked the *Bhutan Times* website for approximately two months owing to antigovernment comments. According to the International Federation of Journalists, authorities also blocked the website of the now defunct *Bhutan News* website in 2007 following its critical coverage of the government.

Bolivia

Status: Partly Free

LEGAL ENVIRONMENT: 10
POLITICAL ENVIRONMENT: 18
ECONOMIC ENVIRONMENT: 11
TOTAL SCORE: 39

Survey Edition	2003	2004	2005	2006	2007
Total Score, Status	30,F	37,PF	35,PF	33,PF	37,PF

Heightened political tensions and the president's antipress rhetoric continued to promote a climate of hostility and violence toward the press from both government and opposition supporters, as press freedom remained compromised by inadequate legal guarantees and the increasing polarization of media outlets. While the constitution provides for freedom of speech and of the press, Bolivia's penal code allows for journalists to be jailed for one month to two years if found guilty of slandering, insulting, or defaming public officials. When the infractions involve criticism of the president, vice president, or a minister, the sentence may be increased by half. Nevertheless, few have been prosecuted under these laws in recent years. The legal norms that will govern the press under the new constitution—should it enter into force—remained unclear at year's end; draft articles included strong language protecting press freedom but also used ambiguous terms such as "veracity and responsibility" when describing media duties. At several points during the year, the ruling MAS party also called for an ombudsman to monitor media content. In May 2006, several journalist groups combined to form a National Ethics Council to act as a self-regulator, but it has so far proven ineffective.

Bolivia's journalists continued to face the challenges of reporting on their country's volatile politics. President Evo Morales repeatedly criticized opposition media outlets during the year, contributing to a permissive atmosphere for attacks against journalists. Media watchdog group Reporters Sans Frontieres reported an estimated 60 physical attacks on journalists throughout the year. In a continuation of the previous year's trends, 2007 began poorly, as at least 11 reporters were harassed and injured by protesters and security forces while covering unrest in Cochabamba in January. In October, at least six journalists were injured by police and soldiers as the government tried to retake Santa Cruz's main airport, which had been occupied by opposition protesters. In late November, rioting in Sucre accompanied the controversial preliminary approval of the draft constitution; during the turmoil, at least five journalists were physically assaulted by the police, while some members of the media were reportedly attacked by demonstrators. The opposition was responsible for several incidents of violence, including on November 27 in Cobija, when protesters threatened journalists of radio stations Digital and Pando, stoning the stations' headquarters for their supposed negative portrayal of the regional protest against the new constitution. Impunity for such attacks is the norm. In September, Minister of the Presidency Juan Ramon Quintana suggested that some opposition journalists were in the pay of the U.S. government, though no proof was provided.

Print media are privately owned and diverse in their editorial views, though many newspapers follow a strongly antigovernment editorial stance. The television industry is privately owned except for one government-run TV network. Broadcast outlets express a variety of political views, but stations have been criticized for their overt partisanship in news coverage, with outlets from the eastern department of Santa Cruz among the most hostile to the new president; some media owners themselves are active in the political opposition. The government has been criticized for allegedly withholding advertising from pro-opposition media. Radio is the major news source in the countryside, with an estimated 800 stations nationwide. With Venezuelan financial support, the government established a new set of over two dozen community radio networks. One of the largest national networks is Radio Erbol, operated by a consortium of 70 churches. In recent years, Bolivia has experienced a growth in alternative media along with new internet news operations, but very few media of any type are profitable. Less than 7 percent of the population was able to access the internet in 2007. According to the U.S. State Department, the president issued a decree in June to increase telecommunications technology to better serve rural areas; however, the decree prohibits the transmission of any partisan messages by stations not affiliated with the government.

Bosnia & Herzegovina

LEGAL ENVIRONMENT: 8
POLITICAL ENVIRONMENT: 21
ECONOMIC ENVIRONMENT: 16

Status: Partly Free

TOTAL SCORE: 45

Survey Edition	2003	2004	2005	2006	2007
Total Score, Status	49,PF	48,PF	45,PF	45,PF	45,PF

Freedom of the press in Bosnia and Herzegovina (BiH) is guaranteed by the constitution as well as the human rights annex to the Dayton Peace Accords, which ended the country's 1992–95 civil war. Bosnia has one of the most liberal legal environments in the world for media freedom, but effective enforcement of these laws is largely absent owing to an overburdened judiciary. Libel and defamation have been decriminalized, leaving civil suits as the main remedy. Government officials have filed lawsuits against journalists, but instances of journalists suing their colleagues are more common. While freedom of information is protected by law, institutions are often slow to respond to journalists' requests. Legislation that would reorganize and unify the country's public broadcasting system has been held up by Croat leaders who argue that it would not serve their community's interests. An independent Communications Regulatory Agency (CRA) licenses and monitors broadcast media. The Press Council, a self-regulatory body for print outlets, responds to alleged violations of the Press Code.

Journalism in both of the country's state entities—the Federation, made up of Bosniak (Muslim) and Croat cantons; and the Serb-dominated Republika Srpska (RS)—continues to be plagued by a relatively low standard of professionalism and a tendency to appeal only to narrow ethnic constituencies. Although attacks are fairly uncommon, journalists throughout BiH remain subject to political pressure and threats of violence, including one uttered in October 2007 by the Serb human rights ombudsman. There is also concern over the influence of organized crime on the media. Meanwhile, the current RS prime minister, Milorad Dodik, has been accused of tightening control over the Bosnian Serb media. His government replaced the leadership of the official SRNA news agency and the semiofficial daily *Glas Srpske* in 2006, and the opposition has alleged that the RS public broadcaster, RTRS, shows a progovernment bias. In January 2007, the RS government initiated a boycott of BHT-1, the BiH public television station, over perceived disrespect for the RS and Bosnian Serb leaders. RS officials refused to give interviews or statements to BHT-1, and the station's reporters were barred from RS press conferences. The boycott was lifted at the end of the month, after the general director of BHT-1 was replaced. The Organization for Security and Cooperation in Europe (OSCE) criticized the RS government's actions, noting that it could have simply filed a complaint with the CRA if it was dissatisfied with BHT-1's coverage. Media in the RS generally supported or remained silent on the boycott, while journalists in the Federation were critical.

In addition to the separate public broadcasters for the RS, the Federation, and BiH as a whole, three major private television stations operate in the country. There is also competition from outlets based in Serbia and Croatia, as well as a glut of more than 40 small television and 140 minor radio stations, many of them supported by municipal governments. Print publications include half a dozen dailies and more than 40 weeklies and monthlies. The crowded media market survives on limited advertising revenue, increasing outlets' dependence on economic and political patronage. Self-censorship is further encouraged by journalists' relatively low salaries and high national unemployment rates; a majority of journalists work without contracts. Internet access is unrestricted, and although the number of users in BiH has increased dramatically in recent years, it remains at about 20 percent of the population.

Botswana

Status: Partly Free

LEGAL ENVIRONMENT: 8
POLITICAL ENVIRONMENT: 17
ECONOMIC ENVIRONMENT: 11
TOTAL SCORE: 36

Survey Edition	2003	2004	2005	2006	2007
Total Score, Status	30,F	30,F	30,F	35,PF	35,PF

Freedom of speech and of the press are provided for in the constitution, and the government generally respects these rights in practice. However, libel is a civil offense, and in past years publications have been charged with defamation and have had to pay large amounts of money in court-ordered damages or as part of a settlement. The 1986 National Security Act (NSA) has been used to restrict reporting on government activities. A 2006 draft version of the Botswana broadcasting bill was debated by the National Assembly during the year. The bill includes plans to establish a new community broadcasting sector as well as a public entity to monitor the quality and objectivity of state-owned media. Botswana does not have a freedom of information law, and critics accuse the government of excessive secrecy. In fact, a draft Mass Media Communications Bill (2001) is due to appear before Parliament that would further limit journalists' abilities to access government information.

Journalists are occasionally threatened, harassed, or attacked in retaliation for their reporting. In 2005, the government employed immigration legislation to deport two Zimbabwean journalists who had criticized state policies and used the NSA to deport an Australian-born academic who criticized the country as undemocratic. In March 2007, seven foreign journalists who had written critically about the government were forced to apply for visas despite being citizens of countries where Botswana visas are not required. The government occasionally censors or otherwise restricts news sources or stories that it finds undesirable, and editorial interference in the state-owned media from the Ministry of Communication, Science, and Technology has increased in recent years. In July, press freedom organizations condemned a ministry announcement that journalists who did not report "correctly" risked losing their licenses. In August, the editor of the independent *Tswana Times* claimed that the state's Botswana Telecommunications Corporation withdrew advertisements from the paper in retaliation for a critical story.

Independent print media and radio stations provide vigorous scrutiny of the government and air a wide range of opinions, mostly without government interference. Several independent newspapers and magazines are published in the capital, Gaborone. However, the state-owned Botswana Press Agency dominates the media landscape via its free *Daily News* newspaper and two nationally broadcast FM radio stations; radio remains the chief source of news for the majority of the population. Botswana Television, also owned by the state, is the country's only source of local television news. Privately owned radio stations and a private television station have a limited reach, particularly within rural districts; however, Botswana can easily receive broadcasts from neighboring South Africa. Government-controlled media generally confine themselves to coverage that is supportive of official policies and do not adequately cover the activities or viewpoints of opposition parties and other critics. Some private media companies have claimed that the government has cut back on its advertising with outlets that fail to cover the administration in a favorable light. In general, financially viable news sources available in languages other than English are rare. Internet access is unrestricted, albeit limited to approximately 3 percent of the population because of income and infrastructural constraints.

Brazil

Status: Partly Free

LEGAL ENVIRONMENT: 15
POLITICAL ENVIRONMENT: 16
ECONOMIC ENVIRONMENT: 11
TOTAL SCORE: 42

Survey Edition	2003	2004	2005	2006	2007
Total Score, Status	38,PF	36,PF	40,PF	39,PF	42,PF

Continuous legal rulings in favor of censorship to protect the reputation of high-ranking officials served to restrict press freedom during 2007, in addition to ongoing violent attacks against the media, including the killing of one journalist. While the 1988 constitution guarantees freedom of expression, several courts continue to prosecute journalists under the 1967 Press Law, which was passed during a military dictatorship. During its sessions in December 2007, Congress debated the possibility of amending the 1967 law to decriminalize defamation offenses. Legal avenues, such as privacy protections under the Brazilian civil code, were often invoked to harass and censor the press in the local courts. While many cases were overturned on appeal, cases of court-imposed censorship to protect politicians, influential business members, and government officials served to limit the public's right to information and promote self-censorship among journalists. Joao Henrique Cameiro, mayor of Salvador, successfully petitioned a Bahia court in June to prevent the Metropole media network from mentioning his name in any of the group's print, broadcast, or web media. The judge also ordered the seizure of 30,000 copies of a Metropole magazine that featured the mayor in an unfavorable light. A few days later, an appeals court judge overturned the sentence. Local courts in the states of Sao Paulo and Santa Catarina also issued preventive censorship rulings. A Sao Paulo local court banned the weekly *Folha de Vinhedo* from publishing an interview in which Paulo Cabral, a former government official, denounced local officials and businessmen of corruption. After an appeal, however, this ban was overturned. According to Reporters Sans Frontieres (RSF), in February, a Santa Catarina local court banned the *Gazeta de Joinville* from mentioning the names of Joinville mayor Marco Tebaldi, his wife, and former Miss Brazil Taiza Thomsen, after the paper referred to an alleged affair between the mayor and the former beauty queen.

Journalists and members of the media also continued to serve as targets for violent physical attacks in 2007, particularly those who reported on organized crime and corruption. On May 5, journalist Luiz Carlos Barbon Filho of the *JC Regional* and *Jornal do Porto* newspapers and Radio Porto FM contributor, was shot and killed in Porto Ferreira in the state of Sao Paulo. Barbon was known for his reports on corruption involving people close to the local government, including a 2003 investigation that accused local businessmen and city officials of being responsible for child sex abuse. The case of Barbon's murder remained under investigation at year's end. Another journalist, Amaury Ribeiro Junior of the daily *Correio Brasiliense*, was shot in September while investigating organized crime in the outskirts of Brasilia. While the attack on Ribeiro was classified as an attempted robbery by local police, the journalist believed it was related to his investigation and left the field of journalism. Four men were arrested in relation to the shooting. Radio host Joao Alckmin, who has been the victim of threats and harassment for years owing to his reporting on corruption and the involvement of local police in illegal gambling in eastern Sao Paulo state, was shot twice in November. Alckmin was the suspected target of an attack in July that wounded Rodrigo Duenhas, a lawyer who worked with Alckmin's wife. Anchor Domingues Junior from Rede TV Rondonia was also attacked in his own home, along with his family, by five unidentified armed individuals. Junior had denounced a money-for-votes scheme by the state government and had received death threats. In a number of cases over the years, former and incumbent government officials have been guilty of both legal and extralegal attacks on the media. In January, former secretary of communication Luiz Gushiken asked the federal police to investigate several reporters from leading news organizations on suspicion of corruption. As reported by RSF, his request, which was publicized by journalist Paulo Henrique Amorim in his blog, included a list of journalists "likely to harm [his] reputation." Gushiken himself was accused by the Ministerio Publico of improper financial management. In August, Eurico Mariano, former mayor of Coronel Sapucaia in the Brazilian state of Mato Grosso do Sul, was convicted of ordering the 2004 shooting of Paraguayan radio journalist Samuel Roma in order to silence his reporting. The former mayor received close to 18 years in prison for his role in the murder.

As South America's largest media market, Brazil boasts dynamic and diverse media, presenting an array of opinions on social and political issues as well as criticisms of the government and its policies. The country is home to hundreds of newspapers and television stations in addition to thousands of radio stations. Nevertheless, vigorous investigative journalism is more often practiced in the main cities as opposed to the interior, where legal and physical threats feed a climate of intimidation. Despite the pluralism of Brazil's media, ownership is highly concentrated, particularly within the broadcast sector. Globo Organizations, a large media conglomerate, continues to enjoy a dominant position, maintaining ownership of Brazil's principal television and cable networks, as well as several radio stations and print media outlets. Another company, Editora Abril, dominates the magazine industry, holding more than two-thirds of the market. Meanwhile, close ties between lawmakers and media owners continue to threaten the development of a fully independent press, particularly in regions where state and federal government representatives own broadcasting licenses and newspapers. The Committee to Protect Journalists reported that in October the president launched a new state-owned media group, Empresa Brasil de Comunicacion, which will run the new channel TV Brasil.

In a country with huge social disparities, Brazil has made tremendous gains in expanding internet access. More than 22 percent of Brazilians accessed the internet in 2007, almost 50 percent of total users in South America. While internet use has been mostly unrestricted in the past, several legal actions in 2007 raised concerns for freedom of expression. Senator Expedito Junior submitted a draft law to the Senate in December proposing to increase the length of prison sentences by one-third for offenses of denigration, defamation, and insult that are committed online. The penalty would be further increased if the victim is a government official, holds a public position, is elderly, or is handicapped. The bill was being examined by a senatorial committee at year's end. Altino Machado, a former journalist for the leading dailies *Folha de Sao Paulo* and *Estado do Sao Paulo*, was forced to pay a fine for posting an image on his blog of a minor sitting on top of the statue of a local poet. The picture had been copied from the boy's web page in a social network site, and the minor's family has asked Machado to withdraw the picture. More than 25 defamation lawsuits have been brought against blogger Alcinea Cavalcanti. Senator Jose Sarney, who felt personally offended by the content of several postings, was responsible for initiating the majority of the lawsuits. In December 2007, a court in the southern city of Porto Alegre forced journalist Vitor Vieira to withdraw content from an internet site that compromised a state representative.

Brunei

Status: Not Free

LEGAL ENVIRONMENT: 28
POLITICAL ENVIRONMENT: 25
ECONOMIC ENVIRONMENT: 22
TOTAL SCORE: 75

Survey Edition	2003	2004	2005	2006	2007
Total Score, Status	76,NF	74,NF	75,NF	77,NF	76,NF

The absolute monarchy of Sultan Hassanal Bolkiah and emergency laws—in effect for nearly half a century—continue to restrict journalists and limit the diversity of media content in Brunei. Harsh press legislation has required that newspapers apply for annual publishing permits and that noncitizens obtain government approval to work as journalists since 2001. The government has the authority to arbitrarily shut down media outlets and to bar distribution of foreign publications. Journalists can be jailed for up to three years for reporting "false and malicious" news. The May 2005 Sedition Act further restricted press freedom by expanding the list of punishable offenses to include criticism of the sultan, the royal family, or the prominence of the national philosophy, the Malay Islamic monarchy concept. Under the amended law, persons convicted of such crimes, or any publishers, editors, or proprietors of a newspaper publishing matters with seditious intention, face fines of up to B$5,000 (US$2,965).

No incidents of attacks on or harassment of the press were reported in 2007. However, in April 2007, the deputy prime minister warned the media not to "play with fire" when reporting on the sultanate, emphasizing that disrespect for government decisions to withhold certain information could be interpreted as subversion. Media are generally not able to convey a diversity of viewpoints and opinions, and criticism of the government is rare. The country's main English-language daily newspaper, the *Borneo Bulletin*, is controlled by the sultan's family and often practices self-censorship to avoid angering the government, though it does publish letters to the editor that criticize government policies. The private press is mostly owned or controlled by the sultan's family or practices self-censorship on political and religious matters. In July 2006, after receiving permission from the sultan, an independent media company run by a group of prominent businessmen launched a second English-language daily, the *Brunei Times*. The paper's global focus is intended to help foster international investment in light of the country's depleting oil and gas reserves, thus falling in line with current government priorities, yet it covers a wider range of international, finance, and opinion pieces, as well as online polls on government policies. A smaller Malay newspaper and several Chinese newspapers are also published within Brunei. The only local broadcast outlets, including the country's one television station, are operated by the government-controlled Radio Television Brunei, but residents can also receive Malaysian broadcasts, and international news is available via satellite channels.

In 2007, roughly 47 percent of the population accessed the internet, which is reportedly unrestricted. Yet the primary internet service provider is state owned, and the country's internet practice code stipulates that content must not be subversive, promote illegitimate reform efforts, incite disharmony or instability, or fall out of line with "Brunei Darussalam's religious values, social and societal mores." It also requires all sites that carry content or discuss issues of a religious or political nature to register with the Broadcasting Authority and makes failure to register punishable on conviction by imprisonment for up to three years and/or a fine of up to US$200,000. In 2006, the government called on internet cafés to install firewalls to prevent users from viewing immoral content and, according to the U.S. State Department, to monitor private e-mail and internet chat room exchanges of citizens believed to be subversive.

Bulgaria

Status: Partly Free

LEGAL ENVIRONMENT: 10
POLITICAL ENVIRONMENT: 12
ECONOMIC ENVIRONMENT: 11
TOTAL SCORE: 33

Survey Edition	2003	2004	2005	2006	2007
Total Score, Status	30,F	35,PF	35,PF	34,PF	34,PF

The constitution provides for freedom of speech and of the press, and the government generally respects these rights in practice. Defamation is punishable by high fines, and in previous years many suits were filed in response to published reports detailing the corruption of high-level officials. Although the courts usually declined to impose fines, the threat of legal action has led to some self-censorship. No libel lawsuits were reported in 2007. The law on freedom of information is considered fairly strong, but in some cases state institutions reportedly resist information requests from journalists despite court rulings in their favor. Press freedom and freedom of information advocates expressed concern in May 2007 after the parliament granted initial approval to proposed reforms that would restrict access to information and increase fees and time limits for information requests. In April, an independent commission tasked with opening the Communist-era archives of the state security service began its work, vetting candidates for European Parliament elections the following month. Prior to the 2006 legislation that created the new panel, the files had been at the disposal of the interior minister, which led to selective leaks on politicians and other public figures, including journalists. In September 2007, the commission identified dozens of public figures who had collaborated with the Communist-era security services, including the president and 19 current members of parliament. The files would eventually be open to the public, subject to certain national security restrictions.

Media outlets express a diverse range of public and political views, in most cases without government interference. However, the country's reporters continue to face pressure and intimidation aimed at protecting economic, political, and criminal interests. The perpetrators often operate with impunity, leading to some self-censorship among journalists. In February 2007, two men entered the offices of the weekly *Politika* and threatened to throw acid at writer Maria Nikolayeva if she continued reporting on possible corruption linked to real estate developments in Strandzha national park. The paper published her follow-up story, but an unidentified buyer purchased all the copies from the distributor in Burgas, the administrative center of the region that includes Strandzha. Nikolayeva's coauthor in the series was beaten by a group of men in Burgas later in the year. In another February incident, Ataka party leader Volen Siderov and a mob of supporters entered the offices of the daily *24 Chasa* and the *168 Chasa* weekly to complain about an article alleging that the ultranationalist Ataka had received funding from an ethnic Turkish party, the Movement for Rights and Freedoms. The men physically threatened and verbally abused journalists at the papers, and a pro-Ataka television station aired their names and addresses, leading to more threats. The party staged a protest against "media lies and manipulation" in early March. In May, five police officers used batons to beat photojournalist Emil Ivanov as he attempted to comply with their order to delete photographs he had just taken of unusually tight security surrounding a witness outside a courthouse in Sofia. The assault was recorded by fellow journalists, but the officers were not punished.

Top private and public media outlets are generally free of political affiliations. The popular state-owned Bulgarian National Television and Bulgarian National Radio are often critical of the government, and large foreign media firms play a major role in the private print and television markets. Germany's Westdeutsche Allgemeine Zeitung (WAZ), for example, owns the two leading dailies, *Trud* and *24 Chasa*. However, smaller regional stations and publications struggle financially, providing low salaries to reporters and weak scrutiny of local officials. Many traditional media outlets have established a presence on the internet, which is unrestricted by the government and used by about 30 percent of the population.

Burkina Faso

LEGAL ENVIRONMENT: 13
POLITICAL ENVIRONMENT: 15
ECONOMIC ENVIRONMENT: 13

Status: Partly Free

TOTAL SCORE: 41

Survey Edition	2003	2004	2005	2006	2007
Total Score, Status	39,PF	39,PF	40,PF	38,PF	39,PF

Although freedom of speech is protected by the constitution under Article 8, in practice journalists occasionally face harassment by public authorities for coverage deemed unfavorable, and many practice self-censorship. Under the 1993 information code, media outlets may be summarily banned if they are accused of distributing false information or endangering national security. Libel laws are unfavorable to the press and put the burden of proof on the defendant. No law exists to guarantee equal access to information. In June 2007, the media came under the control of the newly formed Ministry of Culture, Tourism, Communications, and Spokesman of the Government, which is responsible for developing media policy. The Superior Council of Communication, which is housed in the presidential office and possesses little independence, regulates the media.

The investigation into the 1998 murder of prominent journalist Norbert Zongo continued to demonstrate in 2007 the limits to press freedom in Burkina Faso. Following the July 2006 dismissal of the case against a presidential guard, the only person ever formally charged in the murder, subsequent efforts in 2006 to reopen the case by Zongo's family and Reporters Sans Frontieres were unsuccessful. On February 3, almost 3,000 people demonstrated in the capital against the closing of this case, but no government response was ever forthcoming. In January 2007, a court in Ouagadougou sentenced two journalists with the private monthly *L'Evenement*, director Germain Nama and editor Ahmed Newton Barry, to two-month suspended prison terms and fines of US$680 each on libel charges, associated with a 2006 report connecting President Blaise Compaore's brother with Zongo's murder.

Burkinabe journalists faced other instances of harassment throughout 2007. In April, Karim Sama, the singer and radio host for Radio Ouaga who is also known as Sam's K le Jah, received death threats for publicly criticizing Compaore's government. In September, while Sama was working his parked car was burned; yet by year's end, the government had not taken action to investigate the case. According to the Media Foundation for West Africa, in March, Thierry Nabyoure, a journalist with the private paper *San Finna*, was arrested and held for two days in response to an article critical of the head of the national gendarmerie; in May, formal defamation charges were filed. In June, Abdoul Salam Quarma, a correspondent with the Burkinabe Information Agency based in the northern town of Titao, received death threats from a group of youths dissatisfied with a report he had written about a recent drinking-related death in the town.

Although the state-operated media function with a noticeable progovernment bias, the media are generally free of overt censorship. During 2007, several newspapers were openly critical of the government, despite the threat of censure. Radio is the most popular news medium, owing to the country's literacy rate of only 24 percent and the high cost of newspapers and television sets. There are several private ratio stations in addition to the state-run Radio Burkina, and a small number of private television stations broadcast alongside the state-run Television Nationale du Burkina. Several private daily and weekly papers circulate in addition to *Sidwaya*, the official daily paper. Access to international print and broadcast media and the internet remains unrestricted by the government, while infrastructure limitations and poverty held the percentage of the population able to access the internet at 0.6 percent.

Burma (Myanmar)

LEGAL ENVIRONMENT: 30
POLITICAL ENVIRONMENT: 39
ECONOMIC ENVIRONMENT: 28

Status: Not Free

TOTAL SCORE: 97

Survey Edition	2003	2004	2005	2006	2007
Total Score, Status	94,NF	95,NF	96,NF	96,NF	96,NF

The Burmese media environment remained among the most tightly restricted in the world during 2007, with conditions worsening in August and September owing to the authorities' crackdown on prodemocracy demonstrations led by Buddhist monks. Burmese authorities warned local journalists to refrain from covering the protests, and many local publications did not cover the demonstrations, fearing retaliation. As a result of the demonstrations, as many as 15 journalists were detained, and a Japanese cameraman was killed. The current ruling military junta, which has been in power for 20 years, zealously implements a 1996 decree banning speech or statements that "undermine national stability," and those who publicly express or disseminate views or images critical of the regime are subject to harsh punishments, including lengthy prison sentences. Other laws require private publications to apply for annual licenses and criminalize the use of unregistered telecommunications equipment, satellite dishes, computers, and software. Laws also criminalize the possession or distribution of videos that are not approved by state censors.

Private periodicals are subject to prepublication censorship under the 1962 Printers and Publishers Registration Act, which requires that all content be approved by the authorities. As a result, coverage is limited to a small range of permissible topics, publications are sometimes required to carry government-produced articles, and most publications are forced to appear as weeklies or monthlies. With the April 2005 establishment of the Press Scrutiny and Registration Division (PSRD), under the control of the Ministry of Information, all publications were required to reregister and provide staff, ownership, and financial information to the PSRD. Under new censorship rules in effect since July 2005, media are ostensibly allowed to offer "constructive" criticism of government projects and are allowed to report on natural disasters and poverty, provided it does not affect the national interest. In recent years, however, there are also reports that the government has pressured private media outlets to publish articles critical of the opposition.

Both local and foreign journalists' ability to cover the news is restricted, with conditions worsening following the eruption of demonstrations in August 2007. At year's end, nine journalists were still imprisoned, including the well-known journalist U Win Tin, who recently turned 77 and has been in prison since 1989. On August 20, authorities banned journalists from photographing demonstrations, and on September 27, soldiers shot and killed Japanese cameraman Kenji Nagai as he attempted to record the protests. During the year, as many as nine journalists were forced to leave the country because of the repressive media environment. A few foreign reporters are allowed to enter Burma only on special visas; they are generally subject to intense scrutiny while in the country and in past years have occasionally been deported. Foreign journalists were unable to obtain permits to attend the national convention to cover the drafting of the constitution, and in September, many foreign correspondents found that their telephone lines had been cut. A number of Burmese journalists remain in exile; many work for Burma-focused media outlets in the neighboring countries of India, Bangladesh, and Thailand.

The government owns all broadcast media and daily newspapers and exercises tight control over a growing number of privately owned weekly and monthly publications. While official media outlets serve solely as mouthpieces of the state, private media generally avoid covering domestic political news, and the vast majority of journalists practice extensive self-censorship. Many nominally private outlets are owned by either government agents or supporters. A stagnant economy, increased prices for newsprint, and a limited market for advertising revenue (following a 2002 ban on advertising Thai products) continue to threaten the financial viability of the private press. Following the publication of a subversive advertisement in a state-run paper in August 2007, the government issued 28 new guidelines designed to tighten censorship of advertising. Authorities restrict the importation of foreign news periodicals; for several weeks after the outbreak of protests, publications such as *Newsweek* and *Time*, as well as several Thai newspapers, were not available. Although some people have access to international shortwave radio or satellite television, those caught accessing foreign broadcasts can be arrested, according to the Committee to Protect Journalists. In December, the authorities raised the annual cost of renewing a satellite television license from about US$5 to US$800, far beyond the reach of most Burmese. Nevertheless, as the only source of uncensored information, foreign radio programs produced by the Voice of America, Radio Free Asia, and Democratic Voice of Burma are very popular.

The internet, which operates in a limited fashion in cities and is accessible to less than 1 percent of the population, is expensive, tightly regulated, and censored, with the government controlling all of the several dozen domestic internet service providers. Though relatively limited in their sophistication, the authorities employ filtering and surveillance technologies and actively engage in blocking access to websites run by Burmese exile groups and to international e-mail services such as Yahoo!, Hotmail, and Gmail. Beginning in early 2007, authorities banned a growing number of websites and proxy sites that enabled regime critics to circumvent official censorship and banned the video website YouTube in September. For a few weeks beginning in late September, the internet was virtually inaccessible owing to government controls, and authorities restricted internet usage to only a few hours per day in October and November.

Burundi

LEGAL ENVIRONMENT: 21
POLITICAL ENVIRONMENT: 29
ECONOMIC ENVIRONMENT: 24

Status: Not Free

TOTAL SCORE: 74

Survey Edition	2003	2004	2005	2006	2007
Total Score, Status	76,NF	75,NF	74,NF	74,NF	77,NF

Burundi's media environment was slightly more open in 2007 than the previous year, when authorities severely cracked down on media outlets critical of its policies, although the government continues to dominate the media and does not tolerate criticism of the president. While the constitution provides for freedom of expression, this right is rarely respected in practice; much of the current media legislation is vague about the offenses for which a journalist may be charged. For example, the 1997 Press Law forbids the dissemination of "information inciting civil disobedience or serving as propaganda for enemies of the Burundian nation during a time of war." The November 2003 Media Law also provides for harsh fines and prison terms of up to five years for the dissemination of information that insults the president or is defamatory toward other individuals. In 2006, legislation was proposed that would more accurately define the responsibilities and limitations of journalists, but no progress on this legislation was made in 2007.

Unlike in 2006, when Burundi was ranked as Africa's third leading jailer of journalists by the Committee to Protect Journalists, in 2007 there were no reports that authorities detained or arrested journalists for criticizing the administration. In fact, in January, a court acquitted two journalists with the privately owned Radio Publique Africaine (RPA), Serge Nibizi and Domitile Kiramvu, and the director of Radio Isanganiro, Matthias Manirakiza, who were arrested in November 2006 and charged with "violating state secrecy" for publishing information about an alleged coup. All three journalists were imprisoned through the end of last year. Also in contrast to 2006, there were no reports of journalists being harassed or arrested for critical comments about the authorities. Nonetheless, the events of 2006 created a considerable amount of fear within the private media, causing many journalists to self-censor. Furthermore, in October, authorities in Bujumbura detained Emmanuel Nsabimana, RPA's director, for approximately four hours following a broadcast about a sexual harassment incident involving a Protestant minister.

The government dominates Burundi's media industry; it owns *Le Renouveau*, the country's only daily newspaper, as well as the only television station and the sole national radio station. There are six private newspapers that are able to publish on a weekly basis, but they are generally restricted to the Bujumbura area because of financial and infrastructure constraints. The ownership of private radio stations tends to be highly concentrated, but some, like RPA, are still able to provide diverse and balanced coverage. There are no apparent government restrictions on internet access, although the National Communication Council bans websites from "posting documents or other statements by political organizations that disseminate hate or violence." Owing to economic and infrastructure limitations, less than 1 percent of the population accessed the internet in 2007.

Cambodia

Status: Partly Free

LEGAL ENVIRONMENT: 19
POLITICAL ENVIRONMENT: 22
ECONOMIC ENVIRONMENT: 19
TOTAL SCORE: 60

Survey Edition	2003	2004	2005	2006	2007
Total Score, Status	64,NF	63,NF	62,NF	61, NF	58,PF

Though the press remains vibrant, the Cambodian media environment deteriorated in 2007 as censorship and attacks on the press increased, leading at least two journalists to flee the country during the year out of fear for their safety. The constitution guarantees the right to free expression and a free press, and although the 1995 Press Law also theoretically protects press freedom, the government has used it to censor stories deemed to undermine political stability. Under Article 12, the employer, editor, or author of an article may be subject to a fine of 5 million to 15 million riels (US$1,282–US$3,846). The law also gives the Ministries of Information and the Interior the right to confiscate or suspend a publication for 30 days and transfer the case to court. Article 13 states that the press shall not publish or reproduce false information that humiliates or is in contempt of national institutions. According to the U.S. State Department, in December 2007, the Ministry of Information (MOI) issued a directive reasserting these restrictions and prohibiting the running of stories that defame government leaders or institutions. In May 2006, the National Assembly dropped criminal charges for defamation, though civil suits with potentially onerous fines remain in law, as does potential imprisonment for the charge of "spreading disinformation." An estimated seven defamation suits were filed by government officials against journalists during the year, including three against the *Sralanh Khmer* newspaper. In addition, at least one criminal case of disinformation was filed in Phnom Penh against the editor of the *Samleng Yuveachun Khmer*, a paper associated with the party of former prime minister Prince Norodom Ranariddh, over an article alleging that the municipal governor had sold City Hall to developers. The journalist paid US$500 in bail in November, and the case was still pending at the end of the year.

Press coverage is vigorous, and journalists regularly expose official corruption and scrutinize the government. Partly for this reason, attacks against the press and censorship increased in 2007 after a lull in recent years. These were to a large extent related to the publication in May of a report by the London-based organization Global Witness, accusing individuals close to Prime Minister Hun Sen of involvement in illegal logging. In early June, the MOI ordered the confiscation of print copies of the report and directed newspapers to cease reproducing its contents. A news editor of the French-language daily *Cambodge Soir* was fired several days later, after the paper continued to reprint the report. One of the paper's owners then announced the paper's closure, sparking a strike by its staff and an outcry from international press freedom groups. The situation was somewhat resolved through mediation by the International Organization of La Francophonie, which partially funds the paper, and it was relaunched in October 2007 as a weekly publication, but with approximately half the previous staff. Journalists from other publications who sought to further investigate deforestation also reported being harassed. In June, three journalists reported being beaten at gunpoint by a local official's bodyguard in Pursat province, and Lem Piseth, a reporter for Radio Free Asia (RFA), fled to Thailand for several weeks after receiving death threats. Several other attacks and acts of censorship were reported during the year, including a verbal attack by the prime minister against RFA reporter Um Sarim that was rebroadcast over national television, leading the journalist to flee the country for several weeks. In October, the MOI suspended *Khmer Amatak*, a pro-opposition newspaper, for one month after it refused to publish a "correction" the ministry had requested. In November, the authorities seized 2,000 copies of the debut issue of a foreign-funded magazine called *Free Press*, reportedly because of contents deemed insulting of the king. The publication's editor and distribution director subsequently went into hiding.

Journalists from more than 20 Khmer-language publications aligned with or subsidized by various political factions are unbridled in criticizing their adversaries and public officials but generally do not criticize the king. The ruling Cambodian People's Party (CPP) and its alternating coalition partners, the royalist party Funcinpec and the Sam Rainsy Party, each has its own newspaper. However, the government dominates both radio and television, the main media sources for the two-thirds of the population that are functionally illiterate, and broadcast programming generally reflects official viewpoints. Independent broadcast outlets' operations are constrained by the government's refusal to allocate radio and television frequencies to stations that are aligned with the opposition. This was evident in September 2007 when the MOI refused to issue a broadcasting license to the Cambodian Center for Human Rights for its Voice of Democracy radio station, though the previous month it had awarded a license to a CPP official to open a new Phnom Penh station. Nevertheless, alternative news sources arc available through RFA, Voice of America, and Voice of Democracy programming aired by several local radio stations. According to a 2006 survey by InterMedia, over 30 percent of the population listens regularly to RFA, including 56 percent of those living in proximity to Phnom Penh. The economy is not strong enough to generate sufficient advertising revenues to support truly neutral or independent media. Access to the internet is generally unrestricted, although owing to infrastructure and economic constraints, less than 0.5 percent of the population was able to access the internet in 2007.

Cameroon

LEGAL ENVIRONMENT: 20
POLITICAL ENVIRONMENT: 24
ECONOMIC ENVIRONMENT: 21

Status: Not Free

TOTAL SCORE: 65

Survey Edition	2003	2004	2005	2006	2007
Total Score, Status	65,NF	67,NF	68,NF	65,NF	67,NF

The 1996 constitution provides for freedom of the press and of speech, but the government continued to restrict these rights in practice during 2007. There are no legal provisions guaranteeing equal access to information, and libel and defamation remained criminalized contrary to international standards and best practices. Although much of the independent press reports critically about the government, the threat of prosecution leads many, particularly within the broadcast media, to self-censor. Laws against libel and publishing allegedly obscene materials were used against journalists in several instances during 2007, including in April, when journalist Georges Gilbert Baongla, managing editor of the private weekly *Le Dementi*, was arrested on charges of publishing obscene material related to a story on a government minister's alleged involvement in a homosexual scandal. Homosexuality is a crime in Cameroon and continues to be a taboo subject, making reporting on it dangerous; in May, Baongla received a six-month suspended sentence and was fined approximately US$1,000. Among other reported cases, in August, Wirkwa Eric Tayu, publisher of the private weekly *The Nso Voice*, went into hiding and was shortly thereafter sentenced to one year in prison and fined approximately US$1,800 on charges of criminal defamation following reports the paper published on local government corruption in the northwestern town of Kumbo. At year's end, a warrant was still out for his arrest and Tayu's father, a local tribal leader, had been temporarily detained for failing to turn over his son. Since the verdict and the disappearance of Tayu, *The Nso Voice* ceased publishing.

Journalists were also harassed, intimidated, and physically assaulted during 2007, in some instances by state security forces. While these incidents were less frequent than in 2006, they rarely received the serious attention from law enforcement that they deserved. In January, gendarmes raided the private Ocean City Radio station, based in the southwestern town of Kumba. The officers assaulted several staff members in response to a program airing at the time that detailed corruption within the gendarmerie; acceding to pressure from a local human rights group, the gendarmerie commander subsequently issued an apology. Other instances of harassment included a July 23 attack by riot police on journalist Roland Tsapi with the Doula-based private daily *Le Messager*, while he was covering a protest march by opposition groups against fraudulent legislative and municipal elections that took place earlier in the month.

There are about 25 regularly published newspapers, including the privately owned *Mutations, La Nouvelle Expression*, and *Le Messager*, as well as the state's *Cameroon Tribune*, which toes the government line in the majority of its coverage. Many of the private papers freely criticize government policies and report on controversial issues, including corruption, human rights abuses, homosexuality, and economic policies. Distribution problems and high government tariffs on production ensure that newspapers remain a uniquely urban phenomenon, although there are approximately 70 privately owned but not officially recognized radio stations. State-owned Cameroon Radio and Television (CRTV) broadcasts on both television and radio and was the only officially recognized and fully licensed broadcaster in the country until the much-anticipated move on August 30 when the government granted licenses to two private television stations, Spectrum TV and Canal 2 International; one cable television network, TV+; and one private radio station, Sweet FM. These four stations were the first of over 100 applicants to receive formal permission to operate in Cameroon since legislation was passed authorizing private channels back in 1990. Many of these stations had been allowed to operate unofficially for some time under what the government called a "regime of tolerance." Nonetheless, CRTV continues to receive financial assistance from the state, placing independent broadcasters at a disadvantage. In general, the broadcast media are tightly controlled by the government, and discussion or advocacy of secession is strictly prohibited. Several rural community radio stations were established by UNESCO in 2006, though they are all limited in the range of their broadcast capacity and prohibited from discussing politics at all. While foreign broadcasters, including the British Broadcasting Corporation and Radio France Internationale, are permitted to operate within Cameroon and are widely available to Cameroonians who can afford them, they must partner with the state-owned CRTV. Despite the signing into law of the National Anticorruption Commission, corruption is rampant in numerous sectors of the media; many journalists expect and accept payment from politicians for writing articles containing unsubstantiated allegations against their opponents. Access to the internet is not limited by the government, although slow connections and high fees at internet cafés served to restrict access to approximately 2 percent of the population in 2007.

Canada

Status: Free

LEGAL ENVIRONMENT: 4
POLITICAL ENVIRONMENT: 8
ECONOMIC ENVIRONMENT: 6
TOTAL SCORE: 18

Survey Edition	2003	2004	2005	2006	2007
Total Score, Status	17,F	15,F	17,F	18,F	17,F

Legislation forcing journalists to reveal their sources when pertinent to criminal cases continued to be enacted and to weaken press freedom in an otherwise vibrant and free media environment. Canada's 1982 constitution provides protection for freedom of expression, including freedom of the press. The government may legally restrict free speech, however, with the aim of ending discrimination, ensuring social harmony, or promoting gender equality. While defamation remains a criminal offense, the Ontario Court of Appeals issued a groundbreaking decision in November to allow the press the defense of responsible public interest journalism against libel and slander suits. The case had originally been filed by a police officer against the *Ottawa Citizen* for defamation in 2001. In another defamation case, in February 2007, an Ontario jury found that the *Toronto Star* had libeled businessman Peter Grant and awarded him $1,475,000 in damages, the largest Canadian award to date against a news media defendant. Legislation on access to information guarantees journalists' right to information, but in practice access can be hindered by bureaucratic delays, government interference, and numerous exemptions allowing government officials to reject requests. Following trends from recent years, the courts continued to invoke a 2004 law under which reporters can be forced to present documents to the police if deemed vital to a criminal case. In June,

Ottawa Citizen reporter Gary Dimmock was ordered to produce his notes regarding allegations of bribery against Mayor Larry O'Brien. Ken Peters, a reporter for the *Hamilton Spectator* who was found in contempt of court in 2006, after being fined C$31,600 in 2004 for refusing to give up a confidential source, continued to appeal the decision in 2007. In a positive development, in June, the Ontario Superior Court quashed a subpoena issued to Derek Finkle ordering him to turn over the research materials used in his book relating to a recently reopened murder case. Similarly, the Quebec Labor Relations Board refused to force Karin Gagnon of *Le Journal de Quebec* to reveal confidential sources from a story on asbestos in government buildings.

Journalists in Canada are generally free from violence and harassment. However, Jawaad Faizi, a journalist for the *Pakistan Post*, was injured in April after two men wielding a cricket bat attacked him and his car and ordered him to stop writing critically about the Pakistan-based religious organization Idara Minhaj-ul-Quran and its leader. Press freedom advocates also grew concerned over legal cases filed against journalists who wrote critically about Muslims and Islam, fearing the suits would encourage self-censorship. In 2007, the Canadian Islamic Congress filed complaints with human rights commissions in Ontario and British Columbia against *Maclean's* magazine and its editor in chief, charging that "The Future Belongs to Islam," a 2006 article about global demographic trends by columnist Mark Steyn, subjected "Canadian Muslims to hatred and contempt" and that the magazine had published a number of other articles that were Islamophobic in nature.

Both print and broadcast media, which include the public Canadian Broadcasting Corporation (CBC), are generally free to express diverse views. The CBC broadcasts in French and English and provides television and radio services for indigenous peoples in the north. Broadcasting rules stipulate that 30–35 percent of material must be Canadian. The Broadcasting Act also prohibits programming that could potentially incite hatred or contempt toward any group. Allegations of self-censorship on the basis of economic interests arose in November, when the CBC canceled the showing of a documentary about the Falun Gong spiritual group after coming under pressure from the Chinese authorities. The film was aired several weeks later, but only after certain segments had been removed, including comments by a prominent Canadian lawyer comparing the 2008 Beijing Olympics with the 1936 Berlin Games. The extent of media concentration and the influence of powerful media conglomerates such as CanWest Global Communications continue to limit media pluralism.

The internet is generally unrestricted and is used by roughly 22 million Canadians, or 65 percent of the population. Nevertheless, a number of individuals were fined in 2007 by the Canadian Human Rights Tribunal for hate messages posted on the internet.

Cape Verde

LEGAL ENVIRONMENT: 6
POLITICAL ENVIRONMENT: 10
ECONOMIC ENVIRONMENT: 12

Status: Free

TOTAL SCORE: 28

Survey Edition	2003	2004	2005	2006	2007
Total Score, Status	30,F	36,PF	32,PF	32,PF	29,F

The constitution directly provides for freedom of the press as well as confidentiality of sources, access to information, and freedom from arbitrary arrest. In recent years, the government has consistently demonstrated its ability to respect and protect these rights in practice, making Cape Verde among the freest media environments in Africa. A 1999 constitutional amendment still excludes the use of freedom of expression as a defense in defamation cases; however, there have been no such libel cases since 2002. There were also no reported cases of intimidation or violence against journalists in 2007.

Many media outlets are state operated, although there are a growing number of private publications and broadcast outlets. The law requires broadcasters to obtain operating licenses, and government approval is needed to establish new newspapers and other publications. However, there were no reports that the government denied or revoked licenses for political reasons in 2007, and two new private newspapers were launched in September. Six independent radio stations broadcast regularly in Cape Verde, and there are two foreign-owned television stations in addition to the state-owned radio and television stations. The government does not generally restrict access to the media that it controls, although opposition candidates reported difficulty in accessing airtime on the state broadcasters before the February 2006 presidential election. Self-censorship is widespread among journalists, however, and has been one of the largest obstacles to the creation of a truly free press. Geographic barriers and harsh terrain in a country made up of several islands also constitute impediments to the distribution of newspapers and other media products, including the internet, which was accessed by just over 8 percent of the population in

2007. However, there were no reports that the government restricted internet access or monitored e-mail messages, and foreign broadcasts are uncensored.

Central African Republic

LEGAL ENVIRONMENT: 19
POLITICAL ENVIRONMENT: 23
ECONOMIC ENVIRONMENT: 19

Status: Not Free

TOTAL SCORE: 61

Survey Edition	2003	2004	2005	2006	2007
Total Score, Status	67,NF	64,NF	63,NF	61,NF	58,PF

Status change explanation: Central African Republic's press freedom rating decreased from Partly Free to Not Free as authorities sought to limit commentary on the worsening armed conflict in the north of the country.

The 2005 constitution provides for freedom of the press, though authorities have continued to use intimidation and legal harassment to limit reporting, particularly on sensitive topics such as official corruption and ongoing instability due to antigovernment insurgencies. An overwhelming majority of voters approved the new constitution in a December 2005 referendum, recognizing the freedom to inform and express opinions as fundamental rights of the country's citizens. In addition, the new Press Law, which decriminalized many press offenses such as libel and slander, was approved by President Francois Bozize in early 2005; criminal penalties remain for some defamation charges, for incitement to ethnic or religious hatred, and for the publication or broadcast of false information that could "disturb the peace." Despite the 2005 press reforms and the progress that followed in 2006, authorities disappointed in 2007 by using criminal prosecutions to limit critical reporting with the jailing of a prominent local editor and the banning of a private publication. At the same time, entry into the journalism profession is relatively open and unrestricted as no license is required, and in the majority of cases, access to government information is free for both public and private media outlets.

During the year, the government attempted to restrict local journalists' commentary on ongoing insecurity in the north, where anti-Bozize rebels operate along with militias connected to the ongoing conflicts in neighboring Sudan and Chad and to which the UN Security Council authorized the deployment of forces during the year. In early March, the newly-created independent government media regulator, known as the High Communications Council (HCC), suspended the Bangui-based private weekly *Centrafriqu'Un* owing to an article criticizing alleged human rights abuses by soldiers from Chad, a regional ally of Central African Republic's government. On March 12, police arrested Michel Alkhaly Ngady, editor of the private weekly *Le Temps* and president of a local association of independent publishers known as GEPPIC which had encouraged *Centrafriqu'Un* to continue publishing despite the suspension due to "irregularities" within the HCC. Ngady, one of the journalists who had previously received threats in connection with his own reporting on the conflict, was charged with obstruction of justice for having criticized the HCC's suspension of *Centrafriqu'Un*; he was sentenced on April 2 to two months in prison and fined approximately US$635. Ngady filed an appeal, but it was never heard. In general, local journalists reported that the culture of impunity for crimes committed against media workers was one of the primary restrictions to the practice of journalism.

Several dozen newspapers were published in 2007, though only a handful appeared regularly. Many of these were privately owned, including at least three independent dailies, and most were able to report on political and economic issues. Nonetheless, meager salaries and real or self-imposed censorship in a less than dynamic media market continue to hamper the editorial freedom of news organizations. The private press is restricted almost entirely to the capital, the result of financial constraints and the lack of a reliable postal service as well as the danger of working in the countryside, where armed groups operate with impunity. The state remains dominant in the broadcast sector, and private radio stations, reined in by legal and financial restrictions, are often intimidated by the powerful. A prominent exception is Radio Ndeke Luka, managed by the Switzerland-based Fondation Hirondelle with support from the UN, which broadcasts on FM in the capital and occasionally on shortwave in the rest of the country. At year's end, license applications for two new television stations and one new radio station were pending, according to the U.S. State Department. Internet access is open and unrestricted, and there are no reports that the government monitors e-mail. However, the communications infrastructure is almost nonexistent outside of Bangui, and less than 1 percent of the population was able to access this medium in 2007.

Chad

Status: Not Free

LEGAL ENVIRONMENT: 23
POLITICAL ENVIRONMENT: 30
ECONOMIC ENVIRONMENT: 21
TOTAL SCORE: 74

Survey Edition	2003	2004	2005	2006	2007
Total Score, Status	67,NF	74,NF	73,NF	73,NF	74,NF

Chad's constitution allows for freedom of expression, but authorities have routinely used threats and legal provisions criminalizing defamation and vaguely defined "incitement" to imprison journalists and censor critical reporting. In March, Adji Moussa, director of the bimonthly *Le Mirroir*, received a six-month suspended prison sentence, as well as a fine and damages of approximately US$1,050 for allegedly defaming a Catholic priest over corruption allegations. Critical coverage of President Idriss Deby was treated particularly harshly. In December, authorities arrested the prominent local journalist Nadjikimo Benoudjita, director of the private weekly *Notre Temps*, following an editorial critical of Deby and the French government. Benoudjita was charged with inciting ethnic and religious hatred and was detained for three days before leaving the country; the paper, however, remained closed at year's end. In Chad's conservative, ethnically polarized society, many subjects are considered off-limits to the press, including the armed rebellion on the border with Sudan and recurring tensions among tribal clans. The High Communication Council (HCC), the official media regulatory body, has the authority to suspend publications and broadcast outlets for defamation or excessive criticism of the government and the presidency.

The first five months of 2007 were dominated by a nationwide state of emergency, which subjected local newspapers to prior censorship—forcing many to stop publishing altogether—and barred local media coverage of the opposition and the ongoing conflict in the east. Once the state of emergency was lifted in May, a number of private newspapers were able to print again without censorship and several radio stations returned to the air. But this marginal amount of freedom was short-lived as the government imposed a second state of emergency in October on reporting in eastern Chad. This included a blanket prohibition on travel to or coverage of the region as well as restrictions on interviews with opposition leaders and criticism of the government, depriving Chadians of vital sources of information at a time of domestic conflict and instability.

During the year, journalists throughout Chad faced the threats of harassment and detention. On January 31, Marcel Ngargoto, a journalist with Radio Brakos, a critical station based in the southern town of Moissala, was detained without charge for two days; he was later accused of "ruthless handling of sensitive news which could harm national cohesion," according to Reporters Sans Frontieres. In October, authorities detained three French journalists in eastern Chad who were traveling with Zoe's Ark, the French nonprofit charged late in the year with involvement in child trafficking in response to the organization's attempt to transport more than 100 purported Darfuri orphans to France for adoption. The journalists, who were not directly involved in the organization's operations, were held for 10 days on charges of complicity in kidnapping, but were later released on bail and allowed to leave the country, after intervention from French president Nicolas Sarkozy. Following the incident, authorities in eastern Chad tightened already-strict travel restrictions on journalists and nongovernmental organization workers in the region, according to the France-based newspaper *L'Humanite*. While coverage of the conflict remains easier for foreign correspondents than for their local counterparts, government intimidation frequently results in self-censorship.

Private newspapers, some of which publish commentary critical of the government when not operating under the prepublication censorship requirements that come with the imposition of a state of emergency, circulate freely in N'Djamena, the capital, but they have little impact on the largely rural and illiterate population. The only television station, Teletchad, is state owned, and its coverage favors the government. Radio is the primary means of mass communication and station licenses are granted by the HCC which is considered to be greatly influenced by the government. Despite the high cost of these licenses for commercial radio stations, there are over a dozen private and community-run stations on the air, some operated by nonprofit groups, including human rights organizations and the Catholic Church. These broadcasters are subject to close official scrutiny, and those that fail to pay annual fees to the state are threatened with closure. There are no reports that the government restricts internet access, although according to the U.S. State Department, there are reports that the government occasionally monitors e-mail. The internet infrastructure remains government owned, and less than 1 percent of the population had access to this resource in 2007.

LEGAL ENVIRONMENT: 10
POLITICAL ENVIRONMENT: 12

Chile

ECONOMIC ENVIRONMENT: 8

Status: Free   TOTAL SCORE: 30

Survey Edition	2003	2004	2005	2006	2007
Total Score, Status	22,F	23,F	24,F	26,F	30,F

Violence against journalists decreased in 2007, but efforts by the Supreme Court to limit press access to the courts as well as highly concentrated media ownership served to hinder press freedom. The Chilean constitution provides for freedom of speech and of the press, and these rights are generally respected in practice. The 2001 Press Freedom Law removed many of the preexisting penalties for the libel and slander of senior officials. However, a number of vague provisions still exist that prohibit insulting state institutions such as the presidency, the legislature, and judicial bodies. Those accused of defamation of military personnel may also be tried in military courts. In March, the Supreme Court tried to limit the ability of the press to report in the courts or to interview court officials. The decree was rescinded four days later following heavy local and international criticism. In August, the Supreme Court upheld the conviction of three Chilevision journalists who used hidden cameras, thereby violating the criminal code, to tape a meeting between a judge and a sauna manager of an establishment that catered to homosexuals. The journalists each received a three-month suspended jail sentence. While constitutional provisions allowing censorship have been eliminated, at least two books remain banned under judicial order since 1993. In a positive step, the Bachelet government introduced legislation in October that would help to legally and financially boost the status of the country's 400 licensed community radio stations, such as the extension of the right to earn funds from advertising. While celebrating the proposed bill, the World Association of Community Radio Broadcasters called for additional remaining restrictions to be lifted, including limitations on the territorial range and power of the broadcasting signals.

While violence against the press is limited in Chile, reporting on events that took place during the 1973–1990 dictatorship remains sensitive and can place journalists at risk of violence or harassment. Argentine freelance TV journalist Benjamin Avila and his Chilean assistants Mario Puerto and Arturo Peraldi were arrested while covering a protest at the house of a former military officer suspected of the 1973 killing of foreign journalist

Leonardo Henrichsen. The journalists were allegedly beaten while in custody and then quickly released following protests by the journalist's association. Avila and members of the journalists association received death threats following the event.

Chile has a multitude of both private and state-owned newspapers, radio stations, and television outlets. However, print media ownership is highly concentrated in the hands of two companies that received preferential treatment during the conservative military dictatorship. Leftist media often struggle to survive financially as a result of politically cautious advertisers. In addition, the diversity of the media is affected by an oversupply of Chilean journalists who are forced to protect their jobs and not take too many risks in their reporting, as well as by the low wages and poor benefits they receive. Nevertheless, the media are relatively free to criticize the government and cover sensitive issues. The government does not directly control or heavily influence state-owned print outlets such as *La Nacion*, or broadcast media, including Television Nacional. There are hundreds of radio stations, and cable television provides the public with local and international programming. The internet served as an additional source of unrestricted information, with more than 43 percent of Chileans accessing the internet in 2007.

LEGAL ENVIRONMENT: 28
POLITICAL ENVIRONMENT: 35

China

ECONOMIC ENVIRONMENT: 21

Status: Not Free

TOTAL SCORE: 84

Survey Edition	2003	2004	2005	2006	2007
Total Score, Status	80,NF	80,NF	82,NF	83,NF	84,NF

Despite moderate breakthroughs for investigative journalism and regulations providing somewhat greater access to foreign correspondents, the year 2007 was marked by a tightening of media control and internet restrictions in preparation for the 17th Party Congress, as well as the jailing of additional online journalists and bloggers. Article 35 of the Chinese constitution guarantees freedom of speech, assembly, association, and publication. However, other articles subordinate these rights to the national interest, which is defined by party-appointed courts. The Communist Party maintains direct control over the news media through its Central Propaganda Department (CPD), especially with respect to news deemed politically sensitive. This control is reinforced by an elaborate web of regulations and laws that are worded vaguely and interpreted according to the wishes of the party leadership. Routinely taboo topics include criticism of party leaders, violations of minority rights in Tibet and Xinjiang, Taiwanese independence, and the Falun Gong.

Press freedom was further undermined in 2007 by new legislation aimed at controlling media coverage of unforeseen events. In November 2007, an emergency response law came into effect that allows media outlets' licenses to be revoked if they report "false information" about natural disasters, emergencies, or government responses to them without obtaining prior authorization. Throughout 2007, the CPD and its top officials reportedly issued instructions that restricted media coverage of an estimated 20 new topics, including flaws in the legal system, the work of some human rights defenders, a deadly bridge collapse in Hunan province, and relations with Taiwan surrounding the Olympic torch route. In addition to such preemptive restrictions, the Communist Party implemented postpublication censorship, confiscating publications deemed to have "harmed social stability, endangered national security, or incited ethnic separatism."

Despite such restrictions, some journalists and media outlets were known to push the limits of permissible coverage, particularly in cases of local corruption. In an incident considered by many as a significant step forward for Chinese investigative journalism, in May 2007, Henan Television journalist Fu Zhengzhong exposed slavery in brick kilns in Shanxi province that forced as many as 1,000 people—including abducted children—to work in inhumane conditions without pay. A wave of subsequent reporting led to raids on more than 2,500 kilns, the liberation of hundreds of workers, and the arrest of many officials with ties to the scandal. Nevertheless, within two weeks, the government imposed a media blackout on the subject and foreign journalists who sought to do follow-up reporting on the slavery noted that they were followed by security personnel and harassed.

In general, journalists who attempted to investigate or report on controversial issues, criticized the Communist Party, or presented a perspective contrary to state propaganda continued to suffer harassment, job loss, abuse, and detention. Huang Liangtian, editor in chief of the monthly *Bai Xing*, was removed from his post after investigating harsh living conditions in rural areas. In October, an investigative reporter for the *China Economic Times*, Pang Jiaoming, reported that substandard materials had been used in concrete employed in the construction of the Wuhan-Guangzhou railway. The CPD and the government-sponsored All-China Journalists Association later issued a circular denouncing Pang's reports and barring his employment as a journalist by news organizations nationwide. In an additional push-back against investigative journalism, the government announced a crackdown on "false" news in August 2007 following a report by broadcast journalist Zi Beijia on the use of chemically treated cardboard in pork buns in Beijing; later that month, Zi was sentenced to one year in prison.

According to international media freedom watchdogs, at least 29 journalists and 51 cyberdissidents were in prison in China at year's end, more than in any other country in the world. At least 9 journalists and online writers were detained during the year for information they had published on the internet, particularly on U.S.-based independent Chinese news websites. In March 2007, internet writer Zhang Jianhong was sentenced to six years in prison for publishing online articles calling for political reform on the *Boxun* and *Epoch Times* websites. In May, journalist Sun Lin and his wife were arrested on questionable charges of illegal weapons possession after Sun contributed several reports to *Boxun*, including one about the outlet's inability to receive accreditation to cover the Beijing Olympics. In August, He Weihua was reported to have been forcibly admitted to a psychiatric hospital, apparently in relation to postings on his *Boxun*-linked blog. During the year, writers Yang Zhengxue and Chen Shuqing were also sentenced to long prison terms on charges of "inciting subversion" after they criticized the government in online postings. At year's end, several other cyberdissidents—including prominent human rights defenders Hu Jia and Gao Zhisheng—remained in police custody, potentially awaiting sentencing. Violence against journalists also remained a concern in 2007. In January, a newly hired journalist at the *China Trade News*, Lan Chengzhang, was beaten to death while going to meet the owner of an illegal coal mine, who allegedly believed Lan sought to extort money in exchange for avoiding mention of the mine. In August, five journalists were reportedly beaten by unidentified assailants when they tried to report on a deadly bridge collapse in Hunan province. On a positive note, two journalists were released in 2007: *New York Times* researcher Zhao Yan, who was imprisoned in 2004, and Li Minying, former editor of the Guangzhou-based daily *Nanfang Dushi Bao*, who was released after serving half of his six-year sentence.

Owing to technological advancements and efforts of overseas activists, the regime's task of suppressing information has become more difficult in recent years. For Chinese with foreign language ability, foreign news reports accessible online present an alternate perspective to that available in the official media. A growing number of Chinese use proxy servers to circumvent internet restrictions, receive illegal satellite transmissions, and watch a plethora of pirated media products available in urban areas. However, the government has also taken steps to limit such access to more diverse sources of information, jamming shortwave radio broadcasts by Voice of America, Radio Free Asia, Sound of Hope, and the British Broadcasting Corporation (BBC). In the summer of 2007, the authorities also cracked down on local cable systems illegally transmitting foreign satellite broadcasts, particularly affecting the popular Hong Kong–based Phoenix television station and reportedly causing the outlet to lose millions of viewers.

Despite official pledges to allow international media full freedom to report ahead of the Olympic Games, foreign journalists' ability to work remained severely restricted. On January 1, 2007, a series of new regulations came into effect that removed travel restrictions on foreign media and allowed journalists to interview organizations and individuals without prior government consent. The new regulations, effective through mid-October 2008, apply to reporters from Hong Kong, Macau, and Taiwan but not to mainland citizens. As correspondents sought to take advantage of looser travel regulations, however, incidents of harassment and intimidation of sources reportedly increased compared with previous years. A survey conducted by the Foreign Correspondents Club of China (FCCC) found that while journalists reported improvements in some areas, 40 percent of respondents experienced some form of interference, including intimidation of sources, detention, surveillance, physical violence, and death threats. According to the FCCC, it received 180 reports of violations of the new regulations during 2007, compared with 72 reports of harassment received from 2004 to 2006. Although covering events in the restive areas of Tibet and Xinjiang remained particularly difficult, the FCCC received reports of harassment in at least five other provinces as well as Beijing and Shanghai. Tim Johnson, a reporter for the U.S.-based McClatchy newspaper chain, reported being warned by a Foreign Ministry official that the new rules for foreign journalists did not apply to Tibet. Some international press freedom monitors also reported difficulties in obtaining visas.

Media outlets are abundant in China but remain owned by the state, as media reforms have allowed for the commercialization of outlets without the privatization of ownership. Most cities have their own newspaper published by the local government or party branch, and according to the BBC, provincial and municipal stations of the state-run Chinese Central Television offer over 2,000 channels. Though all Chinese media are state owned, the majority no longer receive state subsidies and now rely on income from advertisements, which some argue has shifted the media's loyalty from the party to the consumer. Economic incentives have also been known to contribute to self-censorship, however, as publications fear losing advertising revenue should they run afoul of powerful societal actors. Salary schemes generally pay journalists only after their reports are published or broadcast. When a journalist writes a report that is considered too controversial, payment is withheld, and in some cases the journalist must pay for the cost of news gathering out of pocket. A small number of elite media outlets combat such deterrents to aggressive reporting by paying journalists for reports that are subject to censorship. This has resulted in a few outlets championing popular causes and printing embarrassing exposures of official malfeasance, though media personnel who engage in such journalism can be fired or arrested. Corruption among Chinese journalists remained common in 2007, with many journalists noting that they received payments from public relations firms for attending press conferences. Other journalists mentioned frequent use of bribery by corporations to pressure officials in Beijing to censor news stories considered harmful to corporate interests.

In 2007, China had the world's second-largest population of internet users after the United States, with an estimated 210 million people online, or just under 16 percent of the country's population. Though the government already employed an extensive surveillance and filtering system to prevent Chinese users from accessing material that was considered obscene, harmful to national unity, or politically subversive, efforts to censor and control internet content have increased in recent years. In 2005, the government introduced new regulations that bar websites from distributing information that violates the Chinese constitution, endangers national security, encourages illegal strikes, contains pornographic or violent content, or promotes unrecognized religious groups. In March 2007, the Ministry of Culture and the Ministry of Information Industries banned the opening of new internet cafés (113,000 were in existence at the time). Internet censorship was further increased prior to and during the 17th Party Congress in October 2007, during which the party leadership for the next five years was endorsed. Between April and September, access to over 18,400 websites was blocked. The Committee to Protect Journalists reported that in September, security agencies in several regions ordered internet data centers, which host large numbers of websites and blogs, to suspend their services or disable interactive features—such as bulletin boards and comment sections—during the congress meeting. In addition to blocking content, the authorities have also taken steps in recent years to proactively guide online discussion. Since 2005, the Communist Party has recruited and trained an army of web commentators, known as the "Fifty

Cent Party," to post pro-government remarks. Some estimates place their number at over 200,000.

Several other steps were taken by the government to restrict internet access during 2007. In an apparent effort to overcome difficulties monitoring audiovisual content with automated filtering technology, on December 20, the State Administration for Film, Radio, and Television (SAFRT) and the Ministry of Information Industries issued a regulation requiring websites with audiovisual content to apply for permits. The regulation, which potentially affects 60,000 sites, also banned audiovisual content deemed to fall into vaguely defined categories such as opposing the principles of China's constitution, harming national unity, contributing to ethnic divisions, or disrupting social harmony. In some instances, restrictions were imposed at a local level. After bloggers supported a protest against construction of a chemical factory near the southern city of Xiamen, the municipal government adopted measures requiring internet users to provide their real names when posting material on more than 100,000 websites registered in the city. Foreign internet companies have largely cooperated with the Chinese government on censorship enforcement. The Chinese-language search engines of the U.S. firms Yahoo!, MSN, and Google filter search results and restrict access to information about topics deemed sensitive by the party such as the Falun Gong, Tibetan independence, and human rights. In August 2007, Yahoo! and Microsoft were among a number of internet companies and service providers to sign on to a "self-discipline code" in which they agreed to encourage bloggers to register under their real names and to delete "illegal and unhealthy" postings. The government has also been known to monitor personal communications that are used to spread news and information, including e-mails and cellular telephone text messaging.

Colombia

Status: Partly Free

LEGAL ENVIRONMENT: 13
POLITICAL ENVIRONMENT: 30
ECONOMIC ENVIRONMENT: 16
TOTAL SCORE: 59

Survey Edition	2003	2004	2005	2006	2007
Total Score, Status	63,NF	63,NF	63,NF	61,NF	57,PF

The status of press freedom deteriorated in 2007 owing to a rise in attacks against journalists by both state and nonstate actors as well as mounting economic uncertainty for media outlets amid the ongoing civil war. Freedom of the press is guaranteed by the 1991 constitution, but journalists have trouble exercising their rights in a country racked by a complex armed conflict involving left-wing guerrilla organizations, drug traffickers, paramilitary groups, and government security forces. Occasional criminal complaints and civil lawsuits continue to be filed against the media with slander and libel filed as criminal charges under Colombia's penal code. In addition, media watchdogs decried as prior censorship a January court decision in Barranquilla that barred a local newspaper from disseminating further information regarding the results of a corruption investigation. In May, a large telephone-tapping scandal was uncovered that included the illegal surveillance of at least 13 journalists. Also in May, the Colombian Federation of Journalists was formed to advocate on reporters' behalf.

The media continued to play an important role in exposing paramilitary activities as well as contributing critical reporting on high-level corruption scandals like the "para-politics" incident, which linked government officials with paramilitary leaders. However, Colombia remains the most dangerous country for journalists in South America, with the violence and harassment of journalists by state and nonstate actors the primary impediments to a free media. Comments made by high-ranking government officials (including President Alvaro Uribe), who have chastised journalists for their reporting on the war, serve to further stigmatize the press and put them at risk of retribution. The Bogota-based watchdog Fundacion para la Libertad de Prensa (FLIP) reported a 16 percent increase in violations of press freedom in 2007, with a spike in incidents occurring in September and October during the run-up to local and regional elections. Security forces were implicated in over a dozen violations of press freedom, often related to press coverage of protests against state policies. Two journalists were killed during the year. In Choco, reporter Elacio Murillo Mosquera was shot and killed on January 10, possibly in retaliation for his reports on the movements of armed groups in the area. A member of criminal group Aguilas Negras was arrested and charged for Murillo's murder two days later, and the investigation continued at year's end. Radio reporter Javier Dario Arroyave was stabbed and killed in his home in Cartago in September; authorities claimed it was unrelated to his work, but past run-ins with local functionaries over corruption denunciations caused doubts among colleagues. Numerous threats against journalists occurred throughout the country, forcing at least 16 journalists to go into hiding or exile; among them, correspondent Gonzalo Guillen of Miami's *El Nuevo Herald* was forced to leave the country after receiving two dozen death threats. President Uribe had publicly accused Guillen of trying to harm him. FLIP reported a total of 85 death threats against journalists in 2007. In sensitive cases, local journalists often consider it safer to practice self-censorship or to leak information to large national outlets for publication or broadcast rather than break the stories themselves. Paramilitaries and the Revolutionary Armed Forces of Colombia (FARC) rebels were implicated in the greatest number of threats and attacks against journalists. In August, the FARC warned various broadcast media outlets in Arauca that they would become military targets if they refused to air rebel communiqués.

Since 2000, the Ministries of Justice and the Interior have operated the Journalist Protection Program to assist endangered journalists with security, transportation, financial aid, and assistance to leave the country; however, FLIP reported that only in 45 of the 102 cases in which protection was recommended were the suggested measures implemented. Government investigations and prosecutions for crimes against journalists have been slow and inconclusive, contributing to an atmosphere of impunity. In 2005, the government established a special unit in the Office of the Public Prosecutor to deal specifically with cases involving the assassination of journalists, but the unit has been hamstrung by insufficient personnel and budgetary resources. Little progress was reported in the investigations into three murders committed in 2006, but several older cases received new boosts owing to information divulged in the courtroom by paramilitaries engaged in a demobilization process. Unfortunately, there has been little consistency with respect to the press' ability to view the testimony of these ex-fighters directly, at times making them reliant on information from prosecutors and often intimidated victims.

Most of the country's media outlets are controlled by groups of private investors. Independent and privately owned print and broadcast media are generally free to express a variety of opinions and cover sensitive issues without restrictions. The government operates one educational and two commercial television stations along with a national radio network. Despite some advances, the hundreds of community radio stations operating in Colombia sometimes come under pressure from both the government and armed actors. Government advertising is an important source of revenue, since local media depend heavily on advertising by provincial and municipal agencies to stay in business. Low salaries add to this financial dependence, which creates a powerful incentive for collusion among media owners, journalists, and officials that affects editorial views and news coverage. There is a widespread perception that journalists accept bribes in exchange for biased coverage. In August, a majority stake in the country's paper of record, *El Tiempo*, was sold to Spanish investors. There were no reported cases of government monitoring or censoring of the internet, which was accessed by close to 23 percent of the population in 2007.

Comoros

Status: Partly Free

LEGAL ENVIRONMENT: 14
POLITICAL ENVIRONMENT: 25
ECONOMIC ENVIRONMENT: 15
TOTAL: 54

Survey Edition	2003	2004	2005	2006	2007
Total Score, Status	43,PF	45,PF	44,PF	47,PF	48,PF

Although the freedoms of speech and of the press are protected by the 2001 constitution, in practice, journalists are subject to harassment and harsh defamation laws. Conditions for journalists worsened during 2007 following the eruption of tensions between the central government and the semiautonomous island of Anjouan, where presidential elections were held in June to reelect Mohamed Bacar despite the central government's opposition. However, the media environment varied considerably among the union's three islands, with slightly greater levels of freedom on Grand Comore and Moheli and greater levels of repression on Anjouan in response to Bacar's attempts to limit criticism of his regime.

On May 16, gendarmes on Anjouan detained four journalists for a day following their attempts to secure transmitters that Bacar's supporters had damaged. On May 30, owing to published pictures of soldiers who had been captured in Anjouan, copies of the independent monthly *L'Archipel* were removed from stores by union police and the paper's director, Aboubacar M'changama, was held for questioning. In June, Elarifou Minihadji, a reporter with Grand Comore's regional government station, Radio Ngazidja, was held for three days and subjected to mistreatment by gendarmes on Anjouan for covering a demonstration at the island's airport in response to the arrival of African Union mediators. Furthermore, in July, the editor of Djabal Television, a private station based in Grand Comore and the only one to cover events in Anjouan since June, was detained and held for questioning about possible links to Anjouan leaders. In August, two journalists with the station were barred from purchasing airline tickets to the island to cover Independence Day events. In December, Kamal Ali Yahoudha, head of the Anjouan branch of the national broadcasting office, was forced into hiding to escape arrest due to his suspected opposition to the Anjouan authorities.

Comoros has several independent newspapers and one state-owned weekly, *Al-Watan*. In addition to the state-owned Radio Comoros and Television Nationale Comorienne, several other regional and private stations have proliferated in recent years and are funded predominantly by donations from locals as well as from citizens living abroad. Although the internet is available and unrestricted by the government, poverty, illiteracy, and a poor telecommunications infrastructure have severely limited access to an estimated 3 percent of the population in 2007.

LEGAL ENVIRONMENT: 17
POLITICAL ENVIRONMENT: 17

Congo, Republic of (Brazzaville)

ECONOMIC ENVIRONMENT: 17

Status: Partly Free

TOTAL SCORE: 51

Survey Edition	2003	2004	2005	2006	2007
Total Score, Status	55,PF	54,PF	51,PF	51,PF	51,PF

The constitution provides for freedom of the press, although several types of expression are considered to be criminal offenses, including incitement to ethnic hatred and violence. Following legal reforms in 2001, many press offenses are punishable by fines rather than imprisonment, including libel and publishing "false news." Nonetheless, these fines are often excessive and quickly handed down to publications critical of the government. Two-time offenders of libel of the president are still subject to criminal prosecution and jail time. Local journalists employed by international media outlets, as well as those employed by the state-run media, have been stripped of accreditation for reporting perceived to be overly critical of the government or covering taboo topics like water and electricity provisions, the armed opposition, or the way in which oil revenues are managed by the government. Freedom of information is barely recognized and access to government records is often easier for foreign correspondents than for local reporters.

According to the Kinshasa–based press freedom organization Journaliste en Danger, no direct attacks on journalists in Congo-Brazzaville were recorded in 2007. However, two local television journalists reported receiving threats in June in connection with their coverage of the opposition during that month's legislative elections. Self-censorship by journalists in response to subtle intimidation remained a problem.

In 2007, over 15 private weekly newspapers were published in the capital, Brazzaville, and provided some scrutiny of the government, although the print media did not circulate widely beyond major urban centers. There was one state-owned newspaper, *La Nouvelle Republique*, as well as a number of private publications believed to be allied with the regime of President Denis Sassou-Nguesso. Radio remains the most popular medium nationwide. While local journalists reported that there were 18 radio stations and 14 television stations, many of these operated unofficially as the cost of a license is often prohibitive. In fact, the government has been slow to loosen its grip on the broadcast sector at all and continues to run three radio stations and one television station of its own. Political parties are not permitted to own radio stations or television channels. Although several private radio and television stations have gained permission to broadcast in recent years, they rarely criticize the government. There are no reports that the government restricts internet usage or monitors e-mail, although less than 2 percent of the population—concentrated mainly in urban areas—had access to this resource in 2007.

Congo,
Democratic Republic of (Kinshasa)

LEGAL ENVIRONMENT: 25
POLITICAL ENVIRONMENT: 32
ECONOMIC ENVIRONMENT: 24

Status: Not Free

TOTAL SCORE: 81

Survey Edition	2003	2004	2005	2006	2007
Total Score, Status	82,NF	80,NF	81,NF	81,NF	80,NF

The law provides for freedom of speech and of the press and even provides for freedom of information, but these rights are restricted in practice by President Joseph Kabila's government and various nonstate actors, including an insurgent movement led by the Rwanda-backed commander Laurent Nkunda. Officials used an array of prohibitive licensing regulations, criminal libel laws, and legal provisions allowing "preventive detention" without due process to restrict free speech and suppress political criticism. At least three local journalists were convicted on criminal defamation charges, for which truth is no defense, in 2007 for articles addressing public sector corruption. Rigobert Kwakala Kash, editor of the private weekly newspaper *Le Moniteur*, was sentenced shortly after Kabila resumed office in January to 11 months in prison for allegedly libeling the transitional governor of the western province of Bas-Congo. Kash received this conviction despite the fact that *Le Moniteur* had itself been suspended for six months only a day before his arrest for the same offense. Fortunately, Kash was released after serving only 35 days of his sentence. Two other journalists went into hiding to avoid arrests for similar convictions. In October, Information Minister Toussaint Tshilombo banned 22 local private television stations and 16 radio stations for alleged noncompliance with national media laws. While most were allowed to resume broadcasting by year's end, the ban came down particularly hard on media outlets associated with the former rebel leader and Kabila's rival in the 2006 presidential election, Jean-Pierre Bemba. Media outlets also remained subject to regulation by the High Authority on Media (HAM), a public agency created under the 2002 peace accord that formally ended the civil war within the Democratic Republic of the Congo (DRC). Some HAM decisions have appeared politically motivated, such as the May closure of the private broadcaster Radio Television Debout Kasai for allegedly defaming the local governor.

Multiparty presidential elections were held in 2006 for the first time since independence from Belgium in 1960. Kabila, who had led the country's transitional government since 2002, won in an October runoff against Bemba. Subsequent violent clashes between government soldiers and fighters loyal to Bemba led to reprisals against media outlets linked to Bemba and journalists who had covered the violence; Bemba went into exile in April 2007 and was charged in absentia with high treason. In March, two television stations and one radio station owned by Bemba were forced to close following a raid by government security forces.

Local journalists were vulnerable to violent assault, harassment, and arbitrary imprisonment; during the year, 2 journalists were killed, 10 served time in jail, and as many as 54 were questioned by security forces, according to Reporters Sans Frontieres. The International Federation of Journalists ranks DRC as the second most dangerous place for journalists to operate in Africa after Somalia. The most serious of these incidents include the June murder of Serge Maheshe Kasole, a journalist with the internationally funded Radio Okapi network, in the eastern city of Bukavu. Two soldiers and two of Kasole's friends were convicted of the murder and sentenced to death despite a complete lack of evidence against them, and all four were still in jail and awaiting appeal at year's end. In August, freelance photojournalist Patrick Kikuku Wilungula was killed by gunmen in the eastern city of Goma. The peaceful march of over 100 journalists protesting Kikuku's murder was violently suppressed by the deployment of

Rapid Intervention Police officers before the journalists could get to the Interior Ministry to make an official statement. While military tribunals convicted several individuals in 2007 in connection with the 2005 murder of investigative journalist Franck Ngyke Kangundu and his wife and the 2006 murder of journalist Louis Bapuwa Mwamba, local press freedom watchdog Journaliste en Danger (JED) criticized the official investigations and reported that these cases remained far from resolved.

Numerous other journalists were also the victims of non-fatal attacks similar to the beating of Faustin Bela Mako, editor of the small private paper, *Congo News*, who was attacked by unknown assailants in March for writing an article in support of an opposition political party. JED staff themselves received death threats during the year, forcing secretary general Tshivis Tshivuadi and president Donat M'baya Tshimanga to go into hiding temporarily in August. Separately, 15 journalists were dismissed without warning from the private television station, Global TV, after demanding the payment of the nine months of arrears on their salaries.

The DRC boasts hundreds of private newspapers, radio channels, and television stations. While not always objective, the private media are often highly critical of the government. As illiteracy rates are high and few newspapers circulate outside of urban centers, the majority of the population relies on radio broadcasts for news. In order to operate legally in DRC, a media outlet must obtain a license and authorization for technical operations from the Ministry of the Post, Telephones, and Telecommunication as well as a separate authorization to open from the Ministry of Information, Press, and National Communication. The state operates two radio stations as well as a television station and an official press agency. Journalists in all major media outlets are usually poorly paid and lack sufficient training, leaving them vulnerable to bribery and political manipulation. Together with the Swiss-funded Fondation Hirondelle, the UN mission in the DRC operates an independent countrywide radio network, Radio Okapi, which has set new standards for reporting and media objectivity in a volatile political scene. There are no reports that the government restricts internet usage or monitors e-mail, although access was limited to less than half of one percent of the population, mainly in urban centers.

Costa Rica

LEGAL ENVIRONMENT: 6
POLITICAL ENVIRONMENT: 7
ECONOMIC ENVIRONMENT: 6

Status: Free

TOTAL SCORE: 19

Survey Edition	2003	2004	2005	2006	2007
Total Score, Status	14,F	19,F	19,F	18,F	20,F

While the government failed to pass much needed reforms to the Press Law, a series of court rulings in favor of the press and convictions in the 2001 killing of a journalist showed progress in a country that is already considered to be among the freest in Latin America. Costa Rica's constitution guarantees press freedom; however, punitive press laws serve to occasionally restrict the rights of the media. In 2004, the Inter-American Court of Human Rights overturned a 1999 conviction of a Costa Rican journalist for criminal defamation, ruling that Costa Rica needed to amend its outdated criminal defamation laws, which are incompatible with international human rights standards. Despite ongoing discussions and a pending proposal to reform the law, libel and insult remain criminal offenses, allowing for prison sentences of up to three years in cases of the insult of a public official. In addition, a Supreme Court ruling in 2006 upheld the Ley de Imprenta, the 1902 statute that imposes a prison sentence of up to 120 days for defamation in print media. The proposed amended law would establish the "actual malice" standard but would maintain "crimes against honor" as a criminal offense.

While journalists are not often victims of physical threats or violence in Costa Rica, challenges to a free media environment tend to stem from the courts, though the majority of the legal decisions in 2007 demonstrated gains for press freedom. In June, a judge overturned an earlier verdict and awarded restitution, at the expense of the government, to the newspaper *La Nacion* for US$120,000, the amount of damages that the publication was forced to pay former diplomat Felix Przedborski for defamation. Two journalists in August were also found not guilty of defamation for corruption allegations made against social security officials in a 2004 report. In April, the Constitutional Chamber issued an important ruling that weighed the public's right to be informed against the right to privacy. At the center of the case was an interview conducted on hidden camera by the television program *Noticias Repretel,* which reported on the issue of the illegal entry of foreigners into Costa Rica and the relative ease with which people obtain entry visas. The Court ruled in favor of the media in deciding that the right to be informed of this issue of public interest took precedence over the right to privacy. In a blow to press freedom, an appeals court upheld an earlier ruling that acquitted two journalists of defamation but ordered them to pay civil compensation to a police officer whose reputation was harmed by inaccurate information the journalists published that had been supplied by a government minister. This case demonstrated the limited options for the defense of a journalist in civil cases, when proof of harm is the only evidence needed to hold a journalist liable.

In a positive development against impunity, two men were found guilty and convicted in December for the murder of Parmenio Medina, a popular radio journalist who was killed in July 2001. A court sentenced businessman Omar Chaves to 35 years in prison for sanctioning Medina's murder and an additional 12 years in prison for fraud. Luis Alberto Aguirre Jaime was sentenced to 30 years for carrying out the assassination, while a third accused plotter, Father Minor de Jesus Calvo Aguilar, was acquitted in the criminal case but received a 15-year sentence for fraud. Medina had been a frequent critic of official corruption, including corruption in the local Catholic radio station to which Chaves and Calvo were connected.

Costa Rica has a vibrant media scene, with numerous public and privately owned newspapers, television outlets, and radio stations. Private media ownership is highly concentrated, however, and tends to be conservative. The press is relatively free to cover sensitive political and social issues and openly criticize the government. Radio is the most popular outlet for news dissemination, in addition to nine major newspapers. Cable television is also widely available. The internet served as an additional source of unrestricted information and was accessed by more than 20 percent of the population in 2007.

Cote d'Ivoire

LEGAL ENVIRONMENT: 20
POLITICAL ENVIRONMENT: 27
ECONOMIC ENVIRONMENT: 19

Status: Not Free

TOTAL SCORE: 66

Survey Edition	2003	2004	2005	2006	2007
Total Score, Status	68,NF	65,NF	69,NF	65,NF	68,NF

The Ivoirian media environment improved slightly in 2007 owing to the signing of a peace accord between the government and rebels and the dismantling of the confidence zone that separated the country into north and south. Improvements in security have made it easier for journalists to travel around the country, and there were fewer instances of extralegal harassment of journalists in 2007 compared with the previous year. Nonetheless, journalists continue to face the almost constant threat of defamation suits and the possibility of interrogation and imprisonment for criticizing the president.

Although the constitution provides for freedom of the press, since the onset of civil conflict in 2002, the government has restricted media freedom in the name of patriotism and national unity. Despite the parliament's elimination of criminal libel and other punitive laws for press offenses in December 2004, the government still retains the power to criminalize any libel suit at its discretion. While authorities did not use this power in 2007, a journalist with the private daily *Soir Info* newspaper was imprisoned for five days in January on contempt of court charges after he published an article accusing the state prosecutor of corruption. While actual imprisonment of journalists was rare in 2007, numerous reporters were charged with defamation in civil courts, often receiving crippling fines. Among other instances, in September, lawyers representing President Laurent Gbagbo demanded financial compensation from five journalists from two pro-opposition newspapers, *Le Jour Plus* and *Le Rebond*, for publishing articles accusing the president of corruption. Gbagbo initially demanded compensation of over US$300,000 from each defendant, although lawyers requested US$43,000 from each—a smaller sum, but still one that would ruin both papers. Both defamation cases were undecided at year's end.

Journalists and media outlets are vulnerable to physical and other abuses by police and extralegal militia, although the situation improved slightly over the previous year. In August, the progoverment student militia, the Student Federation of Cote d'Ivoire (FESCI), attacked the offices of *L'Intelligent d'Abidjan*, a private daily newspaper, demanding that the paper publish a protest letter clarifying the group's political affiliation. The letter was in response to an article the paper had published alleging that FESCI had joined the opposition. In July, members of FESCI also attacked a television station in response to a statement made on air regarding the teacher's union. Similarly, between May and July, four separate media houses—three progovernment and one affiliated with the opposition—were broken into and robbed of documents, equipment, and money. A culture of impunity remains the norm in Cote d'Ivoire owing to a weak rule of law and judiciary; there were no charges or prosecutions for any cases in which journalists were harassed or attacked over the past two years.

The government maintains control over the state-run media with a heavy hand, running two major radio stations, one of which is the only national station and a key source of news throughout the country, as well as a daily newspaper, *Fraternite Matin*, which has the highest circulation in the country and regularly toes the government line. State-run outlets have far greater funding than their private counterparts and can much more easily access government information and documents. While there are no private terrestrial television stations able to operate in Cote d'Ivoire, there are nearly 100 low-power non-commercial community radio stations that are able to operate freely—including Onuci FM, a station operated by peacekeepers that broadcasts in the north—and 2 commercial private stations. Private newspapers and community radio stations are sometimes able to present diverse views and frequently scrutinize the government, but they are regularly harassed for these reports. Laws also ban the broadcasting of political commentary, according to the U.S. State Department, and many journalists, in both the private and state-funded media, are prone to self-censorship for fear of punishment from their superiors or the government itself. The opening seen following the signing of the peace accord has also enabled the reprinting of articles from foreign papers to resume. The internet is unrestricted by the government, although poverty and infrastructure limitations restricted access to less than 2 percent of the population in 2007.

Croatia

Status: Partly Free

LEGAL ENVIRONMENT: 9
POLITICAL ENVIRONMENT: 13
ECONOMIC ENVIRONMENT: 14
TOTAL SCORE: 36

Survey Edition	2003	2004	2005	2006	2007
Total Score, Status	33,PF	37,PF	37,PF	39,PF	37,PF

Freedom of the press is enshrined in the constitution, and it is generally protected in practice. Amendments to the criminal code in 2006 eliminated imprisonment as a punishment for libel, leaving fines as the only sanction. Government officials occasionally use libel laws against the media. Croatian journalists have also faced contempt-of-court charges at the UN International Criminal Tribunal for the former Yugoslavia (ICTY). Previous cases have involved the revelation of information on protected witnesses, but in 2007, the ICTY summoned several journalists for questioning on the leak of a confidential annex to the indictment of three high-profile Croatian defendants. The document named senior public officials as unindicted participants in the alleged criminal enterprise at issue in the case. Press freedom advocates argued that the information was revealed in the public interest and that many of the summoned reporters had merely picked up the story after it was first broken by state-owned Croatian Radio and Television (HRT). Regulatory agencies such as the Council for Electronic Media are seen as politically independent, but critics have complained of poor professional standards and a lack of transparency in regulatory decisions.

State-owned media, which dominate the broadcast market, remain vulnerable to potential political interference. At least two journalists known for favoring the ruling party were appointed to key positions in state media in 2007. However, the outlets have generally operated with independence in recent years, and they complied with rules granting equal airtime to candidates and parties during the 2007 parliamentary election campaign. Croatian newspapers displayed their willingness to publish information embarrassing to the government in December, when photographs of Interior Minister Ivica Kirin on a boar-hunting trip with indicted war crimes suspect Mladen Markac led to Kirin's resignation. Markac was supposed to have been confined to his home pending trial at the ICTY. Journalists are subject to occasional harassment by the authorities, physical threats, and violence, particularly when their reporting touches on Croatia's role in the 1991–95 Balkan conflict. In January 2007, for the second time in as many months, burglars broke into the home of *Globus* magazine investigative journalist Gordan Malic, who had received death threats in the past. Robert Valdec, host of the television program *Istraga* on the private station Nova TV, received a series of death threats during the first three months of the year. *Istraga* regularly investigated criminal cases, including war crimes. Freelance journalist Zeljko Peratovic was arrested and held for one day in October, apparently as part of a probe into the leaking of state secrets involving war crimes.

HRT benefits from both mandatory subscription fees and revenue from advertising. In addition to the public broadcaster, two privately owned national television stations, more than a dozen smaller stations, and approximately 150 radio outlets compete for audiences. Small broadcasters are often owned or financed by local governments, leaving them open to political influence. Many Croats also have access to various European channels via satellite. Ownership of print outlets is increasingly concentrated in the hands of large media groups, including Europa

Press Holdings (EPH), which is half owned by Germany's Westdeutsche Allgemeine Zeitung. Journalists reportedly practice self-censorship to protect the economic interests of owners and major advertisers. In June 2007, the investigative and satirical weekly *Feral Tribune* was shuttered temporarily after the government emptied its bank accounts to recover a tax debt; the paper resumed operations after EPH acquired it and took on the debt. The *Tribune*'s supporters noted that authorities had previously forgiven tax debts owed by state-financed outlets and that top advertisers had essentially boycotted the paper over its critical reports, crippling its finances. The state does not restrict the foreign press or internet access, and some 35 percent of the population used the internet in 2007.

Cuba

Status: Not Free

LEGAL ENVIRONMENT: 30
POLITICAL ENVIRONMENT: 36
ECONOMIC ENVIRONMENT: 28
TOTAL SCORE: 94

Survey Edition	2003	2004	2005	2006	2007
Total Score, Status	94,NF	96,NF	96,NF	96,NF	96,NF

Despite significant government restrictions and the continued imprisonment of 24 journalists, there was a slight decrease in the governmental harassment of journalists, and the growing number of blogs in Cuba provided some new space for free expression. Nevertheless, Cuba continued to have the most restrictive laws on free speech and press freedom in the hemisphere. The constitution prohibits private ownership of media and allows free speech and press only if they "conform to the aims of a socialist society." Cuba's legal and institutional structures are firmly under the control of the executive. The country's criminal code provides the legal basis for the repression of dissent, and laws criminalizing "enemy propaganda" and the dissemination of "unauthorized news" are used to restrict freedom of speech under the guise of protecting state security. Insult laws carry penalties of three months to one year in prison, with sentences of up to three years if the president or members of the Council of State or National Assembly are the objects of criticism. The 1997 Law of National Dignity, which provides for jail sentences of 3 to 10 years for "anyone who, in a direct or indirect form, collaborates with the enemy's media," is aimed at independent news agencies that send their material abroad.

While there was a decrease in governmental harassment of journalists, state security agents continued to threaten, arrest, detain, imprison, and restrict the right of movement of local and foreign journalists throughout the year. Media watchdog group Reporters Sans Frontieres reported an estimated 80 physical attacks, threats, arrests, and unannounced searches of journalists in 2007. During the year, 2 journalists were freed from prison, but 2 more were imprisoned, resulting in a total of 24 journalists remaining in long-term detention. In January, Ramon Velazquez Toranso, of the Libertad agency, was sentenced to three years in prison under a criminal code provision that allows Cuban authorities to imprison any citizen deemed a potential danger to society, even if they have not committed a crime. In April, Oscar Sanchez Madan, correspondent for the Miami-based Cubanet website, was sentenced under the same criminal code by a court in Matanzas province and received the maximum penalty of four years in prison for "social dangerousness." Sanchez had questioned governmental figures on the actual size of Cuba's sugarcane harvest in his reporting. On September 27, 6 journalists were arrested along with an estimated 30 activists at a peaceful demonstration in support of political prisoners staged in the capital, Havana; they were released the next day. Three foreign journalists were forced to leave the country in 2007. Gary Marx, the Havana correspondent of the *Chicago Tribune*, and Cesar Gonzales-Calero, correspondent for the Mexican daily *El Universal*, had their press cards cancelled in February and were told to leave the country. British Broadcasting Corporation correspondent Stephen Gibbs was denied a visa to re-enter the country the following day and was forced to leave his post.

The government owns all media except for a number of underground newsletters. It operates three national newspapers, four national television stations, six national radio stations, and one international radio station, in addition to numerous local print and broadcast media outlets. All media content is determined by the government, and there is no editorial independence. The Catholic Church weekly publication *Vitral*, which had a reputation for being one of the only publications to offer independent opinion and critical commentary, suspended publication in April, citing lack of resources. The paper resumed publication in June, but under new editorial management and with a much less critical focus. Cubans do not have the right to possess or distribute foreign publications, although some international papers are sold in tourist hotels. Satellite television is forbidden. Up until legislative changes on June 1, it was a criminal offense to possess a DVD player.

Cuban officials strictly regulated and monitored internet use, with the threat of 5 years in prison for connecting to the internet illegally and 20 years for writing "counterrevolutionary" articles for foreign websites. Many websites were blocked during the year. The Committee to Protect Journalists reported that the general population could access the internet from hotels or government-controlled internet cafés by purchasing expensive and difficult-to-obtain voucher cards, while others purchased passwords on the black market for a high price that allowed them less restricted access. On a positive note, blogs are a growing trend that allow Cubans to more freely express their opinions; according to the U.S. State Department, these are posted mostly under pseudonyms and contain "confident and caustic references about today's situation in Cuba." Less than 2 percent of Cuba's population accessed the internet in 2007.

Cyprus

LEGAL ENVIRONMENT: 5
POLITICAL ENVIRONMENT: 9
ECONOMIC ENVIRONMENT: 8

Status: Free

TOTAL SCORE: 22

Survey Edition	2003	2004	2005	2006	2007
Total Score, Status	18,F	18,F	22,F	22,F	22,F

Freedom of speech and of expression are guaranteed under Article 19 of the constitution. These rights are generally respected in practice in the Greek part of Cyprus, where the independent press is vibrant and frequently criticizes authorities. Some laws are in place for freedom of the press in the northern, Turkish part of Cyprus, but authorities are overtly hostile to the independent press, and journalists can be arrested, put on trial, and sentenced under the "unjust actions" section of the criminal code. Although Turkish Cypriot journalists can enter the south, Turkish journalists based in the north are often denied entry across the border and are occasionally harassed by Greek Cypriot border guards and ultranationalist Greek Cypriot groups.

The Northern Cyprus government has frequently targeted independent newspapers; in December 2006, Dogan Harman, editor of the *Kibrisli* paper, was charged with defamation of the attorney general following the publication of a critical article. The charges were later dropped after the Supreme Court repealed the law used to charge Harman retroactively. The newspaper *Afrika* has been a particular target for attack in Northern

Cyprus in recent years. In February 2007, *Afrika* cartoonist Huseyin Chakmak, a vocal supporter of the reunification of Cyprus, was attacked by a group of men throwing stones and tomatoes. *Afrika* journalist Ibrahim Aziz was threatened following the publication of an article criticizing the treatment of a Greek Cypriot businessman who died while imprisoned in Northern Cyprus. In October, right-wing groups—including the Grey Wolves, who claimed the newspaper was supporting terrorism—gathered outside *Afrika*'s offices and threatened journalists. The demonstrators claimed that the newspaper was serving as the voice of a Kurdish group by publishing photographs of Turkish prisoners that had earlier appeared on a Kurdish website.

Cypriots have access to Greek and Turkish broadcasts throughout the island. There are 8 major dailies, approximately 27 weekly newspapers, and 6 major magazines available. However, many daily newspapers are closely linked to political parties. The Cyprus Broadcasting Corporation owns two television stations and four radio stations. Several private television and radio stations compete effectively with government-controlled stations. Ownership is highly concentrated. There are several daily newspapers available in Northern Cyprus, although mainland Turkish papers are generally preferred. The broadcasting service is controlled exclusively by the Turkish Cypriot administration. Approximately 45 percent of Cypriots are able to access the internet on a regular basis and are not subject to any known government restrictions.

[The numerical rating for Cyprus is based on conditions on the Greek side of the island.]

Czech Republic

LEGAL ENVIRONMENT: 4
POLITICAL ENVIRONMENT: 7
ECONOMIC ENVIRONMENT: 7

Status: Free

TOTAL SCORE: 18

Survey Edition	2003	2004	2005	2006	2007
Total Score, Status	23,F	23,F	22,F	20,F	18,F

Freedom of the press is constitutionally guaranteed, though the Charter of Fundamental Rights and Freedoms prohibits speech that might infringe on national security, individual rights, public health, or morality, or that may evoke hatred based on race, ethnicity, or national origin. Libel remains a criminal offense, but prosecutions are rare. The Press Law provides a sound basis for independent journalism, and media protections have been bolstered by Constitutional Court and other institutional rulings. No major changes took place in 2007, though top government officials did call for stricter regulation of the media. Media freedom advocates have noted a growing number of articles written to serve the needs of commercial interests. Although press freedom has long been secure in the Czech Republic, observers continue to raise concerns about the quality and depth of reporting, as well as weak accountability among the tabloids in particular.

Most electronic and print media outlets are privately owned, and they generally convey diverse views without fear of government or partisan pressure. Media advocates point out that while public media are widely respected, their financial sustainability has been undermined by tighter control of public funds and increasing restrictions on advertising. As a result, there has been a gradual migration of revenue from public-sector media to commercial outlets in recent years. The internet continues to develop rapidly, with some 50 percent of the population enjoying regular and unrestricted access.

Denmark

Status: Free

LEGAL ENVIRONMENT: 2
POLITICAL ENVIRONMENT: 3
ECONOMIC ENVIRONMENT: 5
TOTAL SCORE: 10

Survey Edition	2003	2004	2005	2006	2007
Total Score, Status	11,F	8,F	10,F	10,F	11,F

Freedom of speech and of expression are protected in Section 77 of the constitution, and the government generally respects these rights in practice. However, certain legal restrictions exist for libel, blasphemy, and racism. In July, a group of Danish Muslim organizations was forced to pay Pia Kjaersgaard of the Danish People's Party US$7,400 after losing a libel case that they brought against her. Kjaersgaard was accused of libeling the group by calling their 2006 trip to the Middle East to raise awareness about the controversial Muhammad cartoons "treasonous." In an unprecedented legal move, an Icelandic bank, Kaupthing Bank, attempted to sue the Danish newspaper *Ekstra Bladet* in a British court for libel; this is the first time a Danish paper has been sued abroad. In 2006, the paper ran a series of articles accusing bank employees of being "tax fiddlers" for a scheme that involved attempting to avoid paying taxes in Denmark by transferring funds between countries. The newspaper translated the articles into English and posted them on the internet, making them vulnerable to legal action in the United Kingdom. The case was still pending at year's end.

In March 2007, reporters at the public Danish Broadcasting Corporation (DR), forced program cancellations when they walked out in protest over planned workforce cuts. Over 300 employees are set to lose their jobs to save money for the broadcaster, whose budget for a new headquarters building is running 250 percent higher than originally planned. At a second protest in June, employees expressed concern that the cuts would also cause the quality of programming to suffer. Separately, in the independently governed province of Greenland, a journalist was forced out of her position at the local public broadcaster, KRN, after she reported critically on a state-owned tannery. The broadcaster was concerned that her reporting would "put Greenland in a potentially bad light."

The private print press is vibrant, although many papers have political affiliations. Government subsidies are available to the press, as are low-interest loans for struggling newspapers. DR TV is the public network operating both DR1 and DR2, while TV2 is a privately run but government-owned television network. State-run television and radio broadcasting is financed by an annual license fee. However, in 2007 it was reported that over 10 percent of the Danish population does not pay the obligatory annual television license fee, an omission that is estimated to cost DR alone almost US$138 million per year. Satellite and cable television are also available. The government does not restrict use of the internet, which was accessed by almost 70 percent of the population in 2007.

Djibouti

Status: Not Free

LEGAL ENVIRONMENT: 24
POLITICAL ENVIRONMENT: 25
ECONOMIC ENVIRONMENT: 23
TOTAL SCORE: 72

Survey Edition	2003	2004	2005	2006	2007
Total Score, Status	65,NF	66,NF	67,NF	69,NF	69,NF

Although Article 15 of the constitution affords the right to free expression, in practice, the government imposes restrictions on the independent press. Free speech is limited by prohibitions on libel and distributing false information, and journalists frequently face harassment. The U.S. military presence in Djibouti creates additional pressures for self-censorship, as journalists are encouraged to refrain from reporting on soldiers' activities.

On February 1, authorities confiscated printing equipment from the Movement for Democratic Revival (MRD), prohibiting the opposition party from printing its newsletter, *Le Renouveau*. The paper's managing director, Houssein Ahmed Farah, and the paper's distributor, Hared Abdallah Barreh, were arrested and detained in May on charges of libel. The arrests followed critical coverage of the governor of the national bank, who is also President Ismael Omar Guelleh's brother-in-law. Authorities subsequently suspended the paper's production for three months. On June 3, authorities arrested Farah Abadid Hildid, a *Le Renouveau* employee and MRD member, and on June 14 he was sentenced to one month's imprisonment on charges of disseminating false information.

According to the advocacy group Reporters Sans Frontieres, Djibouti has joined the ranks of Eritrea and Equatorial Guinea as one of the three sub-Saharan African countries without a private paper, although Djiboutian law technically permits all registered political parties to publish a paper. Because of high poverty levels, radio is the most popular news medium, as few Djiboutians can afford newspapers or televisions. The government owns the country's only radio and television stations, Radio Djibouti and Djibouti Television, respectively, and monitors satellite usage. The British Broadcasting Corporation, Voice of America Radio, and Radio France Internationale are also available, although the latter was closed temporarily in 2005. The country's only newspaper is the government-owned *La Nation*, which is published three times weekly. The only internet service provider is owned by the government. Although there are no reports that the government monitors e-mail or internet activity, only 2.2 percent of the population was able to use this resource in 2007.

Dominica

Status: Free

LEGAL ENVIRONMENT: 5
POLITICAL ENVIRONMENT: 11
ECONOMIC ENVIRONMENT: 6
TOTAL SCORE: 22

Survey Edition	2003	2004	2005	2006	2007
Total Score, Status	14,F	17,F	17,F	19,F	20,F

Dominica's independent media continued to freely express a diversity of opinions and criticisms of the government. However, a lawsuit filed by the prime minister accentuated concerns about the increasing use of libel laws to deter critical journalism. The constitution guarantees freedom of the press, which the government generally respects in practice. The media are often critical of the government, and as a result, relations with the ruling Dominica Labour Party are fractious. In a potentially inhibiting development for press freedom, Prime Minister Roosevelt Skerrit filed libel suits against the *Times of Dominica* weekly newspaper and its editor Matt Peltier in September. The lawsuits followed the publication of articles written by Peltier questioning the means by which, given his salary, the prime minister acquired two pieces of land valued at US$370,300. The Media Workers Association of Dominica deplored the prime minister's response, which was to criticize the brand of investigative journalism used to produce the story. The two suits were before the civil courts at year's end. There is no daily newspaper, but there are several weekly publications. Dominica has four radio stations, including the state-owned Dominica Broadcasting Corporation, and a cable TV network that covers part of the island. The internet, used by an estimated 36 percent of the population, is neither restricted nor censored by the government.

Dominican Republic

Status: Partly Free

LEGAL ENVIRONMENT: 7
POLITICAL ENVIRONMENT: 19
ECONOMIC ENVIRONMENT: 13
TOTAL SCORE: 39

Survey Edition	2003	2004	2005	2006	2007
Total Score, Status	33,PF	39,PF	38,PF	37,PF	40,PF

While positive steps toward press freedom were taken in the courts with both the introduction of a bill to decriminalize press offenses and the prosecution of those responsible for the murder of journalists, there was an increase in violence against media workers during the year. The law provides for freedom of speech and of the press, and the government mostly respects these rights in practice. Steps to decriminalize libel and insult offenses and replace them with fines were taken in September with the introduction of a bill to parliament by a deputy of the ruling Dominican Liberation Party. The courts also began to take action against the killers of journalists after years of impunity. In April, three men, including a retired army general, were sentenced for the March 1975 murder of Orlando Martinez, editor of *Revista Ahora* magazine. In May, Vladimir Pujols, the leader of a drug-trafficking gang, was sentenced to 30 years in prison for the September 2004 murder of Juan Andujar, the Azua correspondent for *Listin Diario*. In October, the Supreme Court made a landmark ruling ordering the state Transport Reform Office to hand over the documents on the construction of the Santo Domingo Metro demanded by journalist Huchi Lora. A number of legal experts had doubted the Supreme Court would rule against the government.

The media are generally free to provide diverse opinions and openly criticize the government. Nevertheless, journalists tend to avoid serious reportage on certain subjects, such as the army, the Catholic Church, and drug smuggling, as well as on topics that could damage the economic or political interests of media owners. While no journalists were killed in 2007, the National Union of Press Workers reported that civil, police, and military authorities, in addition to civilians, assaulted or threatened more than 40 journalists during the year. Particularly worrying were reports that the police and judicial authorities failed to respond to many of the incidents. Among the many cases, media watchdog group Reporters Sans Frontieres reported that radio journalist Hector Abreu had his home in Tamayo attacked with gunfire on July 6 in a possible response to his reporting on local corruption. Two other journalists narrowly escaped with their lives in Maimon on June 22 when angry demonstrators protesting a lack of drinking water turned on the media with threats to lynch them. On November 24, freelance photographer and radio journalist Noel Encarnacion was physically assaulted and threatened by six police officers and military personnel while attempting to cover the refugee crisis in San Jose de Ocoa province.

There are eight national daily newspapers and a large number of local publications. The state-owned Radio Television Dominicana operates radio and television services. Private owners operate over 300 AM and FM radio stations and more than 40 television stations, most of them small, regional broadcasters. There are no government restrictions on internet access; however, high costs limited use to just 23 percent of the population in 2007.

East Timor

Legal Environment: 12
Political Environment: 13
Economic Environment: 13

Status: Partly Free

Total Score: 38

Survey Edition	2003	2004	2005	2006	2007
Total Score, Status	22,F	29,F	30,F	39,PF	42,PF

A slightly improved security situation and increased access to information under a new coalition government brought a modest improvement in press freedom in the latter part of 2007; nevertheless, heightened political tensions surrounding elections yielded some attacks against journalists, and criminal defamation provisions remained in law. Although the 2002 constitution contains provisions protecting press freedom, Section 40 states that the rights to freedom of speech and of information "shall be regulated by law," thereby opening the door to criminal penalties for defamation. In 2005, former prime minister Mari Alkatiri signed an executive decree approving a new penal code that provides for jail terms of up to three years for defaming public officials and doubles the terms of imprisonment when defamation takes place through the media. The code sets no limits on fines or other penalties for defamation. In February 2006, the bill was sent back to the Ministry of Justice for reconsideration, where it remains, and neither the new prime minister nor President Jose Ramos Horta moved to eliminate criminal penalties for defamation. A 2004 court of appeals ruling suggested that until a new Timorese penal code is passed, the Indonesian law, which contains criminal penalties for defamation, still applies.

Despite some improvement in the political climate, tensions surrounding presidential and parliamentary elections and the formation of a new coalition government led to attacks against journalists, particularly by individuals affiliated with the Fretilin party, which was removed from power in the elections. In March, militants from the party beat a *Timor Post* journalist when he tried to take their photograph at a security checkpoint. In April, a Fretilin lawmaker threatened two journalists from the public broadcaster, National Television of Timor Leste (TVTL), when they tried to record images of empty desks and inactivity at the national parliament. In July, a noneditorial staffer from the daily *Suara Timor Lorosae*, generally perceived to favor the CNRT party that had recently formed a coalition government, was beaten after his assailants confirmed his employment at the paper. Several days later, the windows of the newspaper's office were broken. On November 17, a coroner in New South Wales, Australia, issued a report establishing that the Indonesian army had "deliberately killed" the British, New Zealand, and Australian reporters known as the "Balibo Five" who were in East Timor covering the 1975 invasion.

Although severe economic pressures continued to hamper the free flow of information, there were several promising developments, including a government initiative to distribute East Timor's three daily newspapers to each of its 13 districts. Radio Timor Leste is estimated to reach approximately 68 percent of Timorese, and in May 2007, TVTL became available outside of the capital, Dili, via satellite bandwidth leased from Indonesia Telkom. However, a majority of the community radio stations established after independence remain dysfunctional. Infrastructure limitations and poverty restricted access to the internet in 2007 to 0.1 percent of the population; nonetheless, the government does not censor websites or limit users' access to diverse content.

Ecuador

Status: Partly Free

LEGAL ENVIRONMENT: 14
POLITICAL ENVIRONMENT: 17
ECONOMIC ENVIRONMENT: 10

TOTAL SCORE: 41

Survey Edition	2003	2004	2005	2006	2007
Total Score, Status	41,PF	42,PF	41,PF	41,PF	41,PF

While violence against the media decreased, President Rafael Correa, who took office in January, set a divisive tone toward the press, frequently criticizing the media and initiating a criminal defamation lawsuit against the Quito-based daily *La Hora*. The constitution guarantees freedom of the press. However, given that defamation and slander remain criminal offenses punishable by up to three years in prison, these guarantees are often weak in practice. Concern about the implementation of such restrictive libel laws often results in self-censorship, limiting reporting on public officials and the armed forces. In March, journalist Nelson Fueltala of the daily *La Gaceta* received a two-month prison sentence for defamation of the mayor of Pujili, though the case remained on appeal at year's end. On May 10, President Correa filed a libel lawsuit against *La Hora* chairman Francisco Vivanco for an editorial accusing the president of intending to govern the country with "tumult, sticks, and stones." Alternatively, Quinto Pazmino, former government adviser and an assembly candidate, accused President Correa of libel and filed a US$10 million lawsuit against him. The authorities then arrested Pazmino for insulting the president. However, the Supreme Court ruled in September that Pazmino's status as a political candidate granted him special privileges, and he was released after paying a fine. In a separate ruling in July, the administration banned the unauthorized dissemination of clandestinely recorded videos. It was not yet clear at year's end how press issues would be addressed in the drafting of the new constitution; however, during a September radio address, the president called for stronger laws to regulate the media.

Ecuadorian journalists were subject to frequent rhetorical lacerations from the president, though the level of physical attacks was low compared with the regional average. Correa used an array of colorful descriptors, calling the press "savage beasts," mediocre, corrupt, mafiosi, and "more unpleasant than pancreatic cancer." According to the Committee to Protect Journalists, Congress passed a resolution demanding that Correa respect freedom of expression and exercise tolerance for divergent opinions following one of the president's particularly volatile and disrespectful weekly radio addresses in May. In July, the president announced that he would no longer give interviews or press conferences and would communicate with the media only in writing.

Most broadcast and print media outlets are privately owned. The government owns and operates one radio station, the *El Telegrafo* newspaper, which fell into state hands in May following a multiyear legal dispute, and the new Canal Ecuador TV, which premiered in November and is funded by a US$5 million grant from the Venezuelan government. Media outlets express a broad range of editorial viewpoints, many of which are critical of the government. However, most media outlets are heavily influenced by their financiers and often reflect the political perspectives of their sponsors, a situation that contributed strongly to Correa's frequent accusations of bias in the media. As part of his proposed reforms, Correa has called for the redrawing of media ownership rules to encourage "healthy competition." Access to the internet is not restricted by the government, but the medium is used by only 11 percent of the population.

Egypt

LEGAL ENVIRONMENT: 21
POLITICAL ENVIRONMENT: 20
ECONOMIC ENVIRONMENT: 18

Status: Partly Free

TOTAL SCORE: 59

Survey Edition	2003	2004	2005	2006	2007
Total Score, Status	79,NF	76,NF	68,NF	61,NF	62,NF

Status change explanation: Egypt's status improved from Not Free to Partly Free in recognition of the courage of Egyptian journalists to cross "red lines" that previously restricted their work and in recognition of the greater range of viewpoints represented in the Egyptian media and blogosphere. This progress occurred in spite of the government's ongoing—and in some cases increasing—harassment, repression, and imprisonment of journalists.

While Egyptian journalists succeeded in expanding the diversity of media coverage by pushing back the "red lines" that previously restricted their work, press freedom continued to suffer owing to the government's repressive laws and the extralegal intimidation of journalists. The Emergency Law, the Press Law, and other provisions of the penal code circumscribe the press, despite constitutional guarantees of press freedom. Even after the 2006 amendments to the Press Law, dissemination of "false news," criticism of the president and foreign leaders, and publication of material that constitutes "an attack against the dignity and honor of individuals" or an "outrage of the reputation of families" remain criminal offenses prosecuted opportunistically by the authorities. Fines can range from EGP5,000 to EGP20,000 (US$900 to US$3,600) for press infractions and up to five years' imprisonment for criticizing a foreign head of state or the president. Journalists have few professional protections and remain vulnerable to prosecution under these laws.

A series of high-profile legal cases against independent and opposition journalists over the course of the year served to threaten and penalize the media for taking journalistic and editorial risks. In January, security officers detained Al-Jazeera journalist Huwaida Taha Mitwalli, who also writes for the London-based *al-Quds al-Arabi*, and charged her with "possessing and giving false pictures about the internal situation in Egypt that could undermine the dignity of the country;" authorities also confiscated her videotapes and computer in connection with a documentary she was making about torture in Egypt. On May 2, a Cairo criminal court sentenced her to six months in prison for spreading false news that could "harm the national interest" and fined her EGP20,000 (US$3,600) for "possessing TV tapes, with the aim of distributing and broadcasting them, which included events contrary to reality about torture in Egypt, and which are likely to damage the reputation of the country abroad." At year's end, she was free pending appeal. In September, a state security prosecutor brought charges against Ibrahim Eissa, editor of the feisty independent daily *Al-Dustur*, for publishing reports about President Hosni Mubarak's health "that were likely to harm the public interest." According to a member of the Egyptian Journalists Syndicate, this was the first time a member of the media had been summoned before an emergency court, which does not allow appeals and rarely grants acquittals. In a separate case in September, a Cairo court sentenced Eissa and three other editors, 'Adil Hamuda (*Al-Fagr*), Wael al-Ibrashi (*Sawt al-Umma*), and 'Abd al-Halim Qandil (*Al-Karama*), to one year in prison and imposed a fine of EGP20,000 (US$3,600) for publishing "with malicious intent, false news, statements, or rumors likely to disturb public order," based on their criticism both of President Mubarak's stance on Hezbollah and of senior members of the ruling National Democratic Party, including the president's son Gamal. Also in September, a court sentenced three editors—Anwar al-Hawari, Mahmoud Ghalab, and Amir Salem—of the opposition Wafd party's eponymous newspaper to two years in prison for publishing false news "liable to disturb public security, spread horror among the people, or cause harm or damage the public interest." At year's end, they were free pending appeal.

Although there are more than 500 newspapers, magazines, journals, and other periodicals in Egypt, this apparent diversity disguises the government's role as a media owner and sponsor. The government is a partial owner of Egypt's three largest newspapers, whose editors are appointed by the president. In recent years, the Shura Council—one-third of whose members are appointed by the president—has granted newspaper publication licenses to opposition parties and private investors. The Ministry of Information controls the content of state-owned broadcast media, and privately owned domestic broadcasters are not allowed to air news bulletins but must focus instead on music and entertainment. Nevertheless, a new crop of independent newspapers and political talk shows broach topics that would have been unthinkable five years ago. The government did not block foreign satellite channels and permitted the establishment of locally based private satellite television stations.

Thanks in large part to government efforts to aggressively promote internet use, the number of Egyptians with access to this medium has more than quadrupled over the past several years, and an estimated 10 percent of the population used the internet in 2007. The government does not engage in widespread online censorship but occasionally blocks Islamist and secular opposition websites. In one case in May 2007, an appeals judge being sued for plagiarism by several human rights groups asked the Administrative Judiciary Court to shut down up to fifty news and human rights-oriented websites, arguing that they tarnished the country's reputation. In December, however, the higher court rejected the request. In February, Alexandrian blogger Abd al-Karim Nabil Sulaiman, better known by his pen name, Karim Amer, became the first Egyptian blogger to be imprisoned for his writings. He is currently serving a four-year prison sentence for "insulting Islam" and "insulting the president." In April, security agents detained Abd al-Moneim Mahmud, a blogger and journalist for the London-based Al-Hiwar satellite television station, as he was boarding a plane for Sudan to work on a documentary about human rights in the Arab world. According to Mahmud's lawyers, Egypt's domestic intelligence service cited his criticism of torture in Egypt on his blog, at conferences in Doha and Cairo, and in conversations with the press and international human rights groups as justification for his arrest. He was jailed for several weeks on charges of arming students against the government before a prosecutor dropped the charges as groundless.

El Salvador

LEGAL ENVIRONMENT: 10
POLITICAL ENVIRONMENT: 18
ECONOMIC ENVIRONMENT: 14

Status: Partly Free

TOTAL SCORE: 42

Survey Edition	2003	2004	2005	2006	2007
Total Score, Status	38,PF	42,PF	41,PF	43,PF	42,PF

The media continued to be the target of both legal and extralegal harassment, with the murder of one journalist and the first case of a journalist being charged under new antiterrorism legislation occurring during 2007. Freedom of the press is protected under the constitution, and Salvadoran journalists are generally able to report freely on the news, including critical reporting of the government and opposition parties. At the same time, press freedom is hindered by a lack of public transparency, reflected in the absence of freedom of information legislation. The penal code grants judges the right to restrict media access to legal proceedings in cases they deem of importance to national security or where they determine that the publicity would prejudice the case. In a positive development, a court decision in August 2007 was seen to advance protections for the press when it declared that media workers would no longer be summoned to testify in criminal cases. In March, the Legislative Assembly introduced a motion to subject staffers to a polygraph test in order to identify individuals who had leaked information to the media concerning a salary increase for legislators. The request was withdrawn after vocal public opposition. In one of the year's most controversial legal cases involving the press, freelance journalist Maria Hayde Chicas was arrested on July 2, along with 13 other individuals, while reporting on a demonstration in Suchitoto against government plans to privatize water distribution in the region. Chicas was charged with committing an "act of terrorism" under El Salvador's new 2006 antiterrorism legislation. Although Chicas was granted a provisional release on July 23, the government did not lift the terrorism charge, which carries a possible sentence of up to 15 years in prison. While defamation remains a criminal offense, the president, government officials, and the media jointly made recommendations to create access to information legislation and to decriminalize libel and defamation laws as part of the outcome of an Inter American Press Association conference in May.

Although El Salvador is generally a safe place to practice journalism, one journalist was killed in 2007 and others suffered physical attacks related to their work. On September 20, radio journalist Salvador Sanchez Roque was murdered by a group of unidentified gunmen near his home in the municipality of Soyapango, in San Salvador. Sanchez Roque, who had been threatened weeks prior to the killing, had reported on abuses committed by local criminal gangs. A member of the Salvadoran gang Mara Salvatrucha was arrested for the journalist's killing on October 11, while two other suspects remained at large at year's end. On October 25, three journalists were assaulted during clashes between the police and local residents in Cutumay Comones, Santa Ana, while covering a local rally against the construction of a garbage landfill. In addition, representatives of the San Salvador–based newspaper *El Mundo* claimed to have received anonymous calls of death threats in the newsroom at the time it published articles on corruption and on presidential candidacies.

While there are five daily newspapers, each with an estimated circulation of 250,000, most of the country depends on privately owned television and radio networks for the news. Limited resources prevent many media outlets from producing to their full capacity, and self-censorship is often exercised to avoid offending media owners, editors, and government officials. Challenges to economic viability are further exacerbated by the government's refusal to place advertising in outlets viewed as unsympathetic to the administration, as it has done in recent years with *Co Latino,* a newspaper run by a cooperative of journalists. There were no reported government restrictions on the internet; however, less than 10 percent of the population was able to access this medium in 2007.

Equatorial Guinea

Status: Not Free

LEGAL ENVIRONMENT: 27
POLITICAL ENVIRONMENT: 35
ECONOMIC ENVIRONMENT: 27
TOTAL SCORE: 89

Survey Edition	2003	2004	2005	2006	2007
Total Score, Status	81,NF	89,NF	88,NF	88,NF	89,NF

Freedom of expression and of the press are legally guaranteed, but these rights are practically ignored. The 1992 Press Law gives the government unusually extensive authority to restrict press activities through official prepublication censorship. Registration requirements to establish newspapers and periodicals are burdensome. All domestic journalists are required to register with the Ministry of Information, and equally strict accreditation procedures are in place for foreign correspondents. Almost all local coverage is orchestrated or tightly controlled by the government. There are no laws guaranteeing freedom of information, and both local and foreign journalists could not generally access government information. In practice, all information is reserved for journalists with state-run media houses. Conditions improved only slightly in 2007 with televised public events that provided some information on public revenues and expenditures.

Local journalists were subject to systematic surveillance and frequently practiced self-censorship. The few international reporters who managed to obtain government accreditation were constantly monitored, threatened, and harassed by government officials upon arrival. As in 2006, there were no reported cases of physical abuse or imprisonment during the year, a reflection of the government's degree of control over the local press who refrain from reporting on such incidents, even when they happen to their own reporters. Mild criticism of infrastructure and public institutions is allowed, but nothing disparaging about the president or security forces is tolerated. In the past, foreign journalists have been monitored closely and occasionally deported if their coverage is deemed to be sensitive. The opposition had little access to domestic media, and political party publications are not permitted to be publicly distributed; nonetheless, opposition criticism of the government was televised in September during coverage of a legislative session. During the year, authorities announced that they would boost cooperation with the governments of Zimbabwe and China to enhance the production and transmission of official broadcasts; neither partnership boded well for the enhancement of media freedom.

Equatorial Guinea is one of the few African countries with virtually no independent media. Given the high level of poverty and illiteracy throughout the country, the most influential form of media is radio, but all domestic radio and television stations are owned directly by the government or by the president's family. State-owned media are dominated by sycophantic coverage of the government and the president. Applications to open private radio stations have been pending for several years but have thus far not been approved. A dozen ostensibly private local newspapers appeared irregularly due primarily to financial constraints but functioned mainly as political mouthpieces. According to the U.S. State Department, foreign publications are not permitted to be sold or distributed without government permission, there are no newsstands in the country, and the only bookstores are those affiliated with religious organizations. Foreign broadcasts are available, including those of the British Broadcasting Corporation, Radio France Internationale, and Radio Exterior, an international shortwave service from Spain; uncensored satellite broadcasts were increasingly available to those who could afford the service. Through its interviews with opposition politicians, Radio Exterior operates as the only means by which opposition voices can reach rural populations. The government does not restrict internet access, although government operatives are believed to monitor citizens' e-mail and internet use. Owing to high poverty levels, less than 2 percent of the population was able to access the internet in 2007.

Eritrea

Status: Not Free

LEGAL ENVIRONMENT: 30
POLITICAL ENVIRONMENT: 40
ECONOMIC ENVIRONMENT: 24
TOTAL SCORE: 94

Survey Edition	2003	2004	2005	2006	2007
Total Score, Status	83,NF	89,NF	91,NF	91,NF	94,NF

Conditions for Eritrean journalists continued to be dismal in 2007, a year that was marked by tragedy, as several journalists who attempted to flee the country were arrested or killed. The constitution, which guarantees freedom of speech and of the press, has been ratified but never implemented. Meanwhile, the 1996 Press Proclamation Law mandates that all media outlets must be owned by the government and requires all newspapers and journalists to be licensed. It also stipulates that publications be submitted for government approval prior to release and prohibits reprinting articles from banned publications.

Since a government ban on all privately owned media was imposed in September 2001, Eritrea remains one of the harshest environments worldwide for the press and is a leading jailer of journalists in Africa. Following the official ban, an unknown number of government critics were detained, including many journalists. Beginning in November 2006, the government launched a new crackdown, leading to the arrests of at least 9 journalists after several prominent colleagues had defected. According to the Committee to Protect Journalists, at least 14 journalists were imprisoned during 2007, and at least 1 prisoner, Fessehaye "Joshua" Yohannes, a respected journalist, poet, and playwright, reportedly died in detention. In June, Paulos Kidane, a prominent journalist with Eri-TV, died while attempting to flee across the border into Sudan. Many of the jailed journalists are being held incommunicado in undisclosed locations, without access to their families or the Red Cross. Numerous reports of torture have emerged, suggesting that for many journalists, incarceration is life threatening. Despite Eritrean legal guarantees, none of the journalists in prison have ever been brought to trial, and attempting to leave the country is considered treasonous and punishable by imprisonment or "forced disappearance." As a result, there are virtually no independent journalists able to live in Eritrea and certainly none able to work openly.

As bilateral relations with many Western countries, including the United States, continue to deteriorate, foreign journalists are not able to freely enter the country and are generally not welcome unless they agree to report favorably about the regime. Local correspondents for international news organizations such as the British Broadcasting Corporation and Voice of America face heavy restrictions; both local and foreign journalists are required to obtain permits to leave the capital, Asmara.

There is currently no independent or privately owned press. Only three newspapers, one television station, and one radio station operate, and all remain under state control. Journalists working for the state-owned media operate under strict surveillance and severe pressure to report positively on government programs. The importation of foreign periodicals is forbidden, although the purchase of satellite dishes is permitted. The government requires all internet service providers (ISPs) to use government-controlled internet infrastructure and owns a large percentage of them. According to the U.S. State Department, the government restricts the bandwidth available to ISPs, thus hindering their ability to provide services. Authorities are believed to monitor e-mail communication, although internet use is extremely limited, with just under 2 percent of the population able to access this medium in 2007.

Estonia

Status: Free

LEGAL ENVIRONMENT: 4
POLITICAL ENVIRONMENT: 6
ECONOMIC ENVIRONMENT: 6
TOTAL SCORE: 16

Survey Edition	2003	2004	2005	2006	2007
Total Score, Status	17,F	17,F	17,F	16,F	16,F

The constitution provides for and the government respects freedom of speech and of the press. Criminal libel has been removed from the penal code, and there are no legal penalties for "irresponsible journalism." Numerous media outlets operate throughout the country, and the independent media express a wide variety of views without government interference. The Public Information Law, which is the primary legislation governing freedom of information, obliges the authorities to assist the public in accessing public documents. There were no reports of physical harassment or intimidation of journalists in 2007

The country's public broadcasters are Estonian Television and Estonian Radio. The two nationwide commercial television stations, Kanal 2 and TV3, are owned by Scandinavian companies. Residents have access to a number of private radio stations and regional television channels, as well as cable and satellite services. Various public and private media outlets provide Russian-language programming to the country's sizable Russian-speaking population. There are nearly 150 newspapers in the country, but given the small size of the country's media market, most of them are financed by readers or owners, not by advertising revenues. However, according to the market research company TNS Latvia, Estonia's media advertising market volume increased by 28 percent in 2007 compared with 2006, with newspapers accounting for 40 percent of the country's total advertising market share; the largest measure of growth year-on-year occurred in the internet sector. The government allows unrestricted access to the internet, and Estonia remains among the leading countries in the world regarding internet penetration, with nearly 60 percent of the population actively online in 2007. In late April, access to the online versions of the country's two largest newspapers, *Eesti Paevaleht* and *Postimees*, was temporarily disrupted by coordinated large-scale cyberattacks that also targeted government and other commercial websites. The attacks were widely believed to have been conducted in retaliation for the relocation of a controversial World War II monument, an event that sparked two days of rioting in the capital city, Tallinn.

Ethiopia

Status: Not Free

LEGAL ENVIRONMENT: 27
POLITICAL ENVIRONMENT: 30
ECONOMIC ENVIRONMENT: 19
TOTAL SCORE: 76

Survey Edition	2003	2004	2005	2006	2007
Total Score, Status	64,NF	66,NF	68,NF	75,NF	77,NF

Conditions for press freedom improved slightly in 2007, following the government's November 2005 crackdown on opposition political parties and on civil society groups and media outlets that were perceived to support them. During 2007, in advance of the yearlong celebrations planned to mark the new millennium on the Ethiopian Orthodox calendar, the government acquitted political prisoners and journalists and reactivated the text-messaging service that had been shut down after the November 2005 postelection crackdown. In practice, however, press freedom remained limited in 2007, and there were no notable new entrants into the media market to increase diversity.

The constitution guarantees freedom of the press, but this right is often restricted in practice. Authorities frequently invoke the 1992 Press Law regarding publication of false and offensive information, incitement of ethnic hatred, or libel in order to justify the arrest and detainment of journalists. Court cases can continue for years, and journalists often have multiple charges pending against them. A 2003 draft Press Law, which has been criticized by the private press and press freedom groups for imposing restrictions on the practice of journalism and harsh sanctions for violations of the law, remained under consideration by the parliament in 2007, although certain provisions of the law were included in the new penal code that took effect in May 2005. Kifle Mulat, president of the Ethiopian Free Press Journalists Association, which has been a vocal opponent of the draft Press Law, remained in exile at year's end, although he was acquitted in April of antistate charges. Other EFJA members have also been subject to harassment and arrest in recent years. A major ongoing legal problem for the press has been the absence of judicial independence. Journalists have few guarantees that they will receive a fair trial, and charges are often issued in response to arbitrary events or personal disputes. Laws provide for freedom of information, although access to public information is largely restricted in practice, and the administration has traditionally limited coverage of official events to state-owned media outlets, albeit with slight openings beginning in 2006. In June, the government passed a law prohibiting broadcast organizations from owning broadcast companies that were established or received assistance from outside the country and gave the ministry of information control over the administration of those licenses.

The broad political crackdown that began in November 2005, in which several dozen journalists were arrested alongside politicians and were issued charges ranging from treason to subverting the constitution, continued to have negative implications for the media during 2007. Of the 15 journalists who were released during the year, 7 subsequently sought asylum abroad, and the Ministry of Information continued to deny many journalists who were arrested in the 2005 crackdown licenses to resume work on their respective publications, despite previous public assurances that they would be granted. Several journalists remained imprisoned at year's end, and journalists continued to be arrested on charges dating back several years. There is little information about the two ETV journalists, Shiferraw Insermu and Dhabassa Wakjira, who were arrested in 2004 on suspicion of supporting the Oromo Liberation Front. In addition, two Eritrean journalists from Eri-TV who were reportedly arrested by Ethiopian forces in the Somalian capital of Mogadishu continue to be held at an undisclosed location in Ethiopia. Foreign journalists and those working for international news organizations have generally operated with fewer restrictions than their local counterparts; however, they regularly practice self-censorship and face harassment and threats from authorities. In May, three *New York Times* journalists were arrested and detained in the eastern town of Degehabur for five days for reporting on the Ogaden conflict.

The state controls all broadcast media and operates the only television station. A 1999 law permits private radio stations, and the first licenses were finally awarded to two private FM stations in the capital, Addis Ababa, in 2006. However, by the end of 2007, the only station operational is owned by a supporter of the ruling party. Dozens of print outlets publish regularly and offer diverse views, although many are firmly aligned with either the government or the opposition and provide slanted news coverage. Following the November 2005 crackdown, only a limited number of newspapers that do not challenge the federalist constitution or ethnic makeup of the government were allowed to continue publishing without interruption, and only one new private newspaper, *Addis Neger*, was able to begin operations in that two year period. Authorities largely targeted the Amharic-language private press, banning or shutting down more than a dozen opposition-inclined papers that together accounted for more than 80 percent of total Amharic circulation. Fewer than 10 papers are now publishing in Addis Ababa, compared with more than 20 in 2005. Most newspapers struggle to remain financially viable and to meet the Ministry of Information requirement of a minimum bank balance in order to renew their annual publishing licenses.

In past years, access to foreign broadcasts has occasionally been restricted, a trend that continued in 2007 with the jamming of Deutsche Welle and Voice of America signals. Owing to an extremely poor telecommunications infrastructure, internet access is limited primarily to the major urban areas; less than 0.5 percent of the population made use of this medium in 2007, but its popularity is growing with the proliferation of internet cafés. As more citizens, faced with an increasingly restricted print and broadcast media environment, turned to the internet for information, the government responded accordingly. There are reports that the government monitored e-mail, and starting in 2006, access to some websites and blogs was blocked, including news websites run by members of the Ethiopian diaspora who were critical of the government. The Ethiopian Telecommunications Corporation remained the only internet service provider during 2007.

Fiji

Status: Partly Free

LEGAL ENVIRONMENT: 11
POLITICAL ENVIRONMENT: 18
ECONOMIC ENVIRONMENT: 8
TOTAL SCORE: 37

Survey Edition	2003	2004	2005	2006	2007
Total Score, Status	29,F	29,F	30,F	28,F	39,PF

Press freedom in Fiji recovered somewhat from a major reversal suffered in 2006 as a result of a coup by Commodore Voreqe Bainimarama. Following a significant tightening of the media environment at the end of 2006 and the early part of 2007, the latter part of the year was marked by a reduction of government pressure and an improved legal environment. In December 2006, the country endured its fourth coup in almost two decades when the democratically elected government of Laisenia Qarase's Soqosoqo Duavata ni Lewenivanua party was ousted. Immediately following the takeover, the 1999 constitution appeared to have been suspended, removing legal protections for journalists such as provisions in the bill of rights guaranteeing free speech. However, during 2007, the postcoup regime asserted that the constitution had not been suspended, thereby restoring some legal rights. Though no freedom of information legislation exists, the Fijian High Court issued a landmark ruling in October 2007 in which it rejected a request seeking to bar Fiji TV from broadcasting an audit of the country's largest financial institution, the Fiji National Provident Fund; the Court justified the decision by declaring the audit results to be in the public interest. Nevertheless, in August, the Fiji Human Rights Commission, widely regarded as holding a progovernment stance, commissioned a report entitled *Freedom and Independence of the Media in Fiji*. The report, whose final version had not been publicly released at year's end, was considered by news media and the self-regulatory Fiji Media Council as an attempt to restrict media freedom.

Despite increased security in the legal sphere, there were several incidents of soldiers harassing and threatening journalists and activists regarded as overly critical of the government, reportedly contributing to self-censorship. In one incident, Richard Naid, a prominent media lawyer and former journalist who advises Fiji's largest daily newspaper, the *Fiji Times*, was seized by the military and intimidated. Fiji Television's news director, Netani Rika, was also brought in for questioning and reportedly abused by the military in 2007. In June, foreign journalist Michael Field, a correspondent for Fairfax Media in Auckland, was reportedly detained and then expelled after seeking to cover the expulsion of New Zealand's high commissioner, apparently for publicly criticizing the coup. The harassment, particularly intense in the months immediately after the country's coup on December 5, 2006, eased later in the year as the interim administration became more secure in its political and legal control. Nevertheless, to protect their correspondents, many newspapers ceased providing bylines.

In spite of the coup, the economic climate for independently owned media remained stable. The state-run Fiji Broadcasting Corporation operates three main radio stations in English, Fijian, and Hindustani; the state also runs three national newspapers. These compete with two private national newspapers, the *Fiji Times* and the *Fiji Sun*, as well as a privately owned FM broadcaster, Communications Fiji Ltd. The Fijian investment group Yasana Holdings holds a controlling 51 percent stake in Fiji TV, while the government owns 14 percent but plans to sell its stake. According to the U.S. State Department, the government has been known to direct advertising to media outlets in which it has a stake.

In 2007, nearly 9 percent of the population was able to access the internet. Though there were no restrictions on access to this medium, during the year, the authorities attempted to shut down several prodemocracy blogs that emerged in response to the coup. According to the U.S. State Department, the military closely monitored communications on the sites, and in at least one instance, a businessman accused of contributing to one such blog was detained at an army camp and abused. Several other individuals involved with the blogs were also reportedly threatened or intimidated.

Finland

Status: Free

LEGAL ENVIRONMENT: 2
POLITICAL ENVIRONMENT: 3
ECONOMIC ENVIRONMENT: 4
TOTAL SCORE: 9

Survey Edition	2003	2004	2005	2006	2007
Total Score, Status	10,F	9,F	9,F	9,F	9,F

Finland maintained its position as one of the freest environments for the media in the world. Freedom of expression and access to information are guaranteed under Article 12 of the revised constitution, adopted in March 2000. There were no cases of defamation suits filed against journalists or media outlets during the year, nor were there any reports of attacks on the press. However, in September one reporter was arrested, temporarily detained, and forced to surrender his equipment while covering a protest in Helsinki during the Asia-Europe Meeting summit.

Finland has an impressive newspaper readership, ranking third in the world for circulation in relation to population. Two hundred newspapers are published, including 31 dailies, according to the Finnish Newspaper Association, and in 2007, it was found that the average Finn reads three newspapers a day. A total of 150 publications have editions available online. Media ownership is concentrated, with Alma Media and SanomaWSOY controlling most newspaper distribution. Broadcasting was once dominated by the public broadcaster Yleisradio OY and commercial MTV, but 2 new broadcasters have since emerged. Included in the 67 commercial radio stations are 3 national public stations in Finnish, 2 in Swedish, and 1 in the Sami (Lapp) language. The internet is open and unrestricted, and more than 62 percent of all citizens have regular access. However, web publications must name a responsible editor in chief and archive published materials for at least 21 days. In addition, Finnish law gives every citizen the right of reply and the right to have falsely published information corrected, on internet and traditional publications alike.

France

Status: Free

LEGAL ENVIRONMENT: 6
POLITICAL ENVIRONMENT: 9
ECONOMIC ENVIRONMENT: 7
TOTAL SCORE: 22

Survey Edition	2003	2004	2005	2006	2007
Total Score, Status	17,F	19,F	20,F	21,F	21,F

The media environment remained free during 2007, but France continued to struggle to define the rights of journalists, especially those concerning the confidentiality of sources and the dissemination of information. The constitution and governing institutions support an open press environment, although certain laws, like the 1990 Gayssot law against Holocaust denial, limit aspects of press freedom in practice. There are strict antidefamation laws in place with fines for those found guilty; the law also punishes efforts to justify war crimes and crimes against humanity, as well as incitements to discrimination and violence. Freedom of information legislation exists, but it can be restricted to protect the reputation or rights of a third party, and the majority of requests are denied.

In March, France's Constitutional Council passed a law banning the dissemination of images that constitute offenses outlined in the criminal code, including acts of torture and other physical attacks, punishable with up to five years' imprisonment and fines as high as US$110,000. Although the new law does not apply to journalists in the performance of their normal duties, free speech advocates argue that it imposes a dangerous distinction between citizens and journalists and that it could prevent the exposure of abuses by security forces, particularly over the internet. Separately, free speech advocates scored a legal victory in March when a court acquitted Philippe Val, editor in chief of the satirical weekly *Charlie Hebdo*, of a defamation suit brought against him by several Muslim groups. The suit was initially filed in response to three depictions of the prophet Muhammad that the paper had published in 2006.

Throughout 2007, authorities detained journalists to try to pressure them into revealing their sources and attempted to search media houses and personal premises for documents and sources. On May 11, Justice Thomas Cassuto tried to have the office of the satirical weekly *Le Canard Enchaine* searched in order to obtain information related to the Clearstream case, in which several high-ranking French political and business leaders—most notably President Nicolas Sarkozy, then interior minister—were falsely accused of having received kickbacks from arms sales channeled through the Luxembourg bank Clearstream. Owing to the presence of journalists blocking the entrance, the search was never completed, and the case was closed in September without formal charges being made against any of the journalists. In July, four journalists were summoned before police authorities after covering the actions taken by a group of radical wine producers, the Regional Committee of Wine Action, against two wineries on July 2 and 3. The police wanted the journalists to reveal the source that alerted them to the action. Separately, on July 13, authorities detained photographer Jean-Claude Elassi as he was covering a judicial reenactment of a murder near Paris and seized footage he had taken of the event.

In perhaps the most serious violation of free speech during the year, counterterrorism authorities detained *Le Monde* reporter Guillaume Dasquie for 48 hours on December 5 after searching his Paris apartment and tried to make him reveal his sources. An antiterrorism judge charged that earlier in the year, Dasquie published state secrets pertaining to the terrorist attacks of September 11, 2001. If convicted, Dasquie could face up to five years' imprisonment and a fine of over US$100,000. The case was still pending at year's end.

Most of France's over 100 newspapers are privately owned and not linked directly to political parties; however, newspaper circulation continued to decline in 2006. Following the 2004 consolidation of the newspaper market, ownership has become even more concentrated, despite the existence of a law that prevents any single media group from controlling over 30 percent of press outlets. Many media outlets—print as well as broadcast—are owned by companies with close ties to both prominent politicians and the defense establishment. This issue was particularly pertinent following the May 2007 election of Nicolas Sarkozy as president, given that several of his close associates have recently taken over positions at France's leading television network, TF1, and some of his other supporters were already in leadership positions at prominent newspapers and television stations. There is some evidence that pressure from Sarkozy has already begun to influence media content: In 2006, Sarkozy pushed successfully for the dismissal of the editor of the print tabloid *Paris Match* for printing photos of his then wife, Cecilia, with her alleged lover. In addition, the editors of the *Journal du Dimanche*—a weekly paper headed by Arnaud Lagardere, a close Sarkozy associate—were under pressure from Sarkozy to refrain from running a story alleging that Cecilia had not voted in the second round of the presidential election.

The government controls many of the firms that supply advertising revenue to media groups, and an independently administered fund provides some public subsidies to media outlets, particularly regional newspapers. The French broadcasting market continued to be dominated by TF1, although the growth of satellite and cable and the launch of digital terrestrial television in March 2005 have led to a proliferation of channels. This trend has been accentuated by the approval of the merger between two of the biggest satellite pay-TV operators, CanalSatellite and TPS. France abides by a European Union law that requires 60 percent of broadcast content to be of European origin. The internet is generally unrestricted and used by approximately 55 percent of the population; there are no reports that the government has restricted internet access or monitored e-mail or chat rooms.

LEGAL ENVIRONMENT: 24

POLITICAL ENVIRONMENT: 23

Gabon

ECONOMIC ENVIRONMENT: 22

Status: Not Free

TOTAL SCORE: 69

Survey Edition	2003	2004	2005	2006	2007
Total Score, Status	58,PF	62,NF	66,NF	67,NF	69,NF

The media environment remained restricted as the government continued to force journalists to choose between self-censorship and the risk of reprisals for criticism of its policies. The constitution guarantees freedom of expression and of the press, but authorities used legal harassment, threats, and financial pressure to curb critical reporting. Local media professionals face repressive press laws that impose harsh penalties for libel—including a minimum sentence of three months for a repeat offense—particularly with respect to criticism of the president, his relatives, or members of his cabinet. Libel can be treated as either a civil or a criminal offense, and the government is permitted to criminalize civil suits and initiate criminal suits in response to the alleged libel of government officials.

The boundaries of acceptable political commentary in Gabon are ambiguous, frequently leaving journalists and media outlets vulnerable to government retaliation. The National Communications Council (CNC), a government agency charged with upholding journalistic standards, has a history of using intimidation tactics against the independent press and has forcibly shut down more than half a dozen publications since 2003. In March, authorities suspended the bimonthly private *Edzombolo* for three months following an article critical of the authority of President Omar Bongo, Africa's longest-serving head of state. In June, Guy-Christian Mavioga, director of the private *L'Espoir*, was sentenced to one month in jail plus a five-month suspended sentence and fine for allegedly "offending the head of state" owing to an article critical of Bongo. Mavioga was released after 38 days and was hospitalized in a state of poor health, although the paper remained suspended indefinitely because it had allegedly violated a rule prohibiting state employees from controlling news outlets. In October, the CNC suspended another bimonthly, *La Nation*, over an article critical of Culture Minister Blandine Marundu. The same month, the CNC blocked the Paris-based satirical paper *Le Gri-Gri* from printing and distributing in Gabon following its criticism of a government mining contract.

Gabon has several private radio stations and four private television stations, although private broadcasting tends to be nonpolitical; the government owns two radio stations and two television stations that are able to broadcast nationwide. Approximately nine private weeklies and monthlies circulate in the capital, Libreville, although the state-affiliated *L'Union* is the country's only daily newspaper, and local journalists complain that many nominally private publications are controlled by political factions. Much of the private press appears irregularly because of financial constraints and frequent government censorship. Many Gabonese private newspapers are printed in Cameroon because of the high cost at the only local printing company, and publications printed outside the country are subject to review before distribution. Foreign publications and radio broadcasts are widely available. There are no reports that the government restricts internet access or monitors e-mail, although less than 6 percent of the population had access to this electronic resource in 2007.

The Gambia

LEGAL ENVIRONMENT: 25
POLITICAL ENVIRONMENT: 34
ECONOMIC ENVIRONMENT: 20

Status: Not Free

TOTAL SCORE: 79

Survey Edition	2003	2004	2005	2006	2007
Total Score, Status	65,NF	63,NF	72,NF	73,NF	77,NF

The Gambia's poor record on press freedom worsened further during 2007 owing to legal and extralegal intimidation of journalists and media outlets, as well as complete impunity in past cases of press freedom abuse. The constitution guarantees freedom of expression, but the government does not respect it in practice. Constitutional guarantees are particularly undermined by other pieces of legislation, primarily the Newspaper Amendment Act and the criminal code amendment, both passed in 2004. The latter established the publication of "false information" as an offense carrying stiff penalties and mandated harsh punishments for sedition and libel. Lamin Fatty, a journalist for the *Independent* who had been held incommunicado in detention for two months during 2006, was the first to be convicted under this legislation. He was found guilty of a criminal offense and fined US$1,850 for a mistaken detail in an article about a 2006 coup plot for which the paper subsequently apologized. In another case of legal intimidation, in March, the U.S.-based journalist and political commentator Fatou Jaw Manneh was arrested at the airport as she returned to The Gambia for her father's funeral. According to the Committee to

Protect Journalists, Manneh was charged with sedition for a 2004 interview published in the defunct biweekly the *Independent*, in which she strongly criticized the government, calling President Yahya Jammeh "a bundle of terror" and an "egoistic, frosty imam." She was released after a week on bail but was prohibited from leaving the country. In September 2007, Mam Sait Ceesay, former editor in chief of a progovernment newspaper, and Malick Jones, employee of a state-owned radio and television service, were arrested and charged with "passing information to a foreign journalist." The two were imprisoned for several days until they were able to post bail of as much as US$9,500; the case was subsequently suspended and remained so until year's end.

Violence and extralegal intimidation against journalists continued to be an issue in 2007. Chief Ebrimah Manneh, correspondent for the state-owned *Daily Observer*, remained disappeared throughout the year following his arrest in July 2006 by security agents. He was reportedly detained over allegations of passing damaging information to a foreign journalist who wrote an article critical of the regime prior to the 2006 African Union Summit in Banjul. Manneh was later spotted briefly at several prisons and hospitals after his disappearance. The Media Foundation of West Africa filed suit before the Community Court of Justice of the Economic Community of West African States in Nigeria, seeking Manneh's release from detention and compensation. Nevertheless, in September, the International Federation of Journalists expressed fears that Manneh may have died in custody. In another incident in October 2007, two Amnesty International researchers and a local reporter were arrested and detained for three days, accused of spying. Following a raid on his house by state security agents, local journalist Yahya Dampha of the newspaper *Foroyaa* went into hiding. As a result of such legal and extralegal intimidation, many journalists practice self-censorship, while a number of others have fled the country and remain in exile. Impunity for past abuses continued to be an issue during the year, as the murder of journalist Deyda Hydara remains unsolved after three years. Hydara had been managing editor of the *Point* private weekly and a correspondent for both Reporters Sans Frontieres and Agence France-Presse.

The government owns a daily newspaper, a national radio station, and the only national television station. Political news coverage at these outlets generally favors the official line. The Gambia has three private newspapers that publish biweekly or thrice weekly and four private FM radio stations. Many of these private entities are subject to official pressure for publishing criticism of government and public officials, while most businesses avoid advertising in them for fear of government reprisals. A premium television network operates as a satellite station. Internet usage in 2007 increased to 4.9 percent of the population, one of the highest rates in West Africa. Although the government denies it, two U.S.-based websites—*Freedom Newspaper* and All Gambian—were blocked within The Gambia in June. According to journalists working for the two sites, the blocking was linked to their critical reporting about the government.

Georgia

Status: Partly Free

LEGAL ENVIRONMENT: 14
POLITICAL ENVIRONMENT: 28
ECONOMIC ENVIRONMENT: 18
TOTAL SCORE: 60

Survey Edition	2003	2004	2005	2006	2007
Total Score, Status	54,PF	54,PF	56,PF	57,PF	57,PF

The constitution and the Law on Freedom of Speech and Expression guarantee press freedom, but these rights are often restricted. Press laws, as well as most other laws adopted by the government of Mikheil Saakashvili, are very progressive. Libel has been decriminalized, and freedom of information legislation has been adopted. However, in practice, the government's willingness to implement this legislation has decreased. As a result, the relationship between the government and the media has deteriorated recently. While legislation guarantees access to public information, other legislation limits this right. Amendments to judicial legislation banned photo and video records in courtrooms. Media are often forced to go through the court system to uphold the right to access public information when journalists are denied access to public institutions. Throughout the year, media faced illegal searches, closures, and unfair and nontransparent license regulations. The members of the media regulatory body, the Georgian National Communications Commission (GNCC), are appointed by the president; the GNCC has been criticized by media observers for its nontransparent operations and licensing procedures.

During the fall 2007 political crisis, the relationship between the government and the media hit its lowest point. Prior to that period, which was the worst since the 2003 Rose Revolution and dealt a major blow to Georgia's democratic image, media observers actually noted a slight improvement over 2006. Having secured a strong majority in local elections in 2006, the government took a more relaxed attitude toward the media in the first half of 2007. Observers even noted a decrease in indirect pressure on the media, and strong economic growth positively affected the media's financial positions. Nonetheless, on November 7, antigovernment protests and increasing tension between the government and the opposition erupted in violence when the government authorized police to use heavy-handed tactics to disperse protesters. Throughout the day, police illegally raided the independent and pro-opposition Imedi TV station, co-owned by wealthy businessman (and then presidential candidate) Badri Patarkatsisvhili. News Corporation's Imedi TV and the independent local Tbilisi television station Kavkasia TV were both suspended for allegedly inciting antigovernment protests. The following day, President Saakashvili imposed a nine-day state of emergency that banned all local and foreign broadcasts except for public television. While other stations resumed broadcasts once the state of emergency was lifted, Imedi's license remained suspended until December 12. Throughout the fall period, journalists were often the victims of intimidation and attacks.

Through the end of the year, the media environment remained highly politicized. Progovernment stations such as Rustavi-2 and Merz provided positive coverage of the incumbent, while independent stations grew increasingly pro-opposition in their editorial positions. In December, six well-known reporters from Imedi and Rustavi-2 resigned in protest over pressure to maintain pro-opposition or progovernment coverage. Imedi was forced to close down again before the end of the year following the resignations. Authorities in the separatist regions of Abkhazia and South Ossetia continued to restrict media freedom despite the legal protections for it. Local and foreign journalists are frequently intimidated and detained, and there is little access to local or foreign information in these regions.

For a small country, Georgia enjoys a high number of broadcast and print media outlets. Despite the political turmoil in late 2007, most media continued to operate and express diverse views. There are 200 independent newspapers and at least 8 independent or privately owned television stations, 5 of which have nationwide coverage. However, financially the print media are not self-sustainable, and as of January 2007, print media no longer receive tax benefits. Information about media owners is not transparent, and often journalists and reporters do not know the real owner of the media company for which they work. At the end of the year, ahead of the presidential election in 2008, advertising became a political tool, with President Saakashvili able to dominate free and paid airtime. The opposition, already dealing with a short and unexpectedly early campaign period, had poor funding and was left without a major nationwide broadcast platform, first because of the state of emergency and then because of Imedi's suspension. Although internet usage is expanding in Georgia, only 7 percent of the population regularly accessed information online in 2007.

Germany

LEGAL ENVIRONMENT: 6
POLITICAL ENVIRONMENT: 6
ECONOMIC ENVIRONMENT: 4

Status: Free

TOTAL SCORE: 16

Survey Edition	2003	2004	2005	2006	2007
Total Score, Status	15,F	16,F	16,F	16,F	16,F

Germany's media remained free and vibrant in 2007, despite challenges to the right to confidentiality of sources. The constitution guarantees freedom of expression and of the press, although there are exceptions for hate speech, Holocaust denial, and Nazi propaganda. Early in 2007, two men were sentenced to prison for denying the Holocaust and inciting racial hatred. Ernst Zundel was sentenced to five years for running a website from Canada that questioned the Holocaust and presented anti-Semitic and neo-Nazi views. In an unrelated case, Germar Rudolf was sentenced to 30 months in jail for publishing a book that questioned the use of Zyklon B in the concentration camps. Freedom of information legislation finally went into force in January 2006. While the law establishes that information held by public authorities is by definition open, it also contains numerous exemptions and requires the payment of high fees in advance of every request. According to statistics published by the country's Freedom of Information Commissioner, over 2,200 requests were received in 2006. Of those, access to the desired information was denied in 410 cases, but several successful court cases have required the authorities in question to make those documents available. In a positive move, in February 2007, Germany's Constitutional Court ruled that the raid on the *Cicero* office in 2005 had been illegal. In 2005, several months after *Cicero* had published extracts from a confidential report about al-Qaeda, police raided the political magazine's office and the home of the journalist who had written the article. In November 2007, the German government approved a bill requiring telecommunications firms to store data for up to six months, including e-mails, text messages, and cell phone conversations, and make the information available to police upon request. The new law, which will go into effect January 1, 2008, permits the wiretapping of lawyers and doctors as well as journalists under certain circumstances while providing a level of protection to religious clerics, members of parliament, and state prosecutors.

In August 2007, the German government launched a criminal investigation against 17 journalists from a number of influential publications, including *Der Spiegel*, *Die Welt*, and *Suddeutsche Zeitung*. The journalists were accused of breaking Article 353B of the criminal code—the same article that had initially enabled police to raid *Cicero*—which prohibits the "divulging" of state secrets. The journalists had allegedly committed the crime when they published excerpts from secret government documents detailing covert CIA extraordinary rendition flights and allegations of misconduct by German military personnel during the initial invasion of Iraq in 2003. However, by the end of the year, the cases had all been dropped.

The private media are diverse and independent. Each of the 16 local regional governments is in charge of its own public radio and television broadcasting system, and there are also a number of private stations throughout the country. The print press is dominated by numerous regional papers, and only a handful of national papers are published. A small number of centralized editorial offices control most content, and only a few commercial groups, which are some of the largest in the world, dominate the media market. The internet is open and largely unrestricted except for a law banning access to child pornography and Nazi propaganda. As a result, many search engines in Germany have subscribed to the Voluntary Self-Control for Multimedia Service Providers association, filtering websites based on a list created by Germany's Federal Department for Media Harmful to Young Persons. The internet was accessed by over 64 percent of the population in 2007.

Ghana

LEGAL ENVIRONMENT: 8
POLITICAL ENVIRONMENT: 10
ECONOMIC ENVIRONMENT: 9

Status: Free

TOTAL SCORE: 27

Survey Edition	2003	2004	2005	2006	2007
Total Score, Status	30,F	28,F	26,F	28,F	26,F

Ghana's reputation as a country with unfettered freedom of expression was not seriously threatened in 2007. However, there were some worrying signs involving the activities of nonstate actors, the overzealousness of presidential security guards, and clumsiness in managing press access to public events that could collectively sully Ghana's image. Freedom of the press is guaranteed by law, and the government generally respects it in practice. In recent years, President John Kufuor's administration has demonstrated its desire to expand freedom of expression by repealing criminal libel legislation—the only country West African country to do so. Nonetheless, there has been a spate of civil libel cases with cripplingly high fines brought by former public officials and private citizens against media outlets in the past few years. Only one such case occurred in 2007, while a few other cases were dropped by the government during the year. In January, the courts ordered Militant Publications, the producer of the newspaper *Insight*, to pay US$13,000 to the minister of water resources, works, and housing, for defaming him in an article three years earlier. As President Kufuor enters the final year of his last term in office in 2008, a push is under way by media interest groups to have the government pass a promised freedom of information bill. In May, the Freedom of Information Coalition–Ghana launched a campaign to do this under Article 21(f) of the 1992 constitution, which guarantees the right to information. Government ministers have said the bill will be submitted to parliament once reviews of measures to make it enforceable and practicable are complete.

Meanwhile, however, a number of disturbing incidents during the year alarmed the Ghana Journalists Association (GJA). These include the April murder of Samuel Kwabena Eninn, editor of Ashh FM and chairman of the GJA in the Ashanti region. The police suspected robbery as a motive and announced a US$2,000 reward for information leading to the arrest of his killers. At the end of the year, no one had been arrested and there was still no evidence that the incident was linked to Eninn's work. Separately, Henry Addo, an investigative journalist for an independent television station, was attacked in Accra by a group of vigilantes. Charges of rough handling of media personnel were leveled in April against President Kufuor's security detail by journalists who said they were barred from covering the president's visit to flooded areas in the north. In response to the outcry following incidents of local police harassment of journalists in 2006, Ghana's Inspector General of the Police announced in February that the police would work to ensure that the rights of journalists were more fully respected. However, in July, more than 500 local and foreign journalists were barred from the conference hall of the African Union Summit in Accra during the opening session of the gathering. Guards providing security for the visiting African heads of state were also accused of roughing up reporters. Protocol officials claimed that restrictions on press access to the summit were due to security concerns. Following protests, the Ghana deputy minister of information apologized for lapses in arrangements for press coverage. Other complaints about access restrictions were made by sports journalists who said they were prevented from getting direct access to football players and coaches at the ends of matches. No investigations were conducted during the year into any of the incidents of harassment of journalists that took place in 2006. In a sign of politicization ahead of the 2008 presidential election, in December the Ashanti regional chapter of the GJA condemned as unprofessional the endorsement of presidential candidate Alan John Kyerematen by another group of journalists calling itself Media Friends of Alan.

More than 135 newspapers, including 2 state-owned dailies, publish in Ghana, and approximately 110 FM radio stations function nationwide, 11 of which are state run; there are 27 television stations in operation. Radio remains the most popular medium. Poor pay and unprofessional conduct, including newspapers that fabricate highly sensationalist news stories, remain problematic. Limited revenue from advertising and reader subscriptions threatens the financial viability of private media outlets. Journalists regularly complain about the bias they experience when applying for a license to open a media outlet, particularly those in the broadcast sector. Some have even applied for licenses as far back as 2000 and have yet to receive a response. Foreign media content is widely available, including broadcasts from the British Broadcasting Corporation, Radio France Internationale, and Voice of America. Access to the internet is growing. About 2.7 percent of the population used the medium in 2007, primarily through internet cafés.

Greece

Status: Free

		LEGAL ENVIRONMENT: 9
		POLITICAL ENVIRONMENT: 13
		ECONOMIC ENVIRONMENT: 5
		TOTAL SCORE: 27

Survey Edition	2003	2004	2005	2006	2007
Total Score, Status	28,F	28,F	28,F	28,F	25,F

The Greek constitution provides for freedom of speech and of the press. However, there are limits to speech that incites fear, violence, and disharmony among the population, as well as publications that offend religious beliefs, are obscene, or advocate the violent overthrow of the political system. In 2007, the Greek Helsinki Monitor (GHM), a nongovernmental organization that monitors compliance with the human rights provisions of the Helsinki Accords, brought two separate cases to court against media outlets for allegedly expressing anti-Semitic or racist ideas. In the first of these two suits, GHM accused the extreme right-wing newspaper *Eleftheros Kosmos* of having publicly expressed ideas denigrating Jews. In cooperation with the Central Board of Jewish Communities, GHM brought its second suit against the same newspaper and Kostas Plevris, the former Popular Orthodox Rally party candidate and noted author, for racism and anti-Semitism. In December 2007, while the court convicted Plevris and sentenced him to a 14-month suspended sentence for inciting hatred and racial violence in his book, the newspaper was acquitted.

A media bill currently being discussed in parliament has been criticized for deliberately trying to hinder the development of media in the region and for trying to limit minority group access to media. The proposed law states that the main transmission language of a radio station must be Greek in order for it to obtain an operating permit. It also demands that radio stations keep a certain amount of money in reserve as a guarantee, hire a minimum number of full-time staff, and broadcast programming 24 hours a day, all factors that would disproportionately hurt smaller, minority- or community-owned stations. In July, the European Court of Human Rights (ECHR) overturned the original ruling in a Greek court that journalists or radio program coordinators are liable for statements made on their radio shows by guest speakers. In doing so, the ECHR found that Greek law had been in violation of freedom of expression. The journalist in question was originally fined 41,000 Euros (US$63,103) by the Greek court. Separately, the leader of a journalists' union, Dimitris Trimis, was sent to jail in March for his union activities during a 2004 strike.

There are many independent newspapers and magazines, including those that are critical of the government, and many broadcasters are privately owned. Greek law places limits on ownership of broadcast frequencies. The media, both public and private, are largely free from government restrictions, but state-owned stations tend to report with a slight government bias. However, politically sensitive issues—such as the status of Macedonians and other ethnic minorities in the country—still provoke government pressure and lead to self-censorship. Broadcasting is largely unregulated, and many broadcast stations are not licensed. Use of the internet is not restricted by the government, but only 33 percent of the population accessed this medium in 2007, well below the level of most other developed Western European countries.

Grenada

LEGAL ENVIRONMENT: 8
POLITICAL ENVIRONMENT: 11
ECONOMIC ENVIRONMENT: 5

Status: Free

TOTAL SCORE: 24

Survey Edition	2003	2004	2005	2006	2007
Total Score, Status	14,F	16,F	20,F	23,F	23,F

Although freedom of the press is guaranteed by law, the government continued to use the threat of libel laws to apply pressure on the media and to stifle criticism. In January, Prime Minister Keith Mitchell threatened to take legal action against sections of the local media that he claimed had libeled him. At the end of February, a suit was filed against the operators of radio station 90.1FM. The lawsuit was believed to be linked to comments made in various broadcasts calling for the reopening of an inquiry into corruption allegations against Mitchell for his role in the so-called briefcase scandal. At the end of August, the president of the Media Workers Association of Grenada (MWAG), Michael Bascombe, denounced "undue pressures" placed on journalists and media companies by government officials to not report on a controversy related to the failed First International Bank of Grenada and alleged bribes made to Mitchell and other Grenadian officials. On a positive note, MWAG representatives and government officials met in September and agreed to scrap a clause in the forthcoming Broadcasting Authority Law that would imprison media workers for violating the law. There was also agreement on a method to appoint members to the proposed industry regulatory agency, the Broadcasting Commission; amendments to protect the media from political interference; and discussion of an Access to Information Law. Grenada has 5 television stations, 11 radio stations, 4 newspapers, and 5 periodicals. In the past, the MWAG has complained that the governmental process of granting radio licenses is guided by political considerations. The government does not place restrictions on the internet, which was accessed by just under 19 percent of the population in 2007.

	LEGAL ENVIRONMENT: 17
	POLITICAL ENVIRONMENT: 25
Guatemala	ECONOMIC ENVIRONMENT: 16
Status: Partly Free	TOTAL SCORE: 58

Survey Edition	2003	2004	2005	2006	2007
Total Score, Status	58,PF	62,NF	58,PF	58,PF	59,PF

While reports of threats against and intimidation of journalists decreased from the previous year, Guatemalan journalists continued to work under difficult and dangerous conditions, with the murder of one journalist and targeted assassinations of others. Article 35 of the constitution ensures freedom of expression, which is generally respected by the government. In 2006, the government decriminalized press offenses, and the Constitutional Court declared Articles 411 and 412 of the press code unconstitutional; these articles had deemed an insult or slur on a government official as a crime punishable by imprisonment. Without freedom of information legislation, reporters have claimed that obtaining access to government information remains difficult. There were no legal cases during the year that significantly affected press freedom.

Although the independent media are relatively free to express diverse opinions on a variety of issues and criticize the government without many legal repercussions, violence against media workers by nonstate actors continued to impact the press environment. The Public Ministry reported 11 incidents of intimidation of journalists in 2007, down from 67 in 2006. One journalist was murdered in addition to numerous physical attacks and assassination attempts on others. Threats and violence increased during the weeks surrounding the two rounds of presidential elections held in

September and November. In early February, Wilder Jordan, *Nuestro Diario* correspondent and news director for Radio Sultana, was the target of gunfire in Zacapa. The attack was believed to be connected to a January 15 report in which Jordan alleged that a bus driver's apprentice was responsible for a public transportation accident. By year's end, no official action had been taken to investigate the case. In addition, several journalists from separate media outlets received anonymous threats based on their coverage of the February 19 murder of three Salvadoran congressmen and their driver. Radio producer Mario Rolando Lopez Sanchez was gunned down outside his home in Guatemala City on May 3. Lopez produced the often contentious political program *Casos y Cosas de la Vida Nacional* and a variety of socially focused programs on Radio Sonora, a privately held station with nationwide listeners. On September 4, an unidentified gunman fired into the offices of Radio Nuevo Mundo in Guatemala City five days before the presidential elections. These attacks were allegedly in response to the station's critical coverage of the government throughout the presidential campaign. Frequent attacks against the press, combined with the state of impunity for crimes of this nature, have produced a chilling effect on the industry, often leading journalists to practice self-censorship.

Newspaper ownership is concentrated in the hands of business elites with centrist or conservative editorial stances, with one company—Prensa Libre—dominating the newspaper market. There are four major daily papers. Electronic media ownership remained concentrated in the hands of Mexican Angel Gonzalez, a politically connected entrepreneur who favors conservative perspectives and holds a monopoly on all four of the country's private television stations. Only one cable newscast offers a contrasting viewpoint to this on-air news monopoly. Nine community radio stations that were closed in 2006 for reportedly not having licenses remained closed in 2007. The resolution of their legal status was part of the 1996 peace accords but has not been addressed. In a nation where only 60 percent of the population speaks Spanish, the paucity of indigenous-language programming is a severe constraint on freedom of expression and of the press. Indigenous languages are rarely heard in national media. There are no reports of government limitations on internet usage, although the internet was accessed by only about 7 percent of the population in 2007.

LEGAL ENVIRONMENT: 21
POLITICAL ENVIRONMENT: 29

Guinea

ECONOMIC ENVIRONMENT: 16

Status: Not Free

TOTAL SCORE: 66

Survey Editiion	2003	2004	2005	2006	2007
Total Score, Status	74,NF	71,NF	73,NF	67,NF	67,NF

Although long-ruling president Lansana Conte faced increased pressure for power-sharing and reform in 2007, the regime's practice of bullying the media remained largely unchanged. The constitution guarantees freedom of the press, but this right is not respected in practice and has been widely abused, partly through restrictive legislation that designates defamation and slander as criminal offenses and permits the authorities to censor publications. The number of criminal prosecutions of journalists declined during the year, but the criminal libel law continued to be used. In August, a Conakry court imposed suspended sentences of six months in prison on two private newspaper directors in connection with articles alleging corruption by a former government minister. The directors, Thiernodjo Diallo of *La Verite* and Abdoul Azziz Camara of *Liberation*, were also fined $13,000 and ordered to publish the verdict in their newspapers.

The most serious crackdown on the press took place in January and February during an 18-day national strike, called to protest rising prices, in which security forces killed some 137 people. Three of the four private radio stations in Conakry were taken off the air under a presidential decree that authorized the military to muzzle the print, broadcast, and online media. The editor of the private radio station Liberte FM, Mohamed Tondon Camara, was arrested with a staff worker and detained by presidential security guards for two days after the station aired a call-in program in which callers asked for Conte's resignation. Camara said his release came only after the intervention of the president's brother. Another private radio station, Familia FM, was also forced off the air by presidential guards following a call-in program. The strike was called off when Conte agreed to transfer most of his powers to an appointed prime minister. Media restrictions were subsequently eased, but journalists continued to practice self-censorship.

During the crisis, Information Minister Boubacar Yacine Diallo ordered all broadcast stations to black out news of the strike, and most of the country's private newspapers temporarily ceased operations. Diallo also called Liberte FM to halt its broadcast of an interview of a union leader discussing repression of the demonstrations. The new prime minister fired Diallo in May and replaced him with Justin Morel Junior, a popular journalist and communications officer at UNICEF. Diallo had once been a respected independent journalist and newspaper editor, and served in 2006 as the founding chairman of the Conseil National de la Communication, which is credited with beginning programs to improve the professionalism of media practitioners.

State-owned media provide extensive, mostly favorable coverage of the government but also criticize local-level officials and increasingly report on opposition activities. Although there are four private radio stations, the state-owned Radio Television Guinea (RTG) continues to be the only television broadcaster and downplayed the severity of the 2007 crisis. Guinea had been the last country in West Africa to allow private broadcasting, doing so only in 2006. Privately owned print media openly criticize the president and the government. Ten private weeklies publish regularly in Conakry, while a dozen others publish only sporadically. In 2007, the government gave financial subsidies of US$105,000 to private newspapers through the Guinea Association of Independent Editors, which divided the money among various press organizations. It was the second year in a row that the government had given the grant, rejecting calls by the editors for a doubled subsidy that would support more publications. About 80 of the country's 350 media organizations received money from the subsidy during the year. International media operate within the country, including Radio France Internationale, which was forced to suspend its broadcasts for 24 hours during the protests due to power cuts. The government does not directly restrict access to the internet, but use of the medium is still very low, largely due to illiteracy, limited access points, and high cost of access. The proportion of the population estimated to have access to the internet is 0.5 percent.

Guinea-Bissau

LEGAL ENVIRONMENT: 15
POLITICAL ENVIRONMENT: 23
ECONOMIC ENVIRONMENT: 15

Status: Partly Free

TOTAL SCORE: 53

Survey Edition	2003	2004	2005	2006	2007
Total Score, Status	60,PF	63,NF	55,PF	47,PF	48,PF

In 2007, Guinea-Bissau faced significant setbacks in its efforts to protect media freedoms and build on previous gains made in reestablishing civil and political order. The earlier improvements followed the 2005 return from exile of former military strongman Joao Bernado "Nino" Vieira. After he won the presidential election in 2005, his administration had quickly passed a law that provided for freedom of speech and of the press. But the advances in press liberalization were soon followed by troubling cases of intimidation in the wake of political and economic crises in 2006.

Various acts of intimidation and harassment of media practitioners continued throughout 2007, dampening the initial enthusiasm that accompanied Vieria's return. The dangers faced by journalists attempting to cover the activities of drug traffickers in Guinea-Bissau arguably represent the deadliest threat to press freedom, individual liberties, and personal security since the return of democracy. A fact-finding study by Reporters Sans Frontieres (RSF) concluded that journalists face a "precarious situation," warning that they now live with the constant fear of Colombian drug gangs and their local accomplices. Cocaine traffickers have frightened many journalists into silence, and at least two have fled into exile after receiving death threats in connection with stories linking drug traffickers to local security personnel, especially members of the marine unit. Allen Yero Embalo, a correspondent for Radio France Internationale, was one such reporter. He went into exile in France after unknown persons broke into his home and stole his camera, video footage of a report on drug trafficking, and over $1,200.

Other acts of intimidation in 2007 included the detention of Reuters journalist Alberto Dabo, who was held for several hours in June over a quote in which the interior minister supposedly said that soldiers were involved in the drug trade. Dabo was threatened with jail but was eventually released when he agreed to publicly clarify that the quote stemmed from a translator's error. However, the following month he was again arrested on orders from the head of the navy, who was upset that the British news service

ITN had attributed a similar quote to him. In the end, Dabo was charged with four crimes: defamation, abuse of freedom of the press, violating state secrets, and slander. His case was pending at year's end. In late July, Dabo and three other journalists had temporarily gone into hiding after police ordered them to surrender over reports on the connection between the authorities and drug traffickers. In another act of intimidation, a special police unit, the "Ninjas," seized the camera of a journalist in July because he was taking photographs of them as they conducted an operation to clear the streets of hawkers. The camera was later returned after the journalist apologized. Separately, the interior minister ordered the radio station Bombolom to close after it reported on the murder of a state official and the excessive use of force by police to stymie subsequent riots. The police commissioner refused to enforce the minister's instructions and was later fired. The military similarly failed to close the station, which remained open at the end of the year.

The country's only television station continues to be state run, while three private radio stations—Bombolom FM, Radio Pindjiguiti, and Voice of Quelele—compete with the state-run radio broadcaster, Radio Nacional, and the Portuguese-owned public broadcaster, RTP Africa. Three privately run newspapers operate alongside the state-owned weekly *No Pintcha*. The national printing press is the sole printing plant in the country, and because it is poorly funded, there are delays in publishing newspapers. The impact of such financial constraints has been particularly severe for the state-owned media because the government is unable to earmark adequate operational funding and private advertising is directed primarily toward the private media sector. No government interference with or attempts to censor the internet were reported in 2007, and 2.5 percent of the population had access to the internet.

Guyana

Status: Partly Free

LEGAL ENVIRONMENT: 6
POLITICAL ENVIRONMENT: 14
ECONOMIC ENVIRONMENT: 11
TOTAL SCORE: 31

Survey Edition	2003	2004	2005	2006	2007
Total Score, Status	21,F	20,F	23,F	27,F	29,F

Status change explanation: Guyana declined from Free to Partly Free owing to a government decision to withdraw advertisements from the *Stabroek News*, one of the country's leading newspapers, apparently in response to critical reporting, as well as an attack at gunpoint against several reporters from another major paper.

The constitution provides for freedom of speech and of the press, and media are generally allowed to operate without interference. However, long-standing promised legislation to facilitate the distribution of private radio licenses has yet to be introduced, and a freedom of information bill is apparently unlikely to be passed into law. Independent media are able to express a variety of opinions and freely criticize the government. Nevertheless, attacks against media workers served to intimidate the press and promote self-censorship. Violence against media workers erupted in May, when staff at one of the country's main newspapers, *Kaieteur News*, were left traumatized after two men entered the editorial department and held several reporters at gunpoint, demanding to see the newspaper's publisher, Glenn Lall, who was out of the country. The assailants later fled on foot. According to the International Press Institute, the government stated that it viewed the attack as another attempt to undermine press freedom in Guyana and that the gunmen were part of a criminal network seeking to spread panic and fear in society at large.

Including the government-owned daily, the *Chronicle*, Guyana has six national newspapers and six periodicals, all of which are allowed to operate freely. Following the decision by the Government Information Agency to withdraw advertisements from the *Stabroek News*, commencing in December 2006, a number of government agencies and state corporations followed suit, based on directives from the government. The government has repeatedly insisted—including in its response in December to the special rapporteur for press freedom of the Inter-American Commission on Human Rights—that its withdrawal was based on the newspaper's declining circulation. However, most observers believe that the action was taken to constrain press freedom in reaction to critical reporting by the *Stabroek News* of the government and the People's Progressive Party during the 2006 election campaign. The government maintains a long established radio monopoly and operates the country's only 2 radio stations. There are also 23 television stations. Use of the internet is unrestricted by the government, and approximately 20 percent of the population accessed this medium in 2007.

Haiti

LEGAL ENVIRONMENT: 15
POLITICAL ENVIRONMENT: 23
ECONOMIC ENVIRONMENT: 18

Status: Partly Free

TOTAL SCORE: 56

Survey Edition	2003	2004	2005	2006	2007
Total Score, Status	79,NF	79,NF	66,NF	68,NF	59,PF

Haiti showed continued improvement in press freedom owing to a more secure political atmosphere under the 2006 coalition government and the launch of the Independent Commission to Support the Investigations of Assassinations of Journalists, which yielded prison sentences for several individuals guilty of past murders. The constitution explicitly upholds the rights of journalists to freely exercise their profession and forbids censorship except in the case of war. However, in practice, widespread poverty, a corrupt judiciary, and a tradition of excessively partial media coverage mean that journalists operate in extremely difficult conditions. The judicial system's failure to respond to numerous physical attacks against journalists, including murder, has cast a shadow over the media scene for many years. In this context, there was a significant departure from the norm in August, when President Rene Preval joined forces with the media rights organization SOS Journalistes to launch the Independent Commission to Support the Investigations of Assassinations of Journalists. The commission was given access to police and court documents with the aim of reopening investigations into the murders of at least 10 journalists. Within three weeks, two gang members received life sentences for their part in the July 2005 murder of journalist Jacques Roche. The commission's work bore further fruit on December 12, when two members of a pro–Lavalas Family Party community organization were sentenced to life for the December 2001 murder of journalist Brignol Lindor. The court also issued arrest warrants for five other members of the same organization and ordered a new investigation to be conducted with the aim of prosecuting the intellectual authors of the crime. Also in December, former police superintendent Daniel Ulysse was arrested in the capital, Port-au-Prince, in connection with the investigation into the April 2000 murder of Radio Haiti Inter director Jean Dominique.

The UN peacekeeping force, MINUSTAH, together with the national police force carried out an offensive against armed gangs in late 2006 and early 2007. The subsequent reduction in violence in many parts of Port-au-Prince made it easier for journalists to go about their work, but the gangs remained a serious threat, and two journalists were killed in 2007. Freelance photojournalist Jean-Remy Badio was shot dead in front of his home in Martissant, in the south of the capital, on January 19. UN security forces said that he was probably killed because of his photographs of gang members. Alix Joseph, station manager and news journalist at Radio-Tele Provinciale in the city of Gonaives, was shot dead on May 16. A journalist colleague said he had received threatening telephone calls protesting the radio's calls for the disarmament of local gangs. Two gang members were later arrested and charged with involvement in the murder. In February and March, Robenson Casseus, a journalist at Radio Nouvelle Generation in Port-au-Prince, was badly beaten, had his house burned down, and received anonymous telephone death threats. He believed that the attacks and threats were in response to his refusal to make favorable broadcasts on behalf of a candidate of an opposition political party. In November, Guy Delva, a Reuters correspondent, reporter for Melodie FM, and head of SOS Journalistes, left the country for three weeks after he received telephone calls issuing threats and was followed by men who appeared to be preparing an assassination attempt. Delva suggested that the death threats were in retaliation for his reports about the U.S. citizenship of Senator Rudolph Boulos. According to the Haitian constitution, someone who holds a foreign passport cannot be a senator.

There are two newspapers published several times a week and four weeklies, all privately owned. Television Nationale d'Haiti is government owned, and there are several private stations. The illiteracy rate is well over 50 percent, making radio by far the most popular medium. More than 30 stations broadcast to the capital and surrounding areas, and scores more operate in the provinces. Nevertheless, the majority of radio stations rely on a small range of sources for their news. Thus, a concentration of ownership of the main media houses that generate the news and set the news agenda significantly impacts diversity of coverage. There were no government restrictions on internet access, but usage is low—just over 7 percent of the population in 2007.

	LEGAL ENVIRONMENT: 15
	POLITICAL ENVIRONMENT: 22
Honduras	ECONOMIC ENVIRONMENT: 14
Status: Partly Free	TOTAL SCORE: 51

Survey Edition	2003	2004	2005	2006	2007
Total Score, Status	51,PF	52,PF	51,PF	52,PF	51,PF

Tensions between the press and President Manuel Zelaya's government continued in 2007, while one journalist was murdered and others were forced to flee the country owing to death threats and assassination attempts. Freedom of speech and of the press are constitutionally protected; however, the government generally does not respect these rights in practice. Despite the fact that in 2005, Honduras abolished the penal code's *desacato* (disrespect) legislation aimed at protecting the honor of public officials, other restrictive press laws are still often used to subpoena and punish journalists who report on sensitive issues such as official corruption, drug trafficking, and human rights abuses. Nevertheless, positive measures in the legal sphere were taken during the year. The Transparency and Access to Public Information Law, approved by Congress in 2006, was improved after complaints by local watchdog groups. Furthermore, a draft law was introduced in Congress in October to protect journalists and media companies from criminal charges stemming from their work, though the measure stopped short of extending similar protections to private individuals. Journalists still faced a number of legal prosecutions from political figures during the year. In September, Marcelo Chimirri, manager of the national telecommunications agency, Hondutel, filed slander lawsuits against numerous journalists for publishing reports about Hondutel's alleged misappropriation and diversion of funds. The criminal court later dismissed the case. Meanwhile, Chimirri was arrested on November 9 for publicly releasing illegally recorded tapes of government officials threatening the press that were posted on the website YouTube.com in October.

President Zelaya often criticizes the media when he perceives news reports as being unfriendly to his government and has accused journalists of exaggerating the government's mistakes and minimizing its accomplishments. In May, Zelaya announced that all radio and television stations in the country would be required to simultaneously transmit a series of 10 reports and interviews with public officials in order to "counteract media disinformation" about the government. In October, he further criticized the media and characterized their ownership as an oligopoly.

Threats and physical attacks against media workers continued in 2007, particularly targeting journalists reporting on organized crime or corruption. The local group Committee for Free Expression reported that 11 journalists were subjected to threats and intimidation during the year. In February, two journalists from the daily *La Tribuna* received death threats in connection with their investigative reporting on corruption at the Honduran Institute of Social Security. In October, radio journalist Carlos Salgado was murdered by unidentified assailants near his office at Radio Cadena Voces in Tegucigalpa. Salgado was widely known for his satirical criticism of the Honduran government and had requested police protection after he received several death threats. German David Almendarez Amador was arrested as a suspect in Salgado's killing on October 27. The news director of Radio Cadena Voces, Dagoberto Rodriguez, fled the country on November 1 after being informed by the police that his name was on a hit list. Journalist Hector Geovanny Garcia of the local television station Hondured also left the country, first in October after being fired upon in public on September 7 and again in late November as a result of death threats. Garcia had implicated officials in the Public Works Department of corruption stemming from road-surfacing contracts. Also in September, journalist Martin Ramirez was repeatedly threatened after publishing an article in *La Tribuna* suggesting connections between youth gangs and the local police.

Honduras has around nine daily papers, including the popular *El Heraldo* and *El Tiempo*. There are six private television stations and five nationally broadcasting radio stations—one state owned and four independent. Although both print and broadcast outlets are predominantly privately owned, media ownership is concentrated in the hands of a few powerful business conglomerates with intersecting political and economic ties. This has led to self-censorship among media workers. Corruption among journalists also has an unfavorable impact on reporting. In addition, the government influences media coverage through bribes, the granting or denial of access to government officials, and selective placement of official advertisements. Although the government did not restrict access to the internet, it was used by less than 4 percent of the population in 2007.

LEGAL ENVIRONMENT: 11
POLITICAL ENVIRONMENT: 10

Hong Kong

ECONOMIC ENVIRONMENT: 9

Status: Free

TOTAL SCORE: 30

Survey Edition	2003	2004	2005	2006	2007
Total Score, Status	NA	NA	28,F	29,F	30,F

Although freedom of expression is provided for under the law and Hong Kong media remain lively, press freedom has been threatened in recent years by an increase in self-censorship. Under Article 27 of the Basic Law, Hong Kong residents enjoy freedoms of speech, press, and publication. Nevertheless, these rights risk being undermined owing to the power of the Chinese National People's Congress to make the final interpretation of Hong Kong's Basic Law, Chinese surveillance in the territory, economic interests of media owners in the Chinese market, and the chilling effect of the 2005 sentencing of Hong Kong journalist Ching Cheong to a five-year prison sentence in China on charges of spying for Taiwan. In a series of cases that raised concerns over selective application of the Broadcasting Ordinance, several individuals were summoned to court during the year in relation to broadcasts of the prodemocracy pirate radio station Citizens' Radio. Among those charged with "using unlicensed equipment when delivering a political message" was activist Szeto Wah, who had participated as a guest speaker in a May 2007 program on the 1989 crackdown on the prodemocracy movement in Beijing. The station, which has been broadcasting intermittently since 2005, had its license application rejected in December 2006. The cases were pending at year's end.

Outright attacks on the press did not occur in 2007 as they did in March 2006, when four men armed with hammers broke into the office of the *Epoch Times*, a newspaper known for criticizing the Chinese Communist Party and reporting on China's persecution of the Falun Gong spiritual group. Despite the absence of violence, many journalists practice self-censorship. A survey conducted by the Hong Kong University Public Opinion Program found that close to half of respondents believed that news media practiced self-censorship and that nearly 30 percent of journalists admitted to doing so. Another January 2007 survey by the Hong Kong Journalists Association found that 58 percent of local journalists thought press freedom in Hong Kong had deteriorated since the end of British rule in 1997. The most common types of self-censorship were reportedly downplaying negative news about the central government in Beijing, downplaying information on issues deemed to be sensitive by the Chinese Communist Party, and downplaying information detrimental to media owners or their interests. International media organizations operate freely in Hong Kong, and foreign reporters do not need government-issued identification to operate.

Despite self-censorship, media remain outspoken and political debate is vigorous in the extremely diverse and partisan press. Hong Kong has 49 daily newspapers (including 23 in Chinese and 13 in English); 4 of them are funded by pro-Beijing interests and follow the Chinese Communist Party's lead on political and social issues. Controversy continued during the year over the future of the government-owned Radio Television Hong Kong (RTHK) after a review panel recommended that a new public broadcaster be established but did not comment on RTHK's future. The findings were widely interpreted as a threat to media freedom and the continued existence of RTHK, with particular criticism leveled at the absence of public broadcasting experts on the review panel. In the past, RTHK has come under pressure for not defending or promoting government policies, for criticizing Beijing, and for its coverage of Taiwan. There are no restrictions on internet access. Hong Kong has the highest internet usage rate in Asia, with broadband service available in 74 percent of households.

Hungary

Status: Free

LEGAL ENVIRONMENT: 5
POLITICAL ENVIRONMENT: 9
ECONOMIC ENVIRONMENT: 7
TOTAL SCORE: 21

Survey Edition	2003	2004	2005	2006	2007
Total Score, Status	23,F	20,F	21,F	21,F	21,F

Hungary's constitution protects freedom of speech and of the press. Numerous competitive and independent media outlets generally operate without interference from the state, and many clearly reflect the divisions of the national political scene. In 2007, the media scored a victory when it uncovered a number of high-profile incidents of corruption. The Media Law of 1996 continues to be widely criticized as reinforcing entrenched interests and institutionalizing political interference rather than protecting press freedom. Libel remains a criminal offense, and the criminal code holds journalists responsible not only for their own words, but also for publicizing insulting or libelous statements made by others. Restrictive state secrecy legislation has also raised concerns and brought criticism by the Organization for Security and Cooperation in Europe Representative on Freedom of the Media. A Constitutional Court decision to abolish the capacity of the country's media regulatory body, ORTT, to levy fines and sanctions against media outlets has left a regulatory vacuum.

While most media seem to operate freely, media advocates have noted a slight progovernmental bias in most state-owned media. Some individual journalists were also exposed to pressure from state organs, and there were two incidents of detainment and questionings. One television journalist covering politics was pressured into leaving a morning show after a boycott by several political parties. In several isolated incidents, journalists have been harassed by law enforcement authorities and others, including the arrest and fining of two journalists covering an unauthorized demonstration and the questioning of journalists investigating allegedly corrupt public officials. In June, investigative journalist Iren Karman was abducted and severely beaten; the assailants have yet to be identified, but Karman was working on a documentary on the Mafia and had recently published a book on the subject.

The media landscape is dominated by private companies, with high levels of foreign investment in both national and local newspapers. Diversity is on the rise in both print and electronic media; most notably, there has been an increase in vibrant and influential domestically owned electronic media outlets. The internet is widely available, is governed by a voluntary code of conduct introduced by a professional association of internet content and service providers, and was accessed by over 35 percent of the population in 2007. During the year, the government attempted to block the extreme right-wing website kuruc. info for publishing anti-Semitic information and contact information for a number of government officials but was unable to do so because the site was hosted by a foreign server.

Iceland

Status: Free

LEGAL ENVIRONMENT: 1
POLITICAL ENVIRONMENT: 4
ECONOMIC ENVIRONMENT: 4
TOTAL SCORE: 9

Survey Edition	2003	2004	2005	2006	2007
Total Score, Status	8,F	8,F	9,F	9,F	9,F

Freedom of the press and of expression are protected under Article 72 of the constitution, and the government generally does not interfere in the independent media's expression of a wide variety of views. However, there are limitations to these rights, including fines or imprisonment for people who belittle the doctrines of officially recognized religious groups. Additionally, people may face fines and up to two years' imprisonment for assaults against race, religion, nationality, or sexual orientation. In March 2007, Icelandic singer Bubbi Morthens won US$11,000 in a libel case against gossip magazine *Her og no* In June 2005, the magazine featured a cover image of the singer smoking a cigarette and insinuated falsely that he had recommenced using drugs. There were no reports of physical attacks against journalists in 2007.

A wide range of publications includes both independent and party-affiliated newspapers. Icelandic National Broadcasting Service (RUV) runs radio and television stations funded by both a license fee and advertising revenue. RUV was reestablished as a public corporation in March 2007 after having previously operated as a state-owned institution; the switch is expected to help ensure the organization's autonomy. Nonetheless, according to the British Broadcasting Corporation, RUV is obliged to promote Icelandic history, culture, and language. Media concentration is a concern in Iceland since the company 365 controls much of television and radio broadcasting as well as one of the major national newspapers and several magazines. In 2007, 85 percent of the country's population (down from 87 percent the previous year) was reported to have used the internet, which is unrestricted by the government.

India

Status: Partly Free

LEGAL ENVIRONMENT: 10
POLITICAL ENVIRONMENT: 16
ECONOMIC ENVIRONMENT: 9
TOTAL SCORE: 35

Survey Edition	2003	2004	2005	2006	2007
Total Score, Status	45,PF	41,PF	38,PF	37,PF	35,PF

India's media continue to be vigorous and are by far the freest in South Asia, although journalists face a number of constraints. The constitution provides for freedom of speech and of expression, and although there are some legal limitations, these rights are generally upheld. In recent years, the government has occasionally used its power under the Official Secrets Act to censor security-related articles or prosecute members of the press, but no cases were reported during 2007. State and national governments have also on occasion used other security laws, contempt of court charges, and criminal defamation legislation to curb the media and other critical voices. In 2006, parliament had passed an amendment to the Contempt of Courts Act that introduced truth as a defense. However, in a troubling test case that was condemned by local professional groups, in September 2007, a New Delhi court sentenced the publisher of the *Mid-Day* newspaper, as well as two editors and a cartoonist, to four-month prison terms for contempt of court after they ran an article accusing a former senior judge of issuing a ruling that benefited his son; the four were eventually freed pending an appeal. The Press Council of India, an independent body composed of journalists, publishers, and politicians, serves as a self-regulatory mechanism for the print press through its investigations of complaints of misconduct or irresponsible reporting. No similar body exists for the broadcast media, which have become known for undercover sting operations conducted as part of investigative reports. A broadcasting services regulation bill, which was introduced in 2006 and reintroduced in 2007, could give the government greater power over the media, restrict media cross-ownership, and introduce greater content regulation for news channels—all proposals that have been opposed by broadcasters themselves as well as by journalists groups.

Intimidation of journalists by a variety of actors continues; on a number of occasions during 2007, reporters were attacked or detained by police or others while attempting to cover the news, and others were abducted or threatened by right-wing groups, insurgents, local-level officials, or criminals. Offices were also targeted during the year: Two employees of the Tamil newspaper *Dinakaran* were killed in a May arson attack on the paper's Madurai office by supporters of one of the sons of the state's chief minister, and in August, the Mumbai office of the influential national magazine *Outlook* was attacked by members of the Shiv Sena, a Hindu nationalist group.

Members of the press are particularly vulnerable in rural areas and insurgency-racked states such as Chhattisgarh, Kashmir, Assam, and Manipur. Conditions in Manipur worsened in 2007, according to the Committee to Protect Journalists, as journalists faced threats from competing militant groups as well as a new state government directive banning the publication of any statements made by "unlawful organizations." At least twice during the year, media outlets responded to pressure by ceasing operations temporarily, thus depriving the public of news. In neighboring Assam, Afrida Hussain, a reporter for Northeast Television (NETV), was assaulted in March by hospital security guards in Guwahati when she attempted to interview a group of hospitalized women. NETV, the only private satellite channel in northeast India, had also faced threats in January from the outlawed United Liberation Front of Asom (ULFA) militant group and received criticism of its reports from official quarters. Conditions are particularly difficult in the state of Jammu and Kashmir, where the fact that militants routinely issue death threats against local media personnel has led to significant levels of self-censorship. In March 2007, cable operators across the region suspended broadcasts of four popular English-language entertainment channels whose programming militants denounced as obscene. Pressure to self-censor has also been reported at smaller media outlets that rely on state government advertising for the majority of their revenue. Photojournalist Maqbool Sahil has been detained since September 2004 under the Public Safety Act despite repeated high court decisions calling for his release.

Most print media, particularly the national and English-language press, are privately owned, provide diverse coverage, and frequently scrutinize the government. The broadcast media are predominantly in private hands, but the state retains a monopoly on AM radio broadcasting, and private FM radio stations are not allowed to broadcast news content. In November 2006, the government announced a new policy designed to legitimize community radio and enable nonprofit groups and others to apply for station licenses; this improvement has fostered a modest increase in the growth of community radio stations, leading to a greater diversity of voices and topics covered. Doordarshan, the state-controlled television station, has been accused of manipulating the news to favor the government, and some private satellite TV channels also provide slanted coverage that reflects the political affiliation of their owners, according to the U.S. State Department. Foreign media are allowed to operate freely. The internet, accessed by 3.5 percent of the population in 2007, remains unrestricted, although some states have proposed legislation that would require the registration of customers at internet cafés, and the government retains the right to censor the internet, particularly on the grounds of morality or national security.

Indonesia

LEGAL ENVIRONMENT: 17
POLITICAL ENVIRONMENT: 22
ECONOMIC ENVIRONMENT: 15

Status: Partly Free

TOTAL SCORE: 54

Survey Edition	2003	2004	2005	2006	2007
Total Score, Status	56,PF	55,PF	58,PF	58,PF	54,PF

The media landscape saw both positive and negative turns in 2007, with important court rulings and a vibrant press offset by legal harassment from powerful politicians and businesses, as well as continued attacks against journalists. Freedom of speech and of the press are provided for in the constitution and the 1999 Press Law; however, these rights were at times restricted in practice, particularly under criminal defamation provisions. In July 2007, the Constitutional Court declared unconstitutional Articles 154 and 155 of the Penal Code, which criminalized "public expression of feelings of hostility, hatred, or contempt toward the government." This followed a 2006 landmark ruling that decriminalized insults against the president and vice president. In another important case, in April 2007, a South Jakarta district court acquitted *Playboy* editor in chief Erwin Arnada of publishing indecent material, ruling that any charges against the editor should have been made under the Press Law instead of the penal code. The overall legal picture remained mixed, however, with the question of which piece of legislation should be used in criminal defamation cases often depending upon the educational background of the presiding judge. Thus, in September 2007, criminal charges were brought under the penal code against *Koran Tempo* newspaper columnist Bersihar Lubis, who was accused of insulting the Office of the Attorney General in an article criticizing a ban on a high school history textbook. Also in September, in a defamation decision criticized by press freedom groups, the Supreme Court overturned two lower court rulings and ordered *Time* magazine to pay former president Suharto 1 trillion rupiah (US$106 million) in damages over a 1999 story accusing him and his family of embezzling US$15 billion. A spokesman for the Court said it concluded that the story had damaged the former dictator's "reputation and honor."

In 2007, press advocates also expressed concern about what appeared to be a new trend in which powerful corporations tried to obstruct the press through legal harassment, reportedly leading to increased self-censorship. In one such case, the Riau Andalan Pulp & Paper Corporation, owned by business tycoon Sukanto Tanoto, filed a defamation suit against *Koran Tempo* newspaper after it reported on illegal logging in Sumatra. The July 2007 story quoted a local police chief as stating that of the 189 cases of illegal logging in the province of Riau, 25 involved Riau Andalan Pulp & Paper. In another corporate-related case, police tapped the private cell phone of a *Tempo* journalist and circulated transcripts of his text messages after he had reported on a corruption scandal involving crude palm oil producer Asian Agri, also owned by Tanoto.

Violence and intimidation of journalists continued to be an issue in 2007. Nevertheless, the Indonesian press remains vibrant, with journalists aggressively reporting on issues such as high-level corruption and environmental degradation. The Alliance of Independent Journalists (AJI), the country's largest journalists union, recorded 75 cases of press freedom violations in 2007, including incidents of physical violence, verbal threats, and legal harassment, an increase over the previous year's 53 cases. According to AJI, the most dangerous province for journalists was Jakarta. While no limitations exist on local news broadcasts, several implementing regulations passed in 2005 ban live broadcasts of foreign programs by domestic carriers. In May 2007, the Supreme Court refused a request by the broadcasting commission and a coalition of nongovernmental organizations to review the regulations. On November 17, a coroner in New South Wales, Australia, issued a report establishing that the Indonesian army had "deliberately killed" the British, New Zealand, and Australian reporters known as "the Balibo Five" who were in East Timor covering the 1975 invasion. In March, a judge in a coroner's court in Sydney issued an arrest warrant for a former Indonesian army officer, but Indonesia refused to acknowledge the Court's findings. The government continued to ban foreign journalists from entering West Papua.

Indonesia is home to a wide number of independent media outlets that are generally able to provide a wide variety of opinions and perspectives. Obstruction of the press by large corporations and powerful individuals appears to be especially effective at a time of increased media consolidation. With only seven large companies dominating Indonesian mass media, press advocates argued that owners were increasingly cautious about publishing stories that might offend powerful companies or individuals. The broadcast market includes some 60 private radio stations in the Jakarta area alone and 10 private television networks nationwide that operate in competition with the public Televisi Republik Indonesia. Strict licensing laws have created more than 2,000 illegal television and radio stations that operate on a regular basis without a license. In a countrywide survey, half of the journalists questioned revealed that their salaries were too low to cover basic living costs, as more than 60 percent of journalists earn less than US$200 a month. Widespread corruption in the legal system, as well as the perception that a favorable verdict could be bought, kept most newspaper or television journalists from reporting on stories that were likely to lead to lawsuits. Accessed in 2007 by 20 million people—over 8 percent of the population—the internet is gaining popularity; there are no reported government restrictions on access, but the lack of high-speed infrastructure outside the major cities limits its use as a news source. In November, Indonesia held its first national bloggers conference, attended by some 500 bloggers.

Iran
Status: Not Free

LEGAL ENVIRONMENT: 29
POLITICAL ENVIRONMENT: 34
ECONOMIC ENVIRONMENT: 22
TOTAL SCORE: 85

Survey Edition	2003	2004	2005	2006	2007
Total Score, Status	76,NF	79,NF	80,NF	84,NF	84,NF

Press freedom deteriorated in 2007 as the regime's conservative leaders continued to crack down on critical publications, journalists, and bloggers through arrests, detentions, and newspaper closures. The Iranian authorities were especially restrictive on coverage of women's rights issues, antigovernment demonstrations, the ailing economy, and the development of nuclear technology. The constitution provides for limited freedom of opinion and of the press. However, numerous laws restrict press freedom, including the 2000 Press Law, which forbids the publication of ideas that are contrary to Islamic principles or detrimental to public rights. The government regularly invokes vaguely worded legislation to criminalize critical opinions. Article 500 of the penal code states that "anyone who undertakes any form of propaganda against the state...will be sentenced to between three months and one year in prison"; the code leaves "propaganda" undefined. Under Article 513, offenses deemed to be an "insult to religion" can be punishable by death or by prison terms of one to five years for lesser offenses, with "insult" similarly undefined. Other articles provide sentences of up to two years in prison, up to 74 lashes, or a fine for those convicted of intentionally creating "anxiety and unease in the public's mind," spreading "false rumors," writing about "acts that are not true," and criticizing state officials. Iran's judiciary frequently denies accused journalists due process by referring their cases to the Islamic Revolutionary Court, an emergency venue intended for those suspected of seeking to overthrow the regime. The Preventive Restraint Act is used regularly without legal proceedings to temporarily ban publications.

Charges against journalists and publications are often arbitrary. Prosecutions and sentences are drawn out, and bail sums for provisional release while awaiting trial are substantial. Editors and publishers are prohibited from hiring journalists who have previously been sentenced, and many journalists are forbidden to leave Iran. The successive arrests and closures of media outlets have led to widespread self-censorship among journalists. The government's Office of Public Relations announced the creation of a special team in July whose mandate is to confront publications critical of the government.

In 2007, more than 50 journalists were prosecuted or imprisoned, some without charge, according to Reporters Sans Frontieres. At least 10 journalists remained in prison at the end of the year. The Iranian authorities accused several other journalists of having ties to foreign governments, as was the case with Iranian-American journalist Parnaz Azima, who was working for the Persian-language services of the U.S.-backed Radio Farda. She was charged with disseminating propaganda against the Islamic Republic and engaging in activities against national security. Azima was among four people with dual citizenship who were detained during the year. All were later released on bail or allowed to leave the country. The government continued to intimidate and persecute journalists who covered the country's ethnic minority issues. Kurdish journalists Adnan Hassanpour and Abdolvahed Boutimar were sentenced to death in July 2007 for expressing their views on the Kurdish issue, based on charges of endangering national security and engaging in propaganda against the state. The Supreme Court upheld the death sentence for Hassanpour in December but overturned Boutimar's verdict. At least three other Kurdish journalists and one ethnic Arab journalist were imprisoned for their reports on the government's harsh treatment of minorities. The Iranian authorities also monitored student-run media, shutting down student publications and arresting eight student editors at Amir Kabir University in May 2007 for insulting state leaders and inciting public opinion. Three of the students were prosecuted in July and sentenced to between two and three years in prison. Their sentences were eventually reduced in December to four months in prison, and the three were ordered to be released; however, prison authorities refused to release them at year's end. Journalists also fell victim to violent attacks during the year. In November, two journalists were stabbed in separate incidents by unknown assailants.

A report by the Association of Iranian Journalists in 2007 stated that the profession has suffered in quality and financial stability since the conservative government began cracking down on independent newspapers. The Ministry of Culture and Islamic Guidance has banned or closed more than 100 publications since 2000. The crackdown continued in 2007, focusing primarily on reformist media outlets. At least 11 publications were suspended, 4 of them indefinitely. The proreform dailies *Shargh* and *Ham-Mihan* were shut down during the summer, a few months after they had resumed publication following previous suspensions. In September, a Tehran court confirmed the closure of the reformist daily *Golestan-e Iran*, which had been suspended since 2004, charging it with publishing content that was "lying and hostile to the Islamic regime" and "offending against decency." The deputy interior minister announced a new policy on September 30 forbidding any media from reporting on any party or political group that was not licensed by Commission 10 on Political Parties.

In 2007, there were some 20 major print dailies. The most widely distributed newspaper is the government-supported *Keyhan*, with a circulation of 350,000. Owing to limited distribution of print media outside larger cities, radio and television serve as the principal sources of news for many citizens, with more than 80 percent of residents receiving their news from television. The government maintains a direct monopoly of all domestic broadcast media and presents only official political and religious viewpoints. Together with the Persian-language channels, the state-run Islamic Republic of Iran Broadcasting targets Arabic speakers in Iraq and the Middle East via the Al-Alam and Al-Kawthar television networks. A government-run, English-language satellite station, Press TV, was launched in July 2007. President Mahmoud Ahmadinejad said its mission would be "to stand by the oppressed of the world," according to the BBC. Although it is forbidden, an increasing number of people own satellite dishes and access international news sources. Satellite radio stations such as the U.S.-backed Radio Farda and the Dutch-funded Radio Zamaneh also provide international broadcasts to a large part of the population.

Public use of high-speed internet connections was banned in October 2006. However, internet usage continued to increase dramatically in 2007, with a 7,100 percent growth rate since 2000—by far the largest in the Middle Eastern region, according to Internet World Stats. In January, the government announced that all websites and blogs needed to register with the authorities before March 1, yet only a very small number of sites actually registered, leading authorities to change the regulation to apply only to sites or blogs with their own domain. Iranian authorities systematically censor internet content by forcing internet service providers (ISPs) to block access to a growing list of "immoral sites and political sites that insult the country's religious and political leaders." Since the summer of 2006, the censors have focused their efforts on online publications such as *Zanestan* that deal with women's rights issues. In November, online journalist and women's rights activist Maryam Hosseinkhah was charged with disturbing public opinion, engaging in propaganda against the regime, and spreading false news. Hosseinkhah and a number of other women's activists who were charged and detained throughout the year were involved in a web campaign seeking to gather signatures in protest of Iranian laws that discriminate against women. Several Iranian news websites, such as *Emrouz*, *Ruydad*, and *Rooz Online*, were filtered. Conservative news websites were also subject to censorship. In the beginning of the year, the conservative online publication *Baztab* was blocked for publishing reports on Iran's nuclear industry and on corruption, in which President Ahmadinejad was criticized. Access to international news websites and international organizations is increasingly restricted, and there were contradictory reports on the censoring of YouTube, Facebook, MySpace, and Flickr, indicating that the blocking of websites is occurring at the ISP level and not through an official ban. Nevertheless, websites continue to communicate opinions that the country's print media would never publish, with both reform advocates and conservatives promoting their political agendas. Iran's most popular blogs oppose the regime, and many bloggers publish anonymously. The internet has also provided a key platform for international initiatives—such as Article 19's Persianimpediment.org, Freedom House's *Gozaar*, and *Rooz Online*—that promote freedom of expression and inform the Iranian public on human rights issues.

Iraq

Status: Not Free

LEGAL ENVIRONMENT: 22
POLITICAL ENVIRONMENT: 31
ECONOMIC ENVIRONMENT: 16
TOTAL SCORE: 69

Survey Edition	2003	2004	2005	2006	2007
Total Score, Status	95,NF	66,NF	70,NF	71,NF	70,NF

Iraq continued to be the most dangerous place in the world for the press, with several dozen journalists and media workers killed during the year. The two greatest challenges to press freedom remained the ongoing security issues and the restrictions on investigating corruption and abuses of power. Both freedom of opinion and freedom of the press are guaranteed in Article 36 of the 2005 constitution, provided these rights are exercised "in a way that does not violate public order or morality." The constitution also outlines a legal framework for the creation of an independent National Communications and Media Commission to regulate broadcast media. However, Iraqi laws restrict the press and allow for fines and imprisonment of up to seven years for anyone who insults the national assembly, the government, or public authorities. The media are also prohibited from supporting the Ba'ath Party, inciting violence or civil disorder, or calling for a change in Iraq's borders through violent means. In addition, a number of restrictive laws dating from Saddam Hussein's rule remain on the books, and some emergency orders from the Coalition Provisional Authority (CPA) period are still in effect. The press may also still be prosecuted under the 1969 penal code, which criminalizes libel, defamation, the disclosure of state secrets, and the spreading of "false news." Several amendments to laws governing the press have been circulated, and the constitution itself is still being revised, which may or may not improve legal protections for the press.

The parliament of the Kurdistan Regional Government (KRG) approved a new press bill in December that had been drafted in cooperation with the Kurdistan Journalists Syndicate. The draft is rather restrictive, however, and proposes fines of up to 10 million dinars (US$8,200) for various vaguely worded offenses such as disturbing security, spreading fear, and encouraging terrorism. The new law could have a crippling effect on the many journalists already facing a multitude of frivolous libel charges. Owing to pressure from the Kurdish media and watchdog groups like the Journalistic Freedoms Observatory, President Masoud Barzani refused to sign the law and returned it for revision to the KRG parliament.

While the number of arrests and detentions of journalists by Iraqi security forces and U.S. forces declined considerably in 2007, the Iraqi authorities employed other forms of legal harassment of the media. The government maintained its policy of curbing broadcasters using CPA Order 14, which prohibits the media from "inciting violence." The local offices of Sunni TV channels Al-Zaura and Salah al-Din as well as the Dubai-based satellite channel Al-Sharqiya were closed down in late 2006 and early 2007 for airing footage of Iraqis protesting Saddam Hussein's execution. The stations continued to air on satellite channels hosted outside the country. The Iraqi offices of satellite channel Al-Jazeera remained closed after being shut down by the government in 2004. Citing security reasons, the government placed restrictions on reporting on bomb attack sites in May, and starting in November, journalists were forbidden to go to the Kandil Mountains to cover hostilities between the Kurdistan Worker's Party (PKK) and Turkish forces. Eleven employees of Wasan Media were arrested on February 25 and charged with inciting terror for sharing video footage with Al-Jazeera of an interview with a woman who was allegedly raped by police. While all charges were dropped, two of the media workers remained in jail at the end of the year for charges of possessing unlicensed weapons. Harassment and intimidation of independent journalists also increased in the Kurdistan region over the last couple of years, with several editors of independent publications such as the *Hawlati* being jailed and resigning from their posts over threats of imprisonment for publishing articles critical of the KRG.

The case of Associated Press photographer Bilal Hussein, who had been held by the U.S. military without charge for 20 months, finally came before an Iraqi court in December. The hearings were held in secrecy, and Hussein was never formally charged. U.S. officials have claimed that Hussein had been working with insurgent groups who had given him privileged access to their attacks, but the Associated Press was able to discredit some of these claims. Hussein remained in detention at the end of the year. All other journalists detained by U.S. forces have been released, most without being formally charged.

According to the Committee to Protect Journalists (CPJ), 32 journalists and 12 media support staff were killed in 2007. All journalists killed were Iraqi nationals, with the exception of one Russian photographer working for CBS. Although some journalists are caught in the crossfire, most are victims of deliberately targeted attacks by insurgent groups and militias that often go unpunished. Insurgent groups have been known to issue "death lists" of journalists. On June 7, female reporter Sahar Hussein Ali al-Haydari was singled out and killed by four gunmen associated with the al-Qaeda-affiliated group the Islamic State of Iraq. Al-Haydari worked for the National Iraqi News Agency and the independent news agency Aswat al-Iraq. An American air strike killed a Reuters photographer and his assistant on July 12 along with nine other Iraqis. Reuters called for an investigation into the air strike, which eyewitnesses claimed was fired indiscriminately. The CPJ criticized a Pentagon investigation report on the 2004 killing of two employees of the Al-Arabiya satellite television channel by U.S. troops. U.S. forces have been responsible for the deaths of at least 16 journalists since 2003.

According to Reporters Sans Frontieres, armed groups kidnapped 25 media workers in 2007, and although most were freed shortly after, 5 of those kidnapped were killed. Kidnappers still held 14 Iraqi journalists at the end of the year, including 5 who were kidnapped in 2006. On April 3, gunmen seized Othman al-Mashhadani, a reporter for the Saudi Arabian daily *Al-Watan* who had reported on various sectarian militias, including the Shiite Mahdi army and the Sunni Islamic army. The kidnappers called his family and asked for a ransom, but he was found tortured and dead three days later. Many kidnappings target local journalists working for foreign media as correspondents or stringers. Most journalists practice a high level of self-censorship in response to the extralegal intimidation and violence, as well as the threat and implementation of restrictive press laws.

The diversity of the media in Iraq increased dramatically after the fall of Saddam Hussein. Iraq now has more than 100 daily and weekly publications and dozens of private television and radio channels. Nevertheless, the financial viability of these outlets is severely threatened by the security situation, and many publications have very small circulations. Nearly all media outlets are privately owned and operated; many are financially dependent on or affiliated with ethnic, sectarian, or partisan groups, primarily out of economic necessity. In conjunction with poor training for journalists, the media environment reflects a plurality of viewpoints but a lack of balanced journalism. Traditional, independent journalism is spearheaded by successful publications such as *Assabah Aljadeed* and *Hawlati* and news agencies such as Aswat al-Iraq. Media infrastructure has improved with information and communication technologies and new printing presses in Baghdad and Basra. The government-controlled Iraqi Media Network includes Al-Iraqiya television, the *Al-Sabah* newspaper, and radio stations throughout the country. Among the largest domestic television stations is Al-Sharqiya, which broadcasts from Dubai and features news, soap operas, and satire. The popularity of foreign satellite television, previously banned under Saddam Hussein except in the northern Kurdish regions where it was legalized in 1991, has increased immensely since the 2003 invasion. Around one-third of all Iraqi families now own a satellite dish.

Internet use was severely limited during the Saddam Hussein era, but many internet cafés have opened up since 2003. There are no direct government restrictions on internet access, but owing to the security situation, power failures, and lack of infrastructure, the number of private internet users remains small even by regional standards.

Ireland

	LEGAL ENVIRONMENT: 4
	POLITICAL ENVIRONMENT: 6
	ECONOMIC ENVIRONMENT: 5
Status: Free	TOTAL SCORE: 15

Survey Edition	2003	2004	2005	2006	2007
Total Score, Status	16,F	16,F	15,F	15,F	16,F

Press freedom is constitutionally guaranteed and generally respected in practice. However, archaic defamation laws are still in place under which journalists remain guilty until proven innocent. A defamation bill introduced in late 2006 was still under debate in parliament at the end of 2007, though it had been passed in the Senate earlier in the year. The proposed law would abolish criminal, seditious, and obscene libel, although it allows for a sentence of up to five years for "gravely harmful statements." The law also includes the defense of "reasonable publication," under which journalists would not be held liable for defamatory statements if they acted in accordance with professional ethics and the public interest. The law is expected to give official recognition to the independent press ombudsman and the newly formed Press Council. The ombudsman, appointed in August 2007, would be responsible for investigating and adjudicating public press complaints. Unresolved cases would be passed along to the Press Council, which was established in January 2007. A Privacy Law proposed in 2006 was not discussed in the senate in 2007 and is unlikely to be passed in the near future.

In late 2006, *Irish Times* editor Geraldine Kennedy and senior correspondent Colm Keena were accused of publishing classified information in an article disclosing details of the investigation of Bertie

Ahern, the prime minister, by the Mahon Tribunal, a government anticorruption body. Following their indictment, the journalists destroyed all relevant documents in order to protect their source. In October 2007, the high court ordered Kennedy and Keena to answer questions before the tribunal or face up to two years in prison or a fine of 300,000 Euros (US$461,677). The questioning was postponed pending an appeal to the Supreme Court scheduled for early 2008. In February, freelance reporter Mick McCaffrey was arrested in connection with an August 2006 article about police mishandling of the 1997 arrest and imprisonment of an innocent man on murder charges. McCaffrey cited a confidential police report in the article. The police demanded that McCaffrey reveal his source and seized his phone records. McCaffrey refused but was released nonetheless the next day.

The national public broadcaster, Radio Telefis Eireann, dominates the radio and television sectors, but the growth of cable and satellite has begun to weaken the state broadcaster's monopoly over the industry. According to the U.S. State Department, there were 58 independent radio stations and 2 independent television stations operating during the year. British public and private television offers the main competition to Irish programming. According to the BBC, media cross-ownership is permitted within limits—press groups may own no more than 25 percent of local television and radio. Newspapers were dominated by the Independent News and Media Group, though diversity in views and political affiliations was seen across the multitude of dailies and weeklies produced in 2007. Internet access is unrestricted by the government, and 50 percent of Irish citizens use the internet regularly.

Israel

LEGAL ENVIRONMENT: 6
POLITICAL ENVIRONMENT: 14
ECONOMIC ENVIRONMENT: 8

Status: Free

TOTAL SCORE: 28

Survey Edition	2003	2004	2005	2006	2007
Total Score, Status	27,F	28,F	28,F	28,F	29,F

Press freedom is generally respected in Israel, and the country features a vibrant media landscape. Nevertheless, several incidents during the year tested the scope of press freedom, particularly with regard to coverage of events in Lebanon and Syria. In general, an independent judiciary and an active civil society adequately protect the free media. Hate speech and publishing praise of violence are prohibited, and the 1948 Prevention of Terrorism Ordinance prohibits expressions of support for terrorist organizations or groups that call for the destruction of Israel. Journalists operating in Israel require accreditation by the Government Press Office (GPO) to have access to government buildings and official press conferences or passage across military checkpoints. The GPO has been known to occasionally refuse press cards on political and security grounds, especially to Palestinians. Freedom of information is provided for by law and generally respected. However, in recent years, local human rights groups have lodged petitions with the courts against government bodies for not publishing internal regulations or annual reports. A law that forbids Israeli citizens from traveling to "enemy states" without permission from the Ministry of the Interior raised concerns in 2007 when three journalists were interrogated and faced potential prosecution for having reported from Syria and Lebanon. Press freedom organizations condemned the selective application of the law, as well as the implications of such travel restrictions on the diversity of news sources available to the Israeli public.

While newspaper and magazine articles on security matters are subject to a military censor, the scope of permissible reporting is wide and there is a broad range of published material. Editors may appeal a censorship decision to a three-member tribunal that includes two civilians, and publications cannot be shuttered because of censorship violations. Arabic-language publications are censored more frequently than those in Hebrew, while coverage of the Arab minority in the mainstream Hebrew press is limited. The Special Committee of the Israeli Press Council released a report in April concluding that earlier accusations by security officials were false and the media had not in fact endangered lives with their reporting during the July–August 2006 conflict in Lebanon.

Cases of physical threats and the harassment of journalists are rare. However, in recent years, authorities have been known to detain Arab journalists, especially those reporting for media outlets perceived as hostile to Israel. In July, Israel detained Atta Farahat, a correspondent for Syrian Public Television and the *Al-Watan* daily newspaper who was living in the Golan Heights. The Syrian Center for Media and Freedom of Expression speculated that Farahat was suspected of "collaborating with an enemy state" related to his journalism for Syrian media outlets. According to Reporters Sans Frontieres, Farahat remained in custody at year's end, and Israeli courts issued orders prohibiting his lawyers or the

Israeli press from talking about the case. Another media blackout was instituted in September for one month surrounding an Israeli air strike on a Syrian military facility. In addition, media access to the details of a police investigation of Azmi Bishara, an Arab member of the Knesset accused of espionage, was restricted until a court partially lifted the blackout in April. Mordechai Vanunu, who served 18 years for espionage and disclosing information about Israel's nuclear weapons program, was sent back to jail for six months in July after speaking to international journalists about his case, thus violating the terms of his 2004 release. In an incident in November that was condemned by the local Foreign Press Association as endangering reporters, police officers in Tel Aviv disguised themselves as journalists from the Channel 2 television station in an undercover operation to arrest a Palestinian suspect.

Israel has a free and lively press, with 12 daily newspapers, 90 weekly newspapers, and a number of internet news sites that cover a broad range of political viewpoints and religious outlooks. All newspapers are privately owned, freely criticize government policy, and actively investigate high-level corruption. Nevertheless, concentration and cross-ownership have enabled a small number of families—some with close personal ties to prominent politicians—to control the press. A diverse selection of broadcast media is also available. Television started to be privatized in the early 1990s, and since then, the number of commercial networks has grown exponentially. Most Israelis subscribe to cable or satellite services that also provide access to international commercial stations. As a result, the dominance of the state-run Israel Broadcasting Authority (IBA) in the television market has waned significantly. The IBA's radio station Kol Israel and the military-operated Galei Tsahal remain popular, while a diverse range of pirate radio stations also operate, serving the country's ultra-Orthodox, Russian-speaking, and Arabic-speaking populations in particular. The government does not restrict internet access, which is widespread and used by over 55 percent of the population.

[This rating and report reflect the state of press freedom within Israel proper, not in the West Bank and Gaza Strip, which are covered in the following report on the Israeli-Occupied Territories and Palestinian Authority.]

Israeli-Occupied Territories/ Palestinian Authority

LEGAL ENVIRONMENT: 28
POLITICAL ENVIRONMENT: 34
ECONOMIC ENVIRONMENT: 22

Status: Not Free

TOTAL SCORE: 84

Survey Edition	2003	2004	2005	2006	2007
Total Score, Status	86,NF	86,NF	84,NF	86,NF	84,NF

While events in the West Bank and Gaza Strip are covered extensively by the international media, both Israel and the Palestinian Authority (PA) severely restrict press freedom and often impede the ability of the media to report safely and accurately. The environment for reporting from the West Bank and Gaza Strip further deteriorated in 2007 as journalists came under attack from both militant factions and the leadership of the Islamist party Hamas, which took over authority of the Gaza Strip in June. An atmosphere of impunity continued for crimes against the media, with very few prosecutions of perpetrators by either Israel or the PA. Nevertheless, while journalists' ability to report fully on events was severely hampered by threats of violence, the Palestinian press continued to be relatively vigorous and candid in its coverage of political affairs compared with the situation in other countries in the region. The Palestinian Basic Law and the 1995 Press Law provide for freedom of the press and an independent media. However, the Press Law also stipulates that journalists may be punished and newspapers closed for publishing material deemed harmful to national unity or likely to incite crime, hatred, division, or sectarian dissension. In August, Hamas leaders announced that they intended to apply the 1995 Press Law and imprison journalists for violating such provisions, but there were no reports of its enforcement.

Israel's army and security services continued to commit a range of abuses against the press in 2007. Journalists were subject to gunfire, physical abuse, arrest, and substantial limits on their freedom of movement. Reporters Sans Frontieres (RSF) reported that throughout the year, 16 journalists were wounded by fire from Israel Defense Forces (IDF), including live ammunition, rubber bullets, shrapnel, and tear-gas grenades. Among those injured was Imad Ghanem, a cameraman for the Hamas-affiliated satellite channel Al-Aqsa, whose legs were amputated after Israeli tanks opened fire on him in July. The Committee to Protect Journalists reported that during an incursion into Nablus in February, IDF soldiers fired stun grenades and tear gas at 12 journalists and photographers to prevent them from covering a search and seizure operation. During the same military incursion, soldiers detained Nabegh Break, owner and managing director of the local Sanabel TV station, raiding both his home and the station's office. In the West Bank, IDF forces reportedly carried out similar raids on six Palestinian pro-Hamas media outlets in May and three in December, in many cases seizing equipment and thereby forcing the stations to suspend broadcasting. Journalists reporting from the Israeli-occupied territories are required to carry Israeli-issued press cards, which are difficult to obtain, particularly for many Palestinian and Arab journalists. According to the U.S. State Department, on several occasions, IDF soldiers beat, detained, or confiscated press cards from journalists covering protests against construction of the separation barrier in the West Bank village of Bil'in.

Israel denies that it deliberately targets journalists and maintains that reporters covering the conflict bear responsibility for placing themselves in danger. However, international newswires also quoted an Israeli military source as saying that Israel does not recognize as journalists cameramen working for Hamas-affiliated channels because their films are used for intelligence purposes and they are sometimes armed. A new analysis of an audio recording of the 2003 death of British journalist James Miller in Gaza reportedly indicated that the shots that killed Miller were fired from an Israeli military vehicle. In April 2006, a British coroner's court declared that the shooting constituted an unlawful killing on the part of the IDF. The British attorney general wrote to the Israeli authorities in June 2007 requesting that they begin legal proceedings within six weeks against the officer suspected of firing the shots; however, no proceedings had been launched by year's end.

Since the legislative victory of Hamas in January 2006, Palestinian media outlets have become targets of factional violence between Hamas and Fatah. Danger to journalists and the polarization of the Palestinian media were exacerbated during violence that erupted over the summer in the Gaza Strip, which ended in a Hamas takeover of the area. On May 13, Suleiman Abdul-Rahim Al-Ashi, economics editor of the Hamas-affiliated newspaper *Filastin*, and Mohammad Matar Abdo, the paper's distribution manager, were shot and killed by gunmen associated with Fatah. A few days later, Mohammad Awad al-Joujou, a reporter for the Hamas-affiliated website Palestine Live, was killed by unidentified gunmen en route to cover clashes between Hamas and Fatah supporters. A building housing foreign bureaus such as Al-Jazeera and the BBC was also caught in the crossfire between the two sides on May 16. In an incident unrelated to factional fighting, in June 2007, female employees of the state-run Palestinian Broadcasting Corporation received death threats for appearing on camera in Western dress or without headscarves; the threat was issued by an extremist group called the Swords of Truth, which had previously claimed responsibility for a string of internet café bombings.

Press freedom in Gaza further deteriorated under Hamas rule. From June to November, RSF counted at least 9 assaults and 21 arrests of journalists by the Hamas Executive Forces, in what the Foreign Press Association called "a coordinated policy by Hamas security forces." By mid-June, Hamas fighters had forced all Fatah-affiliated television and radio outlets in the strip to stop broadcasting; at least nine media outlets were shut down, including three state owned and six privately owned. In June, Hamas-linked militants conducted an armed raid of the offices of the Gaza branch of the Palestinian Journalists Syndicate (PJS); and in September, a Hamas government representative announced the dissolution of the PJS, while the new Government Committee for the Media was established. In November, the Ministry of the Interior in Gaza declared that journalists would not be allowed to continue working in Gaza without obtaining a Hamas-issued press card. Obtaining a card would reportedly require submitting to editorial restrictions such as a vague ban on articles that "cause harm to national unity"; however, most media organizations operating in the area had refused to comply by year's end.

Continuing a disturbing trend from previous years, several foreign journalists were kidnapped by militants in Gaza in 2007. The most prominent victim was the BBC's Alan Johnston, who was kidnapped in March and held for 114 days, making it the longest abduction in Gaza to date. The year also saw the first Palestinian journalist to be seized, when Hamas supporters held Abu Dhabi TV's Abdelsalam Mussa Abu-Askar for several hours in May. Danger to journalists reporting from Gaza further increased in June owing to the actions of four armed Palestinians who used a jeep with the press markings of a "TV" insignia to attack an Israeli military position.

The Palestinian media have also faced factional violence in the West Bank. The state-owned WAFA TV station had its offices in Nablus stormed by gunmen on January 4, reportedly because their coverage focused on Fatah more than on other factions. In September, Fatah-controlled security forces raided Hebron University to disperse a press conference organized by the pro-Hamas student council, beating students and several journalists in the process. Six pro-Hamas journalists were arrested during the year and eight reporters were attacked by PA security forces within one week during November. These included a correspondent for Al-Jazeera television whose arm was broken when police beat him while he was covering a demonstration in Ramallah against the Annapolis Middle East peace conference.

There are 3 Palestinian dailies in addition to several weekly and monthly periodicals, and the territories host roughly 30 independently owned television stations and 25 radio stations, though several were shut down during the year. The television station and radio station run by the PA function as government mouthpieces, with control exercised primarily by Fatah. Since 2005, Hamas has also run its own al-Aqsa television network, with programming known for its pro-Islamist slant and overt promotion of violence. Cautious self-censorship adopted by most independent media outlets, particularly on the issue of internal Palestinian politics, further increased in 2007 out of fear of attacks by one faction or another. Israeli checkpoints often prevent newspaper distribution in the territories. After the Hamas takeover of Gaza, the Fatah-led West Bank authorities prevented the printing and distribution of the pro-Hamas *Filastin* and *Al-Risala* newspapers in the West Bank for most of the second half of the year. Access to satellite television and the internet remains unrestricted by the government; however, while satellite TV is gaining popularity, use of the internet was limited to just over 10 percent of the population in 2007.

Italy

Status: Free

LEGAL ENVIRONMENT: 10
POLITICAL ENVIRONMENT: 10
ECONOMIC ENVIRONMENT: 9
TOTAL SCORE: 29

Survey Edition	2003	2004	2005	2006	2007
Total Score, Status	28,F	33,PF	35,PF	35,PF	29,F

Freedom of speech and of the press are constitutionally guaranteed and generally respected in practice in Italy, despite ongoing concerns regarding concentration of media ownership. The 2004 Gasparri Law on Broadcasting, which introduced a number of reforms (including preparations for the switch from analog to digital broadcasting), was heavily criticized for providing measures that served then prime minister Silvio Berlusconi's interests and enabling him to maintain his control of the private media market. Libel cases continued to burden Italian journalists throughout 2007. In fact, two separate suits were filed by prominent politicians. Then deputy prime minister Francesco Rutelli sued the private weekly *L'Espresso* for alleging that he used official travel for personal reasons. Separately, parliamentarian Ferdinando Adornato sued *Il Giornale* over a story that criticized an apartment he purchased from a government agency as an example of excessive government privileges.

In January, the government approved new antiracism legislation that criminalizes Holocaust denial and other forms of hate incitement with potential prison terms of up to four years. In October, officials confiscated wine bottles with images of Adolf Hitler on the labels under this new law. Separately, in June, the Chamber of Deputies overwhelmingly passed a bill on telephone tapping. If it passes the Senate, the law would threaten freedom of information by permitting the destruction of a tapped telephone conversation once the legal case it pertains to has been closed. The law would also allow the state to fine or imprison journalists who publish any of these recordings once an investigation is over. In December, the home of Giuseppe D'Avanzo, a journalist for the daily *La Repubblica*, was searched in response to an article he wrote about alleged efforts by Berlusconi to corrupt Italian senators. The story argued that Berlusconi promised a position in his government to an opposition senator if he helped the former prime minister undermine the government of Romano Prodi. Physical attacks against journalists in Italy are rare, although they do face some intimidation and threats from organized crime groups, particularly in the south.

Under the former Berlusconi government, the country suffered from an unusually high concentration of media ownership by European standards. Through his private holdings and political power over state television networks in his role as prime minister, he controlled 90 percent of the country's broadcast media during his 2001–2006 premiership. With the 2006 election of Romano Prodi, overt government interference regarding media content had diminished by 2007, but much of the private broadcast sector remains in the hands of the Berlusconi family, and concentration continues to be an issue, with the state-owned RAI and Berlusconi's Mediaset controlling 87.5 percent of the market share. Nonetheless, a February 2006 Council of Europe report argued that despite the concentration of broadcast media ownership in Italy, there is considerable diversity of content in the country's news and other media. Print media, which consist of several national newspapers (two of which are controlled by the Berlusconi family), continue to provide diverse political opinions, including those critical of the government.

The government generally does not restrict access to the internet; approximately 57 percent of the population accessed this medium in 2007. In fact, blogs have become an increasingly prevalent source of news for many Italians. One such blog, beppegrillo.it, run by the popular Italian comedian Giuseppe Grillo, has been ranked among the 10 most visited blogs in the world and regularly receives over 1,000 comments to each post. Nonetheless, the government can block foreign-based internet sites if they contravene national law, and police regularly monitor websites for illegal child pornography. After the 2005 London bombings by Islamist extremists, Italy's parliament approved a new antiterror law that requires internet cafés to obtain a government license in order to operate, legalizes internet surveillance, and obliges internet café users to show photo identification.

Jamaica

LEGAL ENVIRONMENT: 3
POLITICAL ENVIRONMENT: 6
ECONOMIC ENVIRONMENT: 6

Status: Free

TOTAL SCORE: 15

Survey Edition	2003	2004	2005	2006	2007
Total Score, Status	20,F	17,F	15,F	17,F	15,F

Jamaica continued to uphold its free media environment in 2007, and in a positive step, the new prime minister created a committee to review restrictive press laws. Although the constitution protects freedom of expression, media rights activists continue to argue that existing criminal libel and defamation laws hinder freedom of expression. In particular, it is believed that media owners discourage investigative reporting of certain subjects because of their fear of libel suits. On May 3, World Press Freedom Day, Desmond Richards, president of the Press Association of Jamaica (PAJ), called for reform of the current laws. Bruce Golding, who took office as prime minister in September, stated the new government's commitment to assess and amend defamation legislation. Golding's government appointed a committee, including members of both the PAJ and the Media Association of Jamaica (MAJ), to make recommendations for legislative changes, with the expectation of submitting a report in February 2008. In the run-up to the September general elections, journalists were frequently harangued as the two main political parties stepped up their campaigning. Both the PAJ, representing media workers, and the MAJ, representing owners, expressed concerns over "inflammatory" statements by the leadership of both parties. There were no reports of physical attacks on the press during the year, although some members of the media do face pressure from gangs and other criminal groups.

Jamaica has an active, independent media that is mostly free to express opinions on a diversity of issues as well as criticism of the government. The country has two national daily newspapers and a daily afternoon tabloid. There are a number of national and regional periodicals serving a variety of sectors and interests. The state broadcasting service was largely privatized in 1997, although the Kool FM radio station is still government owned. In March 2006, the Public Broadcasting Corporation of Jamaica—funded by state and private sector contributions—was launched as a radio and television service to replace the state-run Jamaica Broadcasting Corporation. The authorities imposed no restrictions on the internet, which was used by close to 40 percent of the population in 2007.

Japan

LEGAL ENVIRONMENT: 2
POLITICAL ENVIRONMENT: 13
ECONOMIC ENVIRONMENT: 6

Status: Free

TOTAL SCORE: 21

Survey Edition	2003	2004	2005	2006	2007
Total Score, Status	17,F	18,F	20,F	20,F	21,F

Japan's prolific media garner one of the largest readerships in the world, despite criticism about a lack of viewpoint diversity resulting from exclusive press clubs and occasional backlash from ultranationalists. Press freedom is constitutionally guaranteed and generally respected in practice. The independent court system in particular has emerged in recent years as a bulwark against political pressure on journalists. In several prominent cases during 2005 and 2006, courts upheld the right of journalists to refuse to reveal anonymous sources, even when the source is a public official. In January 2007, Tokyo's high court ruled that the public Japan Broadcasting Corporation (NHK) had bowed to political pressure in censoring a 2001 documentary about sex slavery during World War II. Shinzo Abe, prime minister for much of 2007 and the deputy chief cabinet secretary at the time, was among the politicians who had reportedly pressured the station to delete scenes of a mock trial of wartime emperor Hirohito. The court ordered NHK and two production companies to pay US$16,400 in damages to a women's rights group that had staged the mock trial.

Concerns remain regarding the lack of diversity and independence in reporting, especially in political news. The problem is perpetuated in part by a system of *kisha kurabu*, or journalist clubs, in which major media outlets have cozy relationships with bureaucrats and politicians. Exposés by media outlets that belong to such clubs are frowned upon and can result in the banning of members from press club briefings. Journalists therefore tend to avoid writing critical stories about the government, reducing the media's ability to pressure politicians for greater transparency and accountability. Most of Japan's investigative journalism is conducted by reporters outside the press club system. In recent years, the exclusivity of the clubs has eroded as foreign journalists with press cards from the Ministry of Foreign Affairs are now guaranteed access to most official press conferences; according to the International Press Institute, the last significant *kisha kurabu* to bar foreign reporters is the one that deals with the affairs of the emperor and royal family. However, with the exception of Nagano, where former governor Yasuo Tanaka abolished the prefecture's press clubs, Japanese magazine reporters, online writers, and freelance journalists remain essentially barred from club briefings, even as observers.

Physical attacks against the media are rare. However, in July 2006 an ultranationalist hurled a Molotov cocktail at the headquarters of Japan's largest business daily, *Nihon Keizai Shimbun*. No one was hurt in the attack, but the office suffered minor damage. In July 2007, Motohide Hiraoka was sentenced to 10 months in prison for the attack, which he said was aimed at warning the newspaper after it ran a story about Hirohito's refusal to visit the Yasukuni Shrine once it began honoring high-ranking war criminals in 1978.

Japan has vigorous and free media and boasts the highest daily newspaper circulation per capita in the world. Many national dailies have circulations topping one million and often produce both afternoon and evening editions. More than half of the national newspaper market share is controlled by "the big three": the *Yomiuri Shimbun*, the *Asahi Shimbun*, and the *Mainichi Shimbun*. There is considerable homogeneity in reports, which relate the news in a factual and neutral manner. Television news content, once dominated by NHK, has diversified considerably with the rising popularity of TV Asahi, Fuji TV, the Tokyo Broadcasting System, and satellite television. Japan also has 188 community radio stations and over 87 million internet users, representing almost 70 percent of the population. In recent years, the internet has become an increasingly important source of news and revenue, with online ad sales growing by almost 30 percent in 2006 from the year before. No government restrictions on access to the internet were reported in 2007.

Jordan

Status: Not Free

LEGAL ENVIRONMENT: 21
POLITICAL ENVIRONMENT: 24
ECONOMIC ENVIRONMENT: 18
TOTAL SCORE: 63

Survey Edition	2003	2004	2005	2006	2007
Total Score, Status	65,NF	63,NF	62,NF	61,NF	61,NF

Already suffering from oppressive media legislation and government pressure on advertisers, Jordan's media environment deteriorated in 2007 as security agencies continued to harass journalists and a government body prevented the launching of the country's first private television station. In addition to constitutional guarantees of the right to freedom of expression and of the press, the parliament approved a new Press and Publications Law on March 21 that explicitly prohibits "detention as a result of the enunciation of an opinion in speech, writing, or through other means." Despite this positive development, the new law also drastically increased fines for defamation charges to up to 28,000 dinars (US$40,000) for speech that offends religious beliefs, offends the prophets, or slanders the government. Journalists may also still be prosecuted under the penal code, which allows for imprisonment of up to three years for defaming the king or royal family. In practice, limited criticism of the government and its allies is often tolerated, as is speech in favor of Islamist movements. In April 2007, the lower house of parliament passed a draft Access to Information Law; however, it was criticized by press freedom groups for having vague national security exclusions and an oversight mechanism lacking independence. Journalists must be members of the Jordan Press Association (JPA) to work legally. In the past, critical journalists have been excluded from the JPA and prevented from practicing their profession.

Intelligence agencies watch journalists closely, and the government of former prime minister Ma'ruf al-Bakhit, whom Nadir al-Dahabi replaced on November 25, gave free rein to intelligence officials, the police, and prosecutors to clamp down on legitimate speech. As a result of government threats of fines or prosecution, many journalists practiced self-censorship. Editors and journalists claim to have received official warnings to refrain from publishing certain articles and avoid certain topics, and security officials have pressured printers to delay publications until editors agree to remove sensitive stories. On April 18, security officers confiscated videotapes from an Al-Jazeera journalist containing an interview with former crown prince Hassan bin Talal in which he criticized Saudi and U.S. policies in the Middle East. According to the Committee to Protect Journalists (CPJ), security agents banned the April 30 edition of the weekly *Al-Majd* because of a front-page story about a "secret American plan" to topple the Hamas government in the occupied Palestinian territories with the connivance of "unnamed Arab parties." Fahd al-Rimawi, the paper's editor, told CPJ he reached an agreement with the security services whereby he would be permitted to run the story in the paper's next edition, but off the front page. In both cases of censorship, the government claimed to be acting out of fear of harming relations with neighboring countries.

The media were also subject to physical violence and harassment at the hands of state security officials. In January, Khaled al-Khawaja, a journalist with the progovernment daily *Al-Ra'i*, filed a criminal complaint against a public security officer alleging that the officer assaulted him while he was trying to cover the disbursement of government meat rations. The officer responded by filing a countercomplaint, and in February, al-Khawaja was arrested and charged with assaulting a public security officer. State security officers also assaulted Aubaida Dammur and Fady Ramhy, a journalist and a cameraman from the Al-Ghad TV station, in April as they attempted to cover a bus strike in Amman.

The government owns substantial shares in Jordan's two leading daily newspapers, and all publications must obtain licenses from the state. There are high taxes on the media industry and tariffs on paper, and the government has been criticized for advertising primarily in newspapers in which it owns a stake. In 2003, the government officially gave up its monopoly on domestic television and radio broadcasting by creating the Audiovisual Commission (AVC), which in 2004 began to license and regulate private radio and television outlets. Although the first privately owned television station, ATV, was licensed two years ago, by year's end, the station had not yet been allowed to begin programming after the AVC abruptly halted its planned launch in August 2007, citing incomplete paperwork. The country's state-run Jordan Television and Radio serves mostly as a mouthpiece for the government. The new Press and Publications Law requires the licensing of publications and provides the courts with the right to withhold publication of any printed material, as well as the power to withdraw licenses. However, the new law does limit the government's ability to shut down printing presses. No restrictions are placed on satellite broadcasts, and satellite dishes continue to proliferate.

The Jordanian government is actively seeking to promote access to the internet and claims to place no restrictions on the roughly 13 percent of the population that access it. However, online publications became subject to the Press and Publications Law on September 25, 2007. On October 9, former parliamentarian and head of the Jordan National Movement, Ahmad Oweidi Abbadi, was sentenced to two years in prison by a state security court for posting material on his party's website, ostensibly in contravention of the recently reformed Press and Publications Law prohibiting jailing for the expression of opinions. Abbadi had been detained in May on charges of "slandering a public official" and spreading false news abroad that "would impair the prestige of the state," based on a complaint from the interior minister, who took offense to an open letter to U.S. senator Harry Reid that Abbadi posted on the internet accusing the minister and other government officials of corruption.

Kazakhstan

LEGAL ENVIRONMENT: 26
POLITICAL ENVIRONMENT: 30
ECONOMIC ENVIRONMENT: 22

Status: Not Free

TOTAL SCORE: 78

Survey Edition	2003	2004	2005	2006	2007
Total Score, Status	73,NF	74,NF	75,NF	75,NF	76,NF

While Kazakhstan's media environment displayed familiar obstacles to independent reporting in the form of legal restrictions, self-censorship, and harassment in 2007, political events underscored the overwhelming extent of partisan ownership and presidential influence. The country's constitution guarantees freedom of the press but also provides special protection for the president. The restrictive 2006 amendments to media legislation remained in force, imposing costly registration fees for journalists, broadening criteria for the denial of registration, requiring news outlets to submit the names of editors with registration applications, and necessitating reregistration in the event of a change of address or editor. Although a more liberal draft Media Law was introduced to parliament in April, it had not made progress by year's end. August parliamentary elections that produced an opposition-free legislature took place amid biased media coverage, international observers noted.

Journalists continued to encounter harassment and obstacles, including criminal charges and civil libel suits. Kaziz Toguzbayev, a journalist and activist in the unregistered opposition party Alga who had faced criminal charges in 2006 for allegedly "undermining the reputation and dignity of the country's president and hindering his activities" in articles published on the internet, received a two-year suspended sentence. An Astana court closed the independent newspaper *Zakon i Pravosudiye* (ironically, *Law and Justice*) in February for registration violations. Oralgaisha Omarshanova, an investigative reporter for *Zakon i Pravosudiye* who had written about ethnic clashes and dangerous conditions in mines, went missing in March and had not been found by year's end. The nongovernmental organization Adil Soz reported 144 incidents of harassment in the first 11 months of 2007. Outlets that were willing to criticize the president also faced frequent intimidation. In October and November, the opposition newspapers *Svoboda Slova*, *Tas Zhagan*, *Respublika*, and *Vzglyad* faced tax and regulatory investigations and difficulties with their publishers in connection with their coverage of allegations by Rakhat Aliyev, former son-in-law of President Nursultan Nazarbayev, linking the president to the 2006 killing of opposition leader Altynbek Sarsenbayev.

Major broadcast media remained either state run or controlled by members or associates of the president's family. The fall from grace of Aliyev illustrated the negative consequences of partisan ownership in a system with virtually nonexistent checks and balances. When Aliyev faced criminal charges over a bank takeover in early 2007, media he controlled leapt to his defense. In May, a court shut down two of his holdings, the television station KTK and the newspaper *Karavan*, on selectively applied violations of the country's Law on Language. With Aliyev exiled in Austria, the two outlets were allowed to reopen in August under new management and with a different focus in their coverage. Repercussions from the Aliyev case continued to affect the media even after the president's daughter divorced the errant son-in-law, now stripped of his media assets.

The internet, which had provided a refuge of sorts for Kazakhstan's beleaguered independent press, was increasingly a source of contestation amid more frequent reports of blocked websites. In October, the opposition websites zona.kz, kub.kz, geo.kz, and inkar.info were blocked in connection with audio recordings in which high-ranking officials apparently discussed illegal campaign finance tactics. Although three of the websites were unblocked after a meeting with Culture and Information Minister Yermukhamet Yertysbayev in November, the minister reportedly pressured editors and suggested that internet content providers should face "criminal punishment" for certain materials. In August, Nurlan Alimbekov was arrested for e-mails allegedly insulting the president and inciting ethnic hatred; the country's security service argued that the e-mails violated media legislation because they were sent to multiple addresses. Nevertheless, the internet was freer than print and other broadcast media, although even the most optimistic estimates put the proportion of internet users in the country at less than 10 percent of the population.

Kenya

Status: Partly Free

LEGAL ENVIRONMENT: 21
POLITICAL ENVIRONMENT: 21
ECONOMIC ENVIRONMENT: 18
TOTAL SCORE: 60

Survey Edition	2003	2004	2005	2006	2007
Total Score, Status	68,NF	60,PF	61,NF	58,PF	59,PF

Kenyan media have typically enjoyed a reputation for vibrant, aggressive reporting. However, their independence was threatened in 2007 by the government in a number of ways, including the establishment of a statutory media council to regulate the media and the banning of live news broadcasts following the failed presidential election in December.

Kenya's constitution does not explicitly guarantee press freedom. Media operations are still governed by the constitution's Section 79, which does not provide for freedom of speech but does guarantee citizens the broader right to freedom of expression. Nevertheless, the government routinely restricts this right by widely interpreting several laws, including the Official Secrets Act, the penal code, and criminal libel legislation. Although defamation remains criminalized in Kenyan law, the attorney general declared in a 2005 defamation case that the archaic law would no longer be used to suppress freedom of expression. However, in a March 2007 civil libel case, the editor of the privately owned *Independent* newspaper, Mburu Muchoki, was sentenced to one year in prison owing to his inability to pay a US$7,200 fine; he was released in June after a presidential pardon. Muchoki had previously been convicted of libel following an article accusing the father of Martha Karua—the minister of justice and constitutional affairs and a close friend of the presiding judge—of being involved in an abortion scandal. Kenya was still without freedom of information legislation at year's end, although a freedom of information bill was tabled in parliament in May. In August, after months of acrimonious debate between lawmakers and media representatives, parliament passed the Kenya Media Law, which authorized the creation of a statutory media council to replace the voluntary and self-regulatory council in existence since 2002. However, a last minute amendment requiring editors to disclose the identity of their sources if asked to do so in court provoked a large-scale silent demonstration by journalists in Nairobi. President Mwai Kibaki ultimately refused to sign the law with the inclusion of the new amendment and sent it back to parliament, where the amendment was swiftly removed and the legislation passed in October. The following month, a new 13-member Media Council was sworn in that included academics, media workers, and representatives of civil society groups. As it stands, the new law mandates a council of 15 members, with the chair being appointed by the minister of information and communications. It also limits who can be a reporter by defining a journalist as someone who "holds a diploma or a degree in mass communication from a recognized institution of higher learning" and requiring all media practitioners to register with the council for accreditation. Also withdrawn for revision was a communications bill that would have imposed restrictions on media ownership, among other restrictive provisions.

While instances of harassment and intimidation of the media decreased in 2007 from the prior year, the situation deteriorated markedly following the December 27 general election. Journalists, many of whom were unaccustomed to covering civil and political conflict, were threatened by tear-gas attacks and faced intimidation at polling stations. Moreover, on December 30—the same day the electoral commission mistakenly declared that the incumbent, Mwai Kibaki, had won the presidential election—the internal security minister announced that all live television and radio broadcasts would be formally banned indefinitely. This prevented up-to-date coverage of the rapidly changing events and inhibited the media's ability to question the electoral commission's verdict in the face of growing evidence of irregularities. By year's end, the situation for the media was tenuous indeed, with reporters facing violence and outlets themselves subject to overt censorship.

Although the number of private media outlets has risen steadily, the government-controlled public broadcaster, Kenya Broadcasting Corporation (KBC), remains dominant outside of the major urban centers, and its coverage tended to favor the ruling party. KBC also started a new network in 2007, K24, which exhibited signs of a progovernment bias. Nonetheless, private media outlets are generally outspoken and critical of government policies, and considering the limitations, much of the domestic media provided robust coverage of the postelection violence. Two private companies, the Standard Media Group and the Nation Media Group, are influential media houses, running independent television networks and well-respected newspapers. There has been a significant expansion of FM radio, particularly ethnic FM radio stations, increasing public participation as well as commentary unfavorable to the government through call-in shows. Unfortunately, many of these vernacular stations were accused of broadcasting ethnic hate speech in the wake of the election. International news media, including the British Broadcasting Corporation and Radio France Internationale, are widely available in Kenya. There are no reports that the government restricted internet access or monitored e-mails. In fact, the internet is a growing place for vibrant political debate for Kenyan citizens and the diaspora, and blogs were a crucial source for current information, images, and opinions following the ban on other live broadcasts. The percentage of Kenyans accessing the internet more than doubled in 2007 from 3 percent the previous year to 7.5 percent. This percentage is expected to rise in coming years with the anticipated completion of an underwater fiber-optic cable from the Middle East, which will improve internet speed and affordability.

Kiribati

Status: Free

LEGAL ENVIRONMENT: 5
POLITICAL ENVIRONMENT: 8
ECONOMIC ENVIRONMENT: 13
TOTAL SCORE: 26

Survey Edition	2003	2004	2005	2006	2007
Total Score, Status	26,F	27,F	26,F	28,F	26,F

The tiny island nation of Kiribati has a free and open media system. Freedom of expression is safeguarded under Article 12 of the constitution; however, there are some restrictions. Newspapers are required to register with the government under the Newspaper Registration Act. In addition, the Newspaper Registration (Amendment) Act of 2004 gives the government the power to stop publication of newspapers that face complaints. There is no official censorship, although journalists have self-censored under political pressure from the government. In 2007, Kiribati journalists joined the newly formed Micronesian Media Association to protect free and independent journalism and public access to information. During the run-up to the second round of parliamentary elections in August 2007, a member of the opposition party was denied the opportunity to broadcast a speech on the government-owned Broadcasting and Publications Authority (BPA) radio station. A former BPA radio journalist, Taberannang Korauaba, had been fired in 2005 after refusing to reveal his source for a corruption report. He lost his lawsuit over the dismissal in 2006. The state-run newspaper, *Te Uekera*, and the nation's only privately owned newspaper, *Kiribati New Star*, both operate on a weekly basis and offer diverse viewpoints. Newsletters from Catholic and Protestant churches provide additional sources of information. There is one state AM and FM radio station and one private broadcaster in the capital Tarawa. In 2006, the government hired Powercom, a Tasmanian company, to set up the country's first radio contact among the country's coral atolls. The internet is unrestricted; however, with a single provider, access is among the most expensive in the world, and only 2 percent of the country's population was able to make use of the internet on a regular basis during the year. Toward the end of 2007, Fiji-based Digicel sought a license to begin mobile telephone and internet operations in Kiribati, which would put an end to the government's monopoly on telecommunications.

Kuwait

LEGAL ENVIRONMENT: 18
POLITICAL ENVIRONMENT: 21
ECONOMIC ENVIRONMENT: 15

Status: Partly Free

TOTAL SCORE: 54

Survey Edition	2003	2004	2005	2006	2007
Total Score, Status	54,PF	57,PF	58,PF	56,PF	56,PF

The diversity of Kuwait's media environment, already one of the most open in the Middle East, improved slightly in 2007 as a result of the licensing of six new Arabic-language dailies, the first accreditation of any new paper in 30 years. Nevertheless, during the year, the government also continued to censor and prosecute the media for reporting on certain prohibited religious and political topics. Freedom of speech and of the press are protected under Articles 36 and 37 of the constitution, but only "in accordance with the conditions and in the circumstances defined by law." The 2006 revised Press and Publications Law extends some important protections to the media, but it prohibits the publication of material that insults God, the prophets, or Islam and forbids criticism of the king, disclosing secret or private information, or calling for the regime's overthrow. Any citizen may press criminal charges against an author who they believe has violated these proscriptions. Penalties for criticizing Islam were increased under the new Press and Publications Law and can include prison sentences of up to one year and fines of up to 20,000 Kuwaiti dinars (US$69,000). The government occasionally imposed these press penalties in 2007, including for internet-related offenses. On August 18, Bashar al-Sayegh, editor of the daily *Al-Jarida*, was arrested and charged with insulting the emir based on a comment posted by someone else on an open forum news website he was hosting. Jassim al-Qames, another editor of the paper, was arrested, beaten, and detained for photographing the arrest of al-Sayegh. The two journalists were released days later after being interrogated, and the person responsible for the comment, Nayef Abdullah al-Ajmi, was arrested on August 21 after al-Sayegh was reportedly forced to disclose his internet protocol address. In other instances of legal harassment, in May 2007, charges were filed against two weekly newspapers and their editors for articles on corruption. Ten complaints were filed against *Al-Abraj* for an article blaming the prime minister for Kuwait's poor score in Transparency International's Corruption Perceptions Index; and three separate cases were brought against *Al-Shaab* for publishing an article on politics when it was licensed to cover only arts and culture.

In general, the Ministry of Information (MOI) does not actively interfere or restrict access to news, and the Kuwaiti media are considered more critical and outspoken than those in the rest of the region. Greater in-depth reporting and a wider diversity of opinions appear more often in newspapers than in broadcast mediums. Nevertheless, given the ongoing restrictions in the new Press and Publications Law, journalists continued to practice self-censorship. International news is widely available, with a number of international media outlets operating bureaus in Kuwait. News sources originating from outside Kuwait must be reviewed by the ministry before circulation. In September, several Egyptian newspapers were banned from circulation owing to articles considered injurious to Kuwait. The MOI can censor all books, films, and periodicals it deems morally offensive. The Arabic daily *Al-Watan* was banned for three days for publishing an "indecent photo" of the granddaughter of Saddam Hussein in a swimsuit. In March, an episode of the popular television show *Al-Diwaniya* on the subject of Arab blogs was prevented from airing; and a television series was banned in September for its representation of Shiite beliefs and practices. In an apparently related incident, the offices of both the Middle East Broadcasting Center and the Al-Arabiya satellite channel were attacked with rocks in September. Although neither could not confirm the reason for the attacks, both reported having received numerous calls to ban the television series, which is considered offensive to the Shi'a faith.

Kuwait has nine Arabic and three English-language newspapers, all of which are privately owned. Private media have relatively transparent media ownership. All publishers are required to obtain an operating license from the MOI in order to launch a daily under the new Press and Publications Law; however, the MOI must now issue the license or provide an explanation for its refusal within 90 days of application, and those denied licenses can appeal such action in court. In addition, media outlet licenses may not be revoked without a court order. Despite the fact that the new law requires a minimum capital of 250,000 Kuwaiti dinars (US$950,000) to establish a paper, the government licensed six new daily Arabic-language newspapers in 2007 for the first time in 30 years. The old Press Law of 1963 had limited the press to five dailies. Private newspapers have their own presses and are free to set their own prices. The government has started to license private television and radio stations such as the satellite television news channel Al-Rai, but the state still owns the majority of broadcast outlets, with nine local radio stations and four television stations. Although the advertising market is still limited, it continues to grow owing to an increase in advertising agencies. Wage levels for journalists of both state-operated media and private media were not high enough to discourage the occasional acceptance of bribes to influence coverage. Low salaries have also discouraged many Kuwaiti nationals from pursuing the field of journalism; at the end of 2006, only 2 percent of media workers in the local media sector were Kuwaitis.

Of Kuwait's population, 32.6 percent used the internet in 2007, more than four times the number that accessed it in 2000. The government continued to debate how best to regulate this growing means of communication. The state already requires all internet service providers to install and operate systems to block websites with material deemed anti-Islamic, extremist Islamic, or pornographic, as well as certain types of political websites. However, the website-blocking policies were not always clear or consistent. Internet café owners are required to obtain the names and identification of internet users and must submit the information if required by the Ministry of Communication. At year's end, there was talk of a draft Website Censorship Law to be presented to the parliament.

Kyrgyzstan

Status: Not Free

Legal Environment: 22
Political Environment: 28
Economic Environment: 20
Total Score: 70

Survey Edition	2003	2004	2005	2006	2007
Total Score, Status	71,NF	71,NF	71,NF	64,NF	67,NF

Kyrgyzstan's media environment continued to deteriorate in 2007 in the wake of a failure in 2006 to cement the brief gains seen after the fall of long-ruling president Askar Akayev the previous year. Attacks on journalists and crude government attempts to impose censorship were increasingly evident. Legal protections remained uneven, and with the country's political elite polarized in an ongoing standoff between President Kurmanbek Bakiyev and the opposition, reforms stalled. Parliament debated legislation to decriminalize libel but failed to pass it into law. And while the long-awaited transformation of state television into public television took place, its supervisory board was plagued by conflicts amid signs that the president retained control over the state broadcaster.

The October murder of journalist Alisher Saipov, an ethnic Uzbek who ran the Uzbek-language newspaper *Siyosat* in southern Kyrgyzstan, was a disturbing development that brought to light a number of flaws in the country's media environment. Despite credible allegations of a possible Uzbek role in the killing of Saipov, who was known for his opposition to Uzbekistan president Islam Karimov, Kyrgyz authorities pursued a lackluster investigation focused on Saipov's purported ties to Islamic extremists. Moreover, law enforcement authorities in Osh reportedly pressured local reporters not to cover the case and reprimanded Osh TV stations for broadcasting a documentary about the slain journalist.

Opposition demonstrations in April saw assaults on at least five journalists that government officials dismissed as fabrications made by journalists hungry for more publicity. Separately, in March, Kairat Birimkulov, a reporter for state television, was assaulted as he was covering corruption allegations at the state-run railway company. Facing libel charges and continued death threats, Birimkulov left the country in October and obtained political asylum in Switzerland. Also in March, Talantbek Sopuyev, a cameraman for a television station owned by the brother of prominent opposition politician Omurbek Tekebayev, was beaten; Sopuyev was attacked again in September. Daniyar Isanov, an anchor at the independent television station NTS, was abducted and beaten by unknown assailants in March. Anna Mostfa, a reporter for the newspaper *Obshchestvenny Reiting*, was attacked in November. In these and other incidents, the authorities seemed less than eager to pursue investigations to identify the perpetrators and bring them to justice.

In another distressing development, security forces in the capital city of Bishkek raided an independent publishing house (operated by Freedom House) during opposition demonstrations in April and confiscated the print runs of the newspapers *Agym*, *Kyrgyz Rukhu*, *Apta*, and *Aykyn*. The confiscations took place without a court order or warrant, although Prime Minister Almazbek Atambayev later apologized for the raid. And in October, police confiscated the 2,500-copy print run of the independent newspaper *Alkak*, which had decided to publish criticism of a presidential proposal. Separately, the premises of the opposition newspaper *Kyrgyz Rukhu* were broken into and set on fire after the paper published several articles that criticized a presidential aide. Taken together, the increasing number of assaults on journalists, the murder of Alisher Saipov, and the authorities' willingness to impose extrajudicial censorship at politically sensitive moments betokened a clear continuation of the retreat from reformist principles that was already evident in 2006. The end of the Akayev regime in 2005 had raised hopes that Kyrgyzstan might become an exception to regional trends, but the events of 2007 saw those hopes frozen. In its report on December pre-term parliamentary elections, the Organization for Security and Cooperation in Europe termed the elections a "missed opportunity" and noted that the media "did not provide adequate information for voters to make an informed choice." Nevertheless, independent viewpoints were heard and foreign media operated freely.

Nearly 50 newspapers and magazines printed regularly, 8 of which were state owned, with varying degrees of independence. The independent printing press run by local nongovernmental organization Media Support Center surpassed the state-run printing house, Uchkun, as the leading newspaper publisher in the nation. Foreign media are allowed to operate freely, but foreign ownership of domestic media outlets is prohibited. Internet news sites, blogs, and forums provided a lively alternative for the small numbers of citizens with access (approximately 5 percent), with no reports of the content being restricted or censored by the government.

Laos

Status: Not Free

LEGAL ENVIRONMENT: 26
POLITICAL ENVIRONMENT: 32
ECONOMIC ENVIRONMENT: 25
TOTAL SCORE: 83

Survey Edition	2003	2004	2005	2006	2007
Total Score, Status	80,NF	82,NF	83,NF	81,NF	81,NF

Media remained tightly controlled by the authoritarian, one-party state in 2007. Article 6 of the 1991 constitution guarantees press freedom and civil liberties, but only in theory. Few citizens actually feel free to exercise these rights because there are no legal safeguards for voicing dissent in public. Article 7 requires the mass media, particularly Lao-language papers such as *Vientiane Mai* and *Pasason* and the national news agency, Khaosan Pathet Lao, to "unite and mobilize" the country's diverse ethnic groups to support the ruling Lao People's Revolutionary Party. Under the criminal code, individuals may be jailed for up to one year for reporting news that "weakens the state" or for transporting into the country a publication that is "contrary to national culture."

Although central censorship is no longer imposed directly on the press, the Ministry of Information and Culture continues to oversee media coverage and academic publishing, and self-censorship is commonplace. Editors are government appointees and members of the Lao Journalists Association, presided over by the minister of information and culture. Journalists receive salaries from the government. The media's role is to link the people to the party, deliver party policy messages, and disseminate political ideology. Military abuses against the Lao-Hmong people, as well as arrests of Christians for practicing their faith, go unreported in the Lao-language papers. Two Laotian nationals, Thao Moua and Pa Phue Khang, are serving 12 and 20 years in prison, respectively, for attempting to assist foreign journalists reporting on the Lao-Hmong in 2003. To date, there are no international media agencies in Laos. Foreign journalists must apply for a special visa to enter the country and are accompanied by official escorts throughout their stay. Nonetheless, there were no reports of physical attacks on the media in 2007.

The government owns all newspapers and broadcast media, though it has permitted several privately owned periodicals on nonpolitical topics such as business and trade. Little progress was made during 2007 on a draft law that would allow more significant development of private media, and according to Reporters Sans Frontieres, the authorities sought to control a new private English-language newspaper that journalists and investors attempted to launch in 2007. The French weekly *Le Renovateur* and the English daily *Vientiane Times*, which are subsidized by the Ministry of Information and Culture, occasionally report on social and economic problems, framing their content primarily to attract tourists, expatriates, and investors to the country. According to the U.S. State Department, despite close government control over domestic media, no effort was made to block television and radio broadcasts from abroad. A large number of citizens regularly watch Thai television, access international stations via satellite, or listen to Thai radio, which includes news from international sources. Tourism has led to the proliferation of internet kiosks with unrestricted access to foreign news sites. However, language barriers and high monthly connection fees (approximately US$300–400, compared with the average monthly salary of US$20–30) limit regular internet use to only 0.4 percent of the population, or exclusively wealthy individuals, expatriates, and business organizations. Internet service providers must submit quarterly reports to the government to facilitate monitoring, and citizen users are required to register with the authorities. The government also regularly blocked access to websites operated by Hmong groups abroad.

Latvia

Status: Free

LEGAL ENVIRONMENT: 6
POLITICAL ENVIRONMENT: 8
ECONOMIC ENVIRONMENT: 8
TOTAL SCORE: 22

Survey Edition	2003	2004	2005	2006	2007
Total Score, Status	18,F	17,F	17,F	19,F	19,F

Latvia's constitution protects freedom of speech and of the press, and the government generally upholds these rights in practice. Libel remains a criminal offense, though no journalist has been imprisoned or fined during the past two years. The Freedom of Information Law guarantees and provides detailed rules on access to public information. In a high-profile case, a Riga court ruled in February 2007 that the country's financial police had invaded the privacy of LTV journalist Ilze Jaunalksne and awarded her 100,000 lats (US$47,000) in damages; a government appeal of the verdict was pending at year's end. Jaunalksne, who broke a story on government corruption the previous year, had her private mobile phone conversations tapped by the financial police, who then leaked the transcripts to the newspaper *Neatkariga Rita Avize.* At the end of 2007, the Office of the Prosecutor General was reviewing whether criminal conduct had occurred. *Neatkariga Rita Avize* is widely believed to be controlled by the powerful mayor of Ventspils, Aivars Lembergs, who has faced investigations for corruption.

In June, LTV management dismissed Arta Giga, director of the weekly influential news program *De Facto,* which has run stories critical of the government. The dismissal, which was allegedly over relatively minor offenses, occurred shortly before a referendum on two controversial national security amendments and raised concerns among press freedom and corruption watchdog groups over the politicization of public television. The move followed a restructuring of LTV begun in 2006 that was viewed as compromising journalistic and editorial independence. In December, the general director of LTV resigned after a documentary critical of Russian president Vladimir Putin was abruptly pulled from the station's lineup. Originally scheduled to air the day before Russia's parliamentary elections, the program was ultimately broadcast a few days later; the official reason provided for the delay was "technical difficulties," but there were widespread allegations that the government had exerted pressure following complaints from the Russian embassy.

Latvian media are diverse and competitive, offering a wide range of political viewpoints. Four national terrestrial television channels dominate the airwaves: two public channels, LTV 1 and LTV 7, and two private stations, LNT and TV3. A number of privately owned radio and television outlets operate on a regional basis. Primary broadcast media are required to use Latvian, while secondary broadcasters may reserve up to 20 percent of their airtime for non-Latvian-language (Russian) programming; these requirements apply to terrestrial services only. The print media, which include a large number of both Latvian- and Russian-language papers, are independent and privately owned. Foreign companies, including several Swedish firms, own or control a considerable portion of Latvia's print and broadcast media as well as media distribution and printing facilities; in May 2007, LNT was purchased by News Corporation, the media conglomerate controlled by Rupert Murdoch. Transparency of media ownership is not adequately protected by law, and information on owners of media companies, some of whom are believed to be affiliated with political or economic interests, is not easily available in practice. According to the market research company TNS Latvia, Latvia's media advertising market volume in 2007 increased by 24 percent from 2006; television accounted for 35 percent of Latvia's total advertising market share, followed by newspapers with 22 percent. The government does not restrict access to the internet, which was used by an estimated 47 percent of the population during the year.

Lebanon

LEGAL ENVIRONMENT: 18
POLITICAL ENVIRONMENT: 21
ECONOMIC ENVIRONMENT: 16

Status: Partly Free

TOTAL SCORE: 55

Survey Edition	2003	2004	2005	2006	2007
Total Score, Status	71,NF	66,NF	60,PF	60,PF	59,PF

While the media have more freedom in Lebanon than in other countries in the region, they still face political and judicial obstacles. The constitution provides for freedom of the press, and although the media do not face direct interference from the government, political developments in recent years have resulted in increased security risks and self-censorship among journalists. Security services are authorized to censor all foreign magazines, books, and films before they are distributed, as well as pornography and political or religious material deemed a threat to the national security of either Lebanon or Syria. However, the 2005 withdrawal of Syrian troops from Lebanon emboldened critics of the affairs of both countries. Journalists are prohibited from insulting the head of state or foreign leaders, and those charged with press offenses may be prosecuted in a special publications court. In February 2007, the editor in chief of the daily *Al-Mustaqbal*, Tawfiq Khattab, and journalist Fares Khasan were each fined 50 million Lebanese pounds (US$33,000) for libel and damaging the reputation of the president. The original charges had been filed in February 2006 after *Al-Mustaqbal* published an interview in which a former intelligence chief and ambassador to France criticized the president's performance.

Political violence continues to threaten journalists' safety, and past attacks on the media have gone unpunished. A May 30 UN Security Council resolution creating an international tribunal to prosecute those responsible for assassinating former Lebanese prime minister Rafiq al-Hariri also provided the tribunal with enough jurisdiction to cover the killings and attempted murder of three members of the media in 2005. Car bombings that year killed the daily *Al-Nahar's* general manager and columnist Gebran Tueni, as well as another of the paper's journalists and a prominent academic Samir Qassir. Seriously injured in 2005 was May Chidiac, a talk show host for the satellite-based Lebanese Broadcasting Corporation. The three had been outspoken critics of Syrian influence in Lebanon. At year's end, the perpetrators of these attacks had yet to be identified or prosecuted.

Reporters complained that the army kept them out of the Nahr el-Bared Palestinian refugee camp, ostensibly for their own safety, after fighting between the army and the militant group Fatah al-Islam broke out in the camp in May. Three photographers—Wael al-Ladifi of *Al-Akhbar*, Ramzi Haidar of Agence France-Presse, and Assad Ahmad of *Al-Balad*—and videographer Ali Tahimi of Iran's Arabic satellite station Al-Alam said Lebanese soldiers assaulted them on May 24 and told them not to film Palestinian refugees fleeing the camp. According to the Committee to Protect Journalists, Lebanese military officials later called to apologize. Also in May, members of three television crews were attacked by civilians while conducting interviews with local residents at the site of a recent bombing in the town of Aley. The attackers were reportedly presumed to be supporters of anti-Syrian Druze leader Walid Jumblatt.

Lebanon hosts hundreds of periodicals, many of which publish criticism of the government and offer a broad range of opinions. Competition for readers among nearly a dozen daily newspapers is intense. All national daily newspapers are privately owned, as are most television and radio stations, including six television and satellite stations and nearly three dozen radio stations. However, many media outlets are linked to political or sectarian interests that exert significant influence over content. In addition, media outlets have experienced dramatic drops in advertising revenue associated with military conflicts and political crises, including the conflict with Israel in the summer of 2006. Access to satellite television has grown substantially over the last decade, and some 24 percent of the population regularly access the internet, which serves as a relatively free space for individuals and groups to express their beliefs and opinions. The government did not restrict access to the internet in 2007, and there were no reports of government monitoring of websites or e-mail.

Lesotho

LEGAL ENVIRONMENT: 13
POLITICAL ENVIRONMENT: 19
ECONOMIC ENVIRONMENT: 14

Status: Partly Free

TOTAL SCORE: 46

Survey Edition	2003	2004	2005	2006	2007
Total Score, Status	42,PF	40,PF	42,PF	42,PF	42,PF

The media environment worsened in 2007, particularly during the run-up and aftermath of snap elections in February. The government generally respects freedom of speech and of the press, both of which are provided for in the constitution. However, a 1938 proclamation prohibits criticism of the government and provides penalties for seditious libel. In recent years, extremely high fines have been handed down by the courts in libel cases against publications and radio stations known for criticizing the government, forcing some to the verge of closure. Several such libel suits were initiated by government officials in 2007. Journalism groups have urged the government to create a media council or other regulatory body empowered to mediate such defamation disputes before they end up in court. No such body currently exists.

The government periodically attempts to pressure the independent press, and journalists have suffered occasional harassment or attack. In 2007, the run-up to February's election saw journalists at Harvest FM and People's Choice FM threatened and accused of "causing confusion." According to Reporters Sans Frontieres, Harvest FM has been targeted by the government as the "headquarters" of the opposition All Basotho Convention party; the station was shut down for two days while election results were announced. Host Adam Lekhoaba was deported to South Africa after the elections, though he later returned to Lesotho after winning his case of citizenship. In June, Harvest FM's Thabo Thakalekoala was arrested for treason after his on-the-air reading of a letter attacking Prime Minister Pakalitha Mosisili; the host claimed he was forced to read the letter after death threats were made against him. The government later canceled its advertising with the station and a separate private newspaper, *Public Eye*, claiming that both were aligned with the opposition.

Several independent newspapers operate freely and routinely criticize the government, while state-owned print and broadcast media mostly reflect the views of the ruling party. There are four private radio stations, and extensive

South African radio and television broadcasts reach Lesotho, but there is no private television station. Journalists reportedly have trouble gaining free access to official information, and media development is constrained by inadequate funding and resources. Access to international broadcasts, particularly those from South Africa, is available. In 2007, less than 0.5 percent of the population accessed the internet, which remains unrestricted but monopolized by a government carrier.

Liberia

Status: Not Free

LEGAL ENVIRONMENT: 18
POLITICAL ENVIRONMENT: 25
ECONOMIC ENVIRONMENT: 22
TOTAL SCORE: 65

Survey Edition	2003	2004	2005	2006	2007
Total Score, Status	79,NF	75,NF	73,NF	64,NF	65,NF

Despite a small improvement in government relations with the press following the election of Ellen Johnson-Sirleaf as president in late 2005, the press freedom environment remained stagnant in 2007, as journalists continued to face harsh libel laws and harassment by the government and security forces. Liberia's 1986 constitution guarantees citizens the right of free expression but makes them "fully responsible for the abuse thereof," a clause that helped the regime of former president Charles Taylor harass the media with a semblance of legitimacy. Under the transitional government and the administration of Johnson-Sirleaf, respect for freedom of the press improved noticeably. Nonetheless, hopes for a freedom of information bill and a media reform bill that would improve legal protections for media practitioners, both of which have been discussed for several years but which have made little progress in parliament, have dwindled. Constitutional guarantees for access to information are currently vague; budgetary and financial information in particular is difficult to obtain owing to bureaucratic inefficiency and civil servants' frequent requests for additional payment. Strict libel laws remain in place, and in October, the general manager of Renaissance Communication Incorporated, Ambrose Nmah, sued six journalists from different media houses for libel. This followed their publication of a statement calling on the Liberian Press Union to investigate a comment allegedly made by Nmah during his radio program justifying the use of force by the police against journalists. Nmah was demanding US$10,000 in damages.

Throughout 2007, the media faced threats from a number of sources. Journalists were frequently harassed, beaten, and detained, and the outlets for which they worked were occasionally censored, banned, or accused of broadcasting hate messages. The government played a role in this repression, most notably through its announcement in October that the president's press secretary and the Ministry of Information would subsequently select the reporters who would be permitted to cover the president. In February, the government had banned the private biweekly newspaper the *Independent* for a full year after it published sexually explicit photographs of the minister of presidential affairs. The paper's editor, Sam Dean, went into hiding following death threats, but he took the issue to court and eventually won; the paper resumed publishing in May. A number of domestic and international journalists were harassed or beaten by police, UN peacekeepers, and the president's security force in 2007. In September, reporters attempting to cover the arrival of Sierra Leone's president for the signing of a nonaggression treaty were beaten and harassed by security forces. Included were correspondents for the British Broadcasting Corporation, Radio France Internationale, and Reuters as well as local journalists. Similarly, in August, a journalist with the private *Daily Observer* newspaper was beaten and detained by police while trying to cover a counternarcotics operation, and three others were detained in December for photographing the removal of decomposed bodies from a police cell. Also in December, police shut down a radio station for two days after it was accused of siding with striking workers at a rubber plantation. These and other incidents occurring throughout 2007 seriously threatened the progress that has been achieved over the last few years.

Despite such attacks, Liberian journalists regularly report critically about the government and other politicians, and media outlets offer a diversity of views. In 2007, about a dozen newspapers published in the capital, Monrovia, with varying degrees of regularity. However, newspaper distribution is limited to the capital and literacy rates remain low, meaning most Liberians rely on radio broadcasts. There were 15 independent radio stations in Monrovia and 24 local stations outside of the capital. The government runs 1 radio station, as does the UN Mission in Liberia (UNMIL). Though the independent media have grown significantly since the removal of Taylor, the number of outlets has decreased in recent years owing to financial constraints. Such difficulties, which are inevitable in an impoverished country recovering from war, continue to cause some of the largest impediments to unbiased journalism. Reporters commonly accept payment from individuals covered in their stories, and the placement of a story in a paper or radio show can often be bought and influenced by outside interests. Access to foreign broadcasts and the internet is not restricted by the government, though internet usage is limited to less than 1 percent of the population owing to the dire financial situation of most Liberians.

Libya

LEGAL ENVIRONMENT: 29
POLITICAL ENVIRONMENT: 36
ECONOMIC ENVIRONMENT: 29

Status: Not Free

TOTAL SCORE: 94

Survey Edition	2003	2004	2005	2006	2007
Total Score, Status	89,NF	94,NF	95,NF	96,NF	96,NF

Libya's press remains one of the most tightly controlled in the world. Despite continued efforts on the part of the regime to depict the country as a changed nation, little progress has been made in advancing political rights or civil liberties. Libyan law provides for freedom of speech and of the press within the confines of "the principles of the Revolution." The government severely limits the rights of the media in practice, and journalists who violate the harsh press codes can be imprisoned or sentenced to death. The press avoids publishing any material that could be deemed offensive or threatening, particularly to Islam, national security, territorial integrity, or Colonel Muammar al-Qadhafi. Those who criticize the government from outside the country, such as in foreign publications or internet websites, may be arrested upon entering Libya. A vast network of secret police and informers works to ensure that state critics are known to the regime.

A well-known writer and critic of the Libyan government, Jamal al-Haji, was arrested on February 16 along with 11 other men who were planning a peaceful demonstration in the capital, Tripoli, to commemorate a February 2006 clash between police and protesters in which 11 people were killed. According to Human Rights Watch, the 12 men were accused of planning to overthrow the government, arms possession, and meeting with an official from a foreign government. If convicted, they could face the death penalty. Although al-Haji is a Danish citizen, Libyan officials have refused to allow visits by Danish envoys. Human Rights Watch reported that a few days before his arrest, al-Haji wrote an article that called for "freedom, democracy, a constitutional state, and law." Separately, according to the Committee to Protect Journalists, three suspects were sentenced to death in July for the 2005 murder of journalist Daif al-Ghazal al-Shuhaibi. Al-Ghazal had worked for the state-owned daily *Azahf al-Akhdar* and had contributed to London-based websites focused on Libya. In the months leading up to his death, al-Ghazal had published online articles critical of the government. Little information was released on the trial of the three suspects, prompting concerns about the sincerity and veracity of the process.

As Libya has moved to present a more business-friendly face to the outside world, there has been some mild criticism of certain government policies, but this is carefully managed from the top and does not represent spontaneous or sincere opposition. Journalists practice a high degree of self-censorship in all reporting. The General Press Institute, a branch of the Information Ministry, owns three of the four major Libyan newspapers, and the fourth is owned by the Movement of Revolutionary Committees, a state-supported ideological organization. Broadcast media are also controlled by the government and reflect official positions. For the first time under Qadhafi's rule, ostensibly private media were permitted to operate in 2007. A subsidiary of the Qadhafi Development Foundation, the 1/9 Media Group, launched a satellite television station, Al-Libiya; a radio station; and two daily newspapers, *Oea* and *Cyrene*. No foreign publications are available, and although satellite television is easily accessible, popular pan-Arab satellite television stations such as Al-Jazeera and Al-Arabiya do not have local correspondents covering Libya. The internet also serves as an alternate source of news, but internet penetration remains relatively low; only about 4 percent of the population used the medium in 2007. Access is furnished by a single government-owned service provider. Despite occasional government blocks on political opposition sites, Libyans based outside the country use the internet to criticize the authorities. There have been several cases over the past few years in which the government has harassed or imprisoned Libyans who attacked it from Europe-based websites.

Liechtenstein

LEGAL ENVIRONMENT: 1
POLITICAL ENVIRONMENT: 5
ECONOMIC ENVIRONMENT: 8

Status: Free

TOTAL SCORE: 14

Survey Edition	2003	2004	2005	2006	2007
Total Score, Status	11,F	12,F	14,F	13,F	14,F

Liechtenstein's press continued to be one of the freest in the world. Freedom of expression is guaranteed under Article 40 of the 1921 constitution, and no major press freedom violations were reported in 2007. Laws currently being prepared by the government concerning press freedom include one on electronic communication to foster media and to promote smaller media outlets. There were no attacks on the press in 2007.

Liechtenstein has two publicly owned daily newspapers, *Liechtensteiner Vaterland* and *Liechtensteiner Volksblatt*; one Sunday paper, *Liewo*; and the monthly *Der Monat*. Since it encountered financial troubles in 2004, the former private radio station Radio Liechtenstein is now owned by the government and funded by some commercial revenue. The local TV channel Landeskanal broadcasts official information over the cable network. Anyone can submit a request to broadcast material of national relevance. All content has to be authorized by the government. Satellite television is widely viewed. Because of its small size and shared language, Liechtenstein relies heavily on media from neighboring Austria, Germany, and Switzerland. The internet is open and unrestricted, and just over 64 percent of the population accessed this medium on a regular basis in 2007. The government has started to publish information online and has established feedback mechanisms.

Lithuania

Status: Free

LEGAL ENVIRONMENT: 5
POLITICAL ENVIRONMENT: 7
ECONOMIC ENVIRONMENT: 6
TOTAL SCORE: 18

Survey Edition	2003	2004	2005	2006	2007
Total Score, Status	18,F	18,F	18,F	18,F	18,F

Lithuania's constitution provides for freedom of speech and of the press, and those guarantees are respected by the government in practice. According to the criminal code, libel or defamation is punishable by a fine or imprisonment, although no journalists have been imprisoned or fined during the last two years. Hate speech continues to be a criminal offense. In March, the Lithuanian Radio and Television Commission fined the director of the music television channel MTV Lithuania 3,000 litas (US$1,150) for broadcasting the cartoon series *Popetown*, which satirizes the Vatican. The commission had based its ruling on a decision by the journalism ethics inspector that the series incited religious hatred. MTV Lithuania appealed the decision, and the case was pending at year's end. The media freely criticize the government and express a wide variety of views. The Law on the Provision of Information to the Public and the Law on the Right to Obtain Information from State and Local Government Institutions regulate the public's right to freedom of information.

More than 300 privately owned newspapers publish in Lithuanian, Russian, and a few other languages. In addition to the public broadcast media, dozens of independent television and radio stations are available nationally, regionally, and locally. However, media ownership has undergone increased concentration over the last several years, leading to concerns about the possible effects on media independence and quality. Investors in the country's media market include both domestic firms and foreign companies, mainly from Scandinavia. According to the market research company TNS Latvia, Lithuania's media advertising market volume increased by 15.6 percent in 2007 from 2006; television accounted for more than 45 percent of Lithuania's total advertising market share, followed by newspapers with 25 percent. The government does not limit access to the internet, and the popularity of internet news portals continues to grow. Nonetheless, only about 34 percent of Lithuanians made use of the internet—the lowest percentage among the three Baltic countries.

Luxembourg

Status: Free

LEGAL ENVIRONMENT: 2
POLITICAL ENVIRONMENT: 3
ECONOMIC ENVIRONMENT: 7
TOTAL SCORE: 12

Survey Edition	2003	2004	2005	2006	2007
Total Score, Status	14,F	12,F	11,F	11,F	12,F

Luxembourg, one of the world's richest countries, retained its open media environment in 2007. Freedom of speech and of the press are safeguarded under Article 24 of the constitution and are respected in practice, although no freedom of information legislation is currently in place. An independent press council deals with press complaints and ethical questions. Privacy of sources was an issue in 2006 after the Office of the Public Prosecutor searched offices of the Broadcasting Center Europe S.A., but there were no similar reports, and no follow-up reports, in 2007. Owing to an extremely liberal media policy and a long tradition of providing television and radio services to European audiences, Luxembourg has a rich and diverse media whose influence goes beyond its borders. Exemplary of the free and open press environment that exists in Luxembourg, no journalists were subject to violent attacks or harassment in 2007.

Dailies are printed in Luxembourgish, German, and French, and one weekly publishes in Portuguese. Newspapers represent diverse viewpoints and are privately owned, though state subsidies protect presses from closing. Broadcast media are highly concentrated, dominated by the local group RTL. Luxembourg is also home to the largest European satellite operator. There is only one public broadcasting station, CLT. Many broadcasters operate only a few hours a day. There are two national and four regional broadcasters as well as several local radio stations. The internet is open and unrestricted, with an estimated 340,000 users, or just over 70 percent of the population, in 2007.

Macedonia

LEGAL ENVIRONMENT: 12
POLITICAL ENVIRONMENT: 19
ECONOMIC ENVIRONMENT: 16

Status: Partly Free

TOTAL SCORE: 47

Survey Edition	2003	2004	2005	2006	2007
Total Score, Status	50,PF	53,PF	51,PF	49,PF	45,PF

The legal framework contains most of the basic laws protecting freedom of the press and of expression, and government representatives generally respect these rights. Freedom of information legislation was enacted in 2006, but an Open Society Institute report released in late 2007 found that roughly half of all information requests over the preceding year had been ignored by state institutions with impunity. Another measure passed by the parliament in 2006 eliminated imprisonment as a penalty for libel and defamation. The offenses remain punishable by fines, however, and the institutional weakness of the judiciary enhances journalists' vulnerability to prosecutions and lawsuits. The Broadcasting Council, which regulates television and radio outlets, is ineffective and subject to political influence. The collection of broadcast licensing fees broke down entirely in early 2007, adding to the council's funding problems. Separately, a court in June awarded a total of 100,000 Euros (US$150,000) to 17 journalists whose telephones had been tapped illegally by the Interior Ministry and the telecom company MT in 2000. However, the reporters had initially sought 180,000 Euros (US$290,000) each; both the journalists and the government later appealed the awarded amount. No government officials were ever tried for the larger eavesdropping scandal, which came to light in 2001; the interior minister at the time received a presidential pardon.

Most of the country's numerous and diverse private media outlets are tied to political or business interests that influence their content, and the state-owned media tend to support government positions. Journalists faced a series of violent incidents and threats in 2007. Much of the trouble began with a September brawl in parliament among members of rival ethnic Albanian parties. Some reporters covering the disturbance and subsequent police actions were assaulted by security guards or police, and video recordings of the events were confiscated. A number of journalists later protested the abuses by walking out on a subsequent government press conference. In November, the bilingual private television station Alsat-M alleged that the authorities had consistently pressured it since the September unrest, in which two of its cameramen were harassed and temporarily detained by police and a third was severely beaten, leaving him with two fractured ribs. The station cited repeated labor and financial inspections, unexplained break-ins, and damage to its transmission equipment, as well as government threats to pull its license and prosecute it for its coverage of a recent police raid in which six people had been killed. In a separate incident in May, a column by Iso Rusi in the Albanian-language daily newspaper *Koha* prompted a statement by the Democratic Party of Albanians—part of the ruling coalition—that contained ethnic and religious slurs as well as threats of violence.

Macedonia has a high density of media outlets for its population, including five private nationwide television broadcasters (as well as one public one) and dozens of local television and radio stations. Journalists' salaries are low, professionalism and advertising revenue are scarce, and financial weakness often leads outlets to conform to their owners' political and economic interests. A number of major television stations and newspapers are owned by or linked to political party leaders, and outlets are typically divided along ethnic lines. Ownership of the top print publications is concentrated in the hands of a few firms, including Germany's Westdeutsche Allgemeine Zeitung, which holds three leading dailies. The government is a major advertiser and reportedly favors outlets it perceives as friendly. Access to the internet is restricted only by cost and infrastructural obstacles; as a result, usage remains relatively low at just under 20 percent of the population.

LEGAL ENVIRONMENT: 14

POLITICAL ENVIRONMENT: 19

Madagascar
ECONOMIC ENVIRONMENT: 15

Status: Partly Free
TOTAL SCORE: 48

Survey Edition	2003	2004	2005	2006	2007
Total Score, Status	38,PF	41,PF	50,PF	49,PF	50,PF

Although freedom of speech and of the press are protected by the constitution, strict libel laws and other restrictions are used occasionally to muzzle the media. However, as in the previous year, no journalists were convicted of libel during 2007. In addition, unlike in the previous year, there were no reported incidents in which government authorities arrested journalists, and no journalists were attacked because of their work. However, in September Honore Tsabotogay, editor of the Catholic Church–owned Radio Rakama, was assaulted by supporters of the ruling party while he was shooting footage of vehicles transporting voters to polling stations. No action was taken against his attacker, but Tsabotogay was himself charged with "disrupting the election proceedings" by filming the transport; the charges were later dropped.

In 2007, there were approximately 245 licensed radio stations, 12 registered daily newspapers, and 37 licensed television stations. The 1990 Law on Press Freedom was followed by the creation of privately owned FM radio stations and more critical political reporting by the print media. However, President Marc Ravalomanana owns the private Malagasy Broadcasting System, which operates the MBS TV and Radio MBS networks. In addition, many private radio stations in the capital are owned by Ravalomanana supporters. Owing to low pay, journalists are subject to bribery. Occasionally, the government also exerts pressure on private media outlets to curb their coverage of political issues and criticism of the government, causing many journalists to practice self-censorship. Poverty and fairly widespread illiteracy also mean that the print media are accessed primarily by the French-speaking urban elite. The internet is unrestricted by the government but was accessed by less than 1 percent of the population in 2007.

Malawi

Status: Partly Free

LEGAL ENVIRONMENT: 17
POLITICAL ENVIRONMENT: 20
ECONOMIC ENVIRONMENT: 18
TOTAL SCORE: 55

Survey Edition	2003	2004	2005	2006	2007
Total Score, Status	57,PF	52,PF	54,PF	55,PF	53,PF

Freedom of speech and of the press are constitutionally guaranteed in Malawi, although these rights are sometimes restricted in practice. The government has occasionally used libel and other laws to put pressure on journalists. In fact, in April 2007, the Malawi Communications Regulatory Authority (MACRA) went so far as to ban all private media outlets from broadcasting political rallies live without prior permission from the MACRA. This move primarily targeted the main private radio stations, Capital Radio, Joy Radio, and Zodiac Broadcasting Station. MACRA claimed it acted in order to curb the airing of "hate messages," even though no evidence was given to support the accusation that this had been taking place. However, in July, the high court struck down the MACRA order as unconstitutional when a lawsuit was filed by Joy Radio. Later in October, MACRA appeared to retaliate for the ruling by ordering Joy TV—an affiliate of Joy Radio that stood to be the nation's first private television station—to immediately cease all its broadcasts until the station could obtain the necessary licenses. Tailos Bakili, the station manager, claimed that they did indeed have all relevant licenses.

The government does not exercise overt censorship, but freedom of expression in Malawi is threatened in more subtle ways, often resulting in self-censorship. One journalist was reportedly attacked in 2007. Dickson Kashoti, a reporter for the private *Daily Times*, was physically attacked by parliamentarian Joseph Njobvuyalema over an article that had criticized him. Njobvuyalema was later fired from his position and sentenced to three months in prison for assault.

The print media represent a broad spectrum of opinion; 10 independent newspapers are available, and of the 8 major papers in circulation, 6 are privately owned and most are editorially independent. The state-owned Malawi Broadcasting Corporation (MBC) operates the country's 2 largest radio stations, and there are approximately 15 private radio stations with more limited coverage operating mainly in urban areas. Following the ban on Joy TV, state-owned Television Malawi—which generally adheres to a progovernment bias—is now the country's only television station. In 2007, the Malawi parliament again approved only half of the funding for MBC and Television Malawi, accusing the two state broadcasters of bias toward the government and the ruling party. At the same time, independent radio broadcasters receive no support from the state even through advertising revenue. As all equipment must be imported and paid for in US dollars, the high cost of taxes and import duties imposed by the state threaten the economic viability of many independent commercial broadcasters. There are no restrictions on the internet, although with access at less than 1 percent of the population, it is not a major source for news.

Malaysia

Status: Not Free

LEGAL ENVIRONMENT: 24
POLITICAL ENVIRONMENT: 23
ECONOMIC ENVIRONMENT: 18
TOTAL SCORE: 65

Survey Edition	2003	2004	2005	2006	2007
Total Score, Status	71,NF	69,NF	69,NF	65,NF	68,NF

While Malaysian journalists, particularly online, showed greater aggressiveness in covering official corruption and antigovernment protests, press freedom continued to suffer in 2007 owing to significant legal restrictions, intimidation, and an escalating crackdown on the more open online media. Meanwhile, the Barisan National (BN) ruling coalition invoked traditionally tight restrictions on the mainstream media to prevent coverage of heightened opposition activity toward year's end.

The constitution provides each citizen with "the right to freedom of speech and expression" but allows for limitations on this right. The 1984 Printing Presses and Publications Act (PPPA) requires all publishers and printing firms to obtain an annual operations permit and gives the prime minister the authority to revoke licenses at any time without judicial review. The PPPA has been used by authorities to shut down or otherwise circumscribe the distribution of media outlets for material deemed pro-opposition, against the national interest, or "sensitive." The PPPA was invoked in March 2007 to threaten the opposition paper *Harakah* for "violating its permit conditions" after it ran a front-page story criticizing the prime minister, covering controversial toll hikes, and linking the deputy prime minister to a murder case. In September, the Tamil daily *Makkal Osai* was suspended under the same legislation for publishing a picture that associated Jesus with cigarettes.

The 1988 Broadcasting Act allows the information minister to decide who can own a broadcast station and the type of television service suitable for the Malaysian public. The country has no access to information legislation, and officials are reluctant to share controversial data. The Official Secrets Act (OSA), Sedition Act, and harsh criminal defamation legislation are also used to impose restrictions on the press and other critics, and all transgressions are punishable by several years in prison. The government used this restrictive legislation against online media for the first time in 2007 in response to bloggers' and websites' increasing coverage of corruption cases and other controversial matters. In January 2007, defamation charges were first brought against bloggers accused of plagiarism by the publisher and editor of the *New Straits Times*, which enjoys close ties to the ruling United Malays National Organization party. In April, a BN official brought defamation charges against Malaysiakini, a critical website.

Although violence against media workers in Malaysia is relatively uncommon, several instances of physical assault or death threats against journalists were reported in 2007. In the most severe case, in November, photojournalist R. Raman fell into a coma after being beaten by unidentified men, apparently in connection with articles he wrote for a Tamil-language daily on the possible closure and poor state of schools in the community; according to Reporters Sans Frontieres, he awoke two weeks later but remains paralyzed.

The threat of expensive defamation suits, sackings, media closures, media bans, and unannounced interrogation by the Ministry of Internal Security for any "mishandling" of information generally inhibits investigative reporting. Moreover, a history of political interference in media coverage of issues considered by the government to be against the national interest or "sensitive" has fostered a culture of self-censorship on the part of traditional media. While there has been somewhat greater criticism of official policy in the mainstream print press in recent years, both the print and broadcast media's news coverage and editorials generally support the government line. Reporting bans issued in July 2006 in connection with heightened tensions related to matters of race and religion were repeated in July 2007 when the media were prohibited from reporting all negative reactions to the deputy prime minister's assertion that Malaysia had always been an Islamic state. In November, the authorities ordered the mainstream media to refrain from reporting on antigovernment rallies or relaying the organizers' statements; according to Malaysia's Center for Investigative Journalism, news coverage of the rallies neglected the antigovernment stance while reports on clashes between participants and the police were biased in favor of the police.

Online journalists have increasingly defied this tradition, however, and in 2007 played a particularly central role in exposing government corruption and covering antigovernment protests toward year's end. In addition to using defamation suits and other legalistic means to silence criticism, the government responded by issuing coverage directives to online media for the first time. A July statement by the government explicitly warned that bloggers who write about "sensitive issues" would be charged under the Internal Security Act, OSA, and Sedition Act. Also in July, Nathaniel Tan, a prominent blogger and aide to the head of the opposition People's Justice Party, was arrested under the OSA. Tan was charged in connection with his commentary related to corruption in the country's internal security system and was released after his four-day remand expired. Newspapers were specifically warned against covering "rumors" being reported online. In April, Prime Minister Abdullah Badawi rejected a proposal that would require bloggers to register with the government. In June, however, he convened a task force of BN officials to find legislation that would secure control over online content without contradicting the Bill of Guarantees that was passed under the Multimedia Super Corridor in the 1990s and prohibits internet censorship.

Foreign publications are subject to censorship, and the distribution of issues containing critical articles is frequently delayed. In January, the Internal Security Ministry removed an article on Asian Muslims from local copies of the *Economist* magazine for allegedly "contravening Islamic teaching." The government directly censors books and films for profanity, nudity, and violence as well as certain political and religious material. The Malaysian Film Censorship Unit banned a film about former Malay Muslim members of the Communist Party of Malaysia in February 2007 for portraying the Communist struggle as noble. Television stations censor programming according to government guidelines; a talk show was banned for contradicting the values of Islam Hadari advocated by the prime minister in February. The government also maintained a ban on the Chinese-language newspaper *Epoch Times*.

Print journalism is dominated by 11 national daily newspapers—3 in English, 4 in Malay, and 4 in Chinese—all of which are owned or controlled by the ruling coalition or individuals closely connected with the government. A business deal in October 2006 between the Malaysian Chinese Association and media tycoon Tiong Hiew King solidified the monopolization of the Chinese press, with all top four Chinese dailies now concentrated in the hands of a firm political-business alliance. Regional press freedom watchdog groups expressed concern in February 2007 regarding a further consolidation of the Chinese media across countries following a proposed tripartite merger among three media groups, two of them Malaysian and one based in Hong Kong, all owned by Tiong. Such a merger would create the largest Chinese publication group outside China and Taiwan. The state-owned Radio Television Malaysia operates two television and a large number of radio stations, though private radio stations broadcasting in Malay, Tamil, Chinese, and English are also in operation.

With 60 percent of the population accessing the internet, online media have helped minimize the government's monopoly of information in the past few years and bolstered the average Malaysian's access to alternative information sources. Moreover, online media proved a crucial organizing tool and means of publicizing the opposition-led and minority rights demonstrations in November. There were no reported restrictions on internet access; however, according to the U.S. State Department, the government monitored e-mails sent to blogs, and some online authors were known to self-censor.

Maldives

Status: Not Free

LEGAL ENVIRONMENT: 23
POLITICAL ENVIRONMENT: 25
ECONOMIC ENVIRONMENT: 18
TOTAL SCORE: 66

Survey Edition	2003	2004	2005	2006	2007
Total Score, Status	64,NF	64,NF	68,NF	70,NF	68,NF

Continuing a trend from previous years, a modest expansion of media diversity and public debate in 2007 was balanced by official harassment of journalists. Freedom of expression and of the press are not provided for in the constitution and are often disregarded by the government in practice. Although new regulations in January 2007 dramatically reduced damages for defamation, the legal environment remains harsh. The penal code bans speech or actions that could "arouse people against the government"; a 1968 law prohibits speech considered libelous, inimical to Islam, or a threat to national security; regulations make editors responsible for the content of material they publish; and authorities are empowered by law to shut newspapers and sanction journalists for articles containing unfounded criticism of the government. The Information Ministry, which is spearheading reform efforts, submitted four media-related bills to parliament in February 2006, including bills on freedom of information, press freedom, a proposed Media Council, and registration of print media. Though discussion continued on them in the parliament throughout 2007, none had passed by year's end and two had been withdrawn. In a positive development, the Maldives Media Association, which includes representatives from both pro-opposition and state-run media, began operating in October.

Journalists, particularly those who cover demonstrations or who write critical stories, continue to be subject to arrest or other forms of harassment. Many journalists practice self-censorship and do not scrutinize official policies. During 2007, reporters and photographers from both pro-opposition and state-owned media were arrested while covering protests, illegal prayer meetings, and a taxi drivers' strike. In April, Ibrahim Mohamed, a reporter for the progovernment *Miadhu* newspaper, was held by police for more than a day after taking photographs of police beating opposition Maldivian Democratic Party leader Mohamed Nasheed. Several journalists were also detained during a demonstration marking World Press Freedom Day in May. Owing to *Minivan*'s overtly antigovernment stance, its management and employees have been particularly targeted for official intimidation. In January 2007, Phillip Wellman, a foreign reporter for the English-language *Minivan News* website, was expelled and banned for two years. Journalist Abdullah Saeed continued to serve a life prison sentence after being convicted in 2006 of apparently fabricated drug charges. In June, *Minivan Daily* journalist Ali Rasheed was arrested and held for 43 days after being interviewed by the Qatar-based satellite station Al-Jazeera. Following his release, he was sentenced in absentia to life in prison on drug charges and remained in custody at year's end. In a positive development, the government dropped some charges against *Minivan Daily* editor Aminath Najeeb and deputy editor Nazim Sattar, but Najeeb still faced jail time on charges of "disobedience of an order."

Most broadcast media continue to be government owned and operated, and although these outlets have recently provided more diverse and vigorous coverage, they continue to reflect progovernment views. Since a 2005 law liberalized the registration process, scores of publications have been registered, including six daily newspapers. Many of the key periodicals are owned by those connected to the government, but some publications, such as *Adduvas*, *Jazeera*, and *Hamma*, have adopted a more critical, balanced tone. The pro-opposition *Minivan Daily*, which started as an online publication, now circulates a print version in the Maldives. In 2007, the country's first private broadcasters—radio stations Capital and DhiFM as well as Atoll TV—were launched; however, their independence remained limited because operating licenses were granted via individual agreements with the government rather than through reformed broadcasting legislation. The more overtly antigovernment Minivan Radio was unable to obtain a frequency owing to the prohibitive costs of obtaining a frequency license. Although the country's sole internet service provider is state owned, the internet is generally not restricted. However, the pro-opposition *Dhivehi Observer* website has been blocked. The internet was accessed by less than 6 percent of the population in 2007.

Mali

Status: Free

LEGAL ENVIRONMENT: 10
POLITICAL ENVIRONMENT: 9
ECONOMIC ENVIRONMENT: 8
TOTAL SCORE: 27

Survey Edition	2003	2004	2005	2006	2007
Total Score, Status	24,F	27,F	23,F	24,F	24,F

Although Mali's constitution protects the right to free speech and the country's broadcast and print media have historically ranked among the freest in Africa, recent actions by authorities against journalists have contradicted this past trend. Furthermore, severe punishments for libel still exist under a 1993 law criminalizing slander. Legislation passed in 2000 reduced the maximum penalty for those convicted, but the accused still remain guilty until proven innocent.

Libel laws, though not consistently enforced, were applied in 2007. In March, a court in the capital city of Bamako sentenced Diaby Makoro Camara and Oumar Bouare, respectively the managing editor and editor in chief of the private monthly *Kabako*, to four-month suspended prison terms and fines of approximately US$100 for defaming the minister of planning, Marimantia Diarra. The 2006 article that instigated these charges reported that the minister had allegedly attempted to threaten his former fiancée with physical force. On June 14, authorities arrested Bassirou Kassim Minta, a teacher who assigned his 10th-grade students a fictitious essay about a presidential sex scandal, on charges of offending the president, along with Seydine Oumar Diarra, editor of the private daily *Info-Matin*, who reported on the story. The paper's director received an eight-month suspended sentence and a fine of US$450. On June 20, authorities arrested four other editors whose papers republished the story. Diarra was forced to serve 13 days in prison and to pay a fine of approximately US$400; the sentences for the other four editors were eventually suspended, although they were forced to pay similar fines. Minta was sentenced to two months in prison, fined approximately US$1,200, and banned from teaching.

There were other instances during 2007 in which authorities intimidated journalists. In March, the private station Radio Jamakan was evicted from its office in a government-owned building just one month before presidential elections were scheduled following the station's critical coverage of the opposition. In July, a broadcaster with Radio Kafo-Kan, a community station based in the south, was attacked by a local politician for allegedly incorrectly reporting the politician's share of seats won in the June parliamentary election. The government does not restrict access to foreign media.

Today, there are more than 100 private radio stations and over 50 independent newspapers, many of which openly criticize the government. Given the adult literacy rate of only 24 percent, the majority of Malians rely on broadcast media, and private or community radio stations provide a critical service. The country's only national television station remains under state control but generally provides balanced political coverage. Although the government also does not restrict internet use, less than 1 percent of the population was able to access this electronic resource in 2007.

Malta

LEGAL ENVIRONMENT: 3
POLITICAL ENVIRONMENT: 8
ECONOMIC ENVIRONMENT: 9

Status: Free

TOTAL SCORE: 20

Survey Edition	2003	2004	2005	2006	2007
Total Score, Status	13,F	15,F	18,F	18,F	17,F

The constitution guarantees freedom of speech and of the press but also restricts these rights under a variety of circumstances. Malta bases its laws on the European model but is one of only three European Union (EU) members not to have freedom of information legislation. The Broadcasting Authority, an independent regulatory statutory body, sued an independent television station for broadcasting material that could incite racial hatred.

Several journalists were injured while covering a protest by hunters and trappers in the capital city of Valetta. The attack was the latest in a series of threats and attacks against journalists covering public demonstrations and debates in Malta. The police continue to investigate an arson attack directed against a journalist and an editor covering issues of immigration, racism, and intolerance toward immigrants. The growing number of migrants seeking asylum have grown in Malta since the island became a member of the EU in 2004, making the issue a central topic for local media.

There are at least five daily and two weekly newspapers operating in both Maltese and English. Political parties, private investors, and the Catholic Church all have direct investments in broadcasting and print media that openly express partisan views. The only national television broadcaster is TVM, though the island also has access to Italian television, which many Maltese watch. Several domestic radio stations are regulated through the Broadcasting Authority. The government does not block the internet, and 53 percent of households and 90 percent of schools had access during the year.

Marshall Islands

LEGAL ENVIRONMENT: 2
POLITICAL ENVIRONMENT: 6
ECONOMIC ENVIRONMENT: 9

Status: Free

TOTAL SCORE: 17

Survey Edition	2003	2004	2005	2006	2007
Total Score, Status	10,F	12,F	13,F	15,F	17,F

Freedom of speech and of the press are safeguarded in Article 2 of the Marshallese constitution, and the government generally respects these rights. There is no freedom of information legislation, and no plans to draft such legislation are under way. Self-censorship is practiced on occasion over politically sensitive issues. In 2007, a number of leading journalists from the Marshall Islands joined the newly formed Micronesian Media Association to protect free and independent journalism and public access to information. The Marshallese people receive most of their news from the independent weekly *Marshall Islands Journal*, which launched an online edition in 2007, and the state-run V7AB radio. The government also releases a monthly newspaper, the *Marshall Islands Gazette*, and broadcasts MBC TV. American broadcasts are available via satellite. Blackouts occasionally interfere with radio and television broadcasts. The internet is unrestricted but is accessed by just 4 percent of the population. The government launched a new website in October 2006 to facilitate online communication with its citizens.

LEGAL ENVIRONMENT: 18

POLITICAL ENVIRONMENT: 20

Mauritania

ECONOMIC ENVIRONMENT: 18

Status: Partly Free

TOTAL SCORE: 56

Survey Edition	2003	2004	2005	2006	2007
Total Score, Status	61,NF	64,NF	65,NF	57,PF	55,PF

Mauritania's media environment has opened considerably since a bloodless coup in 2005 overthrew the existing authoritarian regime. Starting with reforms initiated by the transitional military government, authorities have subsequently passed numerous reforms to improve media freedom in the country. Reforms enacted in 2006 include the elimination of the requirement for prepublication government approval for newspapers, the granting of journalists the legal right to the protection of sources, and the establishment of the High Authority for the Press and Broadcasting (HAPA), the country's first independent media regulatory body. Although HAPA's independence is compromised by the president's ability to appoint three of the body's six members, including the chair, and it had not fulfilled its mission by year's end to foster private television and radio stations, media coverage of the March 2007 presidential election was relatively balanced, with free newspaper space and airtime allotted to each candidate.

Nonetheless, despite these positive trends and the constitutional guarantee of free expression, newspapers are still subject to closure for publishing materials seen to denigrate Islam or pose a national security risk. During 2007, journalists faced the threats of detention, imprisonment, and even physical harm for publishing or broadcasting stories considered libelous.

In March, assailants, including a supporter of a failed first-round presidential candidate, raided the Al-Jazeera office in the capital, Nouakchott, claiming that the station had not given enough time to lesser-known candidates. In response, authorities arrested four suspects and initiated an investigation to identify the other participants. In May, Isselmou Ould Mustapha, managing editor of the independent weekly *Tahalil Hebdo*, was threatened with physical force by the board chairman of the credit union Mutpeche, Mohammed Ould Saleck, for refusing to disclose his sources on an article accusing Saleck of corruption. Also in May, Abdel Fettah Ould Ebeidna, managing editor of the private daily *Al-Aqsa*, was detained for four days on libel charges brought by Mohamed Ould Bouammatou, a businessman the paper accused of being involved in a drug ring. In November,

Ebeidna was sentenced to one year in prison on the charge of making a "false accusation" and fined approximately US$250. At year's end, Ebeidna was out of the country with an appeal pending.

Throughout 2007, Mauritanian journalists faced other instances of harassment from prominent public figures and their associates. In August, First Lady Khattou bint al-Boukhary charged the private daily *El Bedil Athalith* with libel following a report alleging she attempted to influence hiring in the national television office. In the same month, she also accused Sidi Mohamed Ould Ebbe, the paper's editor, of libel following reports that accused her of using her public role to raise private charity funds. The First Lady withdrew these libel suits in December, however. On August 16, the prime minister's bodyguards assaulted Mohamed Mahmoud Ould Moghdad, a reporter with Radio Mauritanie, for allegedly avoiding a security check at a Health Ministry event. Following an investigation, the government issued a formal apology and Moghdad withdrew his complaint. On August 31, two of the First Lady's bodyguards attacked Elvaka Ould Cheibany, a correspondent with the private daily *Nouakchott Info*, allegedly over a report on the First Lady's increasingly tense relationship with the media.

Mauritania is currently the only West African country without a private radio or television station. However, a new public television station began broadcasting in October that will devote airtime to the country's minority languages—Pular, Soninke, and Wolof. In addition to several state-controlled papers, there are numerous private daily and weekly papers. However, a relatively low literacy rate of 51 percent limits the impact of the print media in general. Internet access is available and is not restricted by the government, although this electronic resource was used by only 3.1 percent of the population in 2007.

Mauritius

Status: Free

LEGAL ENVIRONMENT: 6
POLITICAL ENVIRONMENT: 8
ECONOMIC ENVIRONMENT: 12
TOTAL SCORE: 26

Survey Edition	2003	2004	2005	2006	2007
Total Score, Status	24,F	26,F	28,F	26,F	26,F

Freedom of expression is safeguarded by the 1968 constitution, and this right was generally respected in practice in 2007. Although there are formally harsh punishments for libel, these laws are not regularly upheld in practice, and the independent media were diverse and frequently expressed views critical of the government. However, there is currently no law in place to guarantee access to public information.

In a worrying move that contradicted the traditionally liberal Mauritian media environment, three journalists were arrested for the first time in 13 years. On November 21, authorities in the capital, Port Louis, arrested Annabelle Volbert and Josian Valere of the private station Radio Plus, and Gerard Cateaux, editor in chief of the private newspaper *Weekend*, on charges of defamation and disseminating inaccurate news. These arrests followed coverage of the discovery of money in a safe used by the late former head of the Major Crime Investigation Team, Premnath Raddhoa. The three journalists were provisionally released following several hours of questioning on the day of their arrests and were released on bail after a court appearance the following day.

Mauritians receive the majority of their news from television, which is monopolized by the government. Radio broadcasts are dominated by the government's Mauritius Broadcasting Corporation, which is funded predominantly through a television license fee, although there are several private radio stations. The private print press is vibrant, with 9 daily papers and 33 weeklies, but ownership is concentrated in two main media houses, Le Mauricien Ltd. and La Sentinelle Ltd. The internet is unrestricted by the government, and usage is wide compared with that in other African nations, at 24 percent of all households. However, on November 9, the Information Communication Technology Authority (ICTA) allegedly requested that internet service providers block access to Facebook, the social-networking site, in response to the posting of a fake profile of Prime Minister Navin Ramgoolam. Access to Facebook was reportedly restored later in the day once Facebook had removed the profile, following the ICTA's request.

Mexico

LEGAL ENVIRONMENT: 13
POLITICAL ENVIRONMENT: 25
ECONOMIC ENVIRONMENT: 13

Status: Partly Free

TOTAL SCORE: 51

Survey Edition	2003	2004	2005	2006	2007
Total Score, Status	38,PF	36,PF	42,PF	48,PF	48,PF

Drug-related violence further undermined press freedom in 2007 as attacks on journalists spread geographically, impunity remained the norm, and self-censorship expanded. Furthermore, the Supreme Court blocked a politically sensitive prosecution in the case of a threatened journalist, and the firing of a critical radio journalist raised questions about broadcast concentration. On the positive side, the government eliminated criminal defamation, libel, and slander statutes at the federal level, and the Supreme Court threw out provisions of the country's controversial broadcast reform.

Articles 6 and 7 of the constitution provide for freedom of speech. While President Felipe Calderon and the Congress ended criminal prosecution of defamation, libel, and slander by moving them into the federal civil code on April 12, most states still criminalize these violations. In past years, numerous politicians have used state statutes to pressure critics. The April federal Decriminalization Law obliges states to follow suit and eliminate criminal statutes at the state level. In one of the most controversial cases of the year, on November 29, the Supreme Court cleared Puebla governor Mario Marin of wrongdoing in the arbitrary arrest and harassment of journalist Lydia Cacho, who had linked Marin to a businessman accused of child prostitution. The ruling outraged journalist groups and provoked the resignation of the federal prosecutor of crimes against women. The United Nations High Commissioner for Human Rights recommended Cacho seek refuge abroad to prevent further violations. A report in Spain's *El Pais* suggested big broadcasters had abandoned critical coverage of Cacho as part of a political deal. Legislation that would federalize crimes against the press, criminalizing any violent attempts or actions to hinder freedom of expression, was introduced by the Office of the Attorney General in September. The bill remained pending at year's end.

Most of the worst violence against the press was linked to an expanding drug cartel dispute. Three reporters and three newspaper deliverymen were murdered in connection with their work; three more journalists disappeared and two others survived shootings. Killings marred four states, including two far from the violent border region. In December, a group of unidentified gunmen killed *La Opinion de Michoacan* reporter Gerardo Israel Garcia in Uruapan, Michoacan, a new trafficking hub. Mateo Cortes Martinez, Agustin Lopez Nolasco, and Flor Vasquez Lopez, all workers for the Oaxaca daily *El Imparcial del Istmo*, were shot on October 8 inside their newspaper delivery truck. The newspaper's editor had received e-mails warning him to reduce drug coverage. In April, *Interdiario* crime reporter Saul Noe Martinez Ortega was found dead near Agua Prieta, Sonora, on the Arizona border after being kidnapped by gunmen. Also that month, broadcaster Amado Ramirez was murdered when leaving work near Acapulco's main square. Police charged suspects, but the case weakened when a witness recanted, Reporters Sans Frontieres noted. According to the Committee to Protect Journalists, three journalists disappeared in 2007: TV Azteca correspondent Gamaliel Lopez and cameraman Gerardo Paredes in May and *Tabasco Hoy* crime reporter Rodolfo Rincon Taracena in January. The cases were linked to reporting on drug trafficking.

Media workers received all kinds of threats; gruesomely, severed heads of local people were delivered to two newspapers in Veracruz and Tabasco. This atmosphere took an obvious toll on coverage. Among other incidences: The *Cambio Sonora* newspaper in Hermosillo closed after two grenade attacks; Amado Ramirez's Acapulco radio program was taken off the air in April owing to continued threats to the station following his death; reporters at Oaxaca's *El Imparcial del Istmo* all resigned following the murder of their delivery workers; and big dailies in metropolitan Monterrey eliminated reporters' bylines on drug stories and now adhere to official police narratives. The U.S.-based *San Antonio Express News* removed its border reporter after U.S. government sources received a report that traffickers were targeting a foreign journalist. The Foreign Correspondents Association urged correspondents to be especially cautious. A compounding problem was the abundance of drug money. Like police officers, journalists face the dilemma of *plata o plomo*, receiving silver or lead, and some journalists worried drug money would taint their profession.

Through all the violence, government inaction on press cases persisted. The creation in 2006 of a special federal prosecutor's office for crimes against the press has not led to any successful prosecutions in the 108 cases under investigation. Authorities blamed lack of resources and jurisdictional problems but had not strengthened the office by year's end. The many pending cases include the murder in Oaxaca City of U.S. documentarian Bradley Will, who died while filming political disturbances in 2006. The case stands out because photographers published pictures of the apparent gunmen—identified as government agents—firing at Will. No serious investigations have resulted, press groups charge.

There is a diversity of perspectives represented in media in the largest cities, less so in smaller states and the countryside. An estimated 300 independently owned newspapers are in operation. Television remains limited because of the duopoly (Televisa and TV Azteca) that has dominated Mexican broadcasting since the authoritarian era. A positive development occurred, however, when the Supreme Court tossed out provisions of a 2006 reform of the Broadcasting Law that critics said would have consolidated ownership concentration into the digital age and left noncommercial broadcasters in limbo. Congressional follow-up was slow to materialize, however. The firing of critical radio host Carmen Aristegui for refusing to follow unspecified orders from W Radio owners Televisa and Grupo Prisa of Spain renewed criticism of editorial manipulation for corporate advantage. The Inter-American Commission on Human Rights agreed to discuss the case at a hearing on media ownership concentration. Government officials are known to use public advertising contracts as a means of punishing unfavorable press outlets. After 33 years, Mexico City–based national radio station Radio Monitor went off the air in June owing to the withdrawal of public contracts by the government. The government does not restrict the internet, which was used by close to 22 percent of the population.

Micronesia

Status: Free

LEGAL ENVIRONMENT: 2
POLITICAL ENVIRONMENT: 8
ECONOMIC ENVIRONMENT: 11
TOTAL SCORE: 21

Survey Edition	2003	2004	2005	2006	2007
Total Score, Status	17,F	19,F	18,F	20,F	20,F

Article 4, Section 1, of the constitution states that no law may deny or impair freedom of expression, but there are no specific safeguards for speech or the press. Free speech was generally respected by the government in 2007, and there were no documented attacks on the press. In September, media executives gathered to form the Micronesian Media Association. The organization aims to promote journalistic freedom and the public's access to information. A lack of economic resources is the biggest constraint on Micronesian media. The country has several newspapers; the widest reaching is the state-owned *Kaselehlie Press*, which is published fortnightly. Two independent weeklies, the *Sinlaku Sun Times* and *Da Rohng*, have a reputation as being critical of the government. There is also an online daily, the *Mariana Variety*. Each of the four state governments has a radio station that broadcasts in the local language, but they have been hampered by technical problems and were inoperable throughout most of the year because of weather-related damages to equipment. Two religiously affiliated radio stations were launched in 2007. The states of Pohnpei and Chuuk have commercial television stations, and Yap has a government-run television station. Foreign television content is available via satellite. The internet is not restricted by the government and was accessed by nearly 15 percent of the population in 2007.

Moldova

Status: Not Free

LEGAL ENVIRONMENT: 20
POLITICAL ENVIRONMENT: 25
ECONOMIC ENVIRONMENT: 21

TOTAL SCORE: 66

Survey Edition	2003	2004	2005	2006	2007
Total Score, Status	59,PF	63,NF	65,NF	65,NF	65,NF

Press freedom declined in 2007 as the government restricted independent news reporting in the months ahead of the June local elections. While the Moldovan government has made some attempts to comply with the requirements of European integration in recent years, enacting a number of democratic legal reforms, those reforms have not been properly implemented or enforced and media restrictions have continued.

Although the government often infringes on legally protected press freedoms, libel is for the most part no longer punishable by imprisonment, and in 2006 the parliament approved legislation designed to moderate excessive financial awards in libel cases. No new libel lawsuits were reported in 2007, partly because a series of judgments against journalists have been struck down by the European Court of Human Rights in recent years. The Strasbourg-based court found violations of freedom of expression in seven cases during 2007, most of them libel judgments involving articles that exposed government corruption. Journalists are often not able to get basic public information from the government because a number of officials continue to ignore an existing Access to Information Law.

In July, the nine members of the Audiovisual Coordinating Council, a broadcast media regulatory agency, voted to replace their progovernment chairman with a representative of the opposition. The government refused to recognize the vote, and two months later, authorities reportedly pressured the council to elect a different progovernment chairman. An audiovisual code approved by the parliament in 2006 was used in January 2007 to privatize and rein in two municipal media outlets in the capital, Chisinau, that had previously criticized the government in their news reports. In March, the ruling Communist Party and their Christian Democrat allies passed a law reducing the rebroadcasting of parliamentary debates on public television. This in turn decreased coverage of the political opposition in the months ahead of local elections.

President Vladimir Voronin's government controls the country's public broadcaster, Teleradio Moldova, whose radio and television news programs consistently favored progovernment candidates and ignored opposition candidates during local election campaigns. Owners of both state-run and private media houses continued to promote self-censorship, and police occasionally harassed journalists for reporting on politically embarrassing events. For example, in March, police officers in Chisinau arrested journalists with the television outlets Pro TV and DTV and confiscated their videotapes after they filmed police arresting peaceful protesters.

In the separatist Transnistria region, media are highly restricted and politicized. Most local broadcast media are controlled by the Transnistrian authorities or companies like Sheriff Enterprises, which are linked to the separatist regime. Several small opposition newspapers like *Novaya Gazeta* and *Chelovek i Yevo Prava* criticize abuses committed by the separatist authorities, and their journalists and advertisers are frequently harassed in response. Print media in Transnistria are required to register with the local Ministry of Information in Tiraspol rather than the internationally recognized Moldovan government in Chisinau.

Moldova's print media were able to express diverse political and public views throughout the year. Only government-controlled broadcasters have national reach; there is little private broadcasting, and most programs are rebroadcasts from either Romania or Russia. Distribution of broadcast licenses and privatizations of state outlets are politicized, and the government also influences the media through financial subsidies. Pluralism in the broadcast media declined significantly in January when, as noted above, companies with ties to the ruling Communist Party and the allied Christian Democrats purchased Radio Antena-C and Euro-TV, two popular public broadcasters in Chisinau, and shifted their content toward entertainment and government-friendly news programming. The government does not control internet access, although internet services are limited to just over 16 percent of the population owing to an underdeveloped telecommunications infrastructure.

Monaco

LEGAL ENVIRONMENT: 3
POLITICAL ENVIRONMENT: 7
ECONOMIC ENVIRONMENT: 6

Status: Free

TOTAL SCORE: 16

Survey Edition	2003	2004	2005	2006	2007
Total Score, Status	9,F	13,F	14,F	16,F	16,F

Freedom of expression is guaranteed under Article 23 of the 1962 Monegasque constitution. However, it is prohibited by law to publicly denounce the ruling family. The media generally abide by the prohibition, which leads to occasional self-censorship. No violations of press freedom were reported in 2007. Monaco has no daily newspapers, although French dailies that cover news in Monaco are available, as are French television and radio broadcasts. Several periodicals and two domestic weekly newspapers, the government-produced *Journal de Monaco* and *Monaco Hebdo*, are also available. Monaco has one government-run television station, one privately owned English-language radio station, Riviera Radio, and the government-run Radio Monte-Carlo, which broadcasts in several languages both in and outside of Monaco. The internet is available and unrestricted and used by more than 60 percent of the population.

Mongolia
Status: Partly Free

LEGAL ENVIRONMENT: 13
POLITICAL ENVIRONMENT: 13
ECONOMIC ENVIRONMENT: 12
TOTAL SCORE: 38

Survey Edition	2003	2004	2005	2006	2007
Total Score, Status	36,PF	36,PF	35,PF	34,PF	36,PF

Freedom of speech and of the press are protected by law, and the government generally respects these rights in practice. However, media freedom was compromised somewhat in 2007 owing to ongoing legal harassment and financial difficulties faced by journalists. Censorship of public information is banned under the 1998 Media Freedom Law, but the State Secrets Law limits access to government information to a degree, as many archived historical records have been given classified status. The government monitors media for compliance with antiviolence, antipornography, and antialcohol content restrictions. There is no freedom of information legislation; a draft law was submitted to parliament in May 2007 but had not been passed at year's end. Officials frequently file criminal and civil defamation suits in the wake of critical articles, with a quarter of journalists reportedly affected. In April and May, criminal charges were filed against a reporter and an editor of *Zuuny Medee* newspaper over articles accusing a member of parliament of corruption. The case was pending at year's end. In August, former government spokesperson Ninjiin Demberel was sentenced to four months in prison for criminal defamation linked to an article and television program on political corruption, though the sentence was later reduced to a fine. The courts have failed to thwart such harassment, particularly because the law places the burden on the defendant to prove the truth of the statement at issue. In a recent study of the 151 defamation cases brought against the media between 2001 and 2005, the local press freedom watchdog Globe International found that the media had lost in almost 60 percent of cases, won in only 10 percent, and settled 32 percent. To avoid being sued for libel, many independent publications practice a degree of self-censorship.

Although no direct government censorship exists, journalists complain of harassment and intimidation as well as pressure from the authorities to reveal confidential sources. In February 2007, police prevented journalist G. Erdenetuya from photographing the site of a helicopter crash that killed over a dozen people. In June 2007, the manager of a restaurant in the capital, Ulaanbaatar, beat and kicked a reporter trying to photograph his business. The journalist was turned away when attempting to report the attack at the local police station.

Although independent print media outlets are common and popular in cities, the main source of news in the vast countryside is the formerly state-owned Radio Mongolia. Under the Law on the Public Radio and Television passed in 2005, state-owned radio and television broadcasting outlets, like Radio Mongolia, are transforming into public service broadcasters, but progress has been slow. Both the state-owned and public media still frequently experience political pressure, and most provincial media outlets continue to be controlled by local authorities. According to media watchdogs, journalists frequently seek payments to cover or fabricate stories. Mongolians have access to local, privately owned television stations, to English-language broadcasts of the British Broadcasting Corporation and Voice of America on private FM stations, and, in Ulaanbaatar, to foreign television programming via cable and commercial satellite systems. Owing to widespread poverty in Mongolia, the internet has yet to serve as a significant source of information; only a little over 10 percent of the population uses the internet.

	LEGAL ENVIRONMENT: 12
Montenegro	POLITICAL ENVIRONMENT: 16
	ECONOMIC ENVIRONMENT: 10
Status: Partly Free	TOTAL SCORE: 38

Survey Edition	2003	2004	2005	2006	2007
Total Score, Status	NA	NA	NA	NA	37,PF

The constitution and legislation generally provide for freedom of the press in Montenegro. Nonetheless, the new constitution does not explicitly prohibit restrictions on freedom of expression, while the right of reply and the right to claim damages for inaccurate media reports are given constitutional status. The constitution also does not guarantee the right to access public information, although Montenegro does have legislation that provides for access to public information. Libel is punishable by fines of up to 14,000 euros (US$22,100) or more for certain types of defamation, and lawsuits against journalists threaten to encourage self-censorship.

A lawsuit filed in September by former president Milo Djukanovic against Zeljko Ivanovic, founder and director of the daily *Vijesti*, as well as the editor in chief and the newspaper's publishing company was highly criticized by international media organizations. Djukanovic is seeking 1 million euros (US$1.6 million) in damages for "mental suffering" caused by defamation stemming from comments Ivanovic made after he was attacked by unknown assailants. Ivanovic, believing his attack was related to his work, publicly blamed Djukanovic for creating an environment of impunity. The trial opened in December and was ongoing at the end of the year. Separately, the trial of Ivanovic's assailants also began in December. The president of the higher court in the capital city of Podgorica filed libel charges against two different journalists, including a journalist for the weekly *Monitor*, Petar Komnenic, and the editor in chief of *Vijesti*, Ljubisa Mitrovic. Both charges stemmed from reports alleging the court officials had ties to criminal activities. The 2004 murder of Dusko Jovanovic, editor of the opposition daily *Dan*, was still unsolved despite the 2006 controversial acquittal of the only person charged with the murder. In November, the editor in chief of public Radio Berane was attacked and severely beaten.

Both broadcast and print media are active and express diverse views. The print media consisted of private newspapers and a state-owned newspaper with a national circulation. The legally mandated privatization process for this newspaper was finally initiated in November of this year when the government put 51 percent of its shares up for sale. There are a number of privately owned radio and television stations in addition to the public broadcasters The members of the media watchdog Radio and Television Council are appointed by nongovernmental organizations (NGOs) and professional groups. As happened in 2006, the parliament refused on two occasions to verify some of the NGO appointments to the council. The parliament is meant only to verify the appointments and not make a choice for the appointments. The frequent failure to verify NGO nominations implies that the government was seeking to influence the council. There are no restrictions on foreign news broadcasts. The government does not restrict access to the internet, which was used by close to 40 percent of the population in 2007.

Morocco

Status: Not Free

LEGAL ENVIRONMENT: 24
POLITICAL ENVIRONMENT: 23
ECONOMIC ENVIRONMENT: 17
TOTAL SCORE: 64

Survey Edition	2003	2004	2005	2006	2007
Total Score, Status	57,PF	61,NF	63,NF	61,NF	62,NF

Press freedom in Morocco declined further in 2007, despite the country's efforts to promote itself as a modernizing Muslim state. Although the constitution guarantees freedom of expression, the Press Law prohibits criticism of the monarchy and Islam and effectively bars material challenging the government's position on the status of Western Sahara. Journalists who cross long-established red lines or violate press legislation are subject to heavy fines and prison sentences of up to five years. While the government imprisons journalists less often than in the past, it now employs an array of economic pressures—such as stiff fines and subtler forms of legal harassment—to punish and threaten independent and opposition journalists into practicing self-censorship. After years of promising an updated and more liberal Press Law, King Mohamed VI finally introduced a draft in 2007. However, the bill retained many of the old law's restrictive penalties and increased fines tenfold. The legislation was still pending at year's end.

According to government statistics, 26 complaints were filed against the press in 2007. On January 15, a Moroccan court sentenced director and editor Driss Ksikes and journalist Sanaa al-Aji from the independent weekly *Nichane* to suspended prison terms of three years and one year, respectively, and fines of about US$10,400 for the publication of an article that analyzed popular Moroccan jokes considered offensive to Islam. Also that month, in a major blow to independent journalism, Aboubakr Jamai, one of the deans of Morocco's independent press corps, left the country to avoid government seizure of his assets and closure of his weekly *Le Journal Hebdomadaire*. Jamai's departure stemmed from a 2006 court decision that found him guilty of the defamation of the head of a Belgian think tank, to whom he was ordered to pay over US$300,000. The record-breaking penalty was believed to be politically motivated given the nature of Jamai's publications, which for years were unrelenting in their reporting on government corruption at all levels. Separately, prior to the parliamentary elections in the fall, authorities in August seized copies of *Nichane* and its sister publication, *TelQuel*, after the latter published an editorial that was critical of the election process and the king's role in government. The editor of the publication also faced criminal charges. *Al-Watan* publisher Abderrahim Ariri and journalist Mustapha Hormatallah were arrested in July for an article that revealed information from a confidential military document. Both received prison sentences in August, in part for not revealing confidential sources, although Ariri's sentence was suspended. There were no reports of extralegal physical attacks on journalists during the year, though at least one reporter received death threats. Coverage of human rights abuses in Western Sahara or open debate on its future status remains largely off limits for domestic media. While foreign journalists can work with relative freedom in Morocco, authorities are as sensitive with the foreign press as they are with local journalists when it comes to the issue of Western Sahara. In February 2007, police in the region's capital El Aaiun detained Swedish freelance photographer Lars Bjork for 19 hours, interrogating him and confiscating his camera after he took photos of protestors.

Morocco is home to a large number of private print publications, many of them critical of the government. Seventeen dailies and 90 weekly publications are in circulation. However, circulation is limited, and most papers receive subsidies from the Ministry of Communication. The government has the power to revoke licenses and suspend or confiscate publications. Broadcast news media are still dominated by the state, but residents can access critical reports through pan-Arab and other satellite channels. Francophone Moroccans can also access French-language broadcasts that provide alternative viewpoints. The internet serves as an alternate source of news and perspectives for many Moroccans. There are six online news sites, including three in French, two in Arabic, and one in English. There is no official legislation regulating internet content or access, but the government occasionally blocks certain websites and online tools, including Google Earth and Livejournal. In May 2007, access to the video-sharing site YouTube was temporarily blocked by the state-owned ISP Maroc Telecom though it was still available through smaller, privately-owned providers. Slightly over 21 percent of the population accessed the internet in 2007.

Mozambique

Status: Partly Free

LEGAL ENVIRONMENT: 11
POLITICAL ENVIRONMENT: 15
ECONOMIC ENVIRONMENT: 14
TOTAL SCORE: 40

Survey Edition	2003	2004	2005	2006	2007
Total Score, Status	47,PF	45,PF	45,PF	43,PF	40,PF

The 1990 constitution provides for press freedom but restricts this right according to respect for the constitution, human dignity, the imperatives of foreign policy, and national defense. Reporters also continue to face problems accessing official information. In August 2005, the government introduced a freedom of information bill, the product of five years of consultations with journalists and press freedom advocates, but a final version had not been passed by the end of 2007. The 1991 Press Law, considered one of the more progressive in Africa, was reviewed in 2006 by Gabinfo, the government press office, which suggested possible "improvements" such as provisions for mandatory licenses for working journalists and pointed to the omission of much needed freedom of information legislation. Registration requirements for starting a new radio station remain cumbersome, and license approvals are sometimes made on political grounds, though few license requests have actually been rejected. Defamation of the president is illegal, and libel laws are sometimes used to prosecute media outlets. Although no libel cases were brought before criminal courts in 2007, several civil libel suits with high amounts sought in damages were brought against independent publications, including *Horizonte* and *Faisca*.

Journalists are occasionally threatened, harassed, or detained for short periods of time by officials or security forces as a result of attempting to cover sensitive stories or if they publish viewpoints critical of the government. For example, Celso Manguana, from the private daily *Canal de Mocambique*, was jailed for four days after police accused him of insulting their authority and was released only after protests from a local human rights group and the intervention of the attorney general. Separately, a photojournalist with *Diario de Mocambique* was detained and released the same day by police while photographing an abandoned building. Developments concerning the 2000 murder of prominent investigative journalist Carlos Cardoso were further resolved during the year. In February, the Supreme Court rejected the appeals of the six men who had been convicted of killing Cardoso and upheld their lengthy prison sentences. Against the wishes of the defendants, the Court also took the unprecedented step of allowing the entire proceedings to be broadcast live, citing the public's right to information. Nyimpine Chissano (son of the former president), who had finally been charged with "joint moral authorship" of the crime in May 2006 after several years of stonewalling but had not been arrested, died in November 2007, bringing an end to his possible prosecution. Despite this resolution, the chilling effect cast by Cardoso's murder remains; many investigative reporters are hesitant to examine sensitive topics, and self-censorship continues to be an issue.

The private media have enjoyed moderate growth in recent years, and independent daily and weekly newspapers routinely provide scrutiny of the government. However, publications based in the capital, Maputo, have little influence on the largely illiterate rural population. The state owns a majority stake in the prominent national daily *Noticias* and the largest broadcast networks, Radio Mozambique (RM) and Televisao de Mozambique, although dozens of private radio and television stations also operate. While state-owned media have displayed greater editorial independence, the opposition still receives inadequate coverage and establishment views are favored. Costs of production and distribution are relatively high owing to poor infrastructure and the fact that newsprint has to be imported from South Africa. According to the Media Institute of Southern Africa's African Media Barometer, the development of private commercial radio continues to be hampered by the fact that state advertisements are broadcast exclusively on RM. Instances have also occurred where newspapers have had advertising from state-owned companies withdrawn after publishing unfavorable stories. The financial viability of many outlets is affected as well by a law limiting foreign investment in any media enterprise to a 20 percent stake. Internet access is unrestricted, though less than 1 percent of the population has access because of a scarcity of electricity and computers.

Namibia

LEGAL ENVIRONMENT: 8
POLITICAL ENVIRONMENT: 10
ECONOMIC ENVIRONMENT: 12

Status: Free

TOTAL SCORE: 30

Survey Edition	2003	2004	2005	2006	2007
Total Score, Status	37,PF	34,PF	29,F	30,F	30,F

Namibia's press is generally considered to be one of the freest on the continent. The constitution guarantees freedom of speech and of the press, and the government generally respects these rights in practice. Independent media routinely criticize the government, though government pressure has led to some self-censorship. A proposed Freedom of Information bill, on which work began in 1999, has yet to come into effect, despite efforts to revive it in recent years.

In recent years, the most serious media restrictions in Namibia have been isolated incidents reflecting the government's sensitivity to criticism. A government ban on advertisements in the independent daily *The Namibian*, in place since March 2001, persists to date. In 2006, Sam Nujoma—former president and head of the ruling South West Africa People's Organization (SWAPO)—initiated a N$5 million (approximately US$650,000) defamation suit against *The Namibian* after an August 2005 story implicated Nujoma in a corruption scandal. In February 2007, a parliamentary debate saw a number of SWAPO members call segments of the independent media "unpatriotic" and "disrespectful" toward SWAPO leaders, including Nujoma. A November resolution of the SWAPO Congress calling for the establishment of a media council under government control drew condemnation from local press freedom groups.

Eight newspapers, six of which are privately owned, publish either daily or weekly in a variety of languages, including English, German, Afrikaans, and Oshiwambo. There are at least 11 private radio stations, 2 community radio stations, and 2 private television stations that broadcast in English and German, and a pay satellite television service broadcasts CNN, the BBC, and a range of South African and international news and entertainment programs. Still, the state-run Namibia Broadcasting Corporation (NBC)—including one television station and nine radio stations—dominates broadcast media. Reporters for state-run media have been subjected to indirect and direct pressure to avoid reporting on controversial topics. While many journalists insist that the state-run media enjoy complete freedom to criticize the government, others believe that they are biased toward the ruling party. In 2007, an NBC plan to change the format of popular call-in shows from open to predetermined topics was torpedoed after public outcry. There are no government restrictions on the internet, but usage is limited to 0.2 percent of the population owing to financial and infrastructural constraints.

Nauru

Status: Free

LEGAL ENVIRONMENT: 4
POLITICAL ENVIRONMENT: 11
ECONOMIC ENVIRONMENT: 13
TOTAL SCORE: 28

Survey Edition	2003	2004	2005	2006	2007
Total Score, Status	26,F	25,F	29,F	30,F	28,F

Freedom of expression is safeguarded in Article 12 of the constitution, though there are limitations for libel and national security. There are no protections under the law for freedom of information, and in the past the government has proven uncooperative in granting access to documents. In 2007, a number of media executives from Nauru joined the newly formed Micronesian Media Association to protect free and independent journalism and public access to information. There were no attacks on the press in 2007. Environmental challenges, inadequate facilities, and a failing economy have limited the country's media scene. Nauru publishes no daily papers, though the government releases the weekly *Nauru Bulletin*, and the *Central Star News* and *Nauru Chronicle* are published fortnightly. Opposition newsletters have also been issued. The state runs one radio and one television station that both carry material from foreign media; there is no private broadcasting. The internet is not restricted by the government, although access remains limited to less than 3 percent of the population owing to a poor telecommunications infrastructure.

LEGAL ENVIRONMENT: 15
POLITICAL ENVIRONMENT: 28

Nepal

ECONOMIC ENVIRONMENT: 14

Status: Partly Free

TOTAL SCORE: 57

Survey Edition	2003	2004	2005	2006	2007
Total Score, Status	65,NF	65,NF	69,NF	77,NF	58,PF

The media environment reached a plateau in Nepal during 2007, following significant improvements in 2006 as a result of dramatic political change in which massive street protests forced an end to King Gyanendra Bir Bikram Shah Dev's direct rule in April. Although an interim constitution was promulgated in January 2007, the Nepali government has not been fully successful in implementing the November 2006 Comprehensive Peace Agreement, as tensions with Maoists and Madhesi unrest in Terrai have indefinitely delayed the holding of constituent assembly elections. Despite significant improvements in law and order following the 2006 cease-fire, attacks on the press by both Maoist and Madhesi groups were common in 2007.

Beginning in May 2006, the interim government rescinded many laws that severely limited press freedom, including the government's ability to revoke journalists' press accreditation and to impose high fines for publishing banned items, bans on private radio news broadcasts, and criminalization of criticism of the royal family. In June, a high-level media commission was formed to further review media laws and practices, and in December 2006, an interim constitution was signed that provides for press freedom and specifically prohibits official censorship. Nevertheless, some international and local press freedom watchdogs expressed concerns over provisions that might be misused to obstruct press freedom, such as ones that allow the government to restrict publication of certain information by enacting laws or to completely suspend rights during emergencies. Improvements in the legal environment continued in 2007, with the interim parliament's passage of the Right to Information Act, which gives Nepali citizens the right to obtain information from government bodies and nongovernmental organizations supported by the government, foreign states, or international organizations. Furthermore, in August, the interim parliament amended the Working Journalists Act, which now provides journalists with improved working conditions and legal rights, including the right to unionize.

Although the interim government and Maoist leadership promised to respect press freedom and reduce the violence against journalists that was commonplace under Gyanendra's rule, violence and intimidation toward journalists increased in 2007. Journalists still face harassment from militant Maoist and Madhesi groups, local-level officials and politicians, police and military forces, and criminal groups, especially when reporting on sensitive topics. Between January and June 2007, Reporters Sans Frontieres reported that at least 72 journalists were threatened or attacked, with at least 2 journalists killed. While mainstream Maoist intimidation has decreased, the Maoist-affiliated Young Communist League (YCL) was responsible for attacks, including in August when YCL members attempted to abduct a journalist for *Dristi Weekly's*. Maoist-affiliated unions also threatened newspapers, forcibly shutting down production and advertising of the *Himalayan Times* and *Annapurna Post* for several days in July and August. On October 5, Maoists abducted and killed Birendra Shah, a journalist in Bara affiliated with Nepal FM, *Dristi Weekly's*, and Avenues TV. Journalists have also faced violence related to the Madhesi movement. Nine newspapers in western Nepal were forced to stop publishing in early January following threats from Madhesi groups. In late January, demonstrators set fire to a radio station and attacked journalists in Birgunj, leading several to flee the area after they were included in a published list of reporters against whom action should be taken. In February, cadres of the Madhesi Janatantrik Forum, a Madhesi political party, attacked five journalists covering a protest in eastern Nepal.

Additionally, although those responsible have not been identified, Shankar Panthi, a journalist with the pro-Maoist paper *Naya Satta Daily*, was found dead in September in the western town of Sunawal, upon his return from covering the destruction of a YCL office. During the year, at least two other journalists were abducted, including the Kanchanpur-based journalists Prakash Singh Thakuri in July and Pappu Gurung in October. Although cases involving government forces were less frequent, police and soldiers have mistreated journalists in some instances. In July, two police constables in the eastern district of Morang assaulted editors for the *Samyantra* weekly newspaper after it published an article implicating the two officers in local corruption. On November 16, authorities briefly detained 39 journalists who were protesting the government's failure to investigate Birendra Shah's death. With dozens of cases of threats and attacks documented throughout the year by groups such as the Kathmandu–based Federation of Nepalese Journalists and the Center for Human Rights and Democratic Studies, journalists' ability to operate freely, particularly in the rural areas, remains constrained. In response to the growing threats to Nepalese media workers, a coalition of newspaper, magazine, and television editors established the Editors Alliance in September.

The government owns several of the major English-language and vernacular dailies; these news outlets generally provide progovernment coverage. Hundreds of private publications, some with particular political viewpoints, provide a range of diverse views, and many have resumed their critical coverage of sensitive issues such as human rights violations, the insurgency, and corruption. The government owns both the influential Radio Nepal, whose political coverage is supportive of official policies, and Nepal Television Corporation, Nepal's main television station. Private FM and community radio stations, which together with the national radio network reach some 90 percent of the population, flourished prior to the 2005 coup and are a primary source of information, particularly in rural areas. Although censorship and news bans caused the closure of many stations under Gyanendra's direct rule, since 2006 many radio journalists have returned to their jobs, and by October, the government had awarded licenses for 6 new television channels and 50 FM radio stations across the country. During 2007, there were no reports that access to foreign media was banned or censored. There were also no reports that authorities monitored e-mail or blocked websites, although the internet was accessed by less than 1 percent of the population in 2007.

Netherlands

Status: Free

LEGAL ENVIRONMENT: 2
POLITICAL ENVIRONMENT: 7
ECONOMIC ENVIRONMENT: 4
TOTAL SCORE: 13

Survey Edition	2003	2004	2005	2006	2007
Total Score, Status	15,F	12,F	11,F	11,F	13,F

The media in the Netherlands are free and independent. Rarely enforced restrictions against insulting the monarch and royal family exist and were used twice in 2007. A homeless man was charged for slandering the queen during an unrelated arrest, and in reaction, a young journalist was arrested for wearing a T-shirt that read, "Queen Beatrix is a whore." The Netherlands does not have legislation ensuring the right of journalists to protect their sources, although this right can be invoked under Article 10 of the European Convention on Human Rights. In November, the Dutch Ministry of Social Affairs and Employment acknowledged that its employees had repeatedly since 2006 hacked into the Dutch Geassocieerde Pers Diensten (GPD) press agency computers. Government employees checked unpublished stories, which was how the activity was discovered: The ministry called the GPD to complain about a piece that had yet to be publicized. The social affairs minister denied directing the actions or any knowledge thereof. Action was pending at year's end. This follows the 2006 case involving *De Telegraaf*, which was at the center of a debate over the legality of wiretapping when it was revealed that the Dutch intelligence service had been taping the phone conversations of two of *De Telegraaf*'s leading reporters.

The legacy left by controversial filmmaker Theo van Gogh's 2004 murder by a radical Islamist has been a climate of fear among journalists and filmmakers interested in pursuing controversial topics, particularly those related to immigration and the increasing influence of Islam in the Netherlands. Ayaan Hirsi Ali, the Somali-born Dutch politician known for her outspoken criticisms of Islam and for the film *Submission*, on which she collaborated with Theo van Gogh, also received death threats and was placed under protection. In 2007, the Dutch government announced it would cut off funding for her security while she was living outside of the Netherlands. Funding was eventually found and she was allowed to maintain the necessary protection while living in the United States.

Despite a high concentration of newspaper ownership, a wide variety of opinions are expressed in the print media. In a remnant of the traditional "pillar" system, the state allocates public radio and television programming to political, religious, and social groups according to their membership size. While every province has at least one public television channel, public broadcasting has faced stiff competition from commercial stations since their legalization in 1988. International news sources are widely accessible, and the internet is unrestricted by the government and used regularly by roughly 88 percent of the population.

	LEGAL ENVIRONMENT: 2
	POLITICAL ENVIRONMENT: 5
New Zealand	ECONOMIC ENVIRONMENT: 6
Status: Free	TOTAL SCORE: 13

Survey Edition	2003	2004	2005	2006	2007
Total Score, Status	8,F	10,F	12,F	13,F	13,F

New Zealand's media remained vigorous and free during the year. Press freedom is guaranteed by convention and statute rather than constitutional right, and it is supplemented by freedom of information legislation passed in 1982. Sedition legislation was abolished in 2007. Although the media have been largely unaffected by antiterrorism laws, a contempt of court charge was filed against the *Dominion Post* in 2007 after it published intercepted communications and other inadmissible evidence related to the discovery of an alleged paramilitary training camp in the remote Urewera region. Also during the year, the self-regulatory Press Council conducted its first independent review since its founding in 1972. Recommendations of the resulting report included turning the council into a legal entity separate from its media industry funders, streamlining complaints processes, and conducting further independent reviews every five years. The broadcasting industry is regulated by the Broadcasting Standards Authority, which in 2007 imposed a fine and a five-hour halt in broadcasting on Alt TV. The channel was punished for screening offensive text messages.

While the news media are generally free of interference, there were several instances in 2007 of outlets coming under pressure from political actors. In a June decision that was condemned by the Commonwealth Press Union, a coalition of parliament members supported a rule change that banned satire, ridicule, and denigration of lawmakers using television footage shot from the parliament galleries. In addition, Amnesty International criticized attempts by Chinese authorities to interfere with free expression and media freedom in New Zealand. The group cited eight recent incidents involving Chinese officials, including one in March in which two local journalists were barred from photographing Chinese vice premier Zeng Peiyan.

Four companies, all foreign owned, continue to control a significant portion of the country's print media sector. Australia's John Fairfax Holdings owns 48 percent of New Zealand's daily newspaper circulation. The *New Zealand Herald,* the largest circulation daily, and a significant slice of smaller provincial and suburban newspapers are owned by the rival Australian Provincial Newspapers (APN) group, amounting to 43 percent of the daily newspaper market. The state-owned Television New Zealand dominates television with two free-to-air channels, and Sky TV, owned by U.S.-based News Corporation, holds a monopoly over pay television. A trend emerged during 2007 in which a growing number of media companies were taken over by private equity corporations such as Australia's Ironbridge, which bought out Mediaworks, the operator of a commercial radio network and TV3. Consolidation by media companies, especially APN, forced significant job losses during the year. Concerns over the quality of the news media contributed to a union-led initiative to create the Movement for Democratic Media. Roughly 75 percent of the population accessed the internet, which was open and unrestricted.

Nicaragua

LEGAL ENVIRONMENT: 14
POLITICAL ENVIRONMENT: 17
ECONOMIC ENVIRONMENT: 12

Status: Partly Free

TOTAL SCORE: 43

Survey Edition	2003	2004	2005	2006	2007
Total Score, Status	40,PF	37,PF	42,PF	44,PF	42,PF

Freedom of information legislation was passed during the year, but the harassment and intimidation of journalists continued, and the Daniel Ortega administration criticized the press and favored progovernment media outlets. The Nicaraguan constitution provides for freedom of the press but also allows for some forms of restriction, including criminal defamation legislation. Legal actions to improve the media environment remain stagnant. Judges are often aligned with political parties, and some have restricted reporters from covering certain stories; cases of judicial intimidation have also been reported. In May, a new Access to Public Information Law was approved, and an office was created in December to serve as the clearinghouse for all freedom of information requests. Nevertheless, civil society groups and media members indicated that the Access to Public Information Law includes sections that may undermine the measure's ultimate effectiveness. A court appeal on constitutional grounds against Law 372, which requires all journalists to register with the Colegio de Periodistas, or national journalists' association, was still pending in the Supreme Court at year's end.

Daniel Ortega, who took office as president in January, has so far failed to follow in his predecessor's footsteps to respect press freedom. Ortega frequently discredits the work of the media in his speeches and appointed his wife, Rosario Murillo, as the administration's point person for press relations. Politicians have also criticized the media for trying to undermine their credibility and limit public debate. Journalists, on the other hand, complained that the government provided media loyal to the ruling Sandinista National Liberation Front (FSLN) party with preferential treatment, intimidated media outlets, and pressured journalists into self-censorship.

While physical attacks on journalists have diminished, a number of reporters received death threats or were harassed at gunpoint throughout the year. In February, three members of the ruling party threatened to kill journalist William Aragon reputedly in response to two articles in the Managua-based daily *La Prensa* in which Aragon exposed government corruption. Later in December, *La Prensa* correspondent Jorge Loaisiga was detained briefly by presidential security guards at a public ceremony attended by the president and several ambassadors. Loaisiga was soliciting comments from the American ambassador when he was roughly handcuffed and detained; authorities released him soon after, however, in response to protests by other journalists and local residents.

There are 10 Managua-based television stations, some of which broadcast partisan content, as well as more than 100 radio stations, which serve as the population's main source of news. Print media are diverse, with both progovernment and critical perspectives and several daily papers. Newspaper ownership is concentrated in the hands of various factions of the Chamorro family, while the prominent Sacasa family dominates the television industry. Mexican media tycoon Angel Gonzalez, noted for his holdings in Guatemala and Costa Rica, also owns significant electronic media interests. In September, customs authorities impounded printing materials imported by *La Prensa* for two weeks in an attempt to make the company pay import duties, despite a constitutional provision that provides tax exemption. Two radio programs were also shut down in August by the FSLN mayor and local government of San Carlos in Rio San Juan based on their criticism of municipal authorities. Nicaragua's media rely heavily on government advertising owing to economic necessity. According to the International Press Institute, President Ortega signed an agreement on March 1 with the Colegio de Periodistas to ensure "the just distribution of government advertising contracts to benefit small and medium-sized radio stations," as well as to waive broadcast licensing fees for smaller media outlets. However, a freeze remains on government advertising, which generally appears only in media outlets that belong to the ruling party or that have close ties to the government, or on highway billboards. The poor economic climate leaves journalists vulnerable to bribes; however, a new generation of journalists is trying to reject the traditional practices of self-censorship and bribery. There are no government restrictions on the internet, which was used by less than 3 percent of the population in 2007.

Niger

Status: Not Free

LEGAL ENVIRONMENT: 22
POLITICAL ENVIRONMENT: 24
ECONOMIC ENVIRONMENT: 17
TOTAL SCORE: 63

Survey Edition	2003	2004	2005	2006	2007
Total Score, Status	53,PF	56,PF	53,PF	56,PF	58,PF

Status change explanation: Niger declined from Partly Free to Not Free owing to the government's attempts to control information related to the civil conflict in the north, including suspending the operation of critical media outlets, prosecuting journalists for libel, and harassing journalists who produced controversial reports.

Although Niger's constitution guarantees freedom of expression, it is often not respected in practice. Conditions for the independent Nigerien media deteriorated considerably in 2007 owing to the government's attempts to control information related to the civil conflict in the north with the nomadic Tuareg population, which began in February 2007 when members of the Mouvement des Nigeriens pour la Justice (MNJ) carried out attacks on the army in the northern town of Iferouane. During the year, Nigerien authorities have suspended the operation of critical media outlets, prosecuted journalists for libel, and harassed journalists for controversial materials, particularly those containing coverage of the civil conflict.

As a direct result of the conflict, Nigerien authorities have sharply limited the media's ability to report on events in the north and have suspended a number of stations for their coverage. On June 29, Niger's regulatory body, the Supreme Council for Communications (CSC), suspended *Air Info*, a private paper from the northern Agadez region, for three months for covering the MNJ's activities and withheld the outlet's annual subsidy of US$3,000. On July 19, the government imposed a one-month ban on the retransmission of Radio France Internationale (RFI) owing to alleged bias toward the MNJ. Furthermore, in late August, the government banned live broadcasts of the MNJ, which occurred in the context of a countrywide state of emergency imposed on August 24 in response to heightened rebel attacks. In late October, the CSC issued a warning to media outlets that criticism of it could lead to the revoking of broadcasting licenses.

Throughout 2007, journalists also faced threats of detention and criminal prosecution for coverage of the conflict. On September 21, authorities arrested and later imprisoned Moussa Kaka, director of the private station Radio Saraounya and a correspondent for RFI and Reporters Sans Frontieres. Kaka was later charged with "complicity in a conspiracy against state authority" owing to coverage of the MNJ's activities and the government's counterinsurgency efforts. Although a court in November rejected the evidence against Kaka, he remained imprisoned at year's end. Earlier in July, an army officer threatened Kaka with death for covering the conflict in the north. On October 9, Ibrahim Manzo Diallo, *Air Info*'s managing editor, was arrested prior to boarding a flight to France for his alleged involvement in antigovernment demonstrations. Diallo had been previously arrested in July for operating his publication under a new name, *Info de l'Air*, after the original *Air Info* had been suspended in June. On October 31, Diallo was charged with criminal association for alleged ties to the MNJ rebels, and he remained imprisoned at year's end. Daouda Yacouba, an *Air Info* correspondent, was arrested on October 25, questioned about his links with Tuareg rebels, and released in early November.

Foreign journalists also faced imprisonment for coverage of events in the north. At the end of August, authorities detained the French filmmaker Francois Bergeron for filming a documentary on the Tuaregs in the north; Bergeron was released on October 6. Separately, on December 17, two French citizens on assignment with the French-German television station Arte, reporter Thomas Dandois and cameraman Pierre Creisson, were arrested and later charged with undermining state security upon allegations that they had traveled illegally to the north. At year's end, Dandois and Creisson were still imprisoned near Niamey; this offense is punishable by death.

Journalists faced other instances of intimidation and harassment throughout the year unrelated to the Tuareg uprising in the north. In October, Hamadou Boulama, editor in chief of the bimonthly paper

Alternative, received a death threat allegedly linked to a story published in October suggesting that the 2009 presidential election would not be competitive. In early December, Ibrahim Souley, managing editor of the bimonthly *L'Enqueteur*, and Soumana Idrissa Maiga, the paper's founder, were arrested and held for 72 hours following libel charges brought by the minister of finance and economic planning owing to the paper's allegations of corruption within the ministry. Their case was pending at year's end, and both remained in pretrial detention.

State media continue to dominate the broadcasting landscape and consistently reflect the government line. Nevertheless, there are 15 private radio stations that broadcast in French and other local languages. Although private publications have been very critical of the government, they have limited influence due to a literacy rate of only 29 percent. Restrictive press licensing legislation and a heavy tax on private media outlets continue to inhibit the growth of a dynamic press. Although the government does not restrict internet access, less than 0.3 percent of the population accessed it regularly owing to the high level of poverty and lack of infrastructure.

Nigeria

Status: Partly Free

LEGAL ENVIRONMENT: 14
POLITICAL ENVIRONMENT: 22
ECONOMIC ENVIRONMENT: 17
TOTAL SCORE: 53

Survey Edition	2003	2004	2005	2006	2007
Total Score, Status	53,PF	53,PF	52,PF	54,PF	55,PF

The year 2007 was marked by state harassment of the private media in advance of the April presidential elections, in which the ruling People's Democratic Party (PDP) candidate, Umaru Musa Yar'Adua, was elected to replace Olusegun Obasanjo. Following the elections, state harassment of the media appeared to decrease.

Although the 1999 constitution guarantees freedom of expression, of the press, and of assembly, the state often uses arbitrary actions and extralegal measures to suppress political criticism and expression in the media, and a culture of impunity for crimes against the media persists. Libel remains a criminal offense, and under Nigerian law the burden of proof still rests with the defendant. Criminal prosecution also continues to be used against journalists covering sensitive issues such as official corruption, separatist movements, and communal violence. In addition, Sharia (Islamic law) in place in 12 northern states imposes severe penalties for alleged press offenses. Despite the recent passage of a freedom of information bill by both houses of the National Assembly, which, among other provisions, would criminalize the destruction or falsification of any official record by any officer, government administrator, or public institution, Obasanjo failed to sign the bill into law prior to leaving office in May. The bill was resubmitted under the new administration and had been presented to both the House and the Senate by year's end. Under the current legal framework, access to information remains limited, with laws—such as the 1962 Official Secrets Act and the Sedition Law—restricting public access to government-held information.

Prior to the April presidential elections, various security agencies, particularly the State Security Service (SSS), an elite corps under the president's direct charge, continued to use arbitrary detention and extrajudicial measures in attempts to muffle political activism and restrict press coverage critical of former president Obasanjo and the ruling PDP. No SSS member has ever been prosecuted or sanctioned in any way for violence against journalists. On January 9, SSS agents raided the offices of the daily *Leadership* and detained several staff members following a story alleging that Obasanjo forced fellow PDP candidate Peter Odili out of the party's primary elections. The following day, agents raided the offices of the *Abuja Inquirer* and detained publisher Dan Akpovwa and editor Sode Abbah for over a day following a story about the possibility of a military coup due to hostility between Obasanjo and his former vice president, Atiku Abubakar, who was also campaigning for the presidency. In another incident in April, security forces raided the transmission studio of the private African Independent Television station, preventing the broadcasting of a documentary critical of Obasanjo and the PDP. Authorities also shut down an affiliated radio station, Ray Power FM, for one hour. At the time of the incident, the National Broadcasting Commission (NBC), the body that monitors the broadcast media, threatened the station with sanctions if it aired the program in the future. Intimidation, including use of the SSS, continued under Yar'Adua's administration, albeit at a lower level than during the preelection period. On June 27, a group of armed men, including two police officers, raided the printing office of the private Uyo-based weekly *Events* and reportedly seized several thousand copies of the paper in response to an article on an alleged indictment against the state governor on corruption charges. On October 10, SSS agents arrested Jerome Imeime, editor of *Events*, on sedition charges owing to critical stories about the state governor. Although Imeime was released after three weeks, the Committee to Protect Journalists noted that these were the first such charges imposed since June 2006.

Violence against journalists sadly remains a common occurrence; however, it is more often a result of the violent environments in which journalists report rather than in response to the particular content of their writing. In May, over 100 armed supporters of local politicians raided the Oyo state broadcasting office and stole equipment, causing injuries to a number of employees and interrupted service; the perpetrators had not been identified by the end of the year. Journalists have also come under attack in the Niger Delta region, where control over oil revenues has sparked conflict among various armed groups. Armed men raided the offices of the Port Harcourt papers *Punch* in June and *National Point* in July, allegedly attempting to rob or abduct staff members. Unlike in 2006, no journalists were killed during the year. However, the December 2006 murder in Lagos of Godwin Agbroko, editorial board chairman of the private daily *ThisDay*, remained unsolved at year's end. International journalists were generally able to operate throughout Nigeria but also faced difficulties in the Niger Delta region. Two German documentary filmmakers were arrested in September, detained for two weeks, and charged with breaching Nigeria's Official Secrets Act by taking photographs and videos of the region's oil facilities.

There are more than 100 national and local publications, the most influential of which are privately owned. The press is vibrant and vocal against unpopular state policies and was particularly critical in covering Obasanjo's third-term ambitions and during the run-up to the April election. The broadcast industry has been liberalized since 1992, and by 2006, about 300 licenses had been granted by the NBC, although most licensees continue to experience financial difficulties, limiting their viability. Radio tends to be the main source of information for Nigerians, while television is used mostly in urban areas and by the affluent. Private television stations are restricted by the requirement that 60 percent of their programming be made locally. Foreign broadcasters, particularly the Voice of America and the British Broadcasting Corporation, are important sources of news in the country. Over eight million Nigerians—or six percent of the population—reportedly had access to the internet in 2007. There are no reports that the government restricted access to the internet or monitored e-mail, although online news sites critical of the government have occasionally experienced disruptions, possibly because of authorities' attempts to impair service.

North Korea

Status: Not Free

LEGAL ENVIRONMENT: 30
POLITICAL ENVIRONMENT: 39
ECONOMIC ENVIRONMENT: 29
TOTAL SCORE: 98

Survey Edition	2003	2004	2005	2006	2007
Total Score, Status	96,NF	98,NF	97,NF	97,NF	97,NF

Though some citizens gained access to alternative information via pirated DVDs and illegal shortwave radios, North Korea remained the most repressive media environment in the world in 2007. The one-party regime headed by Kim Jong-il places severe restrictions on media freedom, attempts to regulate all communication, and rigorously limits the ability of North Koreans to access information. Although the constitution guarantees freedom of speech, in practice constitutional provisions for obeying a "collective spirit" restrict all reporting that is not sanctioned by the government. All journalists are members of the ruling party, and all media are mouthpieces for the regime. Journalists are punished harshly for even the smallest errors. The North Korean media portray all dissidents and the foreign media as liars attempting to destabilize the government, and authorities sharply curtail the ability of foreign journalists to gather information by claiming their cellular telephones upon arrival, preventing them from talking to people in the street, and constantly monitoring their movements. Under the penal code, listening to foreign broadcasts and possessing dissident publications are "crimes against the state" and carry grave punishments, including hard labor, prison sentences, and the death penalty. The aid group Good Friends reported that in October 2007, a man was publicly executed for having made a large number of international phone calls.

Newspaper, television, and radio reports typically consist of praise for Kim Jong-il, often focusing on his daily activities. Radios must be registered with the police and are preset to government frequencies. However, the emergence of black markets in the past decade has provided some alternative sources of information, especially for those near the South Korean or Chinese borders. Some entrepreneurs carry cell phones, and a significant portion of North Koreans are aware of the outside world through shortwave radios and pirated DVDs of South Korean dramas smuggled in from China. Surveys of defectors show that a growing, though still unclear, proportion of North Koreans have access to broadcasts by Radio Free Asia, the South

Korean public radio station KBS, or Free North Korea, a radio station run by North Korean refugees living in the South. In an attempt to curb the growing access to outside information, the authorities throughout 2007 took measures such as raiding homes in search of illegal DVDs and players, confiscating television remote controls, and resoldering radios and television sets that had been unsealed. They also renewed efforts to jam South Korean and other foreign radio broadcasts that reach the North, including one aimed at any surviving Japanese abductees.

All media in North Korea are owned by the state. However, in 2007, a Japanese journalist and several North Korean refugees launched the first newsmagazine to be based on independent reporting from inside the country, conducted by specially trained undercover journalists using hidden cameras. The first issue of the bimonthly *Rimjingang*, which aims to cover the general views of North Koreans along with their reactions to unfolding events within the country, was published in November 2007, with plans to distribute it in both North and South Korea. Internet access is restricted to a handful of high-level officials who have received state approval and to 200 or so foreigners living in the capital, Pyongyang; all foreign websites are blocked by the state. For most North Koreans with computer access, web browsing takes place only on the state-run intranet called Kwangmyong, which restricts access to a few dozen government-sponsored websites.

Norway

Status: Free

LEGAL ENVIRONMENT: 3
POLITICAL ENVIRONMENT: 3
ECONOMIC ENVIRONMENT: 4
TOTAL SCORE: 10

Survey Edition	2003	2004	2005	2006	2007
Total Score, Status	9,F	9,F	10,F	10,F	11,F

Freedom of the press and of information are guaranteed under Article 100 of the constitution. However, a government ban on political commercials, designed to ensure equal opportunity to the media for all candidates regardless of varying resources, violates the European Convention on Human Rights, which Norway has signed. In February, the Ministry of Cultural and Church Affairs proposed a bill that would protect editorial freedom. According to *Nordic Media Policy*, the bill would ensure that owners could not reexamine an editor's decision regarding editorial operations. The bill was pending at year's end.

Norway has one of the highest newspaper readerships in the world and distributes over 200 newspapers that express a diversity of opinions. Media concentration is a concern in Norway, with three main companies dominating print media. In July 2007, the Norwegian Media Authority prevented the establishment of Media Norge, a large media consortium. The new media group would be the result of a large-scale merger among several of the country's largest papers, including *Bergens Tidende*, *Aftenposten*, *Stavanger Aftenblad*, and *Fædrelandsvennen*. The internet is widely used in Norway, accessed by 88 percent of the population.

Oman

Status: Not Free

LEGAL ENVIRONMENT: 25
POLITICAL ENVIRONMENT: 27
ECONOMIC ENVIRONMENT: 19
TOTAL SCORE: 71

Survey Edition	2003	2004	2005	2006	2007
Total Score, Status	73,NF	74,NF	72,NF	70,NF	71,NF

The 1984 Press and Publications Law is one of the most restrictive statutes of its kind in the Arab world and serves to create a highly censored and subdued media environment. Articles 29, 30, and 31 of Oman's 1996 Basic Law guarantee freedom of expression and of the press; however, these rights must be exercised "within the limits of the law." While the 2004 Private Radio and Television Companies Law allows for the licensing of the first private broadcast media, the high capital requirement to launch an outlet under the law has discouraged private broadcasting in practice. Libel is treated as a criminal offense, and journalists can be fined or imprisoned for voicing criticisms of the sultan or for printing material that leads to "public discord, violates the security of the state, or abuses a person's dignity or rights." The Telecommunications Act allows the authorities to prosecute individuals for any message, sent through any means of communication, that violates public order and morals or is harmful to a person's safety. Private communications such as mobile telephone calls, e-mail, and exchanges in internet chat rooms are monitored. The Ministry of Information may legally censor any material regarded as politically, culturally, or sexually offensive in both domestic and foreign media. Media managers and editors also serve as censors and refrain from pursuing more investigative stories out of fear of criminal or financial repercussions. Journalists who have been charged with past Press and Publications Law violations often find it difficult to secure work or be published.

Information and news are widely available, and foreign broadcasts are often accessed via satellite in urban areas. However, there is a basic lack of coverage of local topics such as the economy, unemployment, or minority and migrant issues. Candidates for the October 2007 Consultative Council elections were allowed to place campaign advertisements in the local papers for the first time, and foreign journalists were invited to cover the voting. While both private and state-run print and broadcast media tend to support the government's views, some "constructive" criticism of the government is permitted. Journalists, however, still practice a high degree of self-censorship, and reporters have been jailed in the past for coverage of colleagues' arrests. Journalists are required to obtain licenses to practice, and since 2005 they have been obliged to reapply each year as an employee of a specific media outlet, thus forbidding the practice of freelance journalism. Journalists may have their licenses revoked at any time for violating press laws or for crossing red lines.

The Arabic-language daily newspaper *Azzamn* began publication in August, making it the country's fifth privately owned daily in addition to two government-owned papers. Private newspapers sustain themselves largely on local and international advertising revenues rather than sales, and many no longer need to accept state subsidies. No entity exists to verify circulation numbers of print media. *TheWeek*, a free English-language weekly, became the first newspaper to carry out an audit and provide circulation data to its advertisers in 2007 in order to create greater transparency. There are two state-owned television stations and three state-owned radio stations. The state licensed three private radio stations and one private television station for the first time in 2005 (following passage of the Private Radio and Television Companies Law of 2004). Hala FM, the first private radio station, launched in May 2007, and HI-FM followed in October; both stations broadcast mostly music. The government retains the right to close down any media outlet at any time. Bribes to influence journalistic content are rare owing to relatively high wages for journalists and a lack of opportunity to provide critical perspectives.

Ten percent of Oman's population used the internet in 2007, reflecting a growth rate of more than 250 percent since 2000, still low in comparison with other countries in the region. Attempts to increase internet service and usage outside of the capital have been unsuccessful, partly because of technical problems and high prices. Oman's internet and telecommunications sector is monopolized by the government's

Oman Telecommunications Company. The internet is broadly censored, with the *Internet Service Manual* stipulating a lengthy list of prohibited content, including defamation of the ruling family and false data or rumors. Authorities post ads on local websites warning users that they may be censored or questioned for criticizing the government or the sultan. Numerous websites were blocked in 2007, often arbitrarily. In January, the founder of the popular chat room al-Sablah al-Omania and 10 others were arrested for posting comments criticizing government officials. Six of the defendants eventually received fines of up to 4,000 rials (US$10,000), and one defendant received a one-month prison sentence. The founder and three remaining defendants were acquitted, but the site was shut down.

Pakistan

Status: Not Free

LEGAL ENVIRONMENT: 20
POLITICAL ENVIRONMENT: 29
ECONOMIC ENVIRONMENT: 17
TOTAL SCORE: 66

Survey Edition	2003	2004	2005	2006	2007
Total Score, Status	58,PF	59,PF	61,NF	61,NF	63,NF

Press freedom was continuously tested in 2007 as media outlets took a lead role in reporting on the ongoing political turmoil and in turn were targeted in crackdowns by authorities. The constitution and other legislation such as the Official Secrets Act authorize the government to curb freedom of speech on subjects including the constitution, the armed forces, the judiciary, and religion. Harsh blasphemy laws have also been used in past years to suppress the media. The controversial 2004 Defamation (Amendment) Act expanded the definition of defamation and increased the punishment for offenders to minimum fines of 100,000 rupees (approximately US$1,700) and/or prison sentences of up to five years; however, this legislation has not yet been used to convict members of the press. The Pakistan Electronic Media Regulatory Authority (PEMRA), tasked with regulating the broadcast media, was given additional powers by presidential decree in June to be able to halt broadcasts and shutter media premises. PEMRA intervened several times during the year to restrict broadcasts, particularly those critical of the government, and to ban live news coverage during periods of political unrest. The Supreme Court also attempted to restrict media coverage of the ongoing judicial crisis, issuing a directive that would allow contempt of court charges to be filed against any outlets that covered the case.

Restrictions on media coverage increased dramatically as part of the November 3 imposition of martial law in which a number of civil liberties were suspended and political leaders as well as lawyers and civic activists were arrested. The Provisional Constitutional Order, which replaced the constitution, suspended Article 19 of the constitution relating to freedom of the press, and two additional ordinances imposed severe curbs on print and electronic media, respectively, barring them from publishing or broadcasting "anything which defames or brings into ridicule the head of state, or members of the armed forces, or executive, legislative, or judicial organs of the state," as well as any broadcasts deemed to be "false or baseless." Those journalists or outlets considered to be in breach of the ordinance could face jail terms of up to three years, fines of up to 10 million rupees (about US$165,000), and/or cancellation of their broadcaster's license. A special bureau within the Information Ministry was tasked with monitoring the 21 national dailies and 13 leading regional newspapers to ensure that they followed the rules introduced in the print media ordinance. Transmissions of many foreign and private networks were initially suspended and allowed to resume only after each network had signed a new 14-page code of conduct promoted by PEMRA, in which they agreed to discontinue specific types of programming, such as election-related content, talk shows and live phone-in segments. Those channels that did not, including Geo TV, the country's largest private television network, remained off the air at year's end.

The physical safety of journalists continued to be a major issue of concern. On numerous occasions during 2007, police, security forces, and military intelligence officers subjected journalists to physical attacks, intimidation, or arbitrary arrest and incommunicado detention. In addition, Islamic fundamentalists and thugs hired by feudal landlords or local politicians continued to harass journalists and attack newspaper offices. According to Internews, a training and monitoring group, there were 163 attacks during the year, with at least 7 journalists killed and 100 abducted (most were released after a short period of time). Those killed during the year included Zubair Ahmed Mujahid, a Sindh correspondent for the *Jang* daily, in November 2007; Ahmed Solangi, who was ambushed and shot as he was distributing newspapers in June; and Noor Hakim, who was killed in the tribal areas, also in June. In a chilling trend, family members of journalists also continue to be targeted. The widow of slain journalist Hayatullah Khan was murdered in November 2007, while militants killed four family members of Din Muhammad, a journalist based in the northwestern Waziristan region, in March. In addition, the 14-year-old son of Shakil Ahmad Turabi, editor in chief of the South Asian News Agency, was beaten, probably by plainclothes police, as a warning to his father.

Several reporters were either killed or injured as they attempted to cover political developments or were among the victims of suicide bombings that took place. The spring was a particularly bad period for the media throughout the country owing to protracted conflicts stemming from coverage of the unfolding judicial crisis following the sacking of the chief justice of the supreme court in March 2007. For example, the Islamabad offices of Geo TV were raided by police in March, and Aaj TV's Karachi office was subject to a four-hour siege by progovernment political activists in May. Also in May, bullets were found planted on three cars belonging to journalists at the Karachi Press Club. Unions such as the Pakistan Federal Union of Journalists and its affiliates who held demonstrations in order to protest the treatment of the media were assaulted and arrested, and its leaders faced threats. In general, foreign journalists experience visa and travel restrictions that can inhibit their scope of reporting and are subject to arrest and deportation if found in areas not specifically covered by the terms of their visas; a number of such cases have been reported in the past several years. Conditions for reporters covering the ongoing unrest in the tribal areas bordering Afghanistan were particularly difficult, with a number of local and foreign correspondents detained, threatened, expelled, or otherwise prevented from covering events there, either by the Taliban and local tribal groups or by the army and intelligence services. Media remain much more tightly restricted in Pakistani-administered Kashmir, where publications need special permission from the regional government to operate, and pro-independence publications are unlikely to be given permission to publish.

While some journalists practice self-censorship, many privately owned daily and weekly newspapers and magazines provide diverse and critical coverage of national affairs. Restrictions on the ownership of broadcast media were eased in late 2002, and media cross-ownership was allowed in July 2003. The government continues to control Pakistan Television and Radio Pakistan, the only free broadcast outlets with a national reach, where coverage supports official viewpoints. Private radio stations operate in some major cities but are prohibited from broadcasting news programming. In a dramatic change in the media landscape in recent years, dozens of widely available private cable and satellite television channels such as Geo, ARY, Aaj, and Dawn, some of which broadcast from outside the country, focus on providing live domestic news coverage, commentary, and call-in talk shows, which serve to inform viewers and shape public opinion regarding current events. International television and radio broadcasts are usually available. Authorities attempt to wield some control over content by reportedly providing unofficial "guidance" to editors on suggested placement of front-page stories or permissible topics of coverage. Both state-level and national authorities use advertising boycotts to put economic pressure on media outlets that do not heed unofficial directives on coverage. Throughout 2007, the Dawn Group, which had refused to accede to an official request for a news blackout on coverage of Baluchistan and the tribal areas, was targeted as the federal government cut nearly two-thirds of its advertisements and withheld awarding a television broadcast license to the group. Similar though less drastic cuts targeted a number of other media organizations. In addition, the broadcast ban imposed in November exacted a severe financial toll on private television stations, with many losing significant advertising revenues during this period. Both official and private interests reportedly pay for favorable press coverage, a practice that is exacerbated by the low salary levels of many journalists.

The internet is not widely used, with less than 5 percent of the population able to gain access, although blogs are growing in popularity and many news media outlets provide content over the internet. Despite this, the government did invade online privacy by monitoring the e-mail accounts of some journalists. During 2007, authorities blocked access to certain websites, particularly those that concern Baluchi nationalist issues or other sensitive subjects, with several dozen blocked at various points during the year. During the state of emergency, news websites and blogs—some, such as the Emergency Times, started specifically during this period to provide news—emerged as a primary source of information as a result of the ban on many broadcast channels.

Palau

Status: Free

LEGAL ENVIRONMENT: 1
POLITICAL ENVIRONMENT: 5
ECONOMIC ENVIRONMENT: 8
TOTAL SCORE: 14

Survey Edition	2003	2004	2005	2006	2007
Total Score, Status	9,F	11,F	13,F	14,F	14,F

Palau has a small but vibrant media environment, and the constitution protects freedom of expression and the press. Censorship is rare, and the press is free to report on a diversity of issues, including official corruption. In November 2006, the Consolidated Boards Act was passed, combining four government entities—including the Palau National Communications Corporation, which controls internet and satellite television transmissions— into one commission. The officials of the new commission are publicly elected rather than appointed by the government, as was previously the case. In 2007, Palauan media executives joined the newly formed Micronesian Media Association to protect free and independent journalism and public access to information. There were no attacks on the press in 2007. Palau has relatively diverse media considering its small population, including three weekly print publications. President Tommy Esang Remengesau Jr. meets with the press every Wednesday on the government radio station, Eco-Paradise. There are also two private and two church-owned radio stations. WWFM, owned by outspoken journalist and senator Alfonso Diaz, airs a weekly program for Filipinos in Palau. The internet is not regulated by the government, but the medium is not yet a significant news source, as it was accessed by only 1 percent of the population in 2007.

LEGAL ENVIRONMENT: 18

POLITICAL ENVIRONMENT: 17

Panama

ECONOMIC ENVIRONMENT: 9

Status: Partly Free

TOTAL SCORE: 44

Survey Edition	2003	2004	2005	2006	2007
Total Score, Status	34,PF	45,PF	44,PF	43,PF	43,PF

Panama is notable for its harsh legal environment for journalists, and events in 2007 did little to improve the situation. President Martin Torrijos, who ratified the repeal of the country's *desacato* (insult) laws in 2005, signed into law on March 21 two new penal code amendments that restrict press freedom. The articles, which have been strongly criticized by the Panamanian media, were part of a package of 448 amendments to the criminal code, approved by the national assembly on March 6. Article 164 provides for fines or imprisonment for anyone who makes public the recordings, private or personal mail, or documents of another individual without permission, which results in harm. Article 422 punishes anyone who reveals or provides access to confidential government secrets with a sentence of six months to one year in prison or its equivalent in fines. Provisions in the criminal code in effect prior to the amendments, such as Articles 307 and 308, are similar to *desacato* laws and have been used to prosecute journalists in the past. According to the Inter American Press Association, 34 journalists were facing charges of *injuria* (insulting or offensive words or actions) or *calumnia* (false accusations of a crime); the majority of these cases were brought by government officials. In addition to the threat of legal repercussions, judicial intimidation has served as a factor promoting self-censorship. There were no developments in the case against Jean Marcel Chery, a former reporter with the daily *El Panama America*, who was accused of libel by Supreme Court justice Winston Spadafora in 2005. Chery had written an article questioning Spadafora's Supreme Court decision to cancel a US$2 million debt owed by a prominent businessman with close ties to the government. A separate civil lawsuit filed by Spadafora in 2005 also continued throughout the year, this one seeking US$2 million in damages from the publisher of *El Panama America* for a 2001 story that allegedly "insulted" him by questioning the use of public moneys to build a highway that seemed to service only Spadafora and another government official.

Although there were no physical attacks on the media in 2007, four journalists were detained for six hours in November while trying to cover events at La Joya Prison. According to the local Committee for the Defense of Journalists, Hellen Concepcion and Mizael Castro of TVN Channel 2, Rocio Martins of Editora Panama America, photojournalist Omar Batista, and their driver were taken to the office of the minister of government and justice and accused of "trespassing." Despite the existence of transparency legislation, access to public information remains limited. Government officials are not held accountable for refusing to release information, and public institutions still lack an effective mechanism for expediting information requests.

Independent media are active and relatively free to express diverse perspectives. The media often reflect the polarized political scene, with different outlets openly supporting various factions. All Panamanian media outlets are privately owned with the exception of one state-owned television network and one radio station. Regardless of a law that prohibits cross-ownership, there is considerable concentration of media ownership among relatives and associates of former president Ernesto Perez Balladares, whose party is now led by President Torrijos. Poor salaries encourage corruption among some journalists. Press freedom advocacy groups allege that the government manipulates the free flow of information by buying advertising space from progovernment media outlets while withdrawing funding from critical news organizations. A draft bill to standardize government advertising practices continued to be under consideration at year's end. There are no government restrictions on the internet, which was accessed by a little over 9 percent of the population in 2007.

Papua New Guinea

Status: Free

LEGAL ENVIRONMENT: 4
POLITICAL ENVIRONMENT: 13
ECONOMIC ENVIRONMENT: 11
TOTAL SCORE: 28

Survey Edition	2003	2004	2005	2006	2007
Total Score, Status	25,F	25,F	29,F	29,F	30,F

The relatively vibrant media environment improved slightly in 2007 with the lifting of a state of emergency in the Southern Highlands province in August. Media freedom is guaranteed under the constitution adopted at independence in 1975, and the Papua New Guinea Media Council (PNGMC) is a strong lobby group in support of news organizations and professional standards. However, at times the news media have come under pressure from the government. Tensions between the coalition government of Prime Minister Sir Michael Somare and the media peaked in August when news organizations challenged attempts by the administration to bar coverage of a report by the Defense Force board of inquiry. The report implicated Somare in the escape of Solomon Islands lawyer Julian Moti from Australian extradition proceedings in October 2006 and included recommendations that the prime minister be investigated as well as allegations of corruption. The PNGMC is active, with a well-developed code of ethics and a complaints commission. Council president Oseah Philemon praised the country's media for their efforts at defending media freedom during 2007. Nevertheless, in October, the government announced plans to revise the 1994 National Information and Communication Policy, which governs the media industry and publishing houses, raising concerns that such a review might result in more limited press freedom.

Physical violence against journalists in Papua New Guinea remains uncommon. Nevertheless, according to the International Press Institute, in May 2007, a female reporter for the *Post Courier* newspaper was attacked in her home in the capital and threatened at gunpoint, possibly in connection with a series of articles on government corruption.

Two foreign-owned but opposing daily newspapers dominate the country's media. The *PNG Post-Courier*, founded in 1969, is owned by a subsidiary of Rupert Murdoch's News Corporation, and the rival *National* is owned by a prominent Malaysian logging company with major investments in the country. Papua New Guinea's only television station, EM TV, is owned by Fiji Television Ltd., but the country is moving to establish its own state-run television channel. The state-run National Broadcasting Corporation operates two radio stations—Karai National Radio and Kundu Radio Services. Also broadcasting in the country are two private stations—Nau FM and Yumi FM, which are controlled by the partly Fiji-owned PNG FM Pty. Ltd.. The internet is unrestricted by the government but is accessible to barely 5 percent of the population.

Paraguay

Status: Partly Free

LEGAL ENVIRONMENT: 19
POLITICAL ENVIRONMENT: 23
ECONOMIC ENVIRONMENT: 18
TOTAL SCORE: 60

Survey Edition	2003	2004	2005	2006	2007
Total Score, Status	55,PF	54,PF	56,PF	57,PF	60,PF

Although disappeared journalist Enrique Galeano was found alive after 17 months, dangerous conditions for the media continued in 2007, as numerous other journalists received death threats and one journalist was murdered. Although the constitution supports basic press rights, legal loopholes facilitate defamation and libel cases against the media. The continuation of such cases, which are often brought by public officials, not only endangers the financial sustainability of the press, but also discourages journalists from practicing critical and investigative reporting. In November, President Nicanor Duarte Frutos announced his desire for a Press Law that would regulate the content and ownership of media outlets as well as require all journalists to register in order to practice journalism.

In addition to legal obstacles, three problems continue to undermine the emergence of an independent press: the ambiguous commitment of national and local governments to press freedom, the intertwined relations between the Colorado Party and media ownership, and the persistent threat of criminal enterprises. Journalists who denounce political corruption and the linkages between political power and illegal business typically suffer the brunt of the antipress violence, particularly in the interior and border towns, where smuggling and drug trafficking are widespread. As in previous years, journalists in 2007 suffered a string of verbal and physical attacks. Radio journalist Tito Alberto Palma was killed by unidentified assailants in the city of Mayor Otano on the Argentinian border on August 22. A Chilean national who had lived in Paraguay since 1991, Palma had received threats over his exposés of corruption in the local government, including ties with drug traffickers and other criminal interests. Reporter Javier Nunez of the daily *Ultima Hora* and *Canal 9* in Coronel Oviedo also received death threats; it is suspected that they were linked to his denunciation of a criminal network of car thieves. While the reappearance in Sao Paulo, Brazil, of Paraguayan radio journalist Enrique Galeano, who vanished in February 2006, was welcome, the lack of judicial investigation into his case and several past cases of antipress violence and killings remain troubling. Galeano had disappeared after receiving several death threats for his denunciations of drug traffickers and their links to local Colorado Party politicians.

Paraguay's media system is characterized by lively debates and partisanship. Politicians and newspapers usually trade barbs, which at times can be counterproductive for press freedom, particularly when they come from powerful government officials. In a country where public funds are crucial for press economies, hostile comments against news outlets perpetuate a climate of intimidation and self-censorship. Press freedom groups were concerned about President Duarte Frutos's criticisms of the anti-Colorado press amid the campaign leading up to the 2008 national elections. In November, Duarte Frutos stated that the press was more of an enemy than the political opposition. Unchecked political influence also undermines a free press. The influence of a powerful senator of the ruling Colorado Party was suspected in the termination of a radio program in Paraguari. The program had been critical of local politicians and their suspected links to organized crime.

Paraguay has a diverse media system, with a number of private broadcasting stations and three independent daily newspapers. But the dominance of the Colorado Party elite, which has been in power for six decades, and a hostile political environment toward assertive journalism prevent the media from offering a multitude of viewpoints. The authority of the Colorado Party over broadcasting policies and the lack of transparency surrounding the arbitrary allocation of state advertising also remain serious obstacles for many media outlets. The Paraguayan Union of Journalists (SPP) estimates that about 80 percent of radio stations are controlled by members of the Colorado Party. Furthermore, the lack of resolution on the legal status of community radios, which are often targets of intimidation by political officials and unidentified groups, further compromises press freedom and media diversity. The SPP remains concerned about working conditions for reporters, including low wages and lack of benefits. No cases of government restrictions of the internet were reported in 2007, in a country where just under 4 percent of the population had regular access.

Peru

LEGAL ENVIRONMENT: 15
POLITICAL ENVIRONMENT: 18
ECONOMIC ENVIRONMENT: 11

Status: Partly Free   TOTAL SCORE: 44

Survey Edition	2003	2004	2005	2006	2007
Total Score, Status	35,PF	34,PF	40,PF	39,PF	42,PF

Peru's media freedom declined in 2007 amid a series of threats and physical attacks against media workers, an atmosphere of impunity, and the government's closure of several local radio and television stations—reportedly in retaliation for critical coverage. Freedom of the press is guaranteed in the 1993 constitution, but local and international media organizations continued to express concern about the state of press freedom. In 2002 and 2003, the government of President Alejandro Toledo passed laws expanding access to public information. The willingness of many agencies to provide information has grown, despite a July 2005 measure that tightened restrictions on access to information in certain categories and extended the timelines for release of classified information. *Desacato* (disrespect) laws continued to be a problem, with a number of journalists entangled in court cases in 2007 and charged with defamation by public officials and private citizens. Reporters were sentenced to prison in six cases, though the sentences were either suspended or remained under appeal at year's end. Controversy also ensued on several occasions when local radio and television stations were closed. In April, three radio and three television stations were closed in Chimbote, while a radio station in Pisco was closed in September. In each case the government claimed that licenses were missing or expired, while critics noted that in each case the stations had recently been critical of government actions.

In addition to legal difficulties, the hostile climate for the press is evidenced by numerous instances of physical attacks and verbal threats. Local press watchdog Instituto de Prensa y Sociedad dramatically increased the number of alerts it issued, from 96 in 2006 to 121 in 2007. The majority of these violations came in the form of physical aggression (38 percent) and death threats (23 percent). Journalists working in the country's interior provinces are especially vulnerable, as are reporters covering crime stories, scandals, and corruption. In March, Cajamarca journalist Miguel Perez Julca was murdered. Although he had made several corruption accusations on his radio show and several suspects were arrested, other reporters alleged that the real reason for his murder was his announcement that he was going to name corrupt policemen. Journalists in Loreto, San Martin, and Ancash also faced assassination attempts. Attempts by the media to cover protests also resulted in violence against journalists, especially those involving coca growers. Remnants of the Shining Path rebel group, now associated with cocaine production, published a list of threatened journalists in December in Huanuco.

Most cases of violence or harassment of journalists by public officials and private citizens continued to go unpunished. However, on a positive note, in May President Alan Garcia signed the Inter American Press Association–sponsored Declaration of Chapultepec, which commits the government to action against impunity. Several individuals were sentenced on November 14 for the 2004 murder of radio journalist Alberto Rivera Fernandez in the city of Pucallpa, but the ex-Pucallpa mayor viewed as the intellectual author was cleared, leading to the opening of an investigation of the judges who acquitted him. In a separate case, two men were finally convicted and sentenced for the 1988 killing of reporter Hugo Bustios Saavedra.

Peru's media are diverse and express a broad range of viewpoints. Private investors dominate the media industry, and in comparison, the audience for state-run media is relatively small. However, the government owns two television networks and one radio station and operates the print news agency Andina. Radio is an important medium, especially in the countryside. The media corruption that was endemic in the Alberto Fujimori era continues to an extent today, with both owners and individual journalists occasionally accepting bribes in exchange for slanted coverage. One government minister was accused of trying to buy favorable coverage in several print outlets. These activities contribute to a long-standing lack of confidence in the press as a credible institution. National newspapers are also dependent on advertising revenue from a small number of large companies. The internet is open and unrestricted by the government, with over 25 percent of the population accessing the web in 2007.

	LEGAL ENVIRONMENT: 11
	POLITICAL ENVIRONMENT: 23
Philippines	ECONOMIC ENVIRONMENT: 11
Status: Partly Free	TOTAL SCORE: 45

Survey Edition	2003	2004	2005	2006	2007
Total Score, Status	30,F	34,PF	35,PF	40,PF	46,PF

While reports are often rooted in sensationalism and innuendo, media in the Philippines have historically ranked among the freest, most vibrant, and outspoken in Southeast Asia. However, journalists in 2007 continued to face deadly violence and the use of defamation suits to silence criticism of public officials. Furthermore, the arrests of more than 30 media workers covering an attempt by military officers to rally the public against the ruling administration in November and a series of subsequent warnings effectively restricted reporting on a significant national event.

The constitution guarantees freedoms of speech, expression, and peaceful assembly. There are no restrictive licensing requirements for newspapers or journalists and few legal limitations such as privacy or obscenity laws. However, new national security legislation introduced in 2007 may limit journalists' traditional rights and access to sources. On April 20, shortly before the May legislative elections, President Gloria Macapagal Arroyo issued Executive Order 608, which established a National Security Clearance System to "protect and ensure the integrity and sanctity" of classified information against "enemies of the state." The order calls on the heads of government agencies to implement a vaguely defined security clearance procedure approved by the national security adviser. Separately, watchdog groups expressed concerns that a new Human Security Act, or Antiterror Law, which took effect in July, will allow members of the media to be wiretapped based on mere suspicion of involvement in terrorism.

The country's penal code makes libel a criminal offense punishable by prison terms and, in some cases, large fines. The prevalence and severity of libel cases in recent years prompted a broad-based movement calling for the decriminalization of defamation in 2006. Jose Miguel Arroyo, the president's husband, has been the most notorious abuser of libel laws, with 11 suits filed against 46 journalists as of May 2007. He continued to launch defamation suits in early 2007, including charges against several staff members of the *Philippine Daily Inquirer*, despite a major class-action civil suit filed against him by more than 40 media workers in December

2006 for using the courts to harass the media. Arroyo dropped all of his complaints on May 3, World Press Freedom Day, in what he called a "gesture of peace" following his release from the hospital, where he had undergone risky open-heart surgery. Local press freedom groups welcomed the decision but attributed it to the journalists' countersuit, which was causing political damage to his wife's administration. Despite calls for the case against Arroyo to proceed, it was effectively put on hold in September when an appeals court granted his request for a preliminary injunction.

Although a censorship board has the power to edit or ban content for both television and film, government censorship does not typically affect political orientation. Both the private media and the country's many state-owned television and radio stations cover the country's numerous controversial topics, including alleged election fraud, ongoing counterinsurgency campaigns, and high-level corruption cases. Media coverage in the run-up to the May legislative elections was perceived to be generally unbiased, although there were a few cases in which the media were prevented from conducting interviews with senior opposition members. For example, the media were blocked from interviewing Satur Ocampo of the leftist Bayan Muna party, who was arrested in March for alleged involvement in Communist purges in the 1980s, and foreign journalists were prevented from interviewing a jailed opposition candidate, Senator Antonio Trillanes, in May. The arrest of some 30 media workers, including 4 members of the foreign press, at the scene of a failed coup attempt in November was criticized as a serious infringement of the media's ability to report on significant national events. The Department of the Interior and Local Government called the media presence at the site an obstruction of justice and subsequently warned that arrests would be repeated if reporters defied orders to leave similar scenes in the future.

Filipino journalists faced danger in the course of their work throughout the year. Although violence declined slightly in 2007, with two journalists clearly killed in connection with their work as opposed to three in 2006, the Philippines continues to rank as one of the most dangerous places in the world for members of the press. Exposing corruption scandals or criticizing the government, army, or police can prove lethal, with the Committee to Protect Journalists reporting 32 journalists killed since 1992 and citing a 90 percent impunity rate. Both murder victims in 2007 were radio broadcasters: Carmelo Palacios, a frequent critic of police abuses in Nueva Ecija province in the north, was killed in April; and Ferdinand Lintuan, known as a vocal critic of local government corruption in Davao, was killed in December. Radio broadcasters outside major urban centers—known for sensational political reporting intended to attract high ratings—are the most common targets; at least four radio journalists were shot and wounded during the year under unclear circumstances, and others escaped injury in similar attacks.

The nature of advertising and the prevalence of "block timing" in radio broadcasting contribute to sensational reporting, while local political rivalries, corruption, and family vendettas often make the motives and perpetrators behind journalist murders difficult to identify. Only two convictions for the murder of journalists have ever been issued, and because the crimes are often carried out by hired gunmen, no mastermind of such a slaying has ever been held accountable. In 2006, the president established Task Force Usig, a special police unit, and the Melo Commission to Investigate Media and Activist Killings in an effort to address the problem. However, the official findings of the former are disputed by local human rights groups, while the latter lacked any sort of enforcement capacity. Harassment and death threats are common; attorney Harry Roque, who led the class-action suit against Arroyo, received several death threats early in the year.

Most print and electronic media outlets are privately owned, and while some television and radio stations are government owned, they too present a wide variety of views. Since 1986, there has been a general trend toward concentration of ownership, with two broadcast networks controlled by wealthy families dominating audiences and advertising. Often criticized for lacking journalistic ethics, media outlets tend to reflect the political or economic orientations of their owners and patrons, and special interests reportedly use inducements to solicit favorable coverage. Approximately 15.4 percent of the population made use of the internet in 2007, and the government did not restrict their access.

Poland

Status: Free

LEGAL ENVIRONMENT: 8
POLITICAL ENVIRONMENT: 9
ECONOMIC ENVIRONMENT: 7
TOTAL SCORE: 24

Survey Edition	2003	2004	2005	2006	2007
Total Score, Status	18,F	19,F	20,F	21,F	22,F

Even though 2007 saw increased pressure from state institutions and ever more partisan usage of public outlets, the Polish media remained vibrant, independent, and diverse. The constitution forbids censorship and guarantees freedom of the press. Libel and some forms of insult—including defamation of public officials, the state, and constitutional institutions—are criminal offenses punishable by fines and up to two years in prison. Convictions under these charges are rare and often result only in fines but are not unheard of: Two journalists were taken into pretrial detention this year for failure to appear in court to face criminal charges. In a separate case, a Spanish newspaper, *El País*, was charged with "defaming Poland" for a March 2007 article claiming that Poland's government was plagued by "excessive influence from the Catholic Church, homophobia, and racism." This was the first time any individual or outlet had been charged under Article 132 of the criminal code.

Media freedom advocates concur that political pressures on the media increased in 2007. High-ranking politicians, including the prime minister himself, accused journalists on a number of occasions of bias, cooperation with the Communist-era secret services, and corruption. In fact, new legislation known as the Lustration Act required an estimated 700,000 individuals, including a number of journalists, to submit statements detailing the nature of their relationship with members of the former secret service. Failure to produce such a statement could result in a 10-year suspension from practicing one's profession.

Leading up to the 2007 parliamentary election, domestic and international media freedom advocates noted a bias toward the ruling coalition in public media coverage. In fact, the overall election atmosphere resulted in many media outlets, both public and private, becoming more politically engaged. There were even well-documented cases of partisan oversight of evening news programming and vetting of stories that cast the government in an unfavorable light. The most high-profile example of this was the installation of a friend of the minister of justice as the political commissar in the national television company's information agency. In another unprecedented incident, prime-time programming on the most popular public television stations was interrupted to report a corruption scandal and the arrest of an opposition parliamentarian during the 10 days prior to the elections.

Print media and radio are predominantly private and highly diversified, with a number of new national dailies launched in recent years. Government-owned Polish Television (TVP) and its four channels remain a major source of information for most citizens. This dominant position is reinforced by substantial advertising revenues and a mandatory subscription fee collected from radio and television owners. However, private television stations continue to gain a larger share of the market. Electronic media remained under the jurisdiction of the highly politicized National Radio and Television Broadcasting Council (KRRiT). During the 2007 parliamentary elections, the KRRiT was paralyzed when the chair stepped down to campaign for office. The chief of staff for the incumbent president accepted the job of chair of the national television company TVP. Just over 35 percent of the population has regular and unrestricted internet access. However, in several instances public authorities intervened to block internet content of a fascist or pornographic nature.

Portugal

Status: Free

LEGAL ENVIRONMENT: 4
POLITICAL ENVIRONMENT: 6
ECONOMIC ENVIRONMENT: 6
TOTAL SCORE: 16

Survey Edition	2003	2004	2005	2006	2007
Total Score, Status	15,F	14,F	14,F	14,F	14,F

Portuguese media remained free in 2007 despite the parliament's decision in September to pass the Journalists Statute, a law that potentially strips journalists of their right to protect confidential sources. Freedom of the press is guaranteed by the constitution, and laws against insulting the government or the armed forces are rarely enforced. Changes to the country's Journalists Statute, which were originally proposed in 2006, make it easier for courts to order journalists to disclose confidential sources if the courts decide that it would be "difficult to obtain [the] information in any other way." The parliament made minor changes to the law after the Portuguese president vetoed the bill in August and acknowledged that it contradicted some aspects of the code of criminal procedures that respects professional secrecy, an issue he acknowledged is "particularly delicate to journalists' activity." The parliament passed the law by making cosmetic changes to it to conform to the president's concerns but essentially leaving the capacity for officials to gain access to confidential sources from journalists.

The new Journalists Statute also gives journalists' employers and clients the right to reuse work in any way for 30 days following its first publication. Journalists have the right to reject any modifications to their work if such changes might affect their reputation; they can also remove their names from badly edited pieces. However, the European Federation of Journalists has argued that such protections are "impracticable," especially because such "modifications are made without the journalist's knowledge" and will be discovered only after their publication.

Six main national newspapers, four daily and two weekly, make up the bulk of the printed press in Portugal. There are some 300 local and regional private radio stations. The Catholic station Radio Renascenca commands a wide listening audience. Commercial television has been making gains in recent years, providing serious competition for the public broadcasting channels that lack funds. The internet is unrestricted and is used by more than 70 percent of the population.

Qatar

Status: Not Free

LEGAL ENVIRONMENT: 19
POLITICAL ENVIRONMENT: 24
ECONOMIC ENVIRONMENT: 21
TOTAL SCORE: 64

Survey Edition	2003	2004	2005	2006	2007
Total Score, Status	61,NF	61,NF	62,NF	61,NF	63,NF

Despite vibrant coverage of international news by its flagship satellite television channel, Al-Jazeera, the Qatari government continued to restrict all media from reporting on news critical of local authorities. The government professes to respect freedom of the press, but aside from selected constitutional provisions, such as Section 47, there are no laws that protect media freedom. Journalists are forbidden from criticizing the government, the ruling family, or Islam and are subject to prosecution under the penal code for such violations. The 1979 Press and Publications Law is administered by the criminal courts and provides for jail sentences for libel or slander. By law, all publications are subject to licensing by the government. The law also authorizes the government, the Qatar Radio and Television Corporation, and customs officers to censor both domestic and foreign publications and broadcast media for religious, political, and sexual content prior to distribution. According to the U.S. State Department, several Qatari writers reported that articles they had written—particularly ones deemed critical of the government—which were published outside the country, were deliberately banned in Qatar. Media watchdog group Reporters Sans Frontieres reported that all journalists must now have judicial permission to cover court proceedings following a decision issued by the Supreme Judicial Council in October. In a positive step, however, Qatar was the only country to abstain at a

February meeting of the Ministers of Information of the Arab League from approving a new charter to control and censor satellite channels and transmissions.

Although there were no reports of physical violence directed at members of the press during the year, journalists faced multiple forms of intimidation. Disparity exists in the application of press legislation between Qatari and non-Qatari journalists, who represent the majority of media workers in the country. While local journalists often receive warnings and threats when pushing the limits of permissible coverage, noncitizens employed by Qatari media outlets risk facing harsher measures, including termination, deportation, and imprisonment. As a result, self-censorship is reportedly widespread. All foreign journalists working in the country must be accredited by the Qatar Foreign Information Agency and sponsored by a local institution or the Information Ministry. However, journalists in compliance with these rules can still be barred from entering the country. In November, Qatar officials denied entry to French journalist Aurelien Colly to cover a meeting of the Gulf Cooperation Council.

Qatar has seven newspapers that publish in either Arabic or English, which are owned by either members of the ruling family or businessmen with close ties to the ruling family. The state owns and operates all broadcast media, and there are only two television networks in the country, Qatar TV and the Al-Jazeera satellite channel. While Qatar TV broadcasts mostly official news and progovernment perspectives, Al-Jazeera focuses its coverage on international topics. As a government-subsidized channel, Al-Jazeera refrains from criticizing the Qatari authorities, providing only sparse and uncritical local news. Programming on the local radio station, on the other hand, is more accommodating to voices critical of government services and operations. The concentration of media ownership within the ruling family as well as the high financial costs and citizenship requirements to obtain media ownership licenses continue to hinder the expansion and freedom of the press.

Thirty-two percent of Qataris used the internet in 2007. The government censors political, religious, and pornographic content through the sole state-owned internet service provider. Both high-speed and dial-up internet users are directed to a proxy server that maintains a list of banned websites and blocks material deemed inconsistent with the "religious, cultural, political, and moral values of the country."

Romania

Status: Partly Free

LEGAL ENVIRONMENT: 13
POLITICAL ENVIRONMENT: 16
ECONOMIC ENVIRONMENT: 15
TOTAL SCORE: 44

Survey Edition	2003	2004	2005	2006	2007
Total Score, Status	38,PF	47,PF	47,PF	44,PF	42,PF

The constitution protects freedom of the press, and the government has become increasingly respectful of these rights. A law passed in 2006 decriminalized defamation and similar offenses, meaning journalists would no longer face jail time if convicted. However, the Constitutional Court overturned the measure in early 2007 because it deemed the legislation to be unconstitutional, effectively reinstating defamation and libel in the penal code. Freedom of information legislation now applies to state-owned enterprises as well as to government institutions, but implementation remains problematic. The president and the parliament still appoint the National Council of Broadcasting and the boards of the public television and radio operators, leaving them vulnerable to political influence.

The 2004 election of President Traian Basescu brought substantial improvements in the political environment for the press, as he has proven to be less controlling and manipulative of the media than his predecessors. Self-censorship for political reasons also appears to have decreased. However, the government can be sensitive to media criticism, and journalists risk arrest or harassment when working on issues associated with national security. Ongoing political rifts between the president, the prime minister, and their respective allies in parliament may be contributing to the trend toward less government control over the media. In October, public broadcaster Romanian Television aired a video recording of Agriculture Minister Decebai Traian Remes allegedly accepting a bribe, leading to his resignation the next day. The justice minister later suggested that the video could have been leaked by the presidential administration.

In a more pervasive problem, reporters, cameramen, and photographers frequently face minor assaults in the course of their work, at the hands of both state and nonstate actors. In one such instance, members of the Mafia severely beat a television journalist and destroyed his equipment while he was attempting to film them. President Basescu, who has a history of verbally abusing journalists, seized the mobile telephone of a female reporter who attempted to film and interview him in a supermarket in May 2007 on the day of a referendum concerning his removal from office. The phone then recorded him making sexist and racist remarks about the reporter in a conversation with his wife. In February, the mayor of Bacau beat two journalists who had been filming his car while he was stopped by traffic police.

Television is the most popular form of news consumption for most Romanians, and public broadcasters are forced to compete with several large private channels and a multitude of smaller stations. The number of media outlets and news sources has increased in recent years, driven partly by politicians and wealthy businessmen seeking to establish their own press vehicles. At the same time, a small number of major owners have stepped up concentration, acquiring television, radio, and print outlets. The proliferation of media is not supported by the market, and many outlets are not profitable, encouraging self-censorship to please owners and advertisers. The political influence of state advertising is less of a problem than in previous years, and private media do not receive state subsidies. Access to the internet is increasing, with few reports of government interference. More than 30 percent of the population used the new medium in 2007, and Romania is considered a regional leader in high-speed broadband connections.

Russia

Status: Not Free

LEGAL ENVIRONMENT: 21
POLITICAL ENVIRONMENT: 33
ECONOMIC ENVIRONMENT: 24
TOTAL SCORE: 78

Survey Edition	2003	2004	2005	2006	2007
Total Score, Status	66,NF	67,NF	68,NF	72,NF	75,NF

Media freedom continued to decline in 2007 as the Kremlin further restricted independent news reporting and public dissent while preparing for a stage-managed parliamentary election that was held in December. President Vladimir Putin's authoritarian, corrupt, and lawless style of rule appeared set to continue at the end of his second term. A week after the flawed December parliamentary election, Putin endorsed First Deputy Prime Minister Dmitry Medvedev as his presidential successor for an orchestrated presidential election to be held in 2008; Medvedev reciprocated, naming Putin as his prime minister.

Although the constitution provides for freedom of speech and of the press, the Kremlin used the country's politicized and corrupt criminal justice system to harass and prosecute independent journalists. Throughout the year, journalists faced dozens of criminal cases and hundreds of civil cases, particularly in retaliation for reporting on the Other Russia opposition party. Police officers in Samara and Nizhny Novgorod raided the regional bureaus of the independent Moscow newspaper *Novaya Gazeta* and confiscated their computers, while prosecutors opened politicized criminal cases relating to alleged software piracy. In July, the rubber-stamp parliament approved a series of amendments to the criminal code expanding the country's vague antiextremism laws that are used to suppress critics of the Kremlin and encourage self-censorship. According to the Committee to Protect Journalists, the Moscow-based radio station Ekho Moskvy subsequently received over a dozen official warnings from prosecutors, media regulators, and the Federal Security Service for broadcasting allegedly "extremist" statements. In May, immigration officials at a Moscow airport denied entry to Natalya Morar, a Moldovan journalist working for the Moscow weekly magazine *Novoye Vremya*, after she published articles about high-level government officials involved in money laundering and illegal campaign funding.

Russia remained one of the most dangerous countries in the world for the media. In 2007, two journalists' deaths were deemed "suicides" by authorities: Ivan Safronov, a correspondent with the business daily *Kommersant*, who "fell" out of the window of his Moscow apartment building in March just as he was planning to report on politically sensitive Russian weapons sales to Iran and Syria; and Vyacheslav Ifanov, a television cameraman for the independent station Novoye Televideniye Aleiska in Siberia, who was said to have died from a carbon monoxide overdose in April despite having wounds on his body and having previously received death threats from military officials. Although later investigations by local watchdog groups indicated that Ifanov probably did commit suicide, Safronov's death remains unsolved. The trial of two suspects in the July 2004 murder of *Forbes Russia* editor Paul Klebnikov was delayed throughout 2007 because one of the suspects went into hiding. Over a dozen other murders remained uninvestigated, but in a rare example of accountability, five gang members in the city of Kazan were convicted of the 2000 murder of *Novaya Gazeta* journalist Igor Domnikov. Also encouraging was the August arrest of 10 suspects in the high-profile murder of Domnikov's colleague at *Novaya Gazeta*, Anna Politkovskaya.

Journalists remained unable to cover the news freely, particularly with regard to contentious topics—like human rights abuses in the North Caucasus, government corruption, organized crime, the December election, and police torture—and were subject to a variety of abuses. In March, police in Nizhny Novgorod detained nine local journalists and foreign correspondents—and physically assaulted three of them—trying to cover an opposition rally. According to the Center for Journalism in Extreme Situations, during a crackdown on opposition demonstrations in April in Moscow, St. Petersburg, and Samara, over 70 journalists were detained or beaten. In May, police detained three foreign correspondents in a Moscow airport to prevent them from flying to Samara to cover another opposition rally. And on the eve of the parliamentary election, authorities in the northern city of Arkhangelsk seized the entire print run of a local newspaper containing articles critical of the central government and local authorities. Journalists who criticized federal and regional authorities also faced a risk of imprisonment, with three remaining behind bars at the end of 2007: Boris Stomakhin, editor of the monthly Moscow newspaper *Radikalnaya Politika*; Anatoly Sardayev, editor of the weekly Saransk newspaper *Mordoviya Segodnya*; and Nikolai Andrushchenko, editor of the Saint Petersburg weekly *Novy Peterburg*. Authorities also revived the Soviet-era tradition of temporary psychiatric detentions in order to silence a regional journalist and an activist who criticized local authorities—Vladimir Chugunov from the town of Solnechnogorsk and Larisa Arap from the city of Murmansk. Some journalists were forced to flee the country as a result of aggressive harassment by the Federal Security Service and other government agencies. Two journalists who worked for the Associated Press and Radio Free Europe/Radio Liberty in the North Caucasus—Fatima Tlisova and Yuri Bagrov—received political asylum in the United States, while a third journalist—Yelena Tregubova, a reporter for the Moscow business daily *Kommersant*—fled to the United Kingdom after publicly criticizing the Kremlin's media restrictions.

Authorities continued to exert significant influence on media outlets and news content through a vast state media empire—the leading television networks Channel One, Rossiya, and NTV; the news agencies ITAR-TASS and RIA-Novosti; the national radio stations Radio Mayak and Radio Rossiya; the international English-language broadcaster Russia Today; and hundreds of regional newspapers, radio stations, and television channels—that filled the airwaves with pro-Kremlin propaganda, particularly ahead of the flawed December parliamentary elections. International radio and television channels are generally restricted, and in August, the government terminated the BBC's FM Russian-language program on Bolshoye Radio, though the program is still available on short- and medium-wave frequencies. Diversity continued to decline as private companies loyal to the Kremlin and regional authorities purchased influential private newspapers and most media outlets remained dependent on state subsidies as well as government printing, distribution, and transmission facilities. Lively but cautious political debate was increasingly limited to glossy weekly magazines and news websites available only to urban, educated, and affluent audiences. However, television was the primary source of news for most Russians. With online media developing rapidly and an estimated 20 percent of the population now online, there were no reports that the government overtly restricted internet access. However, the Federal Security Service did continue widespread monitoring of e-mails and web posting, while government officials harassed some news websites and federal authorities debated introducing new legal restrictions on the internet. In June, a wide range of opposition websites reported being hacked or receiving "denial of service" attacks, though it was difficult to prove the source. Additionally, Kremlin allies have purchased several independent online newspapers or have created their own pro-government online news websites, as well as reportedly cultivating a network of bloggers who are paid to produce pro-Kremlin propaganda.

Rwanda

Status: Not Free

LEGAL ENVIRONMENT: 24
POLITICAL ENVIRONMENT: 34
ECONOMIC ENVIRONMENT: 26
TOTAL SCORE: 84

Survey Edition	2003	2004	2005	2006	2007
Total Score, Status	80,NF	82,NF	84,NF	85,NF	84,NF

Although there have been some improvements in political rights and civil liberties in Rwanda since the 1994 genocide, authorities continued to restrict the media in 2007 through the illegal imprisonment of critical journalists and the harassment of independent outlets. The constitution provides for freedom of the press "in conditions prescribed by the law," but the government routinely limited the ability of the independent media to operate, often invoking the destructive role that certain radio stations played in the genocide. The media are tightly controlled by the government in practice despite a 2002 law that formally forbids censorship. Libel remains a criminal offense, and there are no laws guaranteeing access to information.

In June 2007, the minister of information arbitrarily revoked the license of the *Weekly Post*, a new private publication, three days after its first edition was issued, despite laws requiring a court order for such a move.

Throughout 2007, the government of President Paul Kagame regularly arrested and illegally detained journalists. In fact, the risk of imprisonment posed by far the greatest threat to independent journalists in Rwanda. On January 12, for example, authorities arrested and charged the editor of the private periodical *Umurabyo*, Agnes Nkusi-Uwimana, with divisionism and discrimination following the paper's publication of an article that was critical of the government. On the belief that Nkusi-Uwimana represented a "threat to state security," a judge kept her in pretrial detention until April, when she was sentenced to a year in prison and fined approximately US$760. Separately, in February, authorities arrested a Congolese journalist and professor who was teaching in Kigali on charges of threatening state security, following his publication of a critical online article; he was released on March 21 and subsequently deported, but his case marked Rwanda's first imprisonment in response to an online publication. Also in March, police detained a reporter and a photographer with the American magazine *U.S. News & World Report*, along with a local journalist for the private newspaper *Umuco*, as they attempted to cover a trial. The two Americans were released after three hours following the confiscation of their equipment, while the local journalist escaped from detention. A number of other incidents of harassment took place during the year. *Umuseso*, a critical independent newspaper, faced repeated hounding by the authorities; its editor, Gerard Manzi, was arrested and held for a week in August on fabricated rape charges.

The aggressive stance of the authorities toward the media could be seen in official rhetoric as well. During a state-run television program in September, government ministers accused many in the media of working with "negative forces" inside and outside of the country, with the interior minister suggesting that any journalist who publishes an official document should be detained until he or she reveals the source of the leak. In response, RIMEG—which produces papers including *Umuseso* and is Rwanda's largest independent private publisher—announced that it would suspend its operations until the government apologized or provided evidence for its accusations. *Umuco* soon followed suit. Both publishing houses remained closed for several weeks but started publishing again despite the government's inaction, citing the ongoing demand for independent news. On a more positive note, Tatiana Mukakibibi, a former presenter for the state-owned Radio Rwanda, was finally acquitted of genocide charges after spending 11 years in pretrial detention.

Most newspapers operating in Rwanda face a number of financial constraints that prevent them from publishing on a daily basis. The *New Times*, a private paper with close government ties, is the only paper that appears daily, and the government refuses to advertise with outlets that regularly produce critical reports. The state broadcasters continue to dominate radio and effectively monopolize television in the country, with the handful of private radio stations focusing largely on entertainment. The British Broadcasting Corporation and Voice of America are available in Rwanda, but Radio France Internationale is still banned after the government severed diplomatic relations with France in 2006. Internet access was not restricted or monitored by the government, but it was available to less than 1 percent of the population in 2007.

St. Kitts and Nevis

LEGAL ENVIRONMENT: 4
POLITICAL ENVIRONMENT: 8
ECONOMIC ENVIRONMENT: 7

Status: Free

TOTAL SCORE: 19

Survey Edition	2003	2004	2005	2006	2007
Total Score, Status	18,F	21,F	23,F	21,F	20,F

Freedom of the press is enshrined in the constitution and is generally respected by the government. The independent media were active in 2007 and expressed a wide variety of views without restriction. A draft freedom of information bill that was submitted to parliament in 2006 continued to be debated throughout the year. In November, the high court ruled against the *Democrat*, the newspaper of the opposition People's Action Movement, in a libel suit brought against it by parliament member Asim Martin, his campaign manager, and the editor of the *Labour Spokesman*, the newspaper of the ruling St. Kitts–Nevis Labour Party. A total of US$168,000 was awarded in damages. In addition to the weekly newspapers published by the two main parties, there are three other nonaligned weekly newspapers. ZIZ Broadcasting Corporation, a company in which the government is a majority shareholder, operates both radio and television services. Additionally, there are seven private radio stations and a multichannel cable television service. There are no government restrictions on the internet, which approximately 25 percent of the population was able to access in 2007.

St. Lucia

LEGAL ENVIRONMENT: 3
POLITICAL ENVIRONMENT: 9
ECONOMIC ENVIRONMENT: 4

Status: Free

TOTAL SCORE: 16

Survey Edition	2003	2004	2005	2006	2007
Total Score, Status	8,F	11,F	16,F	18,F	16,F

Press freedom deteriorated in 2007 as a result of increased political pressure on the media. The constitution provides for freedom of speech and of the press, and the government generally respects these rights in practice. In November 2006, the parliament repealed Section 361 of the criminal code, which had prescribed imprisonment for those convicted of publishing news that endangered the "public good." Following the change of government after the December 2006 victory of the United Workers Party over the St. Lucia Labour Party (SLLP), there were indications of greater interference in the state-owned radio station. Controversy ensued in January when the state-owned Radio St. Lucia (RSL) withdrew an SLLP advertisement calling on party supporters to "take back our country!" In October, Roger Joseph resigned as general manager of RSL. He denied his decision was politically motivated, but the *St. Lucia Star* reported that Joseph resigned because of the immense pressure he was under from the new government. The source said the government had instructed Joseph to send them every release the opposition submitted to the station to allow them to decide whether the station would air the information or not. St. Lucia has three television stations and seven radio stations—all of which are private apart from RSL. There are three weekly newspapers and two that are published three times a week. There are no government restrictions on the internet, which was accessible to over 32 percent of the population in 2007.

St. Vincent & the Grenadines

LEGAL ENVIRONMENT: 4
POLITICAL ENVIRONMENT: 7
ECONOMIC ENVIRONMENT: 6

Status: Free

TOTAL SCORE: 17

Survey Edition	2003	2004	2005	2006	2007
Total Score, Status	17,F	14,F	16,F	16,F	17,F

The government continued to pressure the media for favorable coverage, as the prime minister and government officials filed numerous libel suits against media outlets. The constitution guarantees a free press, and although the government does not often interfere directly with the press, the prime minister, Ralph Gonsalves, and other officials rebuke the media from time to time. In March, Gonsalves filed a libel suit against the Trinidad and Tobago newspaper *Mirror* over an article about the early release of a convicted drug dealer. Gonsalves also threatened to sue a Vincentian political activist for reading the content of the article on a radio program. In July, Gonsalves criticized the mass media for failing to report on what he described as "a major national story"—a high court ruling in favor of the government's request that a foreign company hand over 100 acres of land. In September, Elwardo "E. G." Lynch, who hosts a talk show for the opposition New Democratic Party that is broadcast on Nice Radio, was threatened with legal action for slandering the minister of housing, Senator Julian Francis. Lynch has been involved in similar controversies in the past and in 2005 was ordered to pay damages to Gonsalves. The main newspaper, the daily *Herald*, and the weeklies *News*, *Searchlight*, and the *Vincentian* are all privately owned. The state-run St. Vincent and the Grenadines Broadcasting Corporation operates SVG Television and the Hitz FM music radio station. NBC is a partly government-funded national FM radio service, and there are numerous other private radio stations. There are no government restrictions on the internet, but it is not a significant source of information, with only about 8 percent of the population able to gain access in 2007.

Samoa

Status: Free

LEGAL ENVIRONMENT: 7
POLITICAL ENVIRONMENT: 12
ECONOMIC ENVIRONMENT: 10
TOTAL SCORE: 29

Survey Edition	2003	2004	2005	2006	2007
Total Score, Status	24,F	24,F	25,F	29,F	30,F

The press freedom environment in Samoa remained stable in 2007. While the constitution protects press freedom in Samoa, the Defamation Law of 1992 contains provisions on criminal and civil libel that remain of concern. The most significant media freedom issue in 2007 involved a fire that destroyed the offices of *Newsline Somoa*, hampering one of the country's main publications. Although there were no clear allegations that the fire was intentional, an editor noted that it took place just days before the Pacific Games, the biggest media event of the year. Early in 2007, the chief executive of the privately owned commercial television station LAUTV, Tuiasau Leota Uelese Petaia, was embroiled in a court case over allegations that the company had failed to contribute to the National Provident Fund for six months on behalf of its media workers. The year concluded with concerns about a proposal to privatize the public radio and TV broadcaster Samoa Broadcasting Corporation (SBC). Apart from the state-run SBC, Samoa has five private and religious broadcasters, including the Radio Polynesia group with four FM stations, and access to local and foreign satellite television. There are seven main news publications, including the newspapers *Samoa Observer*, *Newsline*, *Le Samoa*, and the state-run *Savali*, and three newspapers based in Auckland, New Zealand. The internet is unrestricted but was accessed by only 3.2 percent of the population in 2007.

San Marino

LEGAL ENVIRONMENT: 4
POLITICAL ENVIRONMENT: 6
ECONOMIC ENVIRONMENT: 7

Status: Free

TOTAL SCORE: 17

Survey Edition	2003	2004	2005	2006	2007
Total Score, Status	9,F	14,F	16,F	17,F	17,F

The 1974 San Marino Constitutional Order guarantees freedom of expression, and Article 183 of the criminal code protects against libel and slander. However, there are restrictions when freedom of expression comes into conflict with the right to confidentiality and to secrecy. No direct violations of freedom of the press by either state or nonstate actors were reported in 2007. During a public meeting held on World Press Freedom Day, members of the San Marino media requested increased professional training and a new law defining the rights and duties of journalists. Later in the year, Secretariats of State for Labor and Information established a preparatory training course in journalism and public communication. By law, radio and television broadcasting is monopolized by the San Marino Broadcasting Company, which grants concessions to private broadcasters. State-owned San Marino RTV runs both a radio and a television station. Three daily private papers are published in the republic, and a local weekly paper reports on economics, finance, and politics. Italian news is widely available in San Marino, including two private newspapers and several radio and television stations. The internet is available, unrestricted, and used by about 52 percent of the population.

Sao Tome and Principe

LEGAL ENVIRONMENT: 4
POLITICAL ENVIRONMENT: 10
ECONOMIC ENVIRONMENT: 14

Status: Free

TOTAL SCORE: 28

Survey Edition	2003	2004	2005	2006	2007
Total Score, Status	19,F	28,F	28,F	29,F	29,F

The 1990 constitution provides for freedom of the press, and this right is respected in practice and upheld by the state. There were no reported cases of government restrictions on local or foreign media or reports of attacks against the media during 2007. Publications that regularly criticize the administration are circulated freely without government interference, and opposition parties receive free airtime. Nonetheless, self-censorship is widely practiced, and newspapers often depend on official news releases as primary sources of information, which inhibits the growth of investigative journalism. Some writers also accept financial favors from news sources for doing their jobs. Severe problems with infrastructure, including inadequate telecommunications and media distribution networks, constitute a major obstacle for the media. In 2007, there were seven privately owned and two state-run newspapers, all of which typically published infrequently, often because of financial constraints. There were also a number of state-operated radio and television stations. In 2005, the government authorized two new private radio stations to operate within the country, both of which began broadcasting in late 2006. Access to the internet is not restricted by the government but is limited by a lack of infrastructure. Nevertheless, approximately 11 percent of the population accessed this new medium during the year, giving this island republic one of the highest per capita penetration levels in sub-Saharan Africa.

LEGAL ENVIRONMENT: 28

POLITICAL ENVIRONMENT: 29

Saudi Arabia

ECONOMIC ENVIRONMENT: 24

Status: Not Free

TOTAL SCORE: 81

Survey Edition	2003	2004	2005	2006	2007
Total Score, Status	80,NF	80,NF	80,NF	79,NF	82,NF

The media environment in Saudi Arabia remained among the most repressive in the Arab world in 2007. The Basic Law does not provide for press freedom, and certain provisions of the law allow authorities to exercise broad powers to prevent any act that may lead to disunity or sedition. The 49 provisions of the 1963 Publishing and Printing Law govern the establishment of media outlets and the rights and responsibilities of journalists and stipulate penalties for press violations such as fines and imprisonment. According to the official media policy, the press should be a tool to educate the masses, propagate government views, and promote national unity. Avoiding criticism of the royal family, Islam, or religious authorities is an unwritten policy that is followed routinely. Media outlets in Saudi Arabia are administered by the Ministry of Culture and Information, which uses laws, decrees, and interventions by the royal family to restrict media freedom. Nevertheless, Saudi officials have allowed the media to express a moderate level of criticism of the government in recent years, and journalists continued to test the boundaries in 2007 by discussing issues previously considered off-limits.

Journalists face fines and detention upon publishing material deemed objectionable by the authorities, and threats of arrest, interrogation, job dismissal, and harassment contribute to the practice of a high level of self-censorship. The Saudi government has been known to directly censor both local and international media, confiscating print runs and shutting down newspapers temporarily or permanently. In August, the government confiscated copies of the Saudi daily *Al-Hayat* without providing an official explanation and shut down the paper for four days. Some news sources speculated that the seizure was related to the publishing of an article that criticized the Saudi health care system, while others associated it with an article that linked religious scholars with terrorism. All journalists must register with the Ministry of Culture and Information, and foreign journalists face visa obstacles and restrictions on freedom of movement. Elections to the governing board of the Saudi Journalists Association are heavily influenced and controlled by the ministry. Female journalists in Saudi Arabia face multiple forms of gender discrimination such as lesser pay, discouragement from working as freelancers, and limitations requiring them to report solely on topics related to women, family, and children. As a result, many female writers publish under aliases. In January, four female journalists were denied access to the men's campus of the Imam Muhammad bin Saud Islamic University to cover a lecture by the Spanish minister of justice.

There are 10 daily newspapers in Saudi Arabia, and although all are privately owned, most owners are associated with either the government or members of the royal family. Members of the royal family also own two popular London-based dailies, *Asharq al-Aswat* and *Al-Hayat*. Broadcast media are also controlled by the government, which owns and operates all domestic television and radio stations. According to the U.S. State Department, the Saudi Investment Authority had received 30 applications for new private media outlets, but these requests were still pending at year's end. Satellite television has become widespread despite its illegal status and is an important source of foreign news; nevertheless, much of the satellite industry is controlled by Saudi investors and is respectful of local sensibilities.

About 17 percent of Saudi residents used the internet in 2007. However, the Saudi government is one of the most restrictive censors of online material in the Arab region. According to the International Press Institute, over 400,000 websites have been blocked. King Abdul-Aziz City for Science and Technology (KACST)—a government institution charged with developing and coordinating internet-related policies—is the sole gateway for Saudi internet users and manages the connections between the national and international internet, with all privately owned internet service providers linked to the main server at KACST. Through KACST, the government continues to block and filter websites deemed offensive, critical, or immoral. Updated lists of undesirable websites are continuously fed to the filters, and users attempting to access banned sites receive warnings and are told that their attempts are being recorded. E-mail and chat rooms are also reportedly monitored by the Saudi Telecommunications Company. In 2006, the Saudi government approved the first law to combat "electronic crimes," criminalizing defamation on the internet and computer hacking. Given the restricted environment for print and broadcast media, there has been a significant rise in the number of Saudi blogs in recent years, totaling several thousand. The Saudi government has increasingly responded by blocking select blogs and harassing blog authors. On December 10, the authorities detained without charges Saudi blogger Fouad Ahmed al-Farhan, author of a popular pro-reform site. He remained in custody at year's end.

Senegal

Status: Partly Free

LEGAL ENVIRONMENT: 16
POLITICAL ENVIRONMENT: 20
ECONOMIC ENVIRONMENT: 13

TOTAL SCORE: 49

Survey Edition	2003	2004	2005	2006	2007
Total Score, Status	38,PF	37,PF	37,F	44,PF	46,PF

Senegal's steady decline in media freedom comes despite years of promises made by President Abdoulaye Wade to protect it. Article 80 of the penal code is particularly harsh and is used repeatedly to severely punish journalists and offending media. Because Wade had come into power after years in opposition as a persecuted politician, many thought he would usher in a new era in which civil and political liberties would be strengthened, legal backing would be given to shield the independence of the media, and laws like criminal libel legislation would be revoked. At the start of his second seven-year term of office in February 2007, President Wade has not only failed to deliver on prior commitments, he has quickened the pace of persecution of journalists. In December, he "recommended" that journalists obtain feedback from officials prior to the publication of any government-related articles, to better enable the government to maintain a positive image.

A number of press freedom violations occurred in 2007, including harsh criminal libel cases and severe punishments for "threatening state security," which were particularly common. These included the case of Moussa Gueye, managing editor of the private daily newspaper *L'Exclusif*, and Pape Moussa Doucar, the paper's owner. Both men were arrested, imprisoned, and charged with endangering public security after their newspaper ran a front-page story by political reporter Justin Ndoye titled "Late Outings at the Presidency: The Nocturnal Escapades of President Wade." Ndoye went into hiding after the story was published, and police issued an arrest warrant for him. It was only after an executive order was issued that Gueye and Doucar were released from detention. Separately, Pape Amadou Gaye, managing editor of the private *Le Courrier*, was detained and similarly charged with offending the state for an article holding the president responsible for the rising cost of living. He too was released from detention following an executive order seven days after his arrest. In March, facing accusations of defamation by a car dealership, Jean Meissa Diop, director of the private daily *Walf Grand-Place*, and one of the paper's reporters, Faydy Drame, were each sentenced to six months in prison and fined US$23,000. In April, director Ndiogou Wack Seck of the private, progovernment daily *Il Est Midi* was also sentenced to six months in prison, fined US$90,000 for criminal defamation, and barred from working as a journalist for three months. These actions, as well as the suspension of Seck's newspaper, followed the publication of a story criticizing several close associates of President Wade for their role in the 2006 release of an imprisoned former prime minister.

Although physical harassment of journalists was not as common as harsh libel cases, politicians and their supporters occasionally took extraordinary measures to silence critical and opposition viewpoints during the year. Such was the case with ruling party politician Moustapha Cisse Lo, who in April stormed the studios of Radio Disso FM with a dozen supporters following the broadcast of critical comments during a call-in show. The station filed a complaint with the police over the attack, but Lo filed a subsequent suit for defamation worth US$452,000. Separately in May, the government shut down the offices of Premiere FM and confiscated all of its equipment on the grounds of licensing irregularities; Premiere FM was not allowed to reopen for four months.

Institutional bodies like the National Council for the Regulation of Broadcasting (CNRA) with a mandate for monitoring and regulating the media sector were accused of unfairness in their enforcement of standards, fines, fees, and other measures designed to assure equitable access to the airwaves. The CNRA also remained largely silent or was sidelined as pressure was increased on media practitioners on all fronts. Despite the unwholesome climate for media practice, Senegal still has many private, independent print publications. A number of community, private, and public radio stations operate all over the country, and more than 80 radio frequencies have been granted so far. But more criticism has been leveled against the Wade administration for the nontransparent way in which frequencies are allocated and fees charged for access to airwaves. Critics say President Wade's associates in politics, business, and the religious community get preferential treatment. The Wade administration refuses to accept private participation in the television sector except for entertainment channels. The only national television station, Radiodiffusion Television Senegalaise, is required by law to be majority controlled by the state. Its broadcasts generally give favorable coverage of the government. Foreign satellite television and radio stations, including Radio France Internationale and the British Broadcasting Corporation, are available and unrestricted. Internet access is also unrestricted, and penetration is now estimated at over 5 percent of the population.

LEGAL ENVIRONMENT: 13
POLITICAL ENVIRONMENT: 17

Serbia

ECONOMIC ENVIRONMENT: 9

Status: Partly Free

TOTAL SCORE: 39

Survey Edition	2003	2004	2005	2006	2007
Total Score, Status	40,PF	40,PF	40,PF	40,PF	39,PF

The constitution protects freedom of the press, and the Public Information Law states that "no one may exert any form of physical or other pressure on a media outlet or its staff." However, these and other laws protecting the media were not always enforced, and there were numerous instances of pressure on the media that went unpunished. Overall the media environment remained relatively unchanged in 2007. Conservative and nationalist elements in the government have proven to be less tolerant of media criticism. Libel remains a criminal offense punishable with imprisonment or fines up to US$18,000. There are concerns that the process through which the Republic Broadcasting Agency (RRA) grants broadcasting licenses is unfair and nontransparent. Compounding the problem is the complicated procedure for obtaining a license. In July, the Supreme Court ruled in favor of two television stations and six radio stations that were denied licenses in 2006. But the RRA ignored the ruling and upheld its own decision. The RRA was also criticized for interfering in the editorial decisions of the public broadcaster Radio Television Serbia (RTS) when it ordered RTS to broadcast daily parliamentary sessions in their entirety. The parliament controls the budget of the RRA. In 2006, BK Television, the first private television station, was shut down by the police for operating without a license; it resumed operations briefly in 2007 via satellite but was closed by the end of the year.

Media organizations and journalists were frequently the victims of harassment, vandalism, violence, and intimidation. In fact, in November the editor in chief of the daily *Politika* wrote that one of the wealthiest businessmen in Serbia had himself phoned journalists to criticize them for their coverage. In April, Dinko Gruhonjic, a BETA news agency correspondent and chairman of the Independent Journalists Association of Vojvodina, received death threats after reporting on a neo-Nazi group. Separately, in August, the editor in chief of the independent broadcaster TNT, Stefan Cvetkovic, also reported receiving death threats allegedly in response to his station's coverage of a police scandal. The independent broadcaster B92 and its journalists were frequently harassed, and its offices were vandalized throughout the year. On several occasions, nationalist political parties interrupted B92 broadcasts and staged demonstrations outside its offices, protesting its content. In April, a bomb exploded outside the Belgrade apartment of Dejan Anastasijevic, journalist for the weekly *Vreme*, following his critical report of a former Serbian paramilitary group. Such attacks have not been vigorously prosecuted. Local media operate in a more difficult environment, where local governments typically block journalists' access to public information and cooperate mostly with state-owned media. In October, masked assailants simultaneously entered two television stations in Novi Pazar and at gunpoint halted the rebroadcast of an interview with an Islamic leader in Serbia. The International Press Institute has also recorded a number of other attacks against members of the media throughout the year.

Both broadcast and print media in Serbia are highly active and promote diverse views. However, the media environment remains somewhat politicized. Journalists at times practice self-censorship, and many avoid politically charged topics, including war crimes and the Kosovo status negotiations. Serbia's broadcast and print media are for the most part privately owned. The government owns a stake in the daily *Politika* but has little direct editorial influence. Most local media, however, have yet to be privatized, and there is little support from local governments for these types of liberalization reforms. The public RTS was the dominant media source, operating two television stations and Radio Belgrade. While there are no government subsidies for private media, the state-owned media enjoy strong financial support from the government, as does the state-owned news agency, Tanjug. Media ownership in general remains somewhat nontransparent, with indications that some formal owners are a front for real interests behind the asset. Media ownership concentration has increased slightly with the growing presence of foreign firms. Internet access is unrestricted, though the government regularly monitors its content and only 14 percent of the population was able to receive information online in 2007.

The media environment in Kosovo is regulated by the UN Mission in Kosovo and the constitutional framework. The system of licensing broadcast media in Kosovo is complicated and inconsistent. The television regulator Temporary Media Commissioner is generally considered nontransparent. There were several reported incidents of violence during the year, including the assault of Vesna Bajicic, a Pristina-based correspondent for Voice of America. A masked assailant attacked Bajicic in her home, accusing her of "bias in favor of Albanians" in her reporting, and threatened to abduct her child and kill her if she continued. Journalists frequently complained of not being able to access public information. Although many media were able to sustain operations through aid donations, most struggled financially. As a result, editorial independence remains a weakness in Kosovo, with media adhering to business interests. Public broadcaster Radio Television Kosovo is particularly at the whim of political and economic interests. Public media have a financial advantage, as they are exempt from the value-added tax.

Seychelles

Status: Partly Free

Legal Environment: 20
Political Environment: 20
Economic Environment: 19
Total Score: 59

Survey Edition	2003	2004	2005	2006	2007
Total Score, Status	50,PF	52,PF	58,PF	60,PF	60,PF

The constitution provides for freedom of speech but also restricts this right by protecting the reputation, rights, and privacy of citizens as well as the "interest of defense, public safety, public order, public morality, or public health." These restrictions have limited freedom of the press, particularly because libel charges can easily be filed under these laws to penalize journalists. The law also allows the minister of information to prohibit the broadcast of any material that is against the "national interest." While the judiciary is often perceived as favorable to plaintiffs in libel cases, in August 2007, the court of appeals overturned a Supreme Court libel conviction against *Regar*, one of the country's two independent weekly newspapers. *Regar* had closed in October 2006 in protest at an exorbitant US$58,500 fine it had received. The paper resumed operations once the fine was reversed. Attacks against and harassment of media workers are known to occur at times in the Seychelles; in August 2007, a State House security officer physically assaulted the editor of *Le Nouveau Seychelles Weekly*.

The only daily newspaper, *Nation*, is state owned and rarely publishes stories critical of the government. All other papers publish more sporadically and are often affiliated with a political party. The state has a de facto monopoly over the widely consumed broadcast media (both radio and television), and private broadcasters have been slow to develop because of restrictive licensing fees of more than US$185,000 per year. Following one opposition party's efforts to raise enough money for a radio license, the National Assembly passed an amendment to the Broadcasting and Telecommunications Act prohibiting politically affiliated groups from obtaining a license. The constitutionality of the amendment is currently being appealed in court. Telecommunications companies must submit subscriber information to the government. Although the internet was available and unrestricted in the Seychelles, there were reports in 2007 of the government monitoring e-mail, chat rooms, and blogs for the now nearly 40 percent of the population with access.

Sierra Leone

Status: Partly Free

LEGAL ENVIRONMENT: 18
POLITICAL ENVIRONMENT: 23
ECONOMIC ENVIRONMENT: 18
TOTAL SCORE: 59

Survey Edition	2003	2004	2005	2006	2007
Total Score, Status	61,NF	58,PF	59,PF	59,PF	56,PF

Sierra Leone continues to recover from its long civil war and the political instability of earlier years. The constitution guarantees freedom of expression, but the retention of the Public Order Act of 1965 continues to threaten the enjoyment of this freedom in practice. The Public Order Act criminalizes libel and holds accountable not only journalists, but also vendors, printers, and publishers. In these cases, the burden of truth rests with the accused, and even then truth is not always an adequate defense. Under this law, the editor of the *Standard Times*, Philip Neville, was arrested in August and charged with criminal libel after publishing an editorial on the front page of the newspaper critical of the government in the wake of a visit by Colonel Muammar Qaddafi of Libya. The opinion piece alleged that the government did not publicly disclose gifts made to Sierra Leone by the Libyan leader. The office of President Tejan Kabbah issued a statement saying there was "no iota of truth in the publication" and demanded "immediate action" be taken against the newspaper. The *Standard Times* carried the government's rebuttal. When Neville appeared at a court in the capital city of Freetown, bail for his release from prison was set at a record US$68,150 in addition to other stringent conditions. All charges against the editor were later dropped after the newspaper retracted the story.

In May, parliament passed an amendment to the media code of practice that provided guidelines for media coverage of public affairs. The code required media to be guided by broad principles of democratization, pluralism, diversity, cultural sensitivity, and responsibility. The media also signed a code of conduct that was aimed at discouraging hate radio and sensational xenophobic publications ahead of the August–September presidential and parliamentary elections. Although the measures probably helped avert the worst excesses in the preelection period, they did not completely eliminate problematic broadcasts or prevent reprisals against local media in some cases. For example, a station was briefly shut down in Yele for broadcasting material unfavorable to the incumbent Sierra Leone Peoples Party (SLPP). And in June, a member of parliament shut down a community radio station in Pujehun district after a broadcast criticized the SLPP for being corrupt and inept. Separately in February, a radio station in the district of Koinadugu was besieged by a group of youths accusing the station of inciting ethnic hatred and forced it temporarily to cease its broadcast. However, on the whole journalists agree that incidents of violence against the media have decreased markedly in recent years.

Along with the election came a successful transition to a new government; the opposition All Peoples Congress (APC) party won both the presidential election and a majority in parliament, and the SLPP leaders stepped down peacefully. However, the preelection period was predictably charged with tension; politicians and their media allies on both sides traded charges of biased reporting, threats, and physical violence. Radio stations that belonged to the SLPP and the APC helped fuel the tension, prompting the Independent Media Commission (IMC)—which has a reputation for acting independently of government—to ask the two stations to "tone down" for the sake of peace.

Foreign journalists did not entirely escape some of this hostility and violence; they were often similarly accused of partisan support and were required to obtain a license from the IMC upon entry. In September, the IMC issued a directive to media houses barring them from publishing critical comments on or discussing United Nations personnel and other international community members in Sierra Leone. The IMC said it was pressured into issuing the directive by the Office of National Security and the Ministry of Foreign Affairs after it received complaints from the office of the UN Integrated Office in Sierra Leone (UNIOSIL). The UNIOSIL said it was a target of offensive articles in a number of newspapers, including *Awareness Times*, *Democrat*, and *Salone Times*. Despite this IMC directive, the commission is typically credited with helping to improve the professionalism of media practice in Sierra Leone. The boom in the media sector and the improving viability of media ventures can be credited partly to the commission's oversight, despite the fact that capacity constraints have so far prevented the IMC from operating outside of Freetown.

More than 35 newspapers now publish, many of them privately owned, a number affiliated with political parties, and several openly critical of the government. Poor journalistic training, instances of self-censorship, and corruption within the media sector continued to weaken the capacity of professional media practice. Internet access is slowly penetrating the country as it continues to recover from the disruption caused by a lengthy civil war; 0.2 percent of the population accessed the internet in 2007, and at least five separate internet service providers were operating in the country.

Singapore

LEGAL ENVIRONMENT: 24
POLITICAL ENVIRONMENT: 24
ECONOMIC ENVIRONMENT: 21

Status: Not Free

TOTAL SCORE: 69

Survey Edition	2003	2004	2005	2006	2007
Total Score, Status	66,NF	64,NF	66,NF	66,NF	69,NF

Media freedom in Singapore continued to be constrained in 2007, with the vast majority of print and broadcast journalists practicing self-censorship for fear of harsh defamation charges, while a government review raised concerns of increased restrictions for online content in the future. The Singapore constitution provides the right to freedom of speech and of expression in Article 14 but also permits restrictions on these rights. In addition, the Newspapers and Printing Presses Act, the Defamation Act, and the Internal Security Act (ISA) constrain press freedom, allowing the authorities to restrict the circulation of news deemed to incite violence, arouse racial or religious tensions, interfere in domestic politics, or threaten public order, national interest, or national security. The judiciary lacks independence and systematically returns verdicts in the government's favor, further undermining press freedom in the city-state. Singapore law does not recognize journalists' rights to protect the identity of their sources, and in May 2007, Reuters correspondent Mia Shanley was forced to reveal an anonymous source in a commercial case under an order from the court of appeals.

Films, television programs, music, books, and magazines are sometimes censored; all films with a political purpose are banned unless government sponsored. In April 2007, the government banned a film by filmmaker and blogger Martyn See about Said Zahari, a journalist and political activist who was held without trial for 17 years under the ISA. Although *Zahari's 17 Years* was banned under the Film Act from being screened in Singapore, it could still be viewed on the internet. The Singapore government and ruling party members are quick to sue critics under harsh civil and criminal defamation laws in order to silence and bankrupt political opponents and critical media outlets. Foreign media in Singapore are also subject to such pressures and restrictive laws. In October 2007, the *Financial Times* published an apology and agreed to pay damages to the ruling Lee family for a September article that suggested nepotism factored into various appointments allocated to several of its members. Foreign publications are required by the Ministry of Information, Communications, and the Arts to post a bond of S$200,000 (approximately US$127,200) and appoint a local legal representative if they wish to publish in Singapore. In August 2006, after the *Far Eastern Economic Review* (*FEER*) published an interview with opposition party leader Chee Soon Juan, it and four other foreign publications were informed they would no longer be exempt from the regulations as they had been previously and needed to post a deposit. When the *FEER* did not comply, its circulation permit was revoked, effectively banning the publication; the ban remained in effect throughout 2007, though the publication was accessible online. In a corresponding defamation suit filed by the prime minister and his father over the article, a June 2007 ruling by the Singapore Supreme Court rejected the magazine's application for a queen's counsel from the United Kingdom to represent it.

Nearly all print and broadcast media outlets, internet service providers, and cable television services are either owned or controlled by the state or by companies with close ties to the ruling People's Action Party. Annual licensing requirements for all media outlets, including political and religious websites, have been used to inhibit criticism of the government. Internet use is widespread in Singapore, but the government attempts to restrict and control it by licensing internet service providers. Websites offering political or religious content are also required to register with the government's Media Development Authority (MDA), thus making a website's owners and editors criminally liable for any content that the government finds objectionable. Although the ruling party has been successful in curbing dissenting opinion among traditional print and broadcast media, the internet has proven more difficult to control. Bloggers and discussion groups still offer alternative views and a virtual channel for expressing dissent. During the year, an online petition against a proposed salary hike for government ministers collected thousands of signatures as well as comments criticizing the hike and the authorities' lack of accountability. In March 2007, the MDA announced that it was seeking to expand the jurisdiction of its media market conduct code from the traditional print and broadcast sectors to new media markets. Although the MDA said its review was intended "to better address competition issues that may arise under the new landscape," international watchdog groups expressed concerns that the revisions would be used to limit ownership and stifle online dissent. The internet was accessed by over 66 percent of the population in 2007.

Slovakia

LEGAL ENVIRONMENT: 6
POLITICAL ENVIRONMENT: 9
ECONOMIC ENVIRONMENT: 7

Status: Free   TOTAL SCORE: 22

Survey Edition	2003	2004	2005	2006	2007
Total Score, Status	21,F	21,F	21,F	20,F	20,F

Press freedom in Slovakia is constitutionally guaranteed and generally respected, and independent media outlets freely disseminate diverse views. Defamation is not a criminal offense, though some other types of expression—such as Holocaust denial—can, and have been, sanctioned with criminal prosecutions. In 2007, legislators drafted the new Press Act; press freedom advocates criticized several of its provisions, including restrictions on content, the powers of intervention granted to the state executive, and the right of correction and mandatory access to media by interested parties (with no possibility of editorial intervention in terms of content or space). In a surprise decision, the Slovak Supreme Court refused to recognize the overturning of a libel verdict by the European Court of Human Rights, effectively upholding the original decision of a lower Slovak court.

Journalists in both print and electronic media exercise broad editorial independence, and in general the heads of state-owned media enterprises are no longer political appointees. However, media freedom advocates noted that the new management of Slovak Public Television (STV) seemed to be exerting pressure on editors and journalists to provide more favorable coverage of the government. Nearly one-third of the staff of STV news programs quit amid allegations of political interventions in editorial policy. The atmosphere of pressure was enhanced by statements and parliamentary hearings on the media in which, in the opinion of media advocates, parliament impinged on the oversight role of other institutions.

During the year, the prime minister also asked the prosecutor general to investigate a number of journalists who were reporting on government corruption allegations. Critics claimed that this move was an intentional act of intimidation against the media.

Most Slovak media outlets, including all major print outlets, are privately owned. Lack of transparency in media ownership remains a concern, as does inadequate enforcement of regulations on cross-ownership of media outlets. Electronic media are diverse and pluralistic, and many Slovak citizens also regularly watch television from neighboring Czech Republic and Hungary. Slovaks enjoy growing access to the internet; although the government does not censor most content, it does monitor websites hosting hate speech and has, at times, attempted to fine the authors of such sites. Just over 40 percent of the population enjoyed regular internet service in 2007, including the majority of teenagers and young adults.

Slovenia

Status: Free

LEGAL ENVIRONMENT: 6
POLITICAL ENVIRONMENT: 10
ECONOMIC ENVIRONMENT: 7
TOTAL SCORE: 23

Survey Edition	2003	2004	2005	2006	2007
Total Score, Status	19,F	19,F	19,F	20,F	21,F

The Slovenian constitutional and legal system guarantee freedom of the press, and these rights are largely protected in practice. That said, the relationship between the media and the government became tense during the year, and journalists accused the government of both indirect and direct political and economic pressure on the media. Libel remains a criminal offense in Slovenia and is punishable by up to two years in prison; according to the U.S. State Department, one individual was sentenced for three months during the year. The media in Slovenia are diverse and express a wide variety of views. The acrimonious relationship between the government and the media began in 2005 when the government passed a controversial law that increased its influence on public media outlets. The legislation established a programming council and a supervisory board to oversee television and radio networks. The parliament appoints 21 of the 29 Programming Council members and 5 members of the 11-member Supervisory Board. As a result of the legislation, several heads of television and radio broadcasters have been replaced. Concerns were raised by media organizations that a

separate 2006 law intended to increase media plurality through the allocation of government funding has led to disproportionate funding going to
government-friendly media houses and the Catholic Church media.

While most print media are privately owned, the government owns
shares in some companies that were themselves shareholders of large media
houses. According to a petition signed by 517 journalists in September
and backed by the European Federation of Journalists, the government
used its partial ownership of media houses, business relationships, and
share holdings to exert influence over the media. The petition also
alleged that the government used its position to weed out editors and
journalists critical of the government. There are concerns that the increased
government influence led to an increase in self-censorship. The problem
is compounded by the fact that freelance journalists do not fit under the
current labor legislation, leaving them vulnerable to pressure from media
owners. Internet access is unrestricted, and there are no reports of the
government monitoring its content or the e-mail communications of its
citizens; 62 percent of Slovenians are reported to be accessing the internet
on a regular basis.

Solomon Islands

LEGAL ENVIRONMENT: 5
POLITICAL ENVIRONMENT: 14
ECONOMIC ENVIRONMENT: 11

Status: Free

TOTAL SCORE: 30

Survey Edition	2003	2004	2005	2006	2007
Total Score, Status	25,F	30,F	30,F	30,F	30,F

The law provides for freedom of speech and of the press, and provisions
of a draft constitution under consideration would reportedly further
strengthen legal guarantees for freedom of speech. However, the draft
also includes a right of reply section (s39) that enables people harmed by
"inaccurate or offensive" media reports to have a correction published.
The case of Australian citizen Julian Moti, sworn in as the country's
attorney general in July in defiance of Australia's efforts to extradite him
over alleged sex offenses in Vanuatu in the 1990s, was a key media issue
during 2007. As relations with Australia deteriorated over the matter, some
observers predicted that the Solomons government would expel Australians
participating in the Regional Assistance Mission to the Solomon Islands
(RAMSI). This raised concerns among local journalists because RAMSI

had been heavily involved in the country's media development, providing training and support programs to bolster the local press. The bilateral tensions subsided near the end of the year, however, when Prime Minister Manasseh Sogavare lost power in a no-confidence vote in December; Moti was extradited shortly thereafter.

One daily newspaper, the independent *Solomon Star*, dominates the media scene, although readership is limited by the country's low literacy rates. Three private weekly papers—*Solomons Voice, Solomon Times*, and the new *Island Sun*, established in 2006—are also published, along with the monthly newsletters *Agrikalsa Nius* and the *Citizen's Press*. The Solomon Islands Broadcasting Corporation operates several radio outlets, including the national public station Radio Hapi Isles. Several private commercial stations, including Paoa FM, also operate. There are no domestic television stations, but residents have satellite access to the Australian Broadcasting Corporation, the British Broadcasting Corporation, and other foreign channels. The internet is not restricted by the government, but it is accessed by less than 2 percent of the population.

Somalia

LEGAL ENVIRONMENT: 27
POLITICAL ENVIRONMENT: 35
ECONOMIC ENVIRONMENT: 22

Status: Not Free

TOTAL SCORE: 84

Survey Edition	2003	2004	2005	2006	2007
Total Score, Status	80,NF	80,NF	83,NF	83,NF	85,NF

The media environment remained extremely dangerous in 2007 amid ongoing conflict between the internationally recognized Transitional Federal Government (TFG), based in Baidoa, and the Islamic Courts Union, an Islamist alliance that regrouped and has engaged in insurgent attacks against the TFG since late 2006, when the TFG—backed by Ethiopian troops—resumed control of the capital, Mogadishu. In such an environment, it remained difficult for media to be neutral or objective, as alliances were essential for survival and many outlets operate as public information sources for particular parties. The media environment in the self-governing regions of Puntland and Somaliland was markedly better.

In principle, Somalia's charter provides for freedom of the press, but in practice, owing to the lawless nature of the country, journalists continue to face restrictions on their reporting. There are also no freedom of information laws to guarantee access to public information. In December 2007, the TFG parliament approved a media bill, which had not yet been signed into law at year's end but has been criticized by press freedom groups for imposing vague and severe restrictions, including limits on images and speeches. Nonetheless, the potential impact of this law remains unknown, given that the TFG controls only 30 percent of the country. During the year, the TFG continued to enforce restrictions against reporting or photographing the Ethiopian National Defense Forces.

Numerous press freedom attacks occurred throughout 2007, and the Committee to Protect Journalists ranks Somalia as the deadliest country for journalists in Africa. Seven journalists were killed (4 were caught in conflict crossfire, and 3 others were murdered), 4 injured, and as many as 60 arrested, often without warrants, in relation to their work. Among those killed were Mahad Ahmed Elmi, head of the Mogadishu-based Capital Voice, and Ali Mohammed Omar, a presenter with the private Baidoa-based Radio Warsan. A pervasive culture of impunity continues to persist, and by year's end, no arrests had been made in connection with the killings that occurred either in 2007 or during any of the previous years. In March, the TFG closed Al-Jazeera's Mogadishu bureau, and in April, government soldiers shelled the compounds of HornAfrik and Global Broadcasting Corporation (GBC) during an attack against alleged insurgents; GBC subsequently closed in August. In November, Mogadishu's mayor also closed three radio stations on charges that they had aired allegedly subversive news. The stations were allowed to resume broadcasting three weeks later only after intense international pressure.

Photocopied dailies and low-grade radio stations have proliferated in Mogadishu and elsewhere since 1991; there were at least eight radio stations broadcasting in Mogadishu in 2007, many of which were actually not linked to political factions. A number of outlets ceased operations in 2007, however, and of those that continue to operate, many have been accused of bias, particularly in their coverage of the war or clan rivalries. Somalia has a rich internet presence, fueled predominantly by the Somali diaspora in Europe, North America, and the Gulf states. Internet service is widely available in large cities, and users enjoy a fast and inexpensive connection. Nevertheless, owing to pervasive poverty and the internal displacement of many Somalis, only 1 percent of the population had access to this resource in 2007. Although there were no reports of government restrictions on the internet, opposition groups reportedly monitored internet activity.

Although the status of press freedom was visibly better in Puntland, a self-declared autonomous region, restrictions remain harsh and coverage of political and security issues can be particularly dangerous for journalists. Among other instances of violence against the press, in June, the headquarters of the private newspaper *Shacab* was attacked with firebombs, damaging a printing machine, and on December 16, a French journalist with the French-German television station ARTE was kidnapped but released later in the month.

In 2007, the status of press freedom was markedly better in Somaliland—which claimed but has not been granted full independence from Somalia—than in the rest of the country. In advance of elections that are expected in 2008, journalists faced a greater level of harassment by the authorities than during the previous year. The government also drafted and proposed a new Press Law in 2007 to replace the existing liberal one. The Somaliland Journalists Association has criticized the lack of dialogue in the process of drafting the legislation, as well as provisions allowing the Ministry of Information to influence media outlets' managerial, financial, and editorial decisions. Journalists also protested the proposed requirement that they register with the ministry and hold a press card.

Whereas in previous years there existed a relatively conciliatory relationship between the Somaliland government and the press, this trend was sharply reversed in 2007, when several journalists were imprisoned. In January, three journalists with the private daily *Haatuf* were arrested and sentenced to several years' imprisonment for allegedly insulting the wife of Somaliland president Dahir Riyale Kahin; the journalists were eventually pardoned following internal political pressure, widespread domestic protests, and international condemnation. Among other cases of arrests during the year, in the southern Somaliland town of Las Anod, authorities detained two journalists, Abdiqani Hassan Farah and Mohammed Shakale, for reportedly covering the violent conflict along the Puntland-Somaliland border. During the year, at least two dozen Somali journalists fled Mogadishu to seek safety in the western Somaliland town of Hargeisa. Although the journalists who fled were provided sanctuary by local press freedom organizations and fellow journalists, Somaliland authorities eventually forced the journalists to leave following pressure from the Ethiopian government over their critical coverage of the Ethiopian occupation in the south.

In 2007, there were six independent daily newspapers in addition to a government daily operating in Somaliland, although most newspapers were not economically sustainable and were heavily subsidized by the diaspora and journalists' families. There were also two independent television stations in addition to a government-owned station. The government has been reluctant to liberalize the airwaves, however, citing the potential of instigating clan violence, an argument that some Somalilanders support. As a result, the establishment of independent radio stations is banned. The internet is widely available at competitive prices and serves as an active forum through which the diaspora contributes to the local media environment.

South Africa

LEGAL ENVIRONMENT: 7
POLITICAL ENVIRONMENT: 12
ECONOMIC ENVIRONMENT: 9

Status: Free

TOTAL SCORE: 28

Survey Edition	2003	2004	2005	2006	2007
Total Score, Status	25,F	24,F	26,F	27,F	28,F

Freedom of expression and of the press, protected in principle by the constitution, are generally respected in practice in South Africa. Nevertheless, several apartheid-era laws that remain in effect permit authorities to restrict the publication of information about the police and national defense forces and to compel journalists to reveal sources. A proposed film and publication amendment bill was sent to parliament in 2006; it would subject print and broadcast media to the same prepublication screening for "indecent content" that is currently required for films, computer games, and magazines, ostensibly intended to protect primarily against child pornography. However, after vociferous protests from media outlets and press freedom advocates, the bill was revised in June 2007 to exclude print and broadcast media. Recent years have seen an increase in the use of interdictions and gag orders by both governmental and nonstate actors. In July, a high court in the capital city of Pretoria prevented the *Mail & Guardian* newspaper—as well as other media—from publishing details of alleged corruption at the state-owned South African Broadcasting Corporation (SABC).

Journalists are very occasionally harassed and assaulted in South Africa. In July, the editor of an oppositionist online newspaper in Zimbabwe was shot in Johannesburg by three unknown assailants; the journalist survived the attack, which saw the bullet pierce close to his heart, but it is unclear whether the incident was related to his work. More often, members of government and other political figures reveal a heightened sensitivity to media criticism, in some cases by accusing critical journalists of racism and betraying the state. In August, a major controversy emerged after the *Sunday Times* published articles claiming Health Minister Tshabalala Msimang's recent liver transplant was caused by alcoholism, that she jumped transplant queues, and that she had stolen from a patient while a medical superintendent in Botswana. After the minister took legal action, a Johannesburg high court ordered the newspaper to return copies of the minister's records to a Cape Town clinic and to pay legal fees; the paper was allowed to continue reporting on the story. Subsequently, the editor and deputy editor of the *Sunday Times* were the subjects of police investigations for stealing medical records, and President Thabo Mbeki criticized the behavior and ownership structure of the media. In November, close political allies of Mbeki were involved in the purchase of the Johncom media group—which owns the *Sunday Times*. In December, the ruling African National Congress resolved to investigate the establishment of a national media tribunal to regulate irresponsible reporting.

South Africa features vibrant press freedom advocacy and journalists organizations, and a number of private newspapers and magazines— including the *Mail & Guardian*, the *Cape Times*, and the *Sunday Times*—are sharply critical of the government, political parties, and other societal actors. The SABC dominates broadcast media. Although editorially independent, the SABC has come under fire for displaying progovernment bias and for encouraging self-censorship. A 2006 internal SABC report that found several outspoken government critics had been barred from SABC airwaves continued to generate controversy in 2007; in March, prominent civic actors—including the Congress of South African Trade Unions (COSATU) and the Freedom of Expression Institute (FXI)—accused the government of blacklisting and purging critics from the SABC. Also in March, a well-known radio personality at SABC, John Perlman, resigned. Though Perlman himself made no statement, it is believed that his departure was linked to his on-air accusations that outspoken critics of the government were being muzzled at SABC. In July, the SABC dropped legal action to prevent the screening of a documentary about President Mbeki; the SABC-commissioned film had twice been canceled from screening on state television.

Most South Africans receive the news via radio outlets, most of which are associated with the SABC. However, efforts are being made to expand the number and broadcasting range of community radio stations via the Independent Communications Authority of South Africa, and low-power nonprofit radio stations are increasing in prevalence, though they continue to be difficult to maintain financially. While the SABC's three stations claim most of the television market, the country's two commercial television stations, e.tv and M-Net, are reaching ever greater proportions of the population. Internet access is unrestricted and growing rapidly (11.6 percent of the population are currently users), although many South Africans cannot afford the service fee.

South Korea

Status: Free

LEGAL ENVIRONMENT: 9
POLITICAL ENVIRONMENT: 12
ECONOMIC ENVIRONMENT: 9
TOTAL SCORE: 30

Survey Edition	2003	2004	2005	2006	2007
Total Score, Status	29,F	29,F	29,F	30,F	30,F

Despite steps by the government of President Roh Moo-hyun to limit journalists' access to official buildings, South Korea's media environment remained among the freest in Asia in 2007. Freedom of the press is guaranteed under South Korean law and is generally respected in practice. Censorship of the media is against the law, though the government censors films for sex and violence. Article 7 of the 1948 National Security Law allows imprisonment for praising or expressing sympathy for North Korea. Roh's tenure has been marked by disputes with conservative media outlets, and critics alleged that the liberal government was seeking to reduce the media's influence through two reform laws passed in January 2005. The Law Governing the Guarantee of Freedom and Functions of Newspapers included provisions that would require all newspapers to register with the government and would essentially limit the circulation of the three major conservative dailies. In June 2006, however, the Supreme Court struck down these measures by a vote of seven to two.

Violence against journalists is unusual in South Korea, but in March 2007, at least eight journalists were beaten by riot police while covering a protest against a free-trade agreement with the United States. The police later issued an apology and claimed to have punished the offending officers. The Roh government's animosity toward the media was also apparent in measures approved in May 2007 and implemented in October, under which the authorities reportedly closed all but three pressrooms in government buildings nationwide. The Government Information Agency called the closures part of a media reform designed to upgrade the "support system for news coverage," but journalists and international media watchdogs have criticized the measures as an attempt to restrict access to information. Under the new regulations, journalists are not permitted to enter government buildings without prior authorization and can interview ministers and other civil servants only after receiving state permission.

South Korea has vibrant and diverse media, with numerous cable, terrestrial, and satellite television stations and over 100 daily newspapers in Korean and English. Many newspapers depend on large corporations for their advertising revenue. There are both public and private radio and television stations, including an American Forces Network for the U.S. military. The internet is generally unrestricted by government regulations, but some websites have been blocked for posting pro–North Korean content, and the government requires all website operators to indicate whether their sites might be harmful to youth. Approximately 71 percent of the population reportedly accessed the internet in 2007, and a significant number of young people get their news exclusively from online sources. South Korean online media are especially vigorous and innovative. For example, an interactive internet news site called OhMyNews, launched in 2000, allows citizens to submit their own news articles for immediate publication on the site.

Spain

LEGAL ENVIRONMENT: 5
POLITICAL ENVIRONMENT: 13
ECONOMIC ENVIRONMENT: 5

Status: Free

TOTAL SCORE: 23

Survey Edition	2003	2004	2005	2006	2007
Total Score, Status	16,F	19,F	22,F	21,F	22,F

Spain has a free and lively press, with more than 100 newspapers covering a wide range of perspectives and actively investigating high-level corruption. Freedom of speech is protected by Spanish law and is generally respected in practice. Threats to press freedom include antiterrorism legislation and high awards in defamation suits against journalists. Recently, a judge ordered the garnishing of the pension of Patxi Ibarrondo, editor of *La Realidad*, who was originally charged with libel in 2001 for comments about a regional party secretary of the Popular Party. The libel suit forced the closure of *La Realidad* that same year. In July, two cartoonists were fined 3,000 euros each for "insulting the crown" for their depiction of Crown Prince Felipe having sex with his wife, Princess Letizia. The offending issue of the newspaper was ordered to be confiscated by a judge because it violated the criminal code, which punishes "insults" to the royal family.

In January, the political environment worsened following a breakdown of peace talks between the Spanish government and the Basque separatist group Basque Fatherland and Freedom (ETA) after an airport bombing. Journalists who oppose the political views of ETA continue to be targeted by the group, forcing many to employ bodyguards. Daily newspaper ownership is concentrated within large media groups like Prisa and Zeta. Internet access is not restricted; however, authorities monitor websites with material espousing hate speech or advocating anti-Semitism and shut one down in April, according to the U.S. State Department's 2007 report on human rights.

Sri Lanka

LEGAL ENVIRONMENT: 19
POLITICAL ENVIRONMENT: 31
ECONOMIC ENVIRONMENT: 17

Status: Not Free   TOTAL SCORE: 67

Survey Edition	2003	2004	2005	2006	2007
Total Score, Status	52,PF	53,PF	56,PF	58,PF	63,NF

Media freedom continued to decline in 2007 as media outlets faced increased censorship and other restrictions on reporting and journalists faced a heightened level of attacks and intimidation, particularly in the war-torn north and east of the country. Although freedom of expression is provided for in the constitution, a growing number of laws and regulations restrict this right. The 1973 Press Council Law prohibits disclosure of certain cabinet decisions as well as fiscal, defense, and security information, while the decades-old Official Secrets Act bans reporting on information designated "secret." Those convicted of gathering secret information can be sentenced to up to 14 years in prison; although no journalist has ever been charged under the law, it is frequently used to threaten them. Emergency regulations reintroduced in August 2005 allow the government to bar the publication, distribution, performance, or airing of any print or broadcast material deemed likely to cause public disorder; however, it did not generally use this authority. In 2006, unofficial prepublication censorship concerning issues of "national security and defense" was imposed by the government's Media Center for National Security. The Emergency (Prevention and Prohibition of Terrorism and Specified Terrorist Activities) Regulations, introduced in December 2006, were immediately used to arrest and detain journalists, sometimes for months without charge. In addition, contempt of court laws are used occasionally to punish reporters who investigate judicial misconduct.

The distribution and suspension of broadcast licenses appear to be sometimes arbitrary and politically influenced, as seen in the October license suspensions of five private FM stations belonging to the Asia Broadcasting Corporation, a network perceived to report critically on current events. Official rhetoric has become more unfriendly toward journalists and media outlets perceived to be "unpatriotic" or critical, with high-level officials regularly making statements equating any form of criticism with treason. The government's attitude was indicated by an attempt in June—introduced by the justice minister and supported by the president but opposed by other cabinet members and later quietly withdrawn—to reinstate criminal defamation legislation repealed in 2002 that would include prison terms for violators. In another aborted effort, in October, an executive order banning the media from covering military operations and arms deals was issued and then withdrawn after several days.

The level of threats and harassment against journalists and media outlets continued to grow in 2007. Journalists throughout Sri Lanka, particularly those who cover human rights issues, corruption, or official misconduct, face regular intimidation and pressure from both senior- and junior-level government officials. Cases included those of Champika Liyanarachchi, editor of the prominent *Daily Mirror*, who was telephoned by Defense Secretary Gotabhaya Rajapaksa in April, and T. M. G. Chandrasekara, news director of the state-run Sri Lanka Rupavahini Corporation television station, who was physically assaulted by a government minister and a group of his supporters in December. Several other journalists were temporarily arrested. In November, Leader Publications, a major printing house that publishes the *Sunday Leader* and *Morning Leader* newspapers, was targeted in an arson attack that completely destroyed its facilities; both papers are known for their critical, pro-opposition views and have faced numerous threats, including a prior arson attack. In several other instances, police or security forces manhandled reporters as they attempted to cover the news, barring access to certain events and deleting or otherwise censoring photographic images. In a growing trend, journalists and civil society groups perceived as being supportive of Tamil interests have also drawn ire from Sinhalese nationalist groups. Several journalists decided to leave the country for short periods of time, including prominent defense correspondent Iqbal Athas, who fled three times during the year following repeated threats. Increased threats coupled with expanded legal restrictions have led a growing number of journalists to practice self-censorship.

Previous cases of attacks and killings of journalists have not been adequately investigated or prosecuted.

Media freedom is particularly restricted in the war-torn north and east of the country, where journalists are caught between government forces, the Liberation Tigers of Tamil Eelam (LTTE) separatist rebel group (which does not permit free expression in the areas under its effective control), and other armed political factions and paramilitary groups. As a result, journalists' ability to cover the news freely has been severely curtailed, and those that do face steep repercussions for doing so. At least five journalists were killed and numerous others were abducted or otherwise intimidated during the year. Despite its calls for protection, the largest-circulation daily in Jaffna, *Uthayan*, faced repeated attacks and harassment in 2007, including abduction of its staff; accordingly, the paper's editor and news editor lived semipermanently at the paper's offices, as they were too afraid to go outside. A number of Tamil newspapers have been banned or seized by various factions, and distributors have been attacked or warned not to sell certain papers; as a result, several independent outlets have closed owing to threats against them. In November, the air force bombed the LTTE-run Voice of Tigers radio station, killing five media workers. Foreign journalists' ability to cover events in the region was also compromised, with one film crew being expelled from Jaffna in October.

While numerous privately owned newspapers and broadcasters scrutinize government policies and provide diverse views, private outlets have become more polarized, shrinking the space for balanced coverage. The Colombo-based Free Media Movement has noted that state-run media—including Sri Lanka's largest newspaper chain, two major television stations, and a radio station—are heavily influenced by the government, citing cases of pressure on editors, several unwarranted dismissals of high-level staff, and biased coverage. Cases of overt financial pressure on critical outlets were reported during the year. In March, the government froze the assets of the Standard Newspapers group, publisher of the weekly Sinhala-language *Mawbima* and English-language *Sunday Standard*, after they refused to alter their editorial policy; both papers closed shortly thereafter because of the freeze. Business and political interests exercise some control over content through selective advertising and bribery. Owing to the closure of a major road, newspapers on the Jaffna peninsula faced shortages of newsprint and other key supplies, hindering their production abilities.

Access to the internet and to foreign broadcasts is generally not restricted, but only 1.4 percent of the population used the internet in 2006 because of the high costs involved. However, in June, the government reportedly ordered the country's two largest internet service providers to restrict access to *TamilNet*, a pro-LTTE news website; the ban lasted through year's end. In October, several Sinhala-language websites were singled out for criticism by government politicians, and later that same month, unidentified gunmen wounded internet journalist Kumudu Champika Jayawardana of ethalaya.org, which is linked to the Sinhala-language Sirasa TV channel.

Sudan

					LEGAL ENVIRONMENT: 26
					POLITICAL ENVIRONMENT: 29
					ECONOMIC ENVIRONMENT: 23

Status: Not Free   TOTAL SCORE: 78

Survey Edition	2003	2004	2005	2006	2007
Total Score, Status	84,NF	85,NF	86,NF	85,NF	81,NF

Despite the ongoing conflict in Darfur and the failed attempts to broker peace between the government of Sudan and the Darfuri rebel movements, the media environment remained relatively stable during 2007, marked by a freer environment and less violence against journalists in the southern part of the country. The signing of the Comprehensive Peace Agreement in 2005, which ended the civil war between the north and the south, initiated a process of constitutional reform that brought about some positive changes for the media, such as the lifting of official censorship and an interim constitution that provides for freedom of thought and of expression. Nonetheless, there are no existing laws that explicitly guarantee freedom of the press. Sudanese authorities continue to use arbitrary measures to limit press freedom. In fact, the government often invokes the code of criminal procedure to suspend media outlets for covering sensitive issues, including the conflict in Darfur, even though the code was not designed to address the media. Media outlets are also required to employ security personnel to review stories prior to publication. Another way that authorities control the media is through the government-influenced National Press Council, which is responsible for licensing and has the power to suspend journalists and newspapers. Entry into the media is difficult unless you are a supporter of the government, and all journalists must pass a difficult Arabic-language exam regardless of what language they intend to write in. Restrictions on covering the Darfur region continued in 2007 when the National Press Council issued a ban in March on coverage of the prosecution of crimes committed in Darfur and a ban in May on publishing information on

Darfuri rebel activities. Nonetheless, these bans were not always explicitly enforced. Draft media legislation on freedom of information, public service broadcasting, and the establishment of new print and broadcast regulators are in the early stages of review, although press freedom advocacy groups have expressed concerns about the absence of discussion during the drafting process and restrictive provisions that would allow for continued government control over the media.

Throughout 2007, journalists faced harassment, attacks, intimidation, and direct censorship at the hands of both government and nongovernmental forces. Among other instances of harassment, on February 1, authorities closed the private Arabic-language daily *Al-Sudani* for several days because it violated a direct ban against publishing coverage of the murder of Mohammed Taha Mohammed Ahmed, former editor in chief of the private daily *Al-Wifaq* who was beheaded in 2006. The suspension was lifted only after the charges were overturned on appeal based on the claim that only the National Press Council had authorization to ban media outlets. In May, the minister of justice charged *Al-Sudani* with defamation following an editorial calling for the minister's resignation due to corruption allegations and detained the paper's editor along with another journalist for several days. In June, authorities detained four journalists representing private papers based in the capital, Khartoum, for attempting to report on protests against the Kajbar Dam in the northern Nubian region, and several journalists working for the private *Al-Midan* and *Al-Sahafa* newspapers received death threats in December for reporting on the Darfur conflict. Access for foreign reporters to the Darfur region remained sporadic during the year, with severe restrictions in place during the first two months of the year and some correspondents being denied visas or travel permits. Nevertheless, some reporters gained access with government permission or by entering via Chad, though the intensity of the conflict frequently prevented them from traveling around once there. In April, BBC correspondent Jonah Fisher left the country following an expulsion order that was issued in March for his coverage of the region. Separately, Nichola Dominic Mandil, a Sudanese producer for the U.S. government–funded Sudan Radio Service, was abducted and severely beaten by members of the state security forces for allegedly "being a foreign agent in Sudan promoting American ideology." There are many private newspapers in Sudan—though none are currently able to function regularly in Darfur—and private ownership is common. Although most newspapers experienced intense scrutiny from authorities, they represented a wide range of views, from state-owned Arabic and English outlets, to those that offer a southern Sudanese perspective, to critical opposition publications. Some private papers employ columnists who regularly criticize President Omar al-Bashir's policies. Nonetheless, a significant amount of self-censorship, particularly among the Arabic-language outlets, continued to pervade the media even among independent publications. The English-language media were less prone to this problem and often reprinted critical articles from Western media outlets. In late 2007, the country's first free newspaper, *Al-Hadath*, was launched in Khartoum, and while it has since changed its business model owing to distribution problems, it managed to obtain a significant share of the market. The al-Bashir administration in Khartoum runs one Arabic- and one English-language newspaper. In contrast with the more diverse press, the government dominates the broadcast media, the main source of information for much of Sudan's population. Television broadcasts are formally censored, and radio content is required to reflect the government's views. However, Arabic satellite channels such as Al-Jazeera and Al-Arabiya are popular in Sudan and are increasingly relied upon as an alternative to the progovernment domestic television and radio stations. In addition, some foreign radio stations are available, such as the British Broadcasting Corporation, which broadcasts in Khartoum and other points in the north and south, and several opposition and clandestine stations are available via shortwave frequencies.

Internet penetration in Sudan is among the highest in sub-Saharan Africa, with just under 4 percent of the population able to access this medium in 2007. However, internet access is limited to urban areas and is still low by global standards. The government has not traditionally displayed much interest in censoring this new medium, apart from the blocking of pornographic content, other sites that are deemed offensive, and proxy servers, and there were generally no restrictions on access to news websites. Political debates flourished on forums such as sudaneseonline. com, sudaneseoffline.com, and sudanile.com, which are also highly popular among the Sudanese diaspora. However, there were reports that the government monitored e-mail activity and other forms of online communication.

Press freedom conditions in southern Sudan are better than in areas controlled directly by Khartoum. Journalists in the south are not as restricted as those in the north and have more leeway to criticize government policies. Five private media outlets operated in the region throughout the year. Nonetheless, it could not be said that there is a free press environment even in southern Sudan, as security personnel regularly take the liberty of punishing media outlets for negative coverage. There were reports, however, that the editor of the Juba-based English-language newspaper *Citizen* was detained for a day following the paper's coverage of an alleged corruption scandal within the Finance Ministry. In addition, many Sudanese from the south displaced by the civil war still remain in the more populous north of the country, and most facilities for the production and distribution of media content are concentrated in Khartoum.

Suriname

LEGAL ENVIRONMENT: 5
POLITICAL ENVIRONMENT: 12
ECONOMIC ENVIRONMENT: 6

Status: Free

TOTAL SCORE: 23

Survey Edition	2003	2004	2005	2006	2007
Total Score, Status	26,F	18,F	20,F	23,F	22,F

The coalition government generally respects freedom of expression and of the press, as provided for in the country's constitution. However, government authorities used the threat of legal action against newspapers to intimidate and manipulate the press during the year; one case resulted in a court verdict ordering a newspaper to publish a public apology. There were no developments in the 2005 case in which *De West* publisher George Findley was ordered to publish a correction of a *De West* article on the Suriname Currency Board both in *De West* and in the competing paper *De Ware Tijd*, which refused to publish the retraction. In the only overt act of censorship during the year, the state-owned Suriname Television Foundation was forced to cancel its *Suriname Today* discussion program on May 10 after the country's vice president, Ramdien Sardjoe, requested that the producers not air planned segments addressing China-Taiwan relations. Chinese diplomats in the capital, Paramaribo, had also pressed for the program to be dropped and apparently visited the station to speak to the management. Sardjoe said his request was in the national interests of the country, but the Association of Surinamese Journalists (SVJ) denounced this violation of free speech. Little investigative journalism takes place in Suriname, and some journalists continue to practice self-censorship on certain issues. According to the SVJ, poor salaries and lack of training lead to unprofessional conduct that undermines the profession. There are two privately owned Dutch-language daily newspapers, *De Ware Tijd* and *De West*. Seven radio stations, including the government-owned Stichting Radio Omroep Suriname, broadcast in the country, along with a number of community radio stations. Both television stations—Algemene Televisie Verzorging and Surinaamse Televisie Stichting—are state owned. There are no government restrictions on the internet, though only close to 7 percent of the population was able to access it in 2007.

		LEGAL ENVIRONMENT: 25
		POLITICAL ENVIRONMENT: 26
# Swaziland		ECONOMIC ENVIRONMENT: 25
Status: Not Free		TOTAL SCORE: 76

Survey Edition	2003	2004	2005	2006	2007
Total Score, Status	74,NF	77,NF	79,NF	77,NF	76,NF

Freedom of expression is restricted in Swaziland, especially regarding political issues or matters concerning the royal family. There are very few legal protections for journalists and media workers. While the 2006 constitution provides for freedom of speech, the king may waive these rights at his discretion. The 1938 Sedition and Subversive Activities Act bans publication of any criticism of the monarchy, and self-censorship is widespread, particularly regarding the king's lavish lifestyle. The 1968 Proscribed Publications Act also empowers the government to ban publications if they are deemed "prejudicial or potentially prejudicial to the interests of defense, public safety, public order, public morality, or public health." The law has been used several times in recent years to punish newspapers that criticized the monarchy. Access to information is limited. In June, journalists were barred from entering Mbabne Government Hospital and from talking to hospital employees after a series of media reports exposed the allegedly negligent death of a four-year-old girl.

Harsh defamation laws are also used to stifle the press. In March 2007, parliamentarian Maqhawe Mavuso sued the semiprivate *Swazi Observer* for defamation over an article about an alleged assault involving Mavuso. In July, the editor of the private *Nation* magazine, Bheki Makhubu, was sued for defamation in the amount of US$500,000 by member of parliament Marwick Khumalo after Makhubu wrote an article accusing Khumalo of corruption. Neither case has yet gone to trial. Swazi courts do occasionally dismiss and overturn defamation charges against journalists. In 2006, the Supreme Court overturned massive fines (approximately US$116,000) levied against the independent *Times of Swaziland* in a

2005 defamation case brought by the late deputy prime minister Albert Shabangu. In 2007, the government dismissed a similar suit brought against the paper by Education Minister Themba Msibi.

The government routinely warns against negative news coverage, and journalists are subject to harassment and assault by both state and nonstate actors. In July, parliament investigated charges of contempt against *Times of Swaziland* editor Mbongeni Mbingo after Mbingo penned an editorial criticizing Speaker of the House Prince Guduza. Mbingo was cleared of these charges in October. Separately in March, a controversial pastor stated categorically in a sermon that he was praying for the death of two journalists, which would teach the media not to write "badly" about the church, following an article the two had written about an internal church quarrel. The Media Institute of Southern Africa also reported that a number of reporters had received anonymous phone calls advising them to discontinue their investigations of particular stories; in the majority of these instances, the journalists complied with the request.

The two major newspapers in circulation are the *Times of Swaziland* and the *Swazi Observer*. The *Times*, founded in 1897, is the oldest newspaper in the kingdom and the only major news source that is free of government control; the *Swazi Observer*, on the other hand, is owned by a royal conglomerate. Both newspapers continued to criticize government corruption and inefficiency in 2007 but steered clear of the royal family. The Swaziland Television Authority, which is both the state broadcaster and the industry regulatory agency, dominates the airwaves. There is one government-owned radio station and one independent radio station, Voice of the Church, which focuses on religious programming. A member of the royal family owns the country's lone private television station, which influences its content. However, broadcast and print media from South Africa are received in the country, and state broadcasters retransmitted Voice of America and British Broadcasting Corporation programs without censorship. The government does not restrict internet-based media, though only 3 percent of the population used the internet in 2007.

LEGAL ENVIRONMENT: 2
POLITICAL ENVIRONMENT: 5

Sweden

ECONOMIC ENVIRONMENT: 4

Status: Free

TOTAL SCORE: 11

Survey Edition	2003	2004	2005	2006	2007
Total Score, Status	8,F	8,F	9,F	10,F	11,F

Sweden has strong legal protections for press freedom under the Freedom of the Press Law and the Fundamental Law of Freedom of Expression. Journalists' sources are protected by law, as is access to information for all citizens. Tensions continue between the media and Muslim groups in Scandinavia, stemming from the 2005 Danish cartoons depicting the prophet Muhammad. In September 2007, artist Lars Vilke and editor Ulf Johansson of *Nerikes Allehanda* received death threats via the internet for publishing cartoons of the prophet. Al-Qaeda in Iraq offered a bounty for the artists' murders. Also in September, police raided the home of a prizewinning TV reporter, Trond Sefastsson, according to the *Local*. Sefastsson's computer and investigative materials were seized by police. The reporter admitted to collecting 400,000 kroner (US$57,500) from the family of a convicted criminal that he claims was paid to him for legal counsel.

Public broadcasting has a strong presence in Sweden, consisting of Sveriges Television and Sveriges Radio. Public television and radio is funded through a license fee. Private broadcasting ownership is highly concentrated under the media companies Bonnier and the Modern Times Group. The government offers subsidies to newspapers in order to encourage competition, and media content in immigrant languages is also supported by the state. According to the British Broadcasting Corporation, Sweden is among the top consumers of newspapers in the world. Access to the internet is unrestricted by the government, and at 77 percent of the population, Sweden has one of the highest proportions of internet users in the world.

Switzerland

Status: Free

LEGAL ENVIRONMENT: 5
POLITICAL ENVIRONMENT: 3
ECONOMIC ENVIRONMENT: 5
TOTAL SCORE: 13

Survey Edition	2003	2004	2005	2006	2007
Total Score, Status	10,F	9,F	11,F	11,F	12,F

Media freedom is guaranteed in the constitution and generally respected by the government. The penal code prohibits racial hatred or discrimination. Even though the law does not explicitly prohibit anti-Semitic speech or Holocaust denial, there have been convictions for such forms of expression. Dogu Perincek, a Turkish politician who publicly denied the Armenian genocide while in Switzerland, was convicted in March 2007 and ordered to pay a fine; he vowed to appeal. Transparency legislation adopted in December 2004 went into effect on July 1, 2006. The law applies only to documents produced after July 1, 2006, and contains numerous exceptions.

In 1997, a Swiss federal court found two journalists guilty of inciting an official to disclose a secret, an act considered to be a criminal offense under Article 293 of the Swiss criminal code. However, in April 2006, the European Court of Human Rights overturned the ruling, arguing that a reporter's right to protect his or her sources superseded the domestic Swiss judgment. An editor and two journalists working for *Sonntagsblick*—one of the most popular newspapers in the country—were acquitted in April 2007 after being tried by a military tribunal and awarded compensation. The three were responsible for a 2006 story about an Egyptian fax intercepted by the Swiss Intelligence Service that referred to confidential allegations of CIA prisons in Eastern Europe. The Swiss Defense Ministry charged the journalists with violating "military secrecy," which is punishable by up to five years in prison. Broadcast media are dominated by the Swiss Broadcasting Corporation, a public service association subject to private law that operates 7 television networks and 18 radio stations. The corporation is dependent on the government for financing, although its news reporting is politically neutral. Owing to market forces and the multilingual nature of the country, most private stations are limited to local and regional broadcasts. Nearly all homes are connected to cable networks that provide access to international commercial stations. Daily newspapers are owned by large media conglomerates, which have steadily pushed smaller publications out of the market. The internet is unrestricted by the government and accessed by 69 percent of the population.

Syria

Status: Not Free

LEGAL ENVIRONMENT: 29
POLITICAL ENVIRONMENT: 33
ECONOMIC ENVIRONMENT: 21
TOTAL SCORE: 83

Survey Edition	2003	2004	2005	2006	2007
Total Score, Status	80,NF	80,NF	83,NF	84,NF	83,NF

The Syrian government continued to place severe restrictions on press freedom in 2007. Although the constitution provides for freedom of speech and of the press, a constellation of repressive laws restricts such rights in practice. The 1962 Emergency Law supersedes all constitutional protections for the press and broadly mandates the censorship of letters, publications, broadcast media, and other forms of communication. In addition, the 2001 Press Law allows for broad control over all print media and forbids reporting on topics deemed sensitive by the government, such as issues of "national security" or "national unity," as well as the publication of "inaccurate" information. Violations of the Press Law are punishable by fines of up to US$20,000 and prison terms of from one to three years. Decree No. 6 of 1965 criminalizes "publishing news aimed at shaking the people's confidence in the revolution," along with other legislation that criminalizes "opposition to the revolution, its goals, or socialism." The Ministry of Information and the Ministry of Culture and National Guidance are both responsible for censoring domestic and imported foreign press as well as books and films. During a June 2005 conference of the ruling Baath Party, the Ministry of Information announced its plans to introduce a new Press Law; however, old legislation remained in place at year's end. Syria's first independent press freedom organization, Hurriyat, created in 2005, ceased operations in 2007 as two of its founders were in prison and a third had left the country.

Security services detained eight journalists and online writers over the course of 2007, and dozens of other people who had criticized the regime or were suspected of opposition to the government were detained. Syrian human rights organizations reported that security services held Abd al-Razzaq Eid, an academic and prominent civil rights advocate, for 13 hours based on articles written for Beirut's *Al-Safeer*. The domestic intelligence service held Muhanad Abdel al-Rahman and Alaa al-Din Hamdoun, two journalists reportedly affiliated with an exiled opposition group, for the first weeks of March before releasing them on March 27. The two were later arrested in August and charged with "undermining the prestige of the state." According to the U.S. State Department, both were released on September 25 as part of the Eid al-Fitr amnesty. Regionally based journalists were also not immune to the harassment of Syrian state officials, the Syrian Organization for Human Rights reported. Security officials detained Ubayd Muhammed, a reporter for Kurdistan Satellite TV, and his wife for two weeks as they were trying to leave the country on March 23. Muhammed alleged that he was tortured in custody. The International Press Institute reported that an Iraqi journalist for Japanese Jiji Press was arrested, assaulted, and expelled from Syria in August based on his coverage of the presidential referendum. A number of journalists were sentenced to prison during the year. Journalist Michel Kilo, imprisoned since May 2006, received three additional years in May 2007 for "weakening national sentiment" after he (along with 300 other intellectuals) signed the Beirut-Damascus, Damascus-Beirut statement calling for improved relations between the countries. Lawyer Anwar al-Bunni was also sentenced to five years in April for "spreading false news" based on a letter he submitted to the UN High Commissioner for Human Rights on the human rights violations occurring in Syria.

Except for a handful of radio stations that do not broadcast news or report on political issues, Syria's radio and television outlets are all state owned. Private and political party–affiliated newspapers sometimes publish mild criticism of the government and report more freely on social and economic issues. Newspapers such as *Al-Watan* and *Al-Iqtisad*, owned by businessmen with close connections to the government, occasionally criticize the government's performance, but within limits. The political daily *Baladna*, owned by the son of the former head of intelligence, was banned for 47 days in May after it published a cartoon satirizing Syria's legislative assembly. The Ministry of Information bans foreign news publications if they contain material the government deems a threat to public order or national security. The London-based, Saudi-funded, regional daily *Al-Sharq al-Awsat* was unavailable for most of 2007. All Kurdish-language publications are prohibited but were reportedly available. Satellite dishes are common, and the government makes no attempt to interfere with satellite broadcasts. Syrian television has increasingly broached topics formerly considered taboo and conducted interviews with opposition figures.

Despite the government's aggressive crackdown on the internet in recent years, critical journalists have increasingly used this electronic medium to voice their dissent. Close to 8 percent of Syrians accessed the internet in 2007, a slight increase over the previous year. The government censors the internet and monitors its use based on the Press Law, the Emergency Law, and the penal code. Websites are often blocked by Syria's three internet service providers, although some users employ a range of tools to circumvent this censorship. On July 25, Communications and Technology Minister Amr Salem issued a decree requiring websites to publish the names and e-mail addresses of anyone writing on their sites, threatening to ban websites that failed to comply. Soon after, the ministry blocked access to *DamasPost*, a popular news website, after a commentator identified only as "Jamal" accused prominent journalists of nepotism. On June 7, military intelligence officers detained Karim Arbaji, moderator of the website akhawia.net, a popular site for Syrian youth to discuss social and political issues, and held him incommunicado. His whereabouts were still unknown at year's end. On June 30, military intelligence officers arrested blogger Tareq Bayasi and also held him incommunicado throughout the year, apparently for criticizing Syria's security services online. On September 23, the Supreme State Security Court sentenced blogger Ali Zein al-Abideen Mej'an to two years in prison for "undertaking acts or writing or speeches unauthorized by the government...that spoil its ties with a foreign state," for comments posted online that criticized Saudi Arabia.

Taiwan

LEGAL ENVIRONMENT: 7
POLITICAL ENVIRONMENT: 7
ECONOMIC ENVIRONMENT: 6

Status: Free

TOTAL SCORE: 20

Survey Edition	2003	2004	2005	2006	2007
Total Score, Status	24,F	23,F	21,F	20,F	20,F

Taiwan has the freest media environment in East Asia owing to its open legal environment, commitment to judicial independence, economic freedom, and highly competitive media market. The constitution provides for freedom of speech and of the press, and the government generally respects these rights in practice. While publications from mainland China are subject to screening and potential import bans by the Government Information Office (GIO), numerous materials from China were available in stores as well as on the internet. Domestic print media are completely independent of official control, but electronic media and broadcast television stations had previously been subject to government influence through the authority of the GIO to regulate programming and licensing. In a positive development, that arrangement ended in early 2006, when the National Communications Commission (NCC) was established. The NCC's independence was subsequently questioned, however, and provisions of its founding legislation were declared unconstitutional by the Council of Grand Justices in June 2006 because of requirements for partisan membership selection. Following the legislature's amendment of the law in December 2007, new appointments are to be made in 2008 by the premier, with parliamentary approval. Taiwanese media are vigorous and lively, regularly criticizing government policy and top officials. Reports on high-level corruption were particularly common in 2007, with scandals implicating President Chen Shui Bian, his family members, and several opposition politicians a key topic of coverage. Media observers have raised concerns, however, over a rise in sensationalism and potential loss of quality. During the year, the NCC fined several television stations after they ran footage later found to have been misrepresenting events.

Physical violence against journalists is rare, and both local and foreign reporters are able to cover the news freely. In one incident in March 2007, a controversy erupted surrounding an Associated Press (AP) story in which Taiwan's vice president, Annette Lu, was referred to in derogatory terms originating with the Chinese government. Initially, the GIO announced that the responsible reporter's visa would be revoked, but it reversed its position the following day; AP later interviewed Lu, providing an opportunity for her to counter the views expressed in the original article. In another incident related to media certification, international media watchdogs criticized the United Nations for barring accreditation to Taiwanese journalists seeking to cover the World Health Assembly (WHA) in Geneva in May 2007. Prior to 2004, Taiwanese journalists had reportedly been permitted to cover the WHA, but this authorization was withdrawn under pressure from Beijing.

Taiwan has over 360 privately owned newspapers and numerous radio stations, including the English-language International Community Radio Taipei. Satellite television is broadcast on 143 channels. In 2005, cable television was available to 85 percent of the population, the highest cable viewership in Asia. According to a study conducted by Shih Hsin University in Taipei, 95 percent of Taiwanese watch television and 75 percent read newspapers. Legislation approved in 2003 barred the government and political party officials from holding positions in broadcast media companies and required government entities and political parties to divest themselves of all radio and broadcast companies. The government refrains from restricting the internet, which is currently accessed by nearly 70 percent of the population. However, several nongovernmental organizations claimed that law enforcement agencies monitored chat room and bulletin board exchanges among adults in order to identify and prosecute individuals posting sexually suggestive messages.

Tajikistan

Status: Not Free

LEGAL ENVIRONMENT: 25
POLITICAL ENVIRONMENT: 28
ECONOMIC ENVIRONMENT: 24
TOTAL SCORE: 77

Survey Edition	2003	2004	2005	2006	2007
Total Score, Status	76,NF	73,NF	74,NF	76,NF	76,NF

Freedom of speech is guaranteed by the constitution, but the media situation remained largely moribund in the wake of successful government efforts over the last few years to force independent reporting to the margins. President Emomali Rahmon demonstrated his antagonistic approach to the media during his annual address to parliament when he called for the development of a new press policy in which "the media will be expected to raise patriotism." Criticism of the president is off-limits and can lead to prison terms of up to four years for journalists. Worse still, in October, President Rahmon signed amendments to the criminal code extending the criminalization of libel and defamation to internet publications, with the penalty of fines in excess of US$5,000 and up to two years in prison. The new amendments were put to the test almost immediately when the prosecutor's office in the capital, Dushanbe, opened a criminal libel case against three journalists with *Ovoza*, an independent newspaper that had printed an article critical of singer Raikhona Rahimova. Saida Qurgonova, the editor in chief, and Muhayo Nozimov and Farangis Nabieva, both reporters with the outlet, were being held responsible for an article that quoted critical comments from an internet forum discussing a performance Rahimova had given in Afghanistan. Although the case was resolved amicably, it demonstrated that the new amendments were not merely cosmetic and that journalists could be held responsible for their use of online sources. Independent media are also routinely denied access to public documents and information. While a 2005 presidential decree requires government ministries to hold quarterly press conferences, none have done so, and no freedom of information legislation exists. State-run media outlets have only marginally better access to information, as ministries will occasionally provide them with status updates.

There were no reports of violence against journalists in 2007, but many journalists have reported acts of intimidation or harassment committed against them in previous years. In October, Makhmadullo Makhsadullo, a reporter with the independent paper *Tojikiston*, was detained overnight by a police officer while on his way to cover a press conference. Makhsadullo published an article about the incident, and the police officer subsequently sued him and the other outlets that rose to defend Makhsadullo. However, in a welcome development, the Supreme Court sentenced Aslan Usmanov to a 15-year prison term for acting as an accomplice in the 1995 murder of journalist Muhiddin Olimpur, former head of the British Broadcasting Corporation (BBC)'s Persian service in Tajikistan. Olimpur was one of many victims in a string of unsolved murders of journalists dating back to the country's 1992–1995 civil war. Usmanov, a field commander with the United Tajik Opposition at the time of the killing, was convicted of masterminding the murder.

The government maintained its stranglehold on the media in 2007 through direct and indirect ownership, licensing requirements, control of printing and transmission facilities, and subsidies. Although there were over 200 registered newspapers, none operated daily, and the broadcast industry was monopolized by three nationally televised stations—Tajik, Soghd, and Khatlon—that are all government owned. There are a number of independent outlets in operation, but many practice self-censorship for fear of government retribution and the television industry is notoriously difficult for new outlets to enter. The body responsible for issuing media licenses, the Licensing Commission, is neither independent from the government nor transparent. In fact, the commission withdrew the licenses for a number of independent outlets between 2004 and 2006 owing to alleged "licensing irregularities"; while some of the outlets were allowed to reopen in 2007, others remained closed at year's end. Some international outlets were allowed to operate and broadcast within Tajikistan. However, the BBC was unable to regain its FM broadcast license in 2007 after it had been revoked in 2006. Registration difficulties also affected the U.S.-based nongovernmental organization Internews, which was prevented from opening a number of community radio stations.

The internet is still a relatively new media source in Tajikistan, and because of financial and other constraints, less than 0.5 percent accessed it in 2007. Nonetheless, the government still restricts this electronic medium:

Beginning in 2006, websites critical of the government were blocked, and new internet-focused libel legislation was passed in 2007.

Tanzania

Status: Partly Free

LEGAL ENVIRONMENT: 15
POLITICAL ENVIRONMENT: 18
ECONOMIC ENVIRONMENT: 15
TOTAL SCORE: 48

Survey Edition	2003	2004	2005	2006	2007
Total Score, Status	47,PF	50,PF	51,PF	50,PF	51,PF

With few cases of extralegal intimidation of the press during the year, the media environment improved slightly in 2007. Although the constitution provides for freedom of speech, several other laws limit the ability of the media to function effectively, and there are no explicit provisions for freedom of the press. Authorities are empowered to register and ban newspapers under the Newspaper Registration Act "in the interest of peace and good order," while the Broadcasting Services Act provides for state regulation of electronic media, and the National Security Act allows the government to control the dissemination of information to the public. Despite these restrictive laws, journalists reported that they were typically able to operate freely. At the same time, criminal penalties imposed by libel legislation continue to intimidate journalists. There is no freedom of information law in place, though a draft bill was tabled in February 2007. In April 2007, the government also tabled the media services bill, which contains changes to defamation laws that would be more favorable to journalists and provisions on the protection of confidential sources. However, it also requires the licensing of all journalists by the Media Standards Board, members of which are appointed by the government. The bill had not been passed by year's end.

Although reports of attacks against the media were rare, there was one case in 2007 when Minister of Information Omary Mapuki attacked a reporter who had written critically about him. However, in a positive sign, Mapuki was forced to resign from his position given the political outcry following the assault. The situation in Zanzibar still remains more restrictive than in the rest of the country. Journalists in Zanzibar must be licensed and must obtain a permit prior to covering police activities. The state prohibits any independent radio or television broadcasts, although locals can receive private broadcasts from the mainland and opposition politicians did have access to state media outlets. Zanzibar's first independent private newspaper, *Dira*, remains banned, and in August, the government prevented a BBC meet-the-listeners show from broadcasting from the island; the BBC program had earlier broadcast from a number of sites in mainland Tanzania.

There are numerous media outlets throughout Tanzania, including 47 FM radio stations, 537 registered newspapers, and a dozen television stations. Only 4 radio stations have a national reach—state-run Radio Tanzania and privately owned Radio One, Radio Free Africa, and Radio Uhuru—and all are viewed as sympathetic to the ruling party. The government reportedly continues to withhold advertising from critical newspapers or those that report favorably on the opposition, and taxes on the media remain high despite presidential campaign promises that they would be reduced. Private firms keen to remain on good terms with the government allegedly follow suit, thus making it difficult for critical media outlets to remain financially viable. Nonetheless, even though the government occasionally pressures outlets to suppress unfavorable stories, independent media outlets like *Thisday* and even some state-owned newspapers regularly criticize official policies. Although there were no explicit government restrictions on the internet, there were reports that government officials monitored internet content and activity. Only 1 percent of the population accessed the internet in 2007; however, a number of new internet cafés and internet service providers did open throughout the year.

Thailand

Status: Partly Free

LEGAL ENVIRONMENT: 17
POLITICAL ENVIRONMENT: 24
ECONOMIC ENVIRONMENT: 15
TOTAL SCORE: 56

Survey Edition	2003	2004	2005	2006	2007
Total Score, Status	36,PF	39,PF	42,PF	50,PF	59,PF

Although legal protections for freedom of expression were restored when a new constitution was approved in August 2007, Thailand's military-led government continued to significantly restrict media freedom throughout the year. It passed one of the world's harshest internet crime laws, imposed tight controls on the state-run broadcasting sector, and manipulated the media in efforts to influence the outcome of the August constitutional referendum and the long-awaited general elections on December 23. The continuation of martial law in 35 out of the country's 76 provinces for most of the year also hampered the media, especially local radio broadcasters.

The new constitution, which replaced an interim charter that failed to explicitly protect freedom of expression, restores and even extends the 1997 constitution's freedom of expression guarantees. Moreover, the national legislative assembly replaced the country's draconian 1941 Printing and Publishing Act, which reserved the government's right to shut down media outlets, with a new Printing Act in late August. The new law bears fewer restrictions as well as lighter penalties for violations. However, the Computer Crime Act was passed in May and took effect in July, threatening harsh punitive measures—including prison terms of up to five years—for the publication of forged or false content that endangers individuals, the public, or national security and for the use of proxy servers to access government-restricted material. The legislation was first invoked to bring charges against a blogger and a webmaster in late August; the charges were dropped in October without explanation, but watchdog groups fear the new law will have a chilling effect on online media, the country's strongest outlet for free discussion.

An amended Internal Security Act, passed by the outgoing legislature just before the December elections, is also considered a potential menace to press freedom, as it allows the Internal Security Operations Command to use sweeping emergency powers in the face of vaguely defined security threats. Meanwhile, several older laws that reserve the government's right to restrict the media to preserve public order and prevent criticism of the king, royal family, or Buddhism remain in force. In October, the parliament rejected proposals that would have expanded the country's already restrictive lese-majeste laws by barring criticism of the monarch's children and members of the Privy Council. Access to information is guaranteed under the new constitution "unless the disclosure of such information shall affect the security of State, public safety, interests of other persons which shall be protected, or personal data of other persons as provided by law."

Defamation legislation under the penal code is harsh, and former prime minister Thaksin Shinawatra used it routinely to silence critical voices. This use of libel suits has declined since Thaksin's ouster in a 2006 military coup, but defamation charges have been filed against journalists for insulting coup leader and subsequent deputy prime minister Sonthi Boonyaratglin. In March, media mogul Sondhi Limthongkul, a former Thaksin critic, was sentenced to two years in prison for insulting a government official on the air in 2005. In a separate case in December, he was sentenced to three years in prison for libeling Thaksin in 2006. In April, a court in the capital city of

Bangkok sentenced two talk show hosts to two years in prison for accusing deputy Bangkok governor Samart Ratchapolasit of taking bribes.

The country's print media have remained largely unaffected by military rule and continued to present a variety of viewpoints on controversial topics in 2007. The broadcasting sector and online media have been obstructed much more significantly. On January 10, the ruling Council on National Security (CNS) invoked Military Order No. 10, which urged media cooperation in promoting "peace and national unity," for the first time since it was issued after the coup in September 2006. The CNS convened roughly 50 television and radio executives and asked them to keep their media outlets from being used as platforms for Thaksin and his supporters, warning that any programs failing to comply would be removed. CNN broadcasts of Thaksin were blocked the same week, and three community radio stations were closed down temporarily in May for airing interviews with Thaksin.

The CNS used its tight grip on the broadcasting sector to try to influence both the August constitutional referendum and the elections in December. While television programs featured some debate on the referendum, the government threatened sanctions for any "organized campaigns" to reject the charter. Radio commentators in the provinces were reportedly pressured to refrain from speaking out against the new constitution. As part of a host of campaign restrictions issued by the election commission in October, all broadcast media outlets were prevented from hosting candidates from one party without hosting candidates from all parties. Moreover, in another attempt to prevent Thaksin's allies from gaining ground in the elections, the government in March tried to prevent the launch of a pro-Thaksin satellite news station called People's Television (PTV) by denying it the internet access it needed. The station managed to launch anyway, but the authorities blocked it just hours later. PTV programs continued to be blocked in subsequent months, though it was reportedly broadcasting at year's end. Although some print and broadcast media continued to report news critical of the interim government and the CNS as well as Thaksin's statements and activities later in the year, press freedom watchdog groups such as the Southeast Asian Press Alliance have expressed concerns about heightened self-censorship since the September 2006 coup, citing a shift in news coverage among some outlets and websites.

Radio and television remain under the control of the state or formerly state-affiliated private businesses, and many radio stations have been closed since the coup. Government control of the media increased in March 2007 when the Public Relations Department took over Thailand's only independent broadcast television station, iTV. Officials claimed that the station, previously run by one of Thaksin's former companies, had illegally changed its operating concession with the former prime minister's office and thus owed crippling fines. After facing protests against its outright closure, the government opted to relaunch the station with state funds under the name Thailand Independent Television.

The internet is accessed by approximately 13 percent of the Thai population. Government censorship of the internet has occurred since 2003, largely to prevent the circulation of pornography and illegal products. After the coup, priority shifted to prohibiting potentially disruptive political messages, and sites considered a threat to national security, including those of Muslim separatist groups, continued to be blocked in light of persistent violence in the Muslim south. The CNS continued to censor the internet and block websites it deemed a threat to the military regime, including two in May that covered Thaksin in a favorable light and criticized the junta. YouTube was banned in April after it carried videos deemed insulting to the king and thus a violation of the country's lese-majeste laws; the ban was lifted in August when Google, the owner of YouTube, agreed to block any offensive videos.

Togo

Status: Not Free

LEGAL ENVIRONMENT: 23
POLITICAL ENVIRONMENT: 29
ECONOMIC ENVIRONMENT: 22
TOTAL SCORE: 74

Survey Edition	2003	2004	2005	2006	2007
Total Score, Status	74,NF	78,NF	73,NF	78,NF	74,NF

The media environment remained generally repressive in 2007, following a period of heightened attacks against independent media outlets intended to secure Faure Gnassingbe's hold on power after he replaced his father as president in 2005. Freedom of speech and freedom of the press are legally guaranteed, but these rights are often ignored by the administration. In 2004, in a deal to end European Union trade sanctions, then president Gnassingbe Eyadema initiated legal improvements, including the abolition of prison sentences for libel and a ban on government closures of media outlets without judicial approval. However, these reforms were disregarded following Eyadema's death and his son's rise to power in 2005. Gnassingbe's initial crackdowns subsided as his position grew more secure, although his administration's authoritarian habits have not disappeared. In particular, the High Authority for Audiovisual Communications (HAAC), which was intended as an independent body to protect press freedom and ensure ethical standards, is now used as the government's censorship arm and is closely affiliated with the presidency. During 2007, the HAAC temporarily banned four media outlets without a court order, despite the 2004 legal reforms. Among the targeted outlets was Radio Victoire, which was suspended for "unprofessional conduct" after it refused to ban a controversial foreign journalist, Jacques Roux, from a radio discussion. The HAAC also suspended three newspapers beginning in June: *La Trompette* was suspended for four months for a series of articles critical of the University of Lome; *Le Courrier de La Republique* was suspended for three months for criticizing the HAAC; and *Le Perroquet* was suspended for two months for allegedly accepting payment for a story. Similarly, the HAAC banned radio station Nana FM from airing material by journalist and press freedom advocate Daniel Lawson-Drackey after he criticized the minister of territorial administration.

The political environment for the media was stable in 2007, with journalists wary of criticizing the government but only infrequently subject to direct physical attacks. Nevertheless, the independence of the Togolese press is seriously jeopardized by the culture of impunity that has pervaded the country since 2005. A number of direct attacks on journalists were perpetrated that year, and the incidents have not been investigated. While there were no reported instances of physical attacks or harassment in 2007, journalists are well aware that reporting such crimes to the authorities is probably futile.

Despite such obstacles, Togo is home to lively and diverse independent media, though many private print and broadcast outlets are heavily politicized. The country's 15 regularly published private newspapers are plagued by inconsistent readership. The government runs Togo's only daily newspaper, *Togo-Presse,* and the only national television station, Togo Television. The four private television stations have limited reach; there are also a number of private radio stations. Access to the internet was generally unrestricted during the year, despite reports that its content has been monitored. Slightly less than 6 percent of the population was able to access this new medium in 2007.

Legal Environment: 11
Political Environment: 10

Tonga

Economic Environment: 10

Status: Partly Free

Total Score: 31

Survey Edition	2003	2004	2005	2006	2007
Total Score, Status	32,PF	44,PF	37,PF	32,PF	31,PF

Tonga's media environment remained relatively restricted in 2007 as a state of emergency imposed following prodemocracy rioting in the capital in late 2006 continued throughout the year. Freedom of the press is guaranteed under the constitution and generally respected in practice. However, in November, the government announced the formation of a new Department of Information to oversee all media reporting, though at year's end it was unclear how this would be implemented. Government practices such as not publicly releasing draft budgets and bills or charging a fee to obtain court papers effectively restrict transparency and public involvement in policy decisions. In February, Tongan soldiers temporarily closed the offices of the private newspaper *Kele'a* without explanation, charging its editor Tavake Fusimalohi with sedition and criminal defamation. In April, Falisi Tupou, another of the paper's senior editors, was arrested and charged with sedition. On December 21, the government sued the paper for alleged defamation over an unfavorable editorial, prompting criticism from local and international press freedom groups.

Political reporting has been invigorated by the presence of democracy advocates in parliament and broader public pressure for reform, but in June 2007, the Tongan Broadcasting Commission (TBC) was ordered to stop reporting on parliamentary proceedings after several cabinet members accused it of bias. Although the government said the ban was subsequently lifted, political coverage remained restricted throughout the year and journalists reported increased self-censorship.

In spite of the small size of the nation and population, the kingdom has a remarkably diverse range of media. Some of the newspapers, such as *Taimi 'o Tonga* and *Kele'a*, are printed in New Zealand. The government publishes the *Tonga Chronicle* in English and its sister publication *Kalonikali Tonga* in Tongan, while the independent news website *Matangi Tonga* (originally a magazine) is now well established and one of the most reputable publications in the South Pacific. The TBC owns one AM and one FM station and the free-to-air Television Tonga station. Another privately owned station, the

Oceania Broadcasting Network, which provided airtime to the Human Rights and Democracy Movement, was taken off the air following the November 2006 riots and remained out of commission throughout 2007. There is one other privately owned television station and three private radio stations. The government did not impose restrictions on the internet, though the medium was accessed by only 3 percent of the population in 2007 owing to infrastructure limitations.

Trinidad & Tobago

LEGAL ENVIRONMENT: 6
POLITICAL ENVIRONMENT: 10
ECONOMIC ENVIRONMENT: 7

Status: Free

TOTAL SCORE: 23

Survey Edition	2003	2004	2005	2006	2007
Total Score, Status	25,F	25,F	24,F	26,F	24,F

Freedom of the press is enshrined in the constitution, and is usually respected by the government. While freedom of information legislation is in place, the government has been criticized for gradually narrowing the categories of public information accessible under the law. The use of libel laws by government officials to restrict media operations has been a problem in previous years, as has the discriminatory allocation of broadcasting licenses. Another remaining contentious issue was the role of authorities' interference in the media sphere in the context of the country's simmering ethnic tensions between the African and East Indian communities. In January, the ruling People's National Movement, which is generally supported by Afro-Trinidadians, was heavily criticized for state actions taken against television operator and commentator Inshan Ishmael. Owner of the Islamic Broadcasting Network, Ishmael emerged as one of the leaders of a protest movement that in January proposed a shutdown of businesses and schools as a way of registering public dissatisfaction with the government's failure to deal with soaring crime rates. In the lead-up to the protest, the state-run Trinidad and Tobago Telecommunications Authority blocked the broadcast of Ishmael's television program. Then, on January 24, the day before the work stoppage, Ishmael was arrested by armed police. He was later charged under the Antiterrorism Law. The leader of the recently formed political party Congress of the People, Wilson Dookeran, denounced the arrest as a "deliberate move to stifle freedom of the media." In March, the charges against Ishmael were dropped.

There are three daily newspapers—*Trinidad and Tobago Express*, *Newsday*, and the *Trinidad Guardian*—and three political weeklies. Four television stations are in operation, including the state-owned CNMG TV, and a new cable station, WIN TV, was launched in May. In November, the British Broadcasting Corporation joined an already crowded radio field—there are 36 stations—when it launched its FM frequency Caribbean service. There were no government restrictions on the internet, which was accessed by 12 percent of the population in 2007.

Tunisia

Status: Not Free

LEGAL ENVIRONMENT: 27
POLITICAL ENVIRONMENT: 30
ECONOMIC ENVIRONMENT: 24
TOTAL SCORE: 81

Survey Edition	2003	2004	2005	2006	2007
Total Score, Status	78,NF	80,NF	80,NF	83,NF	83,NF

Despite the government's continued prosecution of critical reporters and its tight control over media outlets, citizens' access to information improved slightly in 2007 owing to the increased availability of satellite television and growing internet usage. The constitution guarantees freedom of the press except under "conditions laid down by law," but the government did not respect this right in practice. The Press Law criminalizes defamation, and those who violate the law can be imprisoned and fined; offensive statements about the president carry prison sentences of up to five years. In a move that ended overt censorship, President Zine el-Abidine Ben Ali signed a law in January 2006 abolishing a procedure whereby all printed material had to receive government approval prior to publication. Nevertheless, authorities continue to vet and censor newspapers published locally as well as those coming from outside the country. The responsibility for prior review of all foreign publications and books was transferred from the Ministry of Justice to the Ministry of the Interior in November 2007. Self-censorship among journalists and government interference in distribution following publication remain routine. According to the U.S. State Department, in March 2007, the authorities purchased all copies of the opposition weekly *Al-Mawkif* to prevent circulation of a photo showing Tunisian and Israeli parliament members participating together in a Euro-Mediterranean parliamentary council meeting in Tunis.

Journalists who cross the government's red lines face harassment, beatings, and potential imprisonment. Interrogation and detention of members of the media were also common throughout the year, as were police surveillance and restrictions on journalists' freedom of movement. According to Reporters Sans Frontieres, at least a dozen journalists were physically assaulted by police in 2007. On June 7, Lotfi Hidouri of the online publication *Kalima* was cornered by plainclothes police who forcefully confiscated his cameras, and in a separate incident, Hidouri and reporter Ayman Rezki of an Italy-based Tunisian satellite channel were reportedly beaten by police. Lotfi Hajji, a correspondent for Al-Jazeera and president of the Tunisian Union of Journalists, was reportedly hindered from reporting on five separate events in the month of April, often suffering physical assault at the hands of the police. Slim Boukhdir, a contributor to the London-based *Al-Quds al-Arabi* and several online news sites, was arrested in November 2007 upon inquiring about his passport application and sentenced the following month to one year in prison on questionable charges of "assaulting a government employee in the exercise of his duty." The government continued to refuse to issue Boukhdir a press card.

Tunisia's print media include eight major dailies, with two owned by the government and two owned by the ruling party. Editors of private media are often close associates of President Ben Ali's government and typically praise state leadership and its policies, while the government withholds subsidies and advertising funds from publications that do not provide sufficiently favorable coverage. Print media do not need to be licensed, but they are required by law to obtain from the Ministry of Information a copyright registration, which is valid for one year. In practice, authorities have consistently blocked the registration of new, independent print outlets. There are seven opposition party newspapers, which enjoy greater freedom to criticize the government, including *Attarik al-Jadid* of the Attajdid Party, *Al-Mawkif* of the Progressive Democratic Party, and the weekly *Mouwatinoun* (which began publication in January) of the Democratic Forum for Labor and Liberties. Nevertheless, circulation of opposition papers remains small owing to financial constraints, with private advertisers avoiding papers that are shunned by the government, and the authorities continue to target them for harassment. According to the Committee to Protect Journalists, on October 1, *Al-Mawkif* was evicted from the offices where it had been housed for 13 years; it also had its papers removed from newsstands three times during 2007. Broadcast media are regulated by the Tunisian Frequencies Agency, which tightly controls the allocation of licenses and frequencies. The private channel Hannibal TV has opened up new space for the debate of social, cultural, and economic issues, although it does not cover political issues. Many foreign satellite stations can be viewed in Tunisia, although the government has been known to block France 2 and Al-Jazeera for their negative coverage of President Ben Ali.

Nearly 16 percent of the population accessed the internet in 2007, almost double the proportion from the previous year. However, the government stringently blocks access to a number of sites, particularly those belonging to domestic human rights organizations, opposition groups, and Islamist associations, as well as websites that post material critical of the Tunisian government. The OpenNet Initiative declared Tunisia to be one of the worst offenders in terms of blocking web content and politically filtering information. Punishments for online dissidents are severe and remain similar to those for print and broadcast journalists who publish information deemed objectionable by the government. Both legal and extralegal harassment and intimidation of journalists and editors of online sites remained a problem. According to the Committee to Protect Journalists, Omar Mestiri, managing editor of the online magazine *Kalima*, was brought before a court on defamation charges in August in relation for a September 2006 article that criticized the reinstatement of a lawyer by the Tunisian Bar Association. While the case was dropped unexpectedly on August 28, the offices of Mestiri's lawyer were torched three days later. After serving two and a half years in prison for an online article that had criticized the state use of torture, writer and human rights lawyer Mohammed Abbou was released in July. However, Abbou was prohibited from traveling outside the country by state officials on numerous occasions in October and November.

LEGAL ENVIRONMENT: 20
POLITICAL ENVIRONMENT: 20

Turkey

ECONOMIC ENVIRONMENT: 11

Status: Partly Free

TOTAL SCORE: 51

Survey Edition	2003	2004	2005	2006	2007
Total Score, Status	55,PF	52,PF	48,PF	48,PF	49,PF

With heightened polarization regarding issues of secularism, nationalism, and separatism, reform efforts toward enhanced freedom of expression stalled in 2007. The restrictive measures of the new Turkish penal code, which came into force in June 2005, continued to overshadow and undermine positive reforms achieved in the country's effort to meet European Union (EU) membership requirements, including a new Press Law in 2004 that replaced prison sentences with fines. The EU accession process and perceptions that the ruling Justice and Development Party intends to undermine the country's secular traditions have prompted a nationalist movement that is driving a legalistic crackdown on free expression by journalists and writers.

Constitutional provisions for freedom of the press and of expression exist but are matched with provisions that restrict it and, in practice, are only partially upheld. According to Bianet, a Turkish press freedom organization, the number of prosecuted journalists, publishers, and activists dropped to 254 in 2007 from 293 in 2006 (after a dramatic jump from 157 in 2005). Yet the same organization reports that 55 individuals were tried over the year under the penal code's especially controversial Article 301 alone. This provision allows for prison terms of six months to three years for "the denigration of Turkishness" and has been used to charge journalists for crimes such as stating that genocide was committed against the Armenians in 1915, discussing the division of Cyprus, or writing critically on the security forces. Book publishers, translators, and intellectuals have also faced prosecution for "insulting Turkish identity." In January, Hrant Dink—editor in chief of the Armenian weekly *Agos*, who was prosecuted for a second time under Article 301 in July 2006 for confirming his recognition of Armenian genocide allegations—was the victim of a carefully plotted assassination carried out by a 17-year-old. Charges against Dink under Article 301 were subsequently dropped, but both his son and the owner of *Agos* were convicted on the same charges for the same case in October. In November, two policemen were charged with knowing about plans to kill Dink and failing to report it; the trials of all 19 people charged in connection with the murder were ongoing at year's end.

Article 277 of the penal code was invoked in 2007 to charge 14 people with "attempting to influence court decisions." Article 216 penalizes "inflaming hatred and hostility among peoples" and is used most frequently against journalists who write about the Kurdish population or are perceived to degrade the armed forces. Twenty-three people were charged on this count in 2007, and in May 2007, a court of appeals overturned the prior acquittal of two professors charged under this article in 2005 for a report in which they discussed the term citizenship of Turkey as it relates to minorities, a concept being debated in preparation for a new "civil" constitution. The court ruled that the discussion constituted a "social danger" and more specifically "a danger to the unitary state and the indivisibility of the nation." Nationalist lawyers groups such as the Great Lawyers Union, credited by many human rights groups with leading the push for prosecutions, continued to bring insult suits over the year.

Despite a September 2006 declaration of commitment by Prime Minister Recep Tayyip Erdogan to revise Article 301 and heightened pressure from international press freedom watchdog groups to abolish it following Dink's murder, no progress was made by year's end; many believe the government dropped the issue in the context of election concerns. Erdogan himself continued to launch a number of defamation suits against members of the media; in October, newly elected president Abdullah Gul promised changes in the period ahead. Convictions against journalists are made much less frequently than are prosecutions, but trials are time-consuming and expensive. A total of six convictions were made for charges under Article 301 in 2007 (nine other cases were acquitted). In a positive development, the Supreme Court of Appeals confirmed a lower court's prior decision to drop the Article 301 case against Turkish writer Orhan Pamuk in August.

While Bianet also reports that the number of threats and attacks on the press increased in 2007, threats and harassment remain significantly more prevalent than acts of violence. The Dink assassination marked the culmination of a deliberate plot believed to be developed by nationalist forces, or the "deep state"—a vague network involving members of the state bureaucracy, military, and intelligence apparatus. The murder of journalists is not a common crime, and reporters' work is not regularly compromised by fears of violence. Instability in the southeastern part of the country does infringe upon journalists' freedom to work, however. In April, three employees of a Christian publishing house in the Malatya province of southeastern Turkey were brutally murdered, and a newspaper owner was killed in the southeastern province of Van in September, though that murder did not appear to be related to freedom of the press. The issue of police violence against journalists was raised by the abduction, assault, and death threats against journalist Sinan Tekpetek by police in Istanbul in late July.

June 2006 amendments to the Antiterror Law allow for imprisoning journalists for up to three years for the dissemination of statements and propaganda by terrorist organizations. The new legislation raises concerns that the broad definition of terrorism could allow for arbitrary prosecutions, particularly for members of the pro-Kurdish press who are sometimes charged with collaborating with the Kurdish Workers

Party (PKK). According to Bianet, 83 people were charged in cases of "terrorism" over the year.

The Supreme Council of Radio and Television, whose members are elected by the parliament, has the authority to sanction broadcasters if they are not in compliance with the law or its expansive broadcasting principles. It is frequently subject to political pressure. Some editors and journalists practice self-censorship out of fear of violating legal restrictions, and Turkish press freedom advocates contend that self-censorship has become more prevalent as a result of the onslaught of prosecutions under the new penal code. The owner of the weekly *Nokta* magazine stopped its publication in April after the magazine's investigative articles on the military prompted a police raid on its offices. Charged with spreading PKK propaganda under the Antiterrorism Law, the *Gundem* newspaper was suspended for 15–30-day periods four times over the year. Broadcasting bans were reportedly issued against a few stations during the preelection period, and the government censored coverage of PKK attacks in southeastern Turkey in October.

Turkey's broadcast media are well developed, with hundreds of private television channels, including cable and satellite, as well as numerous commercial radio stations. State television and radio provide limited broadcasting in minority languages, now including four local radio and television stations in Kurdish. This marks a major step forward for freedom of expression, although critics say that the broadcasts are too restricted and quality is poor. Media are highly concentrated in four major conglomerates, which subtly pressure their editors and journalists to refrain from reporting that will harm their business interests. This could include avoiding criticism of the government or potential advertisers, both of which could have contracts with other arms of the companies. The quality of Turkish media is low, with a greater prevalence of columns and opinion articles than pure news, but independent domestic and foreign print media are able to provide diverse views, including criticism of the government and its policies. An estimated 22.5 percent of the Turkish population accessed the internet in 2007. The video-sharing website YouTube was blocked in March and again in September for airing videos perceived to insult government leaders and the founder of the Turkish republic, Mustafa Kemal Ataturk.

Turkmenistan

Status: Not Free

LEGAL ENVIRONMENT: 30
POLITICAL ENVIRONMENT: 37
ECONOMIC ENVIRONMENT: 29
TOTAL SCORE: 96

Survey Edition	2003	2004	2005	2006	2007
Total Score, Status	92,NF	95,NF	96,NF	96,NF	96,NF

While the death of President Saparmurat Niyazov in December 2006 raised hopes for positive change in Turkmenistan's long-oppressed media environment, there was a distinct lack of tangible improvements in 2007. President Gurbanguly Berdymukhammedov, who won a dubious landslide election victory in February, made a number of encouraging promises but failed to follow through on them, keeping the media environment in Turkmenistan one of the most repressive on earth. Libel is a criminal offense, and the burden of proof rests with the defendant. However, libel laws are rarely implemented given how infrequently independent critical reports are even published.

The government failed to investigate the September 2006 death of Radio Free Europe/Radio Liberty (RFE/RL) correspondent Ogulsapar Muradova while in police custody, despite credible reports that she died under torture. Meanwhile, the remaining correspondents for RFE/RL and other news outlets continued to experience harassment in 2007 in the form of surveillance, blocked phone access, threats, and intimidation. Russia's ITAR-TASS news agency maintained the only foreign bureau in Turkmenistan, while other foreign reporters continued to encounter insurmountable obstacles to accreditation, forcing many to work unofficially if at all. The government gives accreditation to foreign outlets only for coverage of specific events, like the election, that are easily monitored. Moreover, many local journalists are fearful of working with foreign correspondents, because those who have worked with them in the past have often been punished. In April, independent journalist Sona Chuli-Kuli was detained for three days and interrogated; the authorities released her only after she pledged never to work with foreign media outlets.

The government retained its absolute monopoly over all media in 2007, directly controlling not only all media outlets, but also the printing presses and other infrastructure on which they depended. Printing presses are prevented from publishing material unpopular with the government, including all fiction. Authorities also maintained a ban on foreign newspapers and periodical subscriptions, with the sole exception of the Turkish newspaper *Zaman*. The dismissal of Culture Minister Enebai Atayeva in June came with criticism that she had allowed excessive liberalization on state-controlled television, although the only evidence to support this claim was the removal of the former president's image from the bottom of the screen on state television broadcasts. The state even began to crack down on satellite dishes, which have been one of the only means of accessing outside information. In November, President Berdymukhammedov called for the removal of satellite dishes from apartment buildings and their replacement by a single dish on each in order to "beautify the city."

The new president began the year with a promise to lift restrictions on internet access. But when the country's first internet café opened in the capital city of Ashgabat in February, it featured armed guards at the door and prohibitive prices. The number of internet cafés in the country reportedly rose from 0 to 15 by year's end, but the government continued to control the sole internet service provider and to restrict access to critical sites, including regional news sources located outside Turkmenistan, opposition websites operated by Turkmen living abroad, and foreign outlets like the British Broadcasting Corporation. Internet usage in the country is estimated to be only 1.5 percent of the population. In October, the government cut short a brief experiment allowing unmonitored comments to be posted on the official government website, Altyn Asyr, after users posted comments critical of the former president.

Tuvalu

LEGAL ENVIRONMENT: 3
POLITICAL ENVIRONMENT: 11
ECONOMIC ENVIRONMENT: 12

Status: Free

TOTAL SCORE: 26

Survey Edition	2003	2004	2005	2006	2007
Total Score, Status	16,F	19,F	20,F	26,F	26,F

The constitution safeguards freedom of expression, though government regulations and a state monopoly over the tiny media market sometimes limit this right in practice. According to the U.S. State Department, the government tried to influence reporting by the public Tuvalu Media Corporation (TMC) in 2007. TMC controls the country's only newspaper, *Tuvalu Echoes*, and radio station, Radio Tuvalu; it reportedly censors content considered to be in opposition to the government. TMC was reabsorbed in December, making it a department in the Office of the Prime Minister starting in 2008. There are no local television broadcasts, although foreign satellite television is popular. Tuvalu ISP is the sole internet service provider for the 17 percent of the population with the means to access this new medium. Access for those with internet connections is limited in practice by a poor telecommunications infrastructure.

Uganda

Status: Partly Free

LEGAL ENVIRONMENT: 20
POLITICAL ENVIRONMENT: 20
ECONOMIC ENVIRONMENT: 13
TOTAL SCORE: 53

Survey Edition	2003	2004	2005	2006	2007
Total Score, Status	45,PF	44,PF	44,PF	52,PF	54,PF

Although the constitution provides for freedom of expression, laws enacted in the name of national security, including the Press and Media Law of 1995 and the Antiterrorism Act of 2002, have negated many of these constitutional provisions in practice. Following persistent protests from the media industry, the government has agreed to begin the process of amending some of these laws. Yet in October, three journalists working for the *Monitor*, a popular private newspaper, were arrested and charged with sedition in relation to a story alleging soldiers were secretly trained as policemen in order to maintain the police forces under military control. Several statutes, most notably the Press and Media Law, also require journalists to be licensed and meet certain standards like the possession of a diploma in journalism. The law further requires journalists to renew their license each year, though this provision is frequently overlooked. Uganda is one of only three nations on the continent with a Freedom of Information Law.

Continuing a trend seen in 2006, journalists were harassed, intimidated, and censored in Uganda in 2007, and punishment of the perpetrators of these incidents was rare. In March, the Ugandan Journalists Association (UJA) called for the government to protect journalists covering court cases against opposition groups and critical demonstrations and end police harassment of these reporters. This push by the UJA came after two separate cases of police brutality against journalists working for the state-owned *New Vision*—Chris Ahimbisibwe, a reporter, and Richard

Semakula, a photographer—while covering cases in regional high courts. In October, Life FM, a private radio station in southwest Uganda, was forced off the air for five days after unknown assailants poured acid on its transmitter in an attack believed to have been prompted by a program critical of the local government. A rival station had earlier dropped the same program after a meeting with local security officials. However, it was the official media regulator, the Broadcasting Council (BC), which was primarily responsible for government efforts to censor the media. In late January, Nation Television Uganda went off the air after officials at the BC switched off the station's transmitter and confiscated its network receivers for alleged "noncompliance of the industry's technical standards." The station was able to return to the air in April. Similarly, in August, the BC suspended a presenter of the popular Capital FM radio station for alleged violation of the "minimum broadcasting standards." During a show in which the station hosted a lesbian gay activist who used what the BC considered to be "unacceptable language," the suspended host said he had "no problem" with homosexuality while the other two presenters opposed it.

Independent media outlets, including more than two dozen daily and weekly newspapers as well as about 100 private radio and television stations, have mushroomed since the government loosened control in 1993; they are often highly critical of the government and offer a range of opposition views. However, high annual licensing fees for radio and television stations place some financial restraints on the broadcast media. A ban on new radio stations, which was imposed in 2003 and widely disregarded in practice without penalty, was lifted this year for upcountry radio stations; however, it still holds for the capital, Kampala. The state broadcasters, including Radio Uganda, the only national radio station, wield considerable clout and are generally viewed as sympathetic to the government. Nonetheless, the state-run print media have gained a reputation for editorial independence despite the fact that many of their top editors are selected by government officials. In fact, the state paper the *New Vision* has reported critically about the government so regularly that the president has on occasion threatened to fire the paper's editors. There are no official restrictions on access to international broadcasting services or the internet. Internet use became more popular during the year, with over 6 percent of the population accessing it in 2007.

Ukraine

Status: Partly Free

LEGAL ENVIRONMENT: 14
POLITICAL ENVIRONMENT: 19
ECONOMIC ENVIRONMENT: 20
TOTAL SCORE: 53

Survey Edition	2003	2004	2005	2006	2007
Total Score, Status	67,NF	68,NF	59,PF	53,PF	53,PF

Much of 2007 was consumed by political conflict within the government among the country's three dominant politicians—President Viktor Yushchenko, pro-Western Yulia Tymoshenko, and pro-Russian prime minister Viktor Yanukovich—which stalled reforms and left journalists working in chaotic and highly politicized conditions. The fragile governing coalition between Yushchenko and Yanukovich collapsed in May, leading to parliamentary elections in September and the appointment of Tymoshenko as prime minister in November.

The legal framework generally provides for media freedom and is one of the most progressive in Eastern Europe, but respect for these laws has decreased in practice over the last few years following the 2004 Orange Revolution, in which Yushchenko won the presidency. Criminal libel was eliminated in 2001, but some officials use civil libel lawsuits filed in the country's politicized court system to silence critical news reporting. In January, a court in the city of Dniprodzerzhynsk fined the newspaper *Dzerzhinets* 140,660 hryvnia (US$29,071) in civil libel penalties and ordered its property seized after the newspaper published articles about a corrupt local police chief. While the Parliamentary Election Law prohibits the media from engaging in vaguely defined "election campaigning" and provides sanctions for this offense, this provision was not used against the media during the September parliamentary election. Access to public information is still cumbersome, while freedom of information legislation has yet to be formally adopted. As a result, official requests for information are often met by little more than silence, particularly at the local level.

In 2007, threats, harassment, and attacks against the media continued as the country's weak and politicized criminal justice system failed to protect journalists from regional politicians, businessmen, and criminal groups. In fact, a majority of journalists reported receiving some form of threats related to their work. In February, in one of many similar incidents Andriy Shynkarenko, the 9 Kanal television news director, was attacked and seriously beaten by two men he said were associates of a local politician he had been investigating. Separately, in September, the editor in chief of the critical online outlet *Ostriv* was the victim of an arson attack when his car was set on fire. Prosecutors and police regularly failed to take action against suspects identified in these previous attacks, leading to a culture of impunity. For example, in July, prosecutors in the capital city of Kyiv cited a "lack of evidence" when stating that they would not press charges against a politician from Prime Minister Yanukovich's conservative Party of Regions who reportedly attacked two STB television journalists outside the parliament in August 2006. Similarly, despite President Yushchenko's promise to solve the September 2000 abduction and murder of journalist Heorhiy Gongadze, his government has made limited progress in the case. The trial of the three police officers charged with the slaying continued throughout 2007, while a fourth suspect, a senior police official, remained a fugitive. Gongadze's family and press freedom advocates question why prosecutors are ignoring evidence that former president Leonid Kuchma ordered Gongadze's murder, suspecting Yushchenko's administration of protecting the former president.

With hundreds of state and private television and radio stations and numerous print and electronic news outlets, Ukraine's media remain diverse. However, many major outlets are owned by regional business magnates with close ties to the government, while others are dependent on state subsidies, making self-censorship widespread and slanting news coverage in favor of specific economic or political interests. In fact, in March, state-run Ukrainian National Television canceled the popular current affairs debate program only a day after Tymoshenko appeared on the program and brought in record approval ratings for the show. During the campaign for the September parliamentary election, hidden political advertising was widespread in the private media, while the state media provided primarily positive coverage for Yushchenko and Yanukovich. Political infighting distracted the government from reforming politicized state media outlets as well as the state bureaucracies, where secrecy and corruption remain widespread. At the beginning of the year, the Party of Regions pressured state media outlets for more favorable news coverage and tried unsuccessfully to oust an outspoken reformist politician as chairman of the parliament's Committee on Freedom of Speech and Information. Transparency of media ownership remains poor because businessmen and politicians often preferred to hide their ownership and editorial influence over news programs. Ukraine's print distribution system also remains problematic and dependent on the national postal service. Some of these deficiencies were partly offset by strong economic growth, which increased media advertising revenues as well as the popularity of business reporting. The government does not restrict access to foreign outlets or to the internet. Although it also does not require internet publications to register with the government, it does retain the ability to monitor websites and the e-mails of the 12 percent of the population that used the internet regularly. The country's growing economy continued to expand demand and readership of news and other websites.

United Arab Emirates

LEGAL ENVIRONMENT: 23
POLITICAL ENVIRONMENT: 23
ECONOMIC ENVIRONMENT: 22

Status: Not Free

TOTAL SCORE: 68

Survey Edition	2003	2004	2005	2006	2007
Total Score, Status	74,NF	75,NF	72,NF	65,NF	68,NF

Despite high-profile attempts to lure international media outlets to Dubai, concentration of media ownership and restrictive legal provisions continued to constrain press freedom in the United Arab Emirates (UAE) in 2007. While the constitution of the UAE provides for freedom of speech and of the press, in practice, the government uses its judicial and executive powers to restrict those rights. UAE Federal Law No. 15 of 1980 for Printed Matter and Publications regulates all aspects of the media and is considered one of the most restrictive press laws in the Arab world. The law authorizes the state to censor both domestic and foreign publications prior to distribution and prohibits criticism of the government, rulers and ruling families, and other friendly governments. Punishments under the 1980 law have included both fines and prison sentences. Journalists can also be prosecuted under the penal code. The National Media Council (NMC), which was created in 2006 and whose members are appointed by the president, is responsible for licensing all publications in addition to issuing press credentials to editors. According to the International Press Institute, editor Shima Kassiril Ganjadahran and journalist Mohsen Rashed of the *Khaleej Times* were each sentenced to two months in jail on libel charges on September 25, only to have their convictions overturned in an appeals court on November 8. Many speculated that the court's decision was in direct response to a decree issued by UAE vice president and prime minister Sheikh Mohammed bin Rashid al-Maktoum on September 26 that called for the decriminalization of press offenses.

Although there were no reported physical attacks against journalists in 2007, reporters in the UAE suffered multiple forms of intimidation and harassment. Journalists native to the UAE often face warnings and threats in response to pushing the limits of permissible media coverage, while noncitizen journalists, who account for more than 90 percent of those working in the UAE, face harsher measures, including termination and deportation. Extreme forms of self-censorship are widely practiced, particularly when covering issues such as local politics, culture, religion, or any other subject the government deems politically or culturally sensitive. The Dubai Media Free Zone (DMFZ), an area in which foreign media outlets produce print and broadcast material intended for audiences outside the country, is the only arena in which the press operates with relative freedom and is now home to important media outlets such as CNN, BBC, and Agence France-Presse. Broadcast media outlets based in the DMFZ are regulated by the Technology and Media Free Zone Authority. While such outlets generally focus solely on international issues and refrain from covering local concerns, they too are subject to the 1980 Law for Printed Matter and Publications and the penal code, and beginning in March, all free zones must now obtain approval from the NMC before licensing any print or broadcast activities. Under pressure from the Pakistani government, the Dubai government shut down two of Pakistan's most independent satellite channels that broadcast from Dubai in November when Pakistan declared a state of emergency. After much international criticism and protest, the two stations resumed broadcasting on November 30.

Media outlets in the UAE are either government owned or have close government affiliations. Privately owned newspapers such as the Arabic daily *Al-Khaleej* and its sister paper, the English-language *Gulf News*, are heavily influenced by the government. Most major papers receive government subsidies and rely predominantly on the official UAE news agencies for content. Almost all Arabic-language broadcast media that target the domestic audience are state owned and provide only the official view on local issues. In 2005, the government of Dubai formed the Arab Media Group to operate as its media arm. The group publishes two newspapers and controls two local radio stations. Even though it promises a freer and more professional perspective, the group still operates under the 1980 Law for Printed Matter and Publications. Satellite television was widespread and provided uncensored access to international broadcasts.

Over 38 percent of the UAE population used the internet in 2007. Nevertheless, the government censors web content, and the only internet service provider in the country is owned and operated by a government corporation, the Emirates Telecommunications Corporation (Etisalat). Both high-speed and dial-up users find themselves directed to a proxy server that maintains a list of banned websites and blocks material deemed inconsistent with the "religious, cultural, political, and moral values of the country." In January 2006, the government enacted a sweeping Information and Privacy Cybercrime Law that criminalizes use of the internet to commit a range of crimes—including violating political, social, and religious norms—and subjects offenders to prison terms and fines. On August 8, Muhammad Rashed Shehhi, owner of the website majan.net, was sentenced in the emirate of Ras Al Khaima to one year in prison and a fine of 70,000 dirhams (US$19,000) for an anonymous comment posted on his site that criticized a government official. Khaled Alasely, a writer for the website, was also arrested, and on September 12, both Alasely and Shehhi were sentenced to 5 months in prison; Shehhi's 5-month sentence was added to his original 12 months. On November 23, the 17-month jail sentence on Shehhi was overturned, but he continued to face multiple charges stemming from other cases brought against the website during the year. The charges against Alasely remained at year's end.

United Kingdom

Status: Free

LEGAL ENVIRONMENT: 6
POLITICAL ENVIRONMENT: 7
ECONOMIC ENVIRONMENT: 5
TOTAL SCORE: 18

Survey Edition	2003	2004	2005	2006	2007
Total Score, Status	18,F	19,F	18,F	19,F	19,F

With a history of aggressive reporting and an editorially independent public broadcasting system, the United Kingdom maintained its free press environment in 2007. The law provides for freedom of the press, and the government generally respects this right in practice. However, several laws are in place that weaken press freedom. Legislation from the 1980s dictates that journalists deemed to have information vital to a police investigation can be forced to give evidence at trial. In the aftermath of the July 2005 bombings on the London underground, the government passed the Prevention of Terrorism Act 2005 (in effect as of April 2006), which includes provisions for the criminalization of forms of free speech considered by the government to be "encouragements of terrorism," even without proof of a direct link to a terrorist act. A religious hatred bill introduced in 2006 criminalized incitement of religious hatred or violence. The Freedom of Information Act has drawn criticism in the past year for a number of broad exceptions and limitations on time-consuming and expensive requests. Libel laws traditionally have heavily favored the plaintiff in the United Kingdom, with the defendant bearing the burden of truth. However, a Law Lords ruling in October 2006 held that if journalists acted "fairly and responsibly," and the article was in the public interest, a newspaper could not be forced to pay damages for "relevant but defamatory allegations."

Several arrests in 2007 raised concern regarding freedom of information and expression in the United Kingdom. In May, civil servant David Keogh and parliamentary researcher Leo O'Conner were sentenced to six and three months in prison, respectively, under the Official Secrets Act for disclosing a confidential memo containing the minutes of a meeting between George Bush and Tony Blair. A gagging order prohibiting the press from reporting on the content of the memo was repealed in August. In July, three men were each jailed for six years for soliciting murder after they participated in 2006 demonstrations outside the Danish embassy in London. The three were caught on camera chanting statements such as "Seven/seven on its way!" and "Bomb, bomb the U.K.!" A fourth man was convicted of inciting religious hatred and jailed for four years. In November, a reporter for the *Milton Keynes Citizen* was charged with abetting misconduct of a public officer after she allegedly received leaked information. She faces possible jail time if convicted. She was detained overnight in May and had her home and office searched.

There were no physical attacks on the media during the year. However, journalists reporting on sensitive political issues regularly face intimidation in Northern Ireland. Continuing investigations into the 2001 murder of journalist Martin O'Hagan have produced few results, with eight separate suspects arrested and released owing to lack of evidence. It is believed that O'Hagan was killed for his investigations into cooperation among Northern Irish police, military intelligence, armed groups, and drug gangs. In September 2007, on the anniversary of O'Hagan's murder, the editor of the *Andersontown News* received a death threat from a loyalist paramilitary group.

British media are free and largely independent from government interference. The United Kingdom has a strong tradition of public broadcasting, and the British Broadcasting Corporation, although funded by the government, is editorially independent. Ownership of independent media outlets is concentrated in the hands of a few large companies, including those headed by Rupert Murdoch, and many of the private national papers remain aligned with political parties. Few commercial radio news stations exist—in fact, 8 of the 11 radio news stations are affiliated with the BBC—but several independent news television channels operate throughout the country, including ITV and British Sky Broadcasting. Authorities may monitor internet messages and e-mail without judicial permission in the name of national security and "well-being." However, surveillance must be approved by the secretary of state, and there are departments in place to handle public complaints of abuse as well as interception warrants. An estimated 62 percent of the population was able to access the internet without restriction in 2006.

United States

Status: Free

LEGAL ENVIRONMENT: 5
POLITICAL ENVIRONMENT: 8
ECONOMIC ENVIRONMENT: 4
TOTAL SCORE: 17

Survey Edition	2003	2004	2005	2006	2007
Total Score, Status	17,F	13,F	17,F	16,F	16,F

Press freedom is vibrant in the United States, with intense coverage devoted to scandals involving government figures, the more controversial dimensions of the "war on terror," and the Iraq war. While the United States has faced controversy over demands by prosecutors that journalists reveal confidential sources or provide access to research material in the course of criminal investigations, 2007 saw progress toward the enactment of "press shield" legislation that would give journalists qualified protection against prosecution in such cases, which continue to be brought against members of the news media. The year was also notable for the adoption of a law strengthening federal freedom of information policies. Despite these advancements, there was a slight increase in physical attacks on the press, including one murder and several cases of intimidation.

Press freedom enjoys a strong foundation of legal protection in the federal constitution, in state and federal laws, and in court decisions. The Supreme Court has repeatedly issued decisions that take an expansive view of freedom of expression and of the press. In particular, court decisions have given broad protection to the press from libel or defamation suits that involve commentary on public figures, although libel remains a criminal offense in a number of states. The Bush administration had come under criticism for what some said were restrictions on the release of documents under the Freedom of Information Act. At the end of 2007, however, Bush signed into law a revised Freedom of Information Act that will expedite the document request process and provide mediation in cases where a federal agency is reluctant to release material.

An exception to judicial support for press freedom involves demands by prosecutors for information gathered by reporters in the course of their journalistic investigations, including material from confidential sources. During 2007, Josh Wolf, a "freelance blogger," was released in April after having spent 226 days in federal custody for refusing to hand over videotapes he recorded of a July 2005 demonstration in San Francisco and later posted on his blog. His period of detention made Wolf the longest-imprisoned journalist in U.S. history. In another case, two *San Francisco Chronicle* reporters, Lance Williams and Mark Fainaru-Wada, were each sentenced to 18 months in prison by a judge in 2006 for refusing to reveal the identity of a confidential source in a case involving steroid use by prominent athletes. The case against the journalists was dismissed in March when the source, a defense attorney, acknowledged his role in leaking grand jury testimony to the journalists; neither journalist spent time in prison, and the attorney was subsequently sentenced to two and a half years in prison for giving these documents to the journalists. As a result of these and other cases, Congress took up a bill that would grant journalists a qualified right not to reveal news sources in federal cases. The law, called the Free Flow of Information Act, passed the House of Representatives by an overwhelming margin in October. The measure would allow journalists to withhold sources except in cases where the testimony would be critical to the outcome of a trial, in cases of potential terrorism, or where the testimony or information would fulfill a "compelling public interest." The measure excludes from coverage amateur bloggers and journalism students. The legislation was still pending at year's end. More than 30 states already have such "shield laws."

Federal authorities continued to detain two foreign journalists in 2007. Sami al-Haj, a Sudanese cameraman for Al-Jazeera, continued to be held without charge by U.S. forces at Guantanamo Bay. He was originally arrested in Pakistan in 2001 in the initial push for results in the "war on terror." However, al-Haj's lawyer contends that his detention is based on the U.S. government's belief that a link exists between Al-Jazeera and al-Qaeda and that no evidence has been produced against his client. American military authorities also continued to imprison Bilal Hussein, a Pulitzer Prize–winning Associated Press reporter who was arrested in Iraq in 2006 on security-related charges. Officials cited alleged involvement with Iraqi insurgents, although no details have been forthcoming.

In a notable change from 2006, there were several reported instances of violence, or threats of violence, to journalists during the year, most of which targeted reporters or editors of media with a predominantly minority or immigrant audience. In the most egregious case, Chauncey Bailey, editor of the *Oakland Post* in California, was murdered on the street in August, apparently in response to articles he had published that alleged the involvement of a local Muslim bakery in criminal activities. A bakery worker was arrested and confessed to the killing but later retracted his confession. A reporter for the *Miami Herald*, Leonard Pitts Jr., was the object of hate calls and intimidating e-mails for articles about race, crime, and media bias. In Los Angeles, three reporters, one of whom suffered a broken wrist from the incident, were physically assaulted by police while they were covering an immigration rights rally. The Los Angeles Police Department later issued an apology, and investigations are scheduled to be completed in 2008. In New York City, editors of two Urdu-language newspapers, the *Pakistan Post* and the *Urdu Times,* were threatened in May, and copies of the newspapers were seized from distribution points and destroyed by nonstate actors.

Media coverage of political affairs is aggressive and in some cases excessively partisan. The press itself is frequently a source of controversy, with conservatives and supporters of the Bush administration accusing the media of antiadministration bias and liberals accusing the press of timidity in coverage of administration misdeeds. The appearance of enhanced polarization is driven to some degree by the growing influence of blog sites, many of which are aggressively partisan. Nonetheless, most American newspapers make a serious effort to keep a wall of separation between news reporting, commentary, and editorials. Ironically, the trend toward fewer family-owned newspapers and more newspapers under corporate control has contributed to a less partisan, if blander, editorial tone.

In recent years, reporters from several prominent newspapers, including the *New York Times,* the *Washington Post,* and the *Wall Street Journal,* have published a series of investigative articles that have called into question various aspects of the Bush administration's "war on terror" and its conduct in the Iraq war. Articles have included details of prisoner abuse in Iraq, extraordinary renditions and "ghost prisoners," allegations of prisoner abuse in Guantanamo, the treatment of Iraq war vets and the army's Walter Reed Medical Center, warrantless surveillance of American citizens, and the American government's unauthorized access to the Society for Worldwide Interbank Financial Telecommunication in search of material that might involve money transfers by terrorists. Some of these journalistic pieces have drawn sharp criticism from President Bush and other administration officials, as well as threats to bring criminal charges against the *New York Times*. By year's end, no charges had been brought against any newspaper.

The media in the United States are overwhelmingly under private ownership. Nevertheless, National Public Radio (NPR), an entity funded partly by the government and partly by private contributions, enjoys a substantial audience. From time to time, conservatives have accused NPR of a liberal bias in its coverage, and Republicans have occasionally tried to reduce funding for the network or eliminate it altogether. More recently, controversy over NPR has abated and congressional funding has been approved by substantial margins. By law, radio and television airwaves are considered public property and are leased to private stations, which determine content. The Federal Communications Commission (FCC) is charged with administering licenses and reviewing content to ensure that it complies with federal limits on indecent or offensive material. On several occasions, the FCC has issued fines against radio and television outlets for what the agency deemed acts of indecency.

The United States is home to more than 1,400 daily newspapers geared primarily toward local readerships. The number of dailies has declined gradually over the past two decades, and many of the country's largest and most prestigious newspapers have encountered financial difficulties in recent years, owing mainly to competition from the internet. Many newspapers have instituted staff reductions, and most have cut back on their coverage of national and international news (particularly through closures of foreign news bureaus) in favor of a more local focus. Many predict a major transformation of the newspaper business in coming years, with some newspapers closing altogether and others focused increasingly on bolstering their electronic editions. However, the primary form of news dissemination in the country is through television news networks like CNN, Fox News, and CBS, which maintain a consistent audience. Media concentration is an ongoing concern in the United States. This problem has intensified in recent years following the purchase of media entities, especially television networks, by large corporations with no previous experience in journalism. The FCC regularly considers policies that would lift restrictions on the monopolization of national or local media markets by a limited number of entities, with a particular focus on policies that limit a single corporation's ownership of both television stations and newspapers in a single local market. In a 2007 ruling, the FCC voted by a narrow margin to lift certain restrictions on television-newspaper cross-ownership in the 20 largest media markets. The action was sharply criticized by some press freedom advocates, and efforts were launched in Congress to reverse the decision.

At the same time, diversity of the U.S. media has expanded with the mushrooming of cable television and the internet. Nearly 72 percent of Americans are internet users, placing the country ninth in the world in an assessment of internet penetration. The number and influence of internet sites and blogs have expanded greatly in recent years, and blogs have proven to be an important source of information in certain political controversies. Blogs devoted to public policy questions often lean to the highly partisan, and though their proliferation adds to the richness of press diversity, it also contributes to ideological polarization.

Uruguay

Status: Free

LEGAL ENVIRONMENT: 10
POLITICAL ENVIRONMENT: 10
ECONOMIC ENVIRONMENT: 10
TOTAL SCORE: 30

Survey Edition	2003	2004	2005	2006	2007
Total Score, Status	30,F	26,F	29,F	28,F	30,F

Uruguay's media environment remained relatively free in comparison with those of other countries in the region. While the government took positive steps to legalize community broadcasting, the use of defamation laws to prosecute and intimidate journalists continued to hinder press freedom in 2007. The constitution provides for freedom of speech and of the press, and the government generally respects these rights. Access to public information remains a problem, however. In September, the Uruguayan Press Association (APU) brought a denunciation against the state to the Inter-American Commission on Human Rights. The complaint was triggered by the rejection of a journalist's request for information to the city of San Jose concerning statements made by the general accountant regarding the city's budget. Other cases that exemplified obstacles in accessing public information included a judge's decision to reject a petition filed by journalists to attend a legal hearing on the situation of street children and the rejection of the APU's request to the National Telecommunications Agency for information on official advertising. However, on a positive note, a bill to legalize community media, originally drafted with the help of press associations and civil society groups, was passed into law in December. The law established that one-third of available broadcasting frequencies will be granted through "open, transparent, and public" competition to community media, mainly to small radio stations, of which there are an estimated 200 in the country.

Defamation laws also create persistent troubles for journalists. In April, the Supreme Court upheld the 2006 criminal libel conviction of journalist Gustavo Escanlar Patrone of Canal 10 television, which carried a three-month prison sentence for "insulting" a media proprietor during his talk show. In a separate case, Maria Celeste Alvarez, niece of former military president Gregorio Alvarez, brought a lawsuit against Canal 5 journalist Ana Maria Mizrahi for statements made by Jose Luis Rodriguez, whom Mizrahi interviewed in May. Rodriguez, a former member of Tupamaros (the leading guerrilla movement in the 1970s), stated during the interview that Maria Celeste Alvarez's father (brother of Gregorio Alvarez) assassinated one of his comrades in prison. Journalists are not legally responsible for declarations made by third parties. In addition, the defamation case that condemned journalist Carlos Dogliani to five months in prison in 2006 continued to attract a great deal of debate and concern as the case was presented to the Inter-American Commission on Human Rights in February 2007. The APU and the Uruguayan Institute for Legal and Social Studies submitted a draft law to Congress in October that would eliminate desacato offenses (contempt of a public official) and amend defamation definitions; at year's end, the bill was under review by the executive branch.

Uruguayan journalists expressed concerns over several incidences of censorship and interference in the work of the media by political and economic actors. Journalists accused the leading daily, *El Pais*, of censoring an investigative report on the company that controls the television rights for soccer games. They also denounced pressures placed on a journalist by the local mayor and the owner of a radio station in reaction to derogatory comments made about the mayor by a city council member whom the journalist had interviewed. Another journalist received death threats for reporting on untruthful advertising for a chat/electronic mail service. Government officials such as Vice President Rodolfo Nin Novoa and the mayor of Rio Negro were critical of the media and launched numerous verbal assaults against journalists and the press.

While Uruguay has a diverse media environment, with more than 100 privately owned papers, media ownership is relatively concentrated. There are over 100 private radio stations and at least 20 television stations, as well as 1 state-owned radio station and 1 television station that are regulated by the official broadcasting service, SODRE. Discretionary allocation of official advertising discourages news organizations from producing reports critical of the national and state governments. There were no government restrictions on the internet, which was accessed by about 32 percent of the population in 2007.

Uzbekistan

Status: Not Free

LEGAL ENVIRONMENT: 29
POLITICAL ENVIRONMENT: 38
ECONOMIC ENVIRONMENT: 25

TOTAL SCORE: 92

Survey Edition	2003	2004	2005	2006	2007
Total Score, Status	86,NF	84,NF	85,NF	90,NF	91,NF

The aftermath of government crackdowns over the last two years left an already barren media landscape even more desolate in 2007. Despite nominal constitutional guarantees of freedom of the press and restrictions on prepublication censorship, Uzbek authorities showed no respect for these rights, and criticism of the president is a crime punishable by up to five years in prison. Libel is a criminal offense, but very few journalists have been prosecuted under this law, as most independent reporters have either fled or censored themselves. After a new media resolution tightened controls in 2006, President Islam Karimov approved new legislation in January 2007 that holds the media accountable for "objectivity" and defines websites as media outlets, thereby requiring them to register annually with the Ministry of Information and to submit regular content reports to the authorities.

In 2007, state-controlled Uzbek media mounted a coordinated smear campaign against Alisher Saipov, an ethnic Uzbek and Kyrgyz citizen in southern Kyrgyzstan who ran the Uzbek-language newspaper *Siosat*, which was critical of President Karimov. The campaign described Saipov as a Western stooge and traitor. Shortly thereafter, Saipov was shot dead in Kyrgyzstan in October, although no direct evidence has emerged to support the widely held belief that Uzbek authorities were involved in the killing. In a separate care, Umida Niyazova, a journalist with the Central Asian news website Oasis and a stringer for a number of international organizations like Internews and Human Rights Watch, was arrested in January and charged with transporting contraband. She was convicted in May, sentenced to a seven-year prison term, and subsequently freed, but only after she was forced to sign a confession blaming international organizations for her plight. The incident took on a dark light in view of past evidence of coerced confessions in the Uzbek justice system. Meanwhile, Dzhamshid Karimov, an independent journalist and the president's nephew, was one of five journalists who remained in prison in 2007. Karimov was forcibly hospitalized in a psychiatric ward in September 2006 and remains there despite reports of his deteriorating health.

International journalists were also subject to government pressure. In fact, Uzbek authorities have undertaken a concerted campaign against foreign-funded media following the outbreak of domestic unrest in 2005, and local reporters are formally forbidden from working for international outlets. In 2007, the British Broadcasting Corporation, Radio Free Europe/Radio Liberty, and Voice of America remained unable to broadcast from within Uzbekistan. Stringers for Deutsche Welle, one of the last remaining international news outlets operating within the country, were subject to harassment. Correspondent Natalya Bushuyeva fled the country after authorities charged her with tax evasion and working with foreign media outlets—charges that could have led to a three-year prison sentence. Three other Deutsche Welle stringers were also charged with tax evasion and working without accreditation. Although these charges were later dropped, it had the effect of silencing a number of the reporters. In October, Sid Yanyshev, a reporter for the U.K.-based Institute for War and Peace Reporting, was attacked by unidentified individuals.

The government in 2007 continued to control most national dailies and television stations, as well as the publishing houses and printing presses that are responsible for the majority of the country's print media. A few private printing presses were in operation printing independent publications, but the circulation of these was severely limited. Virtually all media were linked either directly or indirectly to the state and were manipulated by the government to present a carefully constructed picture of an ideal reality, with occasional forays into limited criticism. While it is relatively straightforward to enter the media business, as taxes and licensing fees are not exorbitant, outlets with 30 percent or more foreign ownership are prohibited from operating at all, and the requirement to pay reregistration fees each year is a constant disincentive. The closure in July of *Odam Orasida*, an Islamic-oriented weekly in the capital city of Tashkent, may have been linked to its willingness to write about such taboo issues as prostitution and homosexuality; however, other reports suggested that authorities decided to close it when its circulation rose to 24,000 and its popularity began to outpace that of staid publications.

The Uzbek authorities also appeared to step up their efforts to crack down on freedom of speech online in 2007. While exiled Uzbek journalists were able to operate news sites from abroad with a focus on human rights issues, reports indicated an increase in government efforts to block opposition and independent websites in the lead-up to the December presidential election that saw President Karimov reelected easily to a constitutionally dubious third term. Blocking efforts extended beyond websites with materials critical of the government to tools intended to retain the user's privacy online, including proxies and anonymizers, which further hampered access to outside points of view. Although 6 percent of the Uzbek population is estimated to be online (a relatively high percentage by regional standards), many users access the internet in institutional settings, where state controls and the possibility of surveillance cripple the ability to obtain sorely needed independent perspectives on events inside the country.

Vanuatu

LEGAL ENVIRONMENT: 6
POLITICAL ENVIRONMENT: 8
ECONOMIC ENVIRONMENT: 9

Status: Free

TOTAL SCORE: 23

Survey Edition	2003	2004	2005	2006	2007
Total Score, Status	21,F	23,F	24,F	25,F	24,F

Vanuatu continues to have a small but vibrant press. Freedom of expression is protected under the constitution, and this right is generally respected in practice. In 2007, the government agreed to join Transparency International Vanuatu and the Media Association of Vanuatu in drafting the country's first freedom of information bill. The draft was pending at year's end. Although officials do not actively interfere with media coverage, journalists have been censored or intimidated on occasion. There are private print media, but the state owns the only radio and television stations. Radio broadcasts have increased since the installation of new transmitters at the beginning of 2006. The internet is run by the Vanuatu Broadcasting and Television Corporation and is not restricted by the government, but it is accessed by only 3.4 percent of the population.

LEGAL ENVIRONMENT: 26
POLITICAL ENVIRONMENT: 29

Venezuela

ECONOMIC ENVIRONMENT: 19

Status: Not Free

TOTAL SCORE: 74

Survey Edition	2003	2004	2005	2006	2007
Total Score, Status	68,NF	68,NF	72,NF	72,NF	74,NF

A hostile political atmosphere over the past several years under the government of President Hugo Chavez has fostered a steady decline in press freedom that continued in 2007. The major event of the year was the government's refusal to renew the broadcast license of the popular opposition-aligned television station Radio Caracas Television (RCTV). In general, state initiatives have gradually eroded the influence of private media and pro-opposition outlets. Among other actions, the government has enacted legislation prohibiting the broadcast of certain material, intimidated and denied access to private media, and harassed journalists and media outlets that are critical of the government.

The legal environment for the press remains poor. While the law guarantees freedom of speech and of the press, the Law of Social Responsibility in Radio and Television, signed in December 2004, contains vaguely worded restrictions that can be used to severely limit freedom of expression. For example, the law forbids graphic depictions of violence between 5:00 a.m. and 11:00 p.m. on both television and radio. In March 2005, the penal code was revised to make insulting the president a crime punishable by six to 30 months in prison. Furthermore, comments that could "expose another person to contempt or public hatred" constitute a crime punishable by one to three years in prison as well as a severe fine. Inaccurate reporting that "disturbs the public peace" carries a prison sentence of two to five years. Dozens of legal proceedings against media workers and outlets remained open in 2007, and there were several convictions, including of the opposition daily *Tal Cual,* which was fined some $75,000 for seemingly innocuous comments in a satirical piece that mentioned Chavez's daughter. However, in December, Venezuelans rejected by a narrow margin a package of constitutional amendments that would have given the president greater power to declare states of emergency and eliminated the requirement that freedom of information be maintained during these periods. Despite weeks of student-led protests and denunciations by numerous human rights and media groups, RCTV was forced off the air on May 27. Media watchdogs questioned the decision's motivation, legality, and lack of transparency. In a survey by regional watchdog Instituto de Prensa y Sociedad (IPYS), 30 percent of journalists declared that the station's closure would make them think twice about publishing certain information.

Direct assaults on the media continued to occur regularly in 2007. Political polarization remained high, and numerous journalists were injured by either supporters or opponents of the government during street protests, which peaked during the periods preceding the May RCTV closure and the December constitutional referendum vote. One of the only remaining local opposition television stations, Globovision, remained a primary target for physical aggression, lawsuits, the denial of access to information, verbal attacks, and threats to cancel its license. A survey by IPYS revealed that 56 percent of journalists had suffered some sort of verbal or physical threat or attack during the previous year. The state does little to nothing to discourage such harassment. The same survey noted that only 9 percent of reporters were inclined to formally complain about threats, attacks, and harassment. In May, prominent government ally Eva Golinger unveiled a list of 33 journalists who had participated in cultural exchange programs financed by the U.S. State Department. Along with some congressional allies, she called for investigations into whether the reporters were engaged in espionage. However, even some government supporters, notably National Assembly president Desiree Santos and former vice president Jose Vicente Rangel, acknowledged that the accusations were extreme. In general, independent journalists complained that a lack of access impeded their reporting; they were often denied entry to military ceremonies and other official events that state media representatives were allowed to attend.

In addition to fostering the proliferation of community-based media outlets, the government controls five national television stations, a national radio network, and a wire service, all of which have benefited from budget increases. Government-run stations operate alongside a shrinking number of private television and radio stations. The country's leading newspapers are privately owned and most identify with the opposition, but they are subject to threats and violence by the government and its supporters, sometimes leading to self-censorship. Local and regional media are particularly dependent on government advertising revenue, leaving them vulnerable to economic retaliation for criticism. According to responses to the IPYS study, fear of offending the government and a reluctance to antagonize ad buyers were the two primary reasons for a high level of editorial-directed self-censorship. The president has a weekly television show and exercises his power to preempt regular programming to ensure extensive coverage of government *cadenas* (announcements) in private media. During the run-up to the constitutional referendum, the local Media Monitoring Group analyzed time spent by media in discussing the two alternatives that either rejected or supported the referendum and found that while some private stations were quite lopsided against the referendum, state outlets were even more dramatically tilted in favor. There are no government restrictions on the internet, which was used by about 20 percent of the population in 2007.

Vietnam

LEGAL ENVIRONMENT: 27
POLITICAL ENVIRONMENT: 33
ECONOMIC ENVIRONMENT: 22

Status: Not Free

TOTAL SCORE: 82

Survey Edition	2003	2004	2005	2006	2007
Total Score, Status	82,NF	82,NF	82,NF	79,NF	77,NF

Following a relative easing of restrictions on the press in 2006 as Vietnam prepared for accession to the World Trade Organization, Human Rights Watch in 2007 reported "one of the worst crackdowns on peaceful dissent in 20 years." Over a dozen journalists and activists who had pushed for a more open media or had posted online essays calling for democratic reform were sentenced to long prison terms or house arrest. Nevertheless, several media outlets continued to press the limits of permissible coverage, and internet access increased.

Although the 1992 constitution recognizes the rights to freedom of opinion, of expression, and of association for all citizens, the propaganda and training departments of the ruling Communist Party of Vietnam (CPV) control all media and set press guidelines. In addition, a 1999 law requires journalists to pay damages to individuals or groups found to have been harmed by press articles, even if they are true. Reporting considered to be against the national interest can bring charges under the criminal code and antidefamation provisions. During 2007, several writers imprisoned for online postings were sentenced under the penal code's Article 88, which covers antigovernment propaganda. In July 2006, in response to increasingly vibrant reporting by both the traditional and internet-based news media, the government had issued a decree that defined over 2,000 additional violations of the law in the areas of culture and information and imposed hefty fines for offenders, with a particular focus on protecting "national security."

The CPV generally views the media as a tool for the dissemination of party and state policy. Although journalists cannot cover sensitive political or economic matters or openly question the CPV's single-party rule without fear of reprisal, they are more often allowed to report on crime and official corruption, and such reports have become increasingly common. Nevertheless, several media outlets suffered retribution for testing the limits of permissible coverage in 2007. According to the U.S. State Department, two deputy chief editors of the *Tuoi Tre* daily were removed from their posts over a series of 2006 articles on corruption. In addition, the popular online news outlet *VietnamNet* was fined US$2,000 after publishing an editorial about disputed islands in the South China Sea despite a government order to remain silent on the issue. As part of a broad crackdown on those calling for democratic reforms, staff members of several underground publications were imprisoned during the year. Father Nguyen Van Ly, a Catholic priest and editor of *Tu Do Ngon Luan*, which launched in April 2006, was sentenced in March to eight years in prison. Six other individuals involved in the publication were also sentenced to prison or placed under house arrest during the year. In April, police detained journalist and writer Tran Khai Thanh Thuy, who serves on the editorial board of the dissident newsletter *To Quoc*; she remained in custody at year's end. In 2007, the government also cracked down on Vietnam's fledgling community of online prodemocracy writers, sentencing six cyberdissidents to prison terms within one week in May; one of them was Nguyen Van Dai, a prominent human rights lawyer, who was sentenced to five years in prison as a result of essays published on the internet, including on the BBC's Vietnamese-language website. In a more positive development, cyberdissident Nguyen Vu Binh was granted an early release by the president in June, apparently because of bad health. Nguyen had served nearly five years of a seven-year sentence for posting articles about democracy on the internet and maintaining e-mail contact with prodemocracy groups abroad. Though restrictions on the hiring of local journalists by foreign media outlets have reportedly eased somewhat, foreign reporters continue to be monitored closely, and their movements within the country are restricted. In March, the authorities refused to renew the visa of BBC correspondent Bill Hayton, forcing him to leave the country.

There is only one national television station in the country, state-owned Vietnam Television, although cable does carry some foreign channels. Radio is controlled by the government-run Voice of Vietnam or other state entities.

While all print media outlets are owned by or under the effective control of the CPV, government organs, or the army, several newspapers—including *Thanh Nien, Nguoi Lao Dong,* and *Tuoi Tre* (owned by the Youth Union under the CPV)—have attempted to become financially sustainable and to stop relying on state subsidies. Several underground publications have been launched in recent years, including *Tu Do Ngon Luan, To Quoc,* and *Tu Do Dan Chu;* they reportedly continue to circulate despite recent arrests of staff members. Foreign periodicals, although widely available, are sometimes censored, and the broadcasts of stations such as Radio Free Asia are periodically jammed.

Access to satellite television broadcasts and the internet is growing, especially in urban areas. More than 21 percent of Vietnamese reportedly have internet access. The online news site VietnamNet publishes in Vietnamese and English, while vietnamjournalism.com, a blog run by a local journalist, discusses professional and ethical issues. Website operators continue to use internet service providers (ISPs) that are either publicly or semipublicly owned, like Vietnam Data Communications, which is controlled by the Ministry of Post and Telecommunications and caters to nearly a third of all internet users. ISPs are required by law to block access to websites that the government considers politically unacceptable, though many foreign news sites remain accessible. Cybercafés are required by law to register the personal information and record the sites visited by users. In September, the government shut down *Intellasia,* an online news and investment site, blocking access from inside the country and causing the server to crash. Following a raid on the offices and repeated threats from the authorities, *Intellasia's* Australian owner and publisher, Peter Leech, fled the country. The site was operating from Australia at year's end.

Yemen

Status: Not Free

LEGAL ENVIRONMENT: 26
POLITICAL ENVIRONMENT: 31
ECONOMIC ENVIRONMENT: 21
TOTAL SCORE: 78

Survey Edition	2003	2004	2005	2006	2007
Total Score, Status	69,NF	67,NF	76,NF	81,NF	80,NF

While the rights to freedom of expression and a free press are guaranteed under Article 41 of the constitution, the government continues to use the restrictive 1990 Press and Publications Law to prosecute journalists and violate the rights of the media. Steps initiated in 2004 to enact a revised Press and Publications Law have yet to bear fruit. Article 103 of the 1990 law prohibits journalists from criticizing the head of state or publishing material that undermines public morality, prejudices the dignity of individuals by smears and defamation, or distorts the image of the Yemeni, Arab, or Islamic heritage. Penalties for such press violations can range from fines to prison sentences of up to one year. Journalists can also be prosecuted under the penal code for such crimes as apostasy, which may carry the death penalty. The Press and Publications Prosecution Office normally handles cases involving press violations. However, three journalists were referred to the prosecutor's office specializing in terrorism and national security cases in July 2007 after the Ministry of Defense filed a complaint against their newspaper, the independent *Al-Shara'a*, for a series of articles on the conflict in the northern province of Sa'ada. Armed confrontations between the government and followers of the assassinated Zaidi cleric Hussein Badreddin al-Houthi have persisted there for three years. The charges against the journalists included harming national security and stability, undermining the morale of the army, and publishing military secrets. If convicted, the defendants could face the death penalty. On July 30, the offices of *Al-Shara'a* were attacked by armed men who threatened to kill the owners and editors, Nabil Subaie and Nayef Hassan.

Terrorism charges were also brought against Abdel Karim al-Khaiwani, editor of the opposition news website *Al-Shoura*, after his home was raided on June 20. Al-Khaiwani was accused of conspiring with antigovernment rebels and belonging to a terrorist cell, based on material confiscated from his home that included photographs of the conflict area in Sa'ada. A media blackout was imposed in Sa'ada in January, and journalists were forbidden from entering the area. After being released on bail in July, al-Khaiwani was abducted and physically assaulted on August 27 by a group of men who threatened to break or sever his hand to keep him from continuing to criticize the president. At year's end, al-Khaiwani was still awaiting trial on terrorism charges.

Local press freedom group Women Journalists Without Chains reported 113 violations against the press in 2007, close to double the number recorded for 2006. Throughout the year, journalists were fined, arrested, imprisoned, abducted, threatened, subjected to home and office raids, and prevented from reporting on a spectrum of issues and events. A number of journalists were physically assaulted by security forces while covering the weekly peaceful sit-ins organized by the Civil Society Coalition in the capital's Freedom Square. These demonstrations, which started in June, protested press freedom violations such as the blocking of numerous websites, the banning of mobile telephone news services, and the lack of the right to operate private media. Foreign correspondents for satellite television stations such as the Dubai-based Al-Arabiya also faced harassment and were detained by government officials while trying to cover local demonstrations. The government seems to support an environment of complete impunity for crimes against the press, failing to conduct serious investigations or even denounce attacks. There were no further developments in the investigation of the 2006 murder of *Al-Nahar* journalist Abed al-Osaily, who had criticized the government's handling of a local water project.

Fear and intimidation served to perpetuate the widespread practice of self-censorship among journalists and media owners. Investigative journalism is hampered by potential penalties under the Press and Publications Law and the obstacles posed by media outlets' low budgets, small staffs, and poor institutional infrastructure. Nevertheless, Yemen's print media continued to offer relatively diverse coverage of local and international news in 2007. In the last few years, criticism of the government and reporting on issues that were previously considered taboo have increased. However, the government has responded with a media crackdown. Newspapers may be confiscated and withheld from distribution owing to content considered potentially damaging to national security or in violation of the press laws, though articles are not reviewed by a state censorship board prior to publication. Supporting institutions for journalists' rights include the Yemeni Journalists Syndicate and a number of nongovernmental organizations whose mandates focus specifically on freedom of the press.

Three official newspapers and 2 independent papers circulate daily, in addition to an estimated 50 independent and 30 party-affiliated papers that are published less frequently. While a number of licenses for new print media were issued during the year, over 60 requests have been denied since 2006. Newspaper licenses must be renewed every year and may be revoked at any time. Media revenue based on sales or subscriptions is minimal given the country's economic situation; almost half of Yemenis live beneath the poverty line, and about two-thirds live in rural or remote areas. Low salaries leave many journalists susceptible to bribes. The government maintained its complete monopoly on broadcast media in 2007, with two television channels and two national and four regional radio channels. With a national illiteracy rate of roughly 50 percent, many Yemenis relied on state-run television and radio programs for news. For those who can afford it, satellite television provides access to international news and entertainment programs. While only 1.2 percent of the population used the internet in

2007 given economic obstacles, the number of users grew by some 1,700 percent between 2000 and 2007. The Ministry of Telecommunications filters internet content and censors websites, particularly during political events such as the 2006 elections. The state owns the country's two internet service providers, TeleYemen and YemenNet. Prohibitions on what can be published online include material deemed obscene or subversive on either political or religious grounds. Although a number of opposition political websites and independent news sites were blocked during the year, the censoring of web content was not as widespread as in some neighboring Arab countries.

Zambia

LEGAL ENVIRONMENT: 20
POLITICAL ENVIRONMENT: 24
ECONOMIC ENVIRONMENT: 20

Status: Not Free

TOTAL SCORE: 64

Survey Edition	2003	2004	2005	2006	2007
Total Score, Status	63,NF	63,NF	65,NF	64,NF	64,NF

Freedom of speech is constitutionally guaranteed in Zambia, but the provisions can be broadly interpreted, enabling the government to restrict many rights in practice. The Public Order Act, among other statutes, has at times been used to harass journalists. The Independent Broadcasting Authority (IBA) and Zambia National Broadcasting Corporation (ZNBC) Acts which together set up independent boards for the regulatory body and the national broadcaster, have not yet been fully implemented despite being passed in December 2003. Until early 2007, there was a major controversy over the appointment of the ZNBC board of directors under the new legal framework. While media institutions interpreted the new law to mean that the minister of information had no say over the names presented to him, the government took the opposite view. In March 2007, the Supreme Court overturned an earlier judgment by the high court that had confirmed the media institutions' interpretation. As a result of the Supreme Court ruling, it is now clear that the government has the final say in appointments to the board of directors. Even so, in spite of promises from the government that the IBA board would be appointed in August 2007, no appointments have yet been made. The draft freedom of information bill has also yet to be passed, and many officials are noticeably unwilling to talk to journalists. Libel can be prosecuted in either a civil or a criminal court, and defamation of the president is explicitly a criminal offense. Yet the burden of proof rests with the plaintiff, and it is rare that a journalist receives jail time as a result of a libelous article. Journalists are not required to obtain a license in order to report, although it is recommended by the Ministry of Information.

Government officials continued to harass journalists in 2007. On May 17, Information and Broadcasting Services Minister Mike Mlongoti threatened to revoke an operating license for Petauke Explorers, a local commercial radio station, for featuring the president of one of the leading political parties in an on-air paid-for interview. Separately in July, police in the capital city of Lusaka prevented Q-FM, a private radio station, from mounting broadcasting equipment that would enable it to cover live a demonstration outside the gates of parliament. Police said that the permit issued to the conveners of the demonstration did not include live coverage of the event. The government has attempted to limit live Q-FM broadcasts in the past, particularly in the period leading up to the 2006 general election. In November, Radio Lyambai was banned from broadcasting live call-in shows because the station was "becoming a platform for confrontation, controversies, and a channel of insults and misinformation." Unlike in previous years, in 2007, the government did not arrest individual journalists, but there was one reported incident of members of the Anticorruption Commission searching the premises of a local radio station and confining station staff during the search.

The government controls two widely circulated newspapers, the *Times of Zambia* and *Zambia Daily*, and the state-owned, progovernment Zambia National Broadcasting Corporation dominates the broadcast media. Owing to prepublication review at government-controlled newspapers, journalists at those outlets commonly practice self-censorship. In fact, in September, the information minister threatened journalists at a number of state-owned outlets with losing their jobs if they criticized him or the government. Opposition political parties and nongovernmental organizations complained of inadequate access to mass media resources, and the process by which these outlets must obtain a license is cumbersome and expensive. However, a group of independent newspapers widely criticizes the government, and an independent radio station, Radio Phoenix, presents nongovernmental views, though few others report on politics. The available privately owned television stations are not locally owned and relay content primarily from foreign networks. International outlets were able to operate freely throughout the country. The government does not restrict internet access, though its use is hindered by lack of widespread access—only 4.3 percent of the population was online in 2007.

Zimbabwe

Status: Not Free

LEGAL ENVIRONMENT: 29
POLITICAL ENVIRONMENT: 33
ECONOMIC ENVIRONMENT: 27
TOTAL SCORE: 89

Survey Edition	2003	2004	2005	2006	2007
Total Score, Status	88,NF	89,NF	89,NF	90,NF	89,NF

Press freedom in Zimbabwe remained extremely restricted, as President Robert Mugabe's government continued to exert tight control over domestic media and attempted to block the efforts of foreign outlets to circulate unfiltered news within the country. Despite constitutional provisions for freedom of expression, officials display an openly hostile attitude toward media freedom, and a draconian legal framework continues to effectively inhibit the activities of journalists and media outlets. The 2002 Access to Information and Protection of Privacy Act (AIPPA) requires all journalists and media companies to register with the government-controlled Media and Information Commission (MIC) and gives the information minister sweeping powers to decide who is able to work as a journalist. A number of private newspapers have been denied licenses since the AIPPA came into force, most notoriously the *Daily News*, Zimbabwe's only independent daily, which was shuttered in 2003. Repeated constitutional challenges to the AIPPA by the Associated Newspapers of Zimbabwe (ANZ), publisher of the *Daily News*, have proven unsuccessful. Although the MIC was restructured in October, its chairperson, Dr. Tafataona Mahoso, who had been found in previous court rulings to be biased against the ANZ, was retained, casting doubts on the commission's ability to adjudicate fairly on the case.

Authorities continue to employ a range of restrictive legislation—including the Official Secrets Act, the AIPPA, the Public Order and Security Act (POSA), and criminal defamation laws—to harass and charge journalists. Section 15 of the POSA and Section 80 of the AIPPA criminalize the publication of "inaccurate" information, and both laws have been used to intimidate, arrest, and prosecute reporters. The 2005 Criminal Law (Codification and Reform Bill) increased prison sentences for similar violations to a maximum of 20 years, and a February 2006 amendment tightened the "presidential insult" and "communication of falsehoods" provisions of the POSA. Both local and foreign journalists are regularly arrested on charges of practicing journalism without a license. Cases in 2007 include those of Bright Chivburi, editor of the Zimbabwe Congress of Trade Unions magazine, the *Worker*, who was charged in Plumtree in March, as well as Peter Moyo of South Africa's private E.TV station and several other local journalists, who were arrested in Mutare in February while covering a story on illegal mining activities, and *Time* correspondent Alex Perry, arrested in March for covering a similar story. However, in most cases, such charges are often dismissed by the courts.

Professional and media monitoring organizations—such as the Zimbabwe Union of Journalists, the Media Monitoring Project of Zimbabwe, and the local chapter of the Media Institute of Southern Africa (MISA)–Zimbabwe—are subjected to official harassment. These three groups were jointly involved in advocating for the introduction of an independent media council, intended to replace the MIC as part of a self-regulatory system. In December, the government proposed amendments to the AIPPA and POSA, but these were dismissed by MISA as cosmetic changes that would not radically improve the legal environment for media freedom.

Journalists are routinely subjected to verbal intimidation, physical attacks, arrest and detention, and financial pressure at the hands of the police, government officials, and supporters of the ruling party. Instances of arbitrary arrest and detention occur primarily when reporters are trying to cover politically charged stories, and perpetrators are rarely (if ever) punished, leading to a culture of impunity throughout the country. In early 2007, a particularly bad wave of repression occurred in the context of the government's crackdown on the opposition Movement for Democratic Change (MDC) party. Several journalists were arrested and mistreated in detention, including Gift Phiri, a reporter for the *Zimbabwean*. In April, a former cameraman for state television, Edward Chikomba, was abducted, beaten, and murdered, allegedly for leaking footage to foreign news outlets of the beating of MDC leader Morgan Tsvangirai. Watchdog groups raised concerns following the leaking in September of a purported government "blacklist" of 27 journalists who had been targeted for surveillance and possible arrest; those named included Phiri and others who had already been subjected to threats, such as Abel Mutsakani, a former *Daily News* editor and founder of ZimOnline, who survived an assassination attempt in South Africa in July, as well as Bill Saidi, acting editor of the *Standard*, who received an envelope in January containing a bullet and a threatening message following the publication of several articles on desertions and lack of funding within the army.

Foreign journalists are not allowed to reside full-time in the country and are regularly denied visas to file stories from Zimbabwe. Locally based correspondents for foreign publications, particularly those whose reporting has portrayed the regime in an unfavorable light, have been refused accreditation or threatened with lawsuits and deportation. In March, Jan Raath and Peta Thornycroft, prominent correspondents for the United Kingdom's *Times* and *Daily Telegraph*, were accused of reporting "fabricated stories" and were threatened with unspecified reprisals in a government press release, according to the Committee to Protect Journalists (CPJ). Publisher Trevor Ncube, who owns several newspapers in both Zimbabwe and South Africa, has faced harassment as authorities have repeatedly attempted to strip him of his citizenship and confiscate his passport; the Central Intelligence Office (CIO) had previously confiscated his passport in 2005, allegedly because his father was Zambian and not Zimbabwean. During the past several years, dozens of Zimbabwean journalists have fled the country, and according to a report by CPJ, Zimbabwe has the highest number of exiled journalists in the world, with more than 90 currently living outside the country, predominantly in South Africa and the United Kingdom.

The government, through the Mass Media Trust holding company, controls several major daily newspapers, including the *Chronicle* and the *Herald*; coverage in these news outlets consists of favorable portrayals of Mugabe and the ruling party and attacks on perceived critics of the regime. Several independent weeklies such as the *Standard* and the *Zimbabwe Independent* continue to publish, although many journalists practice extensive self-censorship. Newspapers must register with the MIC, which regularly shutters outlets for critical reporting. In March, Sunsley Chamunorwa, editor of the *Financial Gazette*, was dismissed from his job after he reportedly refused to bow to pressure from the CIO regarding the paper's editorial line and published a story concerning the business dealings of a powerful official. The privately owned *Daily Mirror*, which is controlled outright by the CIO, was forced to stop publishing during the year owing to lack of funds. Some foreign newspapers, mostly from South Africa, are available, although the authorities have threatened to restrict their importation. In October 2006, police raided the Harare distribution offices of the *Zimbabwean*, an independent weekly printed in South Africa, and confiscated documents. In general, newspapers have poor distribution networks outside the urban areas and have become relatively expensive, placing them beyond the reach of most Zimbabweans. Printing expenses have increased dramatically because of soaring prices for newsprint and paper, causing many outlets to restrict their print runs. According to MISA's African Media Barometer, state-run companies do not advertise in private papers, and state-run media outlets do not accept advertising from companies known to be aligned with the opposition. Owing to poor economic conditions and salaries that do not keep pace with inflation, corruption and cash incentives for coverage have become rampant.

The state-controlled Zimbabwe Broadcasting Corporation runs all broadcast media, which are subject to overt political interference and censorship. The Broadcasting Services Act bans foreign funding and investment in this capital-intensive sector, making it very difficult for private players to enter the market. Additionally, it provides for a monopoly by the state-owned Transmedia Company regarding the ownership of frequency transmitters, even though Transmedia is currently not able to provide adequate service even to existing broadcast outlets. Broadcasting licenses have been consistently denied to independently owned radio stations, despite calls by a parliamentary committee for the broadcast sector to be opened up. Access to broadcast media in rural areas is hampered by deteriorating equipment and a lack of transmission sites; according to MISA, only 30 percent of the country receives radio and television coverage from the state-controlled broadcaster, although the government has reached an agreement with China to help upgrade this infrastructure. Meanwhile, also using Chinese technology, authorities began jamming the signals of the increasingly popular foreign-based radio stations that broadcast into Zimbabwe in 2005, including those of SW Radio Africa, a London–based station run by exiled Zimbabwean journalists; the Voice of America's Studio 7 service; and the Voice of the People. In April, the Iranian government agreed to help fund a new state radio station designed to counter Western broadcasts. Although satellite television services that provide international news programming remain largely uncensored, their prohibitive cost places them out of reach for most of the population.

Access to the internet is limited by the high costs at internet cafés and service disruptions caused by frequent power outages. Nonetheless, Zimbabwe has a relatively high rate of internet access for Africa, at more than 10 percent of the population. Online newspapers run by Zimbabweans living abroad are popular among those with internet access. The law allows the government to monitor e-mail content, and one individual was arrested and sentenced to a US$33 fine or seven days in prison for possessing an e-mail that contained critical comments about President Mugabe. In August, the government passed the controversial Interception of Communications Act, which would allow officials to intercept telephonic and electronic communications to prevent a "serious offense" or a "threat to national security"; the law would establish a monitoring center and would require internet service providers to pay the cost of surveillance.

About Freedom House

Freedom House is an independent private organization supporting the expansion of freedom throughout the world.

Freedom is posible only in democratic political systems in which governments are accountable to their own people, the rule of law prevails, and freedoms of expression, association and belief are guaranteed. Working directly with courageous men and women around the world to support nonviolent civic initiatives in societies where freedom is threatened, Freedom House functions as a catalyst for change through its unique mix of analysis, advocacy and action.

▮ **Analysis.** Freedom House's rigorous research methodology has earned the organization a reputation as the leading source of information on the state of freedom around the globe. Since 1972, Freedom House has published Freedom in the World, an annual survey of political rights and civil liberties experienced in every country of the world. The survey is complemented by an annual review of press freedom, an analysis of transitions in the post-communist world, and other publications.

▮ **Advocacy.** Freedom House seeks to encourage American policymakers, as well as other governments and international institutions, to adopt policies that advance human rights and democracy around the world. Freedom House has been instrumental in the founding of the worldwide Community of Democracies, has actively campaigned for a reformed Human Rights Council at the United Nations, and presses the Millennium Challenge Corporation to adhere to high standards of eligibility for recipient countries.

■ **Action.** Through exchanges, grants, and technical assistance, Freedom House provides training and support to human rights defenders, civil society organizations, and members of the media in order to strengthen indigenous reform efforts in countries around the globe.

Founded in 1941 by Eleanor Roosevelt, Wendell Willkie, and other Americans concerned with mounting threats to peace and democracy, Freedom House has long been a vigorous proponent of democratic values and a steadfast opponent of dictatorships of the far left and the far right. The organization's diverse Board of Trustees is composed of a bipartisan mix of business and labor leaders, former senior government officials, scholars, and journalists who agree that the promotion of democracy and human rights abroad is vital to America's interests abroad.

1301 Connecticut Avenue, NW, Floor 6
Washington, DC 20036
(202) 296-5101

120 Wall Street, Floor 26
New York, NY 10005
(212) 514-8040

www.freedomhouse.org